Additional praise for

THE INSURGENTS

"Thrilling reading. . . . There is no one better equipped to tell the story . . . than Fred Kaplan, a rare combination of defense intellectual and pugnacious reporter. . . . He brings genuine expertise to his fine storytelling. . . . An authoritative, gripping and somewhat terrifying account of how the American military approached two major wars in the combustible Islamic world."

—Thanassis Cambaniss, *The New York Times Book Review*

"Serious and insightful. . . . *The Insurgents* seems destined to be one of the more significant looks at how the US pursued the war in Iraq and at the complex mind of the general in charge when the tide turned."

—Tony Perry, *Los Angeles Times*

"Riveting . . . essential reading. . . . Kaplan's meticulous account of the ways Petraeus found to bring together and nurture the counterinsurgency 'cabal' might profitably be read by anyone interested in bringing change to a giant bureaucracy."

—John Barry, *The Daily Beast*

"Excellent . . . Poignant and timely. . . . A good read, rich in texture and never less than wise."

—Rosa Brooks, *Foreign Policy*

"Kaplan has a gift for bringing to life what might otherwise seem like arcane strategic debates by linking them to the personalities and biographies of the main participates, and he vividly captures the drama of Petraeus' struggle against a Pentagon establishment."

—Lawrence Freedman, *Foreign Affairs*

"Compelling"

—Dexter Filkins, *The New Yorker*

"A very readable, thoroughly reported account of how, in American military circles, 'counterinsurgency' became a policy instead of a dirty word."

—Janet Maslin, *The New York Times*

"The book's strength lies in the rich detail Kaplan offers the reader as he traces the network of colleagues all dedicated to stopping the violence in Iraq by employing classic counterinsurgency techniques. He untangles the web of professional connections much the same way an intelligence analyst might track down the associates of an al-Qaeda cell. . . . What emerges is a meticulously researched picture."

—Laura Colarusso, *The Washington Monthly*

"A tremendously clear and informative guide to the strengths and weaknesses of the military we have today and to the decisions we are about to make. . . . Anyone who reads *The Insurgents* will be better prepared to understand what America has done right and wrong with its military over the past generation."

—James Fallows, *The American Prospect*

"A dramatic and also damning analysis. . . . An absorbing and informative account."

—William W. Finan, Jr., *Current History*

"A must-read for military and national security professionals . . . Prodigious detail . . . earthy information about the human foibles of the participants."

—Gary Anderson, *Washington Times*

"Fascinating . . . One of the most interesting books I've read in the past seven years about the US in Iraq and counterinsurgency. . . . It is also one of the rare books that links personal histories, political maneuvers inside the national-security apparatus, and strategy on the ground."

—Stéphane Taillat, *Alliance Géostratégique*

"A fascinating . . . fast-moving, insider account . . . of how the 'insurgents'—savvy officers with big brains and advanced degrees in history and the social sciences—came to develop a new counterinsurgency doctrine, push the careers of their friends, form alliances across the government, influence the development of the surge in Iraq and generally succeed against the wishes of many in Congress, the Joint Chiefs and the previous theater commanders."

—Joseph J. Collins, *Armed Forces Journal*

"A compelling story combined with thoughtful analysis of the development, application and limitations of a new model of applying American military power."

—*Kirkus Reviews*

"An illuminating and frequently infuriating examination of how the US views warfare. Measured and meticulous, Kaplan's account is informative, detail-laden, and tempered by sharp analysis."

—*Publishers Weekly*

"Fred Kaplan has written a dazzling, compulsively readable book. Let's start with the fact that it is so well written, a quality so often lacking in books describing counterinsurgency. Let's also throw in the facts that it is both deeply researched and also devoid of cheerleading for the military or indeed any other kind of political bias. This book will join a small shelf of the most important accounts of the wars America has fought and will likely continue to fight in the twenty-first century."

—Peter Bergen, author of *Manhunt: The Ten-Year Search for Bin Laden from 9/11 to Abbottabad*

"Fred Kaplan, one of the best military journalists we have, tells the compelling story of how a cadre of officers and civilians tried to rescue victory from defeat in Iraq and Afghanistan by putting the theory of counterinsurgency into practice, revolutionizing the US Army from within. His narrative is vivid and revelatory, dramatizing a crucial piece of recent history that we shouldn't allow ourselves to forget, however painful the memory."

—George Packer, author of *The Assassins' Gate: America in Iraq*

"Fred Kaplan is one of the best in the business, a top-notch journalist and military analyst with serious intellectual chops and a killer pen. His new book, *The Insurgents,* tells the story of the rise and fall of the COINdinistas from Iraq to Afghanistan and beyond, and it's not only a great read—it's a major contribution to one of the most important strategic debates of our time."

—Gideon Rose, editor, *Foreign Affairs*, and author of *How Wars End*

"A fascinating and powerful work by America's wisest national-security reporter about an epic battle: the Army's search for a way to win the wars of the twenty-first century. If you love your country, if you care about its soldiers, if you wonder about the wisdom of their commanders, read this book now."

—Tim Weiner, author of *Legacy of Ashes: The History of the CIA* and *Enemies: A History of the FBI*

ALSO BY FRED KAPLAN

1959: The Year Everything Changed

Daydream Believers: How a Few Grand Ideas Wrecked American Power

The Wizards of Armageddon

DAVID PETRAEUS

AND THE PLOT TO CHANGE

THE AMERICAN WAY OF WAR

THE INSURGENTS

FRED KAPLAN

SIMON & SCHUSTER PAPERBACKS
New York London Toronto Sydney New Delhi

Again, and always—for Brooke, Maxine, and Sophie

Simon & Schuster Paperbacks
A Division of Simon & Schuster, Inc.
1230 Avenue of the Americas
New York, NY 10020

First Simon & Schuster trade paperback edition January 2014

SIMON & SCHUSTER PAPERBACKS and colophon are registered trademarks of Simon & Schuster, Inc.

For information about special discounts for bulk purchases, please contact Simon & Schuster Special Sales at 1-866-506-1949 or business@simonandschuster.com.

The Simon & Schuster Speakers Bureau can bring authors to your live event. For more information or to book an event, contact the Simon & Schuster Speakers Bureau at 1-866-248-3049 or visit our website at www.simonspeakers.com.

Designed by Renata DiBiase

Manufactured in the United States of America

10 9 8 7 6 5 4 3 2 1

The Library of Congress has cataloged the hardcover edition as follows:
Kaplan, Fred M.
The insurgents : David Petraeus and the plot to change the American way of war / Fred Kaplan.
p. cm.
Includes bibliographical references and index.
1. Counterinsurgency—United States—History. 2. Petraeus, David Howell. 3. Strategic culture—United States—History. 4. United States—Armed Forces—Officers—Education. 5. Generals—United States—Biography. 6. United States—Military policy—Planning. 7. United States—Military policy—History. 8. Counterinsurgency—Iraq—History—Twenty-first century. 9. Counterinsurgency—Afghanistan—History—Twenty-first century. 10. Iraq War, 2003–2011—Campaigns. 11. Afghan War, 2001- —Campaigns. I. Title. II. Title: David Petraeus and the plot to change the American way of war.
U241.K37 2013
355.02'180973—dc23 2012022268

ISBN 978-1-4516-4263-6
ISBN 978-1-4516-4265-0 (pbk)
ISBN 978-1-4516-4266-7 (ebook)

PHOTO CREDITS: 1. US Marine Corps photo by Sgt. J. R. Stence; 2. Courtesy of Daniel Galula; 3. US Military Academy, Social Science Department; 4. Courtesy of the Petraeus family; 5. Charlie Riedel/Associated Press; 6. US Army photo by Spc. Chris McCann; 7. Kaveh Sardari/sardari.com; 8. Courtesy of Kalev I. Sepp; 9. Courtesy of Kalev I. Sepp; 10. Courtesy of Celeste Ward Gventer; 11. Combined Arms Center, US Army; 12. Courtesy of Conrad Crane; 13. American Enterprise Institute; 14. US Army photo by Ashley Cross; 15. Jeff Hutchens/Getty Images; 16. US Army photo; 17. Charles Dharapak/Associated Press; 18. Photo by US Army Cpt. Craig Giancaterino; 19. DOD photo by Cherie Cullen; 20. Photo by US Navy Chief Petty Officer Joshua Treadwell

Contents

THE INSURGENTS

1.

"What We Need Is an Officer with Three Heads"

A few days shy of his twenty-fifth birthday, John Nagl saw his future disappear.

The first tremors came at dawn, on February 24, 1991, as he revved up the engine of his M-1 tank and plowed across the Saudi Arabian border into the flat, endless sands of southern Iraq. For the previous month, American warplanes had bombarded Saddam Hussein's military machine to the point of exhaustion. Now the ground-war phase of Operation Desert Storm—the largest armored offensive since the Second World War—roared forth in full force, pushing Iraq's occupying army out of Kuwait.

Lieutenant Nagl was a platoon leader in the US Army's 1st Cavalry Division, which, on that morning, mounted the crucial feint along the route where Saddam's commanders were expecting an invasion. While Nagl and the rest of the 1st Cav pinned down the Iraqi troops with a barrage of bullets, shells, and missiles, the offensive's main force—a massive armada of American soldiers, nearly a quarter million strong, along with their armored vehicles, artillery rockets, and a fleet of gunship helicopters overhead—swept across the desert landscape from the west in a surprise left-hook assault, enveloping Saddam's troops and crushing them into submission after a mere one hundred hours of astonishingly lopsided fighting.

Nagl had graduated from the United States Military Academy at West Point two-and-a-half years earlier, near the top of his class, and then won a Rhodes Scholarship to Oxford University. Highly ranked cadets got their pick of Army assignments, and Nagl chose the armor branch. Tanks would be the spearhead of the big war for which the Army was ceaselessly preparing—the titanic clash between the United States and the Soviet Union across the East-West German border—and so, tank commanders were prime candidates for fast promotion through the ranks. Nagl even studied German while at West Point and became fluent in the language, figuring that Germany was where he'd be spending the bulk of his career.

Then, not quite a year before he deployed to the Gulf, the Berlin Wall fell, the two Germanys merged, the Cold War ended—and now, right before his eyes, the Iraqi army, the fourth-largest army in the world, was crumbling on contact.

It was a moment of unaccustomed triumph for the US military, still haunted by the defeat in Vietnam. But to Nagl, it also signaled the end of the era that made the triumph possible. Tank-on-tank combat had been the defining mode of warfare for a modern superpower; now it teetered on the verge of obsolescence. The Soviet Union and Iraq had been the last two foes that possessed giant tank armies. With the former gone up in smoke and the latter crushed so easily on the battlefield, it seemed implausible that any foreign power would again dare challenge the United States in a head-on contest of strength. The premise of all Nagl's plans—to say nothing of the rationale for his beloved Army's doctrines, budgets, and weapons programs—seemed suddenly, alarmingly irrelevant.

Nagl didn't think that any of this necessarily meant the coming of world peace. If "major combat operations" (the official name for big tank wars) were no longer likely, there was still plenty of room for minor ones, especially the "shadow wars" mounted along the peripheries of vital interests by insurgents, guerrillas, or terrorists. Nagl didn't know much about these kinds of wars. Neither did the Army. He hadn't learned about them as a cadet at West Point. Nor had he since read about them in Army field manuals or practiced fighting them in officers' training drills.

There was a reason for this gap in his education. In the mid-1970s, after the debacle of Vietnam, the Army's top generals said "Never again" to the notion of fighting guerrillas in the jungle (or anyplace else). Instead, they turned their gaze once more to the prospect of a big war against the Soviet Union on the wide-open plains of Europe—a war that would play to America's traditional strengths of amassing men and metal—and they threw out the book (literally: they *threw out* the official manuals and curricula) on anything related to what were once called "irregular wars," "asymmetric wars," "low-intensity conflicts," or "counterinsurgency campaigns." To the extent that these types of wars were contemplated at all, the message went out that there was nothing distinctive about them. For decades,

Army doctrine had held that wars were won by superior *firepower*. This idea was taken as gospel, whether the war was large or small, whether the enemy was a nation-state or a rogue guerrilla. As one adage put it, if you can lick the cat, you can lick the kitten. Or, in the words of another: war is war is war.

But Nagl suspected that, like it or not, America might find itself drawn into fighting these "small wars" again; that if the Army had a future, these wars would play a key part in it; and (though he didn't grasp this idea at first) that these wars were different from large wars in ways other than mere size and, therefore, had to be fought in different ways by soldiers trained in different skills.

Not long after Desert Storm, Nagl persuaded the Army to send him back to Oxford for graduate school, where he embarked on a historical study of these kinds of wars. The study evolved into a doctoral dissertation, which he published as a book, which he then hoisted as a weapon—an intellectual weapon—in a policy war back home. He sought and found a cadre of allies to fight this war with him: mainly fellow Army officers, along with a few marines and civilian defense analysts, who were reaching similar conclusions through their own experiences, and who, once they grew aware of one another's existence, formed a community—a "cabal" or "mafia," some frankly called it—dedicated to the cause of reviving counterinsurgency doctrine and making it a major strand, even the centerpiece, of American military strategy.

To pull off this feat, they had to act like insurgents: subversive rebels within their own military establishment, armed not with weapons but with ideas and, in some cases, a mastery of bureaucratic maneuvering.

Most of them fully grasped the irony, and the stakes, of what they were doing. One of these rebels would title a PowerPoint briefing about this community's emergence, and his role in it, "An Insurgent Within the COIN Revolution."

Critics derided them as "COINdinistas," a wordplay that combined the abbreviation for counterinsurgency (COIN) with the name of the leftist insurgency that seized power in Nicaragua in the late 1970s (Sandinistas). The COIN rebels took to the name, invoking it with a self-aware smirk and a missionary pride. For it was a serious struggle they were waging: a campaign to overhaul the institutional culture of the US military establishment—the way it groomed new leaders, adapted to new settings, and adopted new ideas.

A few years into the twenty-first century, a second American war in Iraq—this time an outright invasion for the purpose of "regime change"—triggered the rise of sectarian militias. Simultaneously, Islamist insurgents renewed a fight for power in Afghanistan. And the battle of ideas between the COINdinistas and the traditionalists took on an urgent intensity. The stakes were suddenly very high. It was no longer an esoteric quarrel over history and theory, but a struggle whose outcome meant life or death, victory or defeat—not only in those two wars but possibly in other theaters of conflict for years or decades to come. It was a battle for how the Pentagon does business and how America goes to war.

At first the rebels would win the battle. A cultural upheaval would seize the military at its core. A new kind of officer would rise through the ranks. And the Army would shift from a static garrison establishment to a flexible fighting force, more adaptable to the dangers and conflicts of the post–Cold War era.

Yet, as often happens with revolutions, the new doctrine, enshrined in the first flush of victory, would harden into dogma. And its enthusiasts, emboldened in their confidence, would—often with good intentions—lure the nation more deeply into another war that it lacked the ability or appetite to win.

The seeds of the COIN revolt first sprouted in the Army's own hothouse: the military academy at West Point, the gleaming granite fortress overlooking the Hudson River, fifty miles north of New York City, where cadets had been molded into officers since the early years of the republic. A reverence for tradition was carved into its foundations, piped into its air. West Point was where, in 1778, General George Washington built the Continental Army's most critical strategic fortress. It had remained an Army holding ever since—the oldest continuously occupied military post in North America. President Thomas Jefferson signed the bill establishing the United States Military Academy on West Point's land in 1802. Fifteen years later, Colonel Sylvanus Thayer, one of the academy's early superintendents, issued its first curriculum and honor code, which survived so many otherwise tumultuous eras that one cadet, in the mid-twentieth century, scribbled out a proposed new motto: "Two Hundred Years of Tradition, Unhindered by Progress."

Some on the faculty read it as a benediction, not a joke.

The COIN rebellion was fomented by a subculture within the academy, composed of officers who venerated tradition but also embraced strands of progress. They saw themselves as apart from (some would say *above*) the rest of West Point. They were the faculty and students of its Social Science Department, known to members and detractors alike as "Sosh."

Sosh was the brainchild of George Arthur Lincoln, who graduated from West Point in 1929, ranking fourth in his class. There were no majors or even electives at the academy in those days; everyone took the same courses, most of them in engineering. (Throughout the nineteenth century, West Point alumni had played a leading role in constructing the nation's rail lines, bridges, harbors, and interstate roads.) Lincoln, nicknamed Abe by his friends, won a Rhodes Scholarship after graduating and spent the next three years at Oxford, studying philosophy, politics, and economics. It was a heady experience for the son of a farmer from Harbor Beach, Michigan, a small town on the shore of Lake Huron. Afterward, he came back to West Point to teach.

When the Japanese attacked Pearl Harbor, Lincoln was assigned to a high-level staff job in London, where he planned the logistics for the Normandy invasion. His talents were quickly recognized, and in the spring of 1943, he was ordered back to Washington to serve as deputy chief of the Strategy and Policy Group, the US Army's brain trust, located on the third floor of the Pentagon, next to the office of the chief of staff, General George Marshall. In the fall of 1944, at age thirty-seven, Lincoln was promoted to brigadier general—making him the Army's youngest general officer—and took over as the S&P Group's chief. He coordinated operations for every major military campaign in the war's final year and advised Marshall on a daily basis, accompanying him to the conferences at Yalta and Potsdam, where he had a hand in drafting the treaties that shaped the political map of postwar Europe.

By the end of the war, Lincoln had earned enough plaudits to win whatever plum assignment a one-star general might want. He stayed on with the S&P Group for another year, helping Marshall's replacement, General Dwight Eisenhower, organize the newly created Department of

Defense. But what he really wanted to do was to go back to West Point and start a new department that combined the study of history, government, international politics, and economics—a department of social sciences.

While working with Marshall at the various Allied planning conferences, Lincoln had noticed that much of the crucial staff work was performed by just a handful of military officers and that nearly all of them had been, like him, Rhodes Scholars. He calculated that West Point had produced a total of thirteen Rhodes Scholars in its history. Of the six still alive, four were currently holding senior policy-making positions. Throughout the war, those four had planned several major military operations—crossing the English Channel and the Rhine, attacking the islands off Shanghai, arranging the surrenders of Germany and Japan—and now, in the war's unsettled aftermath, they were working out the terms of peace treaties, arms accords, and international boundaries. Emerging as a global power with global responsibilities, the United States would need leaders—or at least staff officers advising the leaders—who were well versed in politics, diplomacy, economics, and military strategy. But few such people existed, in or out of the military.

West Point, Lincoln mused, was good at training mess officers and battalion commanders, and maybe that was enough for an earlier time. But the commanders and chiefs of the postwar American Army would have to be "very broad-gauged individuals," as he put it to one colleague. The problem was that by the time officers were promoted to such a high position, it was "a little late to start instilling the broad approach." Their education had to begin much sooner.

On May 20, 1945, less than two weeks after the war in Europe ended, Lincoln wrote to Colonel Herman Beukema, one of his former mentors back at West Point: "I am beginning to think that what we need is a type of staff officer with at least three heads—one political, one economic, and one military." Over the next year, the two officers struck up a correspondence, pondering the role that West Point might play in breeding this new type of officer for a new Army in a new world.

In one letter, Lincoln proposed "baptizing practically all officers" with a "sprinkling" of education in politics, history, and economics, while taking "certain selected" officers and "dunking" them in those waters much more deeply.

Beukema agreed. The sorts of challenges that Lincoln had described confronting during the war made it clear, Beukema wrote, "that the Army can no longer afford to depend on the fortuitous assembly of Rhodes Scholars . . . There must be an integrated system of high-level training if Army policy and national policy are properly to be served, a system which begins here at West Point."

And so was hatched the idea of starting the Department of Social Science. In August 1945, soon after Japan's surrender, West Point's superintendent announced that the academy would soon resume its four-year course of study, which had been suspended during the war while most of the cadets and instructors had gone off to fight. In June 1946, Congress passed a bill expanding the size of the academy's faculty. In July, Lincoln told Beukema that he might be interested in coming back to West Point.

Beukema was sixteen years older than Lincoln, so he would be the Sosh department's first chairman, but Lincoln would be his deputy—for all practical purposes, running its operations—and formally succeed him when he retired.

There was one hitch. By Army regulations, a department chair or deputy chair at West Point was to be filled by a colonel, not a general. But Lincoln thought this was the most important thing he could do, so he requested a demotion—an almost unheard-of move, which carried a cut in authority and pay.

Lincoln started his new job on September 1, 1947. Another seven years would pass before Beukema retired and Lincoln rose to chairman; meanwhile, together they set about turning their vision into reality. Before Lincoln returned, West Point's curriculum had been very thin in the social sciences. It had offered several full-year courses in engineering, math, chemistry, physics, military tactics, even military bridges, but only a semester each in military history and political science, and only a half semester in economics. Lincoln and Beukema created courses in history, government, foreign affairs, geography, national-security economics, and international relations. (There were no college-level American textbooks on international politics, so Lincoln wrote one, which also wound up being assigned at several civilian colleges across the country.)

From the beginning, there was something clearly different about the Sosh department. A few months before coming back to West Point, Lincoln had written to Beukema, "I am certain that we must make strenuous efforts . . . to improve the so-called Army mind." This would mean, above all, "impressing the student with the fact that the basic requirement is to learn to think—sometimes a very painful process." So, unlike most of the departments, where instructors recited hard facts in straight lectures, Sosh courses were taught more like seminars, allowing, even encouraging, questions, discussion, to some degree dissent. There was no major in Social Science just yet; there were no majors of any sort. (They wouldn't come to West Point until the reforms of the mid-1980s.) All cadets took the same core courses. But a few of the core courses were now Sosh courses, and cadets could sign up for a handful of electives. Those who took Sosh electives felt a sense of separate space for critical inquiry, more like what students at a liberal-arts college were experiencing. It was something that cadets and faculty in other departments at West Point viewed with a little distrust, resentment, envy, or all three.

The act of asking questions and talking back was itself a cause for suspicion in the Army, an institution that, by nature, demanded obedience to authority, especially in a time when American society and culture rewarded conformity. Sosh students and faculty were commonly derided as "communists," sometimes in jest, sometimes not. As late as 1991, when General Norman Schwarzkopf, the hero-commander of Operation Desert Storm, came back to West Point to deliver a rousing victory speech, he reminisced about his own days as a cadet and, at one point, poked fun at the crazy ideas advanced by "a couple of left-wing pinko Social Science instructors." He was joking, sort of, but the laughter and applause from the audience reflected at least a lingering trace of the stereotype.

In a move that only intensified this sense of an elite enclave, Lincoln established a rule allowing cadets who did especially well in Sosh courses to go study at a civilian graduate school, with West Point paying the tuition. In exchange, these cadets, after earning their doctorate degrees, would come back and teach in the Sosh department for at least three years. Once they fulfilled that obligation, Lincoln would use his still-considerable connections in Washington to get them choice assignments in the Pentagon, the State Department, the White House, a foreign embassy, or a prestigious command post.

The idea of all this was to boost the quality of education at West Point, to create an esprit de corps within the Sosh department in particular, and, from that, to cultivate an elite within the Army's officer corps, the new type of officer that Lincoln envisioned in his letter to Beukema just after the war: the "staff officer with at least three heads," instilled with a knowledge of political, economic, and military matters, at a level of breadth and depth that the nation would demand of its top officers in an age of global reach and rivalry.

Lincoln would later articulate a philosophy of personnel policy: "Pick good people, pick them young before other pickers get into the competition, help them to grow, keep in touch, exploit excellence."

Over the years, a network of Lincoln's acolytes—and the acolytes of those acolytes—emerged and expanded. They called themselves the "Lincoln Brigade" (an inside joke on their left-wing stereotype, referring to the Abraham Lincoln Brigade, the group of American leftists who, in the 1930s, had gone off to fight against fascists in the Spanish Civil War). Over the years, when these alumni-officers were appointed to high-level positions, they'd usually phone Colonel Lincoln—or, later on, his successors as department chairmen—and ask for the new crop of top Sosh cadets, or the most promising junior faculty members, to come work as their assistants.

When John Nagl passed through the gates of West Point in the fall of 1983, as a visiting high school senior who'd applied for admission the following year, he knew right away that this was where he wanted to be.

His father, a retired Navy officer who worked at a nuclear power plant, had driven him all the way from their home in Omaha, Nebraska, where John was an honors student at Creighton Prep, an all-boys' Jesuit school. John had grown up in a conservative Catholic family, the oldest of six children, four of them boys, each named after a Gospel in the New Testament (John, Matthew, Luke, and Mark). His hometown served as the base for the Strategic Air Command and was thus America's most likely ground zero—the Kremlin's number-one target—in the event of nuclear war. At the time of Nagl's West Point visit, the Cold War was heating up, and President Ronald Reagan was pouring tens of billions of dollars into a new generation of major Army weapons: M-1 tanks, Bradley Fighting

Vehicles, Apache helicopters, and the Multiple Launch Rocket System. It was a logical fit for Nagl to go to one of the military academies; the Army seemed right for the time.

He was dazzled by the grandeur of the buildings and the grounds, the vista views of the Hudson, the hallowed history all around him. Nearly every prominent Army general had walked these grounds as a cadet, and Nagl fully expected to join their ranks.

He wouldn't make it that far; he'd wind up retiring from the Army before making even full colonel. But along the way, he made a deeper mark, and garnered more fame, than most generals ever had in their lifetimes. And he did this while climbing through the ranks of the Lincoln Brigade—initially as a cadet, then as an acolyte, and finally as a network-builder himself. His first and pivotal mentor in this fraternal order of soldier-scholars was an Army major named David Howell Petraeus.

2.

"Another Type of Warfare"

The Sosh department at West Point in the mid-1980s was teeming with confident, ambitious young officers, but few scaled the cliffs of self-confidence or raced through ambition's fast track with quite the zest of Dave Petraeus.

His competitive streak was the first thing that anyone noticed about him, dating back to his time as a cadet in the class of 1974. In that decade before the reforms, West Point was a merciless place to live and study. Each cadet's grades were posted publicly after every test in every course, and the seating arrangements in each classroom were altered accordingly, with the highest scorers placed in the front row and the lowest scorers in the back. Every minute, a cadet knew where he stood in relation to his fellow cadets, and this awareness didn't end with the school day or school *days*. A cadet's class rank determined how good his stadium seats were during football season. It determined who got the first, and thus most desirable, pick of assignments upon graduating. Years later, if an officer came back to West Point to teach, his class rank from cadet days would determine the size and quality of faculty housing he'd be awarded, thus extending his self-consciousness about hierarchy and status to the pride or shame of his wife and children.

Many dropped out under the pressure. Petraeus thrived on it; he'd discovered his element. But his was an odd streak of drive and ambition. It wasn't dark or scheming, but rather bright, even sunny, bursting with outsized enthusiasm. He was intense and bone skinny. He punctuated his speech with boyish exclamations: "Super!" "Jeepers!" "Holy cow!" And when he challenged a friend to a foot race or a push-ups contest, as he did incessantly, it was with more an unflagging energy than an intimidating dare.

His father was a Dutch immigrant, a proverbially crusty sea captain who taught him the importance of winning. His mother was a librarian, from a family of Oberlin College graduates, who taught him the importance of reading. They raised him in Cornwall-on-Hudson, New York, a small town seven miles from West Point, and he felt the academy's force as an everyday influence. Senior faculty could live off base, and many of them settled in Cornwall, playing active roles in the town's life. Petraeus's high school math teacher was a retired Army colonel and former West Point professor. His soccer coach had once led the West Point soccer team to a national championship. His Sunday School teacher was West Point's ski instructor.

Ever since the 1920s, when General Douglas MacArthur mandated stiff physical fitness standards as West Point's superintendent, the academy had thrived on the playing fields of intercollegiate sports. ("Every cadet an athlete, every athlete challenged," MacArthur had trumpeted.) It was this aspect of the school's legacy that lured Petraeus most of all. In his first year as a cadet, he played on varsity teams all three seasons—soccer in the spring and fall, skiing in the winter—and neglected his studies in the process. He ended the year ranked 161st in a class of just over 800: not bad by most standards, but dismal by his own.

During his second year, he got serious. West Point had a pre-med program that awarded full medical-school scholarships to its top nine students. Petraeus beamed in on that target. He took science courses for most of his electives and earned high marks. Midway through his senior year, he made the grade of "star man": one of the cadets awarded a silver star for his lapel to indicate his ranking in the top 5 percent of his class. Petraeus also suddenly realized that he ranked sixth among the cadets in the pre-med program. He was on track to win one of those scholarships.

Then, in a moment of introspection, he asked himself if he really felt the calling to be a doctor, and he had to admit that he did not; that he'd signed up for the pre-med program mainly because it was one of West Point's hardest and most prestigious competitions. But in the meantime, he was doing well in all the other cadet activities: the core curriculum, the upper-level seminar on military strategy, the officers' training drills. His options were open to a wide range of possibilities.

In the fall of his senior year, Petraeus began dating an attractive blonde named Holly Knowlton, the daughter of Lieutenant General William Knowlton, West Point's superintendent. A few weeks after graduating, he married her. Petraeus's detractors, at the time and for many years afterward, cited his whirlwind courtship as the ultimate in careerist audacity. His friends waved away the accusation as silly jealousy. The two had met on a blind date—Petraeus hadn't been stalking her—and they simply turned out to be a good match. Both were athletic, very smart, and, in their own ways, accomplished and driven. (She was studying French literature at Dickinson College, finishing an honors thesis on the novelist François Mauriac.) Still, even Petraeus's friends joked about the feat; they couldn't help but shake their heads and whistle. There were no women at West Point (the first female cadets wouldn't be admitted for another two years), and out of the 833 graduating men on campus, it was Petraeus who'd won the hand of the superintendent's daughter. A lot of his classmates, friendly and otherwise, saw it as a sign, maybe the most persuasive of several, that if one cadet among them climbed the ranks to four-star general, it would be Dave Petraeus.

Petraeus wasn't yet sure whether he wanted to make a career in the military. But his taxpayer-funded education at West Point carried a contractual obligation to give the Army at least five more years of his life. So he would see how things went.

That May, all the cadets gathered for a ceremony to declare which branch of the service they'd chosen to enter—as with everything else, in order of class rank. When the roll call came to Petraeus, who was ranked forty-third, he called out "Infantry." It was a surprising move for someone of his promise. Only one of the forty-two classmates ahead of him had chosen that branch. Infantry meant foot soldier; it invoked Vietnam. The cadets in his class had watched the Army collapse in Vietnam on the nightly newscasts for their entire time at the academy. Most of their instructors were Vietnam vets. Vietnam came up repeatedly in class discussions, mostly in a cautionary or outright negative way. The class on military ethics discussed the 1968 My Lai massacre; the class on military tactics discussed battlefield errors and the implications of the Tet offensive; the class on foreign policy discussed whether the United States should ever again intervene in that kind of war. Outside the gates of West Point, the Army's top commanders were openly moving on, focusing again on the plains of Europe and the threat of a big war against the vast armies of the Soviet Union and the Warsaw Pact.

Petraeus's higher-ranking classmates chose assignments in armor, artillery, even aviation and engineering. Those branches would lead the fight in the big war; in the meantime, they'd pave the most promising paths to promotion. Infantry seemed like a loser in every sense; it was the branch that the Army's top officers seemed eager to diminish.

But Petraeus saw infantry as the most physically challenging branch, the branch where an individual could leave a mark, leading troops into battle on the ground, out in the open, not cooped up in a tank. He was particularly keen to join one of the elite Ranger units in airborne infantry. He'd trained as a parachutist at West Point's jump school the summer before his senior year. If nothing else, it was exciting, fun.

Shortly after graduating, Petraeus went to Ranger School, a brutal, two-month regimen of mock battles and long marches through the dense woods, muddy swamps, and scraggly mountains of Georgia and Florida, all on just three-and-a-half hours of sleep per night and meager rations. The school was designed to discourage all but the most serious comers and to disqualify all but the fittest among those who dared sign up. Petraeus finished first in his group.

From there, he was assigned to the 509th Airborne Battalion Combat Team, stationed in Vicenza, Italy, where he spent much of the next four years jumping out of airplanes, then meeting up with his French or Italian counterparts for joint training exercises, marching and maneuvering for days or weeks at a time, with heavy rucksacks on their backs, through some of the lushest hills and valleys in all Europe. Some of these jumps were dangerous, especially those over the Pyrenees Mountains along the Spanish-French border: often he couldn't see the landing zone through the clouds, and he could hurt himself badly if he didn't glide just so around the sharp thickets of the shrubs.

It was a magical time for Petraeus: the beauty, the adventure, the tight camaraderie among the men, and maybe especially the danger. He knew, almost right away, that this was the life for him.

Early on in the posting, Petraeus was sent to an advanced training course with the French army's 6th Parachute Regiment at its jump school in Pau, a village on the northern edge of the Pyrenees. At every French officers' club, where the men ate or drank after coming in from the field, he noticed behind the bar a large framed portrait of an officer—always the same officer. He learned from one of his fellow jumpers that the portrait was of General Marcel "Bruno" Bigeard. Petraeus figured that he should find out more about him.

Back at Vicenza, he did some research. Bigeard, it turned out, was the most highly decorated and famous officer in France. During World War II, he'd been a national hero. Captured by the Nazis, he escaped from a POW camp soon after and made his way to northern Africa, where he joined the Free French militia; he then parachuted into Vichy-occupied France with a four-man team of Resistance commandos who gave him the radio code name "Bruno," which his friends and admirers had called him ever since. After the Allied victory, Bigeard fought against the communist Viet Minh in France's war to regain control of its colony in Vietnam, making his reputation in the battle of Dien Bien Phu, where the Viet Minh surrounded and finally routed a badly outnumbered French army force. Defeat was inevitable, but Bigeard fought them off valiantly, succumbing only when he and his extremely loyal men were captured. Released after the signing of the Geneva Peace Accords, Bigeard returned to France and took command of the 3rd Colonial Parachute Regiment, which proceeded to Algeria, where it crushed the National Liberation Front's campaign of urban terrorism against the French occupation of Algeria (at least for a few years). He also wrote a number of books on counter-guerrilla tactics and, years later, two bestselling memoirs.

Petraeus didn't read French well enough to tackle Bigeard's books. But he found a few others, written or translated in English, that recounted the general's exploits, most notably the journalist Bernard Fall's volumes about Vietnam, *Street Without Joy* and *Hell in a Very Small Place,* which contained a detailed account of the battle at Dien Bien Phu. He also devoured Jean Larteguy's bestselling novel *The Centurions,* whose hero, Colonel Raspeguy, was clearly modeled on Bigeard. The novel was about a small band of French airborne infantry soldiers, captured at Dien Bien Phu, who stick together on a forced march to POW camps and, after repatriation, prepare for deployment to Algeria, where they're determined to apply the lessons they learned—and to avoid the mistakes their commanders committed—in Vietnam. The novel romanticized the life of elite soldiers, out on their own, along the edge of civilization, surviving on their wits, integrity, and courage. It all resonated with Petraeus, as it did with many airborne officers. For decades after, he would cite it as his favorite novel—one of his favorite books, period—and he would frequently retrieve it from his bookshelf, not just for pleasure but to consult its meticulous descriptions of small-unit tactics and morale-building rituals.

Later, in the early 1990s, when Petraeus commanded his first battalion, he ordered his men to fasten the top button on their uniforms, the "battle button." Yes, he told them, it was uncomfortable, and other soldiers might mock them for it, but the discomfort and the mockery would set them apart—bind them more tightly—as a unit. He got the idea from a strange hat that Raspeguy had his men wear in *The Centurions,* a plot point that, Petraeus learned, was based on a ritual that Bigeard had ordered his own men to follow.

Bigeard was also an expert self-promoter. He would frequently invite journalists (among them Bernard Fall) into his headquarters and outline his battle plan, tell them his life story, treat them as peers. This practice, which some of his brother officers disparaged, had the effect of building popular support for his mission—and carving a myth about himself. When Petraeus became a commanding general, during the insurgency wars of his own generation in Iraq and Afghanistan, he followed this lesson from Bigeard's playbook with particular vim, and with similar results.

But Petraeus also absorbed intellectual lessons from his self-taught crash course in recent French military history. He took particular note of a passage midway through *The Centurions* in which a French officer first realizes that the Viet Minh had a different concept about how to wage war. Talking with a fellow officer in the POW camp, he likens it to the difference between the card games *belote* and bridge: "When we make war, we play *belote* with thirty-two cards in the pack. But the Viet Minh's game is bridge, and they have fifty-two cards, twenty more than we do. Those twenty cards short will always prevent us from getting the better of them. *They've got nothing to do with traditional warfare,* they're marked with the signs of politics, propaganda, faith, agrarian reform."

Just before this monologue, the two officers had been wondering why their captain was so annoyed. The first officer says, "I think he is beginning to realize that we've got to play with fifty-two cards, and he doesn't like it at all . . . Those twenty extra cards aren't at all to his liking."

Those twenty extra cards, the insight that these kinds of wars were not just clashes of arms but also struggles over ideology and economic well-being, fought in a way that had "nothing to do with traditional warfare"—this was a new idea to Petraeus, and it was an idea, he suspected, that his own Army's commanders wouldn't find to their liking, either.

As much as the Vietnam War was discussed back at West Point, none of Petraeus's instructors had ever taught it systematically. There was no course on the history of the war or the politics of the country. The core course on military history included one section on irregular warfare, but it was glossed over; it included no detailed analysis of counterinsurgency as a separate type of combat that might require different methods, principles, or goals—a whole other set of playing cards.

Intrigued by Fall and Larteguy, Petraeus expanded his reading list. There turned out to be a small stack of books in English about these kinds of wars, and he set out to plow through all of them. Some, like Sir Robert Thompson's *Defeating Communist Insurgency* and Frank Kitson's *Low Intensity Operations,* were by veterans of Britain's colonial campaigns in Kenya or Malaya. But the clearest and most compelling treatise on the subject, the one that had the greatest influence on Petraeus's thinking, was a thin volume called *Counterinsurgency Warfare: Theory and Practice* by a retired French officer named David Galula. It was out of print and hard to find. But Bernard Fall, in the bibliography of *Street Without Joy,* had touted it as "the 'how-to' book in the field—and the best of them all." So Petraeus was determined to hunt down this book and to read it very closely.

Galula had written the book during the academic year of 1962–63 while on a fellowship at Harvard University's Center for International Affairs. He had just retired from the French army as a lieutenant colonel and meant for the book to sum up the lessons he'd learned from witnessing a half dozen insurgency wars—as a French military attaché in China from 1945 to 1948 (during which time he was captured and briefly imprisoned by Mao Zedong's guerrillas), as an observer with the United Nations Special Committee on the Balkans in 1948–49 (where he took notes on counter-guerrilla tactics in the Greek civil war), as a military attaché in Hong Kong in the early-to-mid-1950s (from which he made several trips to Malaya, the Philippines, and Vietnam), and, finally, from 1956 to 1958, as the leader of a small combat unit fighting insurgents and "pacifying" mountain villages during the anticolonial revolts in Algeria.

From the first few pages, Galula's book read like nothing Petraeus had ever been taught at West Point. "Revolutionary war," the book stated, using the French term for this kind of combat, has "special rules, different from those of the conventional war." Moreover, the rules that apply for one side in this sort of war don't work for the other side. "In a fight between a fly and a lion," Galula wrote, "the fly cannot deliver a knockout blow and the lion cannot fly. It is the same war for both camps in terms of space and time, yet there are two distinct warfares—the revolutionary's and, shall we say, the counterrevolutionary's." (A page later, he would call them the "insurgent" and the "counterinsurgent," perhaps coining the terms.) The lion could whack at the fly, with occasionally lethal effect, but there would always be more flies, an endless swarm of them, harassing and stinging the lion into a state of exhaustion and retreat, until someone drained the swamp that was breeding them—a feat that couldn't be managed through whacking alone.

The metaphor appealed to Petraeus. It reminded him of the passage in Larteguy's novel about the two sides playing with different decks of cards. But Galula's aim, much more ambitious, was to outline the rules and to devise systematic guidelines on how to win the game—or, as he put it with an alluring air of scientific certitude, "to define the *laws* of counterrevolutionary warfare, to deduce from them its principles, and to outline the corresponding strategy and tactics."

To Galula, the essence of this kind of warfare wasn't so much the clash of arms (although arms were certainly involved) but rather a competition for the loyalty, or at least complicity, of the local population. The insurgents, animated by an ideological cause, could sow *disorder anywhere,* with the ultimate aim of overthrowing the government or building up parallel structures of governance that, whether through popular appeal or coercion, would grow stronger until the established order collapsed. All the while, the counterinsurgents, as protectors of the existing regime, must maintain *order everywhere.* The advantage, at least initially, is with the insurgent, who "is fluid because he has neither responsibility nor concrete assets," whereas "the counterinsurgent is rigid because he has both." The insurgent can choose to fight or not fight, as it suits him, mounting attacks and ambushes, then falling back into the population, mixing with the people inconspicuously, like a fish swimming in water, as Mao put it in his own book, *On Guerrilla Warfare.*

In his days as a military attaché in Shanghai and Beijing, Galula had learned Chinese; he'd studied Mao's book and, although extremely anti-communist, came to appreciate, even admire, Mao's strategic wisdom. Smart counterinsurgency tactics, Galula realized, involved turning Mao's doctrine on its head. A Maoist insurgency sought above all to win the support of the people by living among them and gradually supplanting the functions of the government. So, Galula reasoned, the counterinsurgents must also live among the people: to isolate them from the insurgency, keep the area secure, and thus earn their trust, so that they in turn provide intelligence about the identity and whereabouts of the surviving rebels.

Galula laid out a "step-by-step" process for how to do this, in one area of the country at a time. First, concentrate enough armed forces to push the insurgents out of the area. Second, keep enough troops there to repel a comeback, eventually turning it over to well-trained local soldiers or police. Third (and here was where things differed considerably from conventional warfare), establish contact with the people, earn their trust or control their movements, and cut off their ties to the insurgents. Fourth, destroy the insurgents' local political organization and create new ones. Finally, mop up or win over the insurgency's remnants.

Some counterinsurgency enthusiasts would later dub this technique "winning hearts and minds," although the term implied a gentler approach than Galula prescribed (or, as a commander in Algeria, practiced). A more fitting phrase, adopted later, was "clear-hold-build": clear an area of insurgents, hold the territory, then build up government services while the area was still secure.

Whatever the shorthand, the point was that winning this kind of war involved more than just fighting. It required military, political, and judicial operations—and all three were essential. The outcome was a matter not of adding the three elements but of multiplying them: if one of the elements was zero, the product of all three would be zero; that is, if one prong of the operation failed, the entire campaign would fail, and thus the insurgents would win.

One of Mao's generals had written that revolutionary war is "20 percent military action and 80 percent political," and Galula endorsed the formula. "[C]onventional operations by themselves," he wrote, "have at best no more effect than a fly swatter. Some guerrillas are bound to be caught, but new recruits will replace them as fast as they are lost." The insurgents will always return unless and until the population begins to cooperate with the counterinsurgents—that is, with the regime. "The population therefore becomes the objective for the counterinsurgent as it was for his enemy." At various stages in the conflict, a counterinsurgent soldier must "be prepared to become a propagandist, a social worker, a civil engineer, a schoolteacher, a nurse, a Boy Scout." Likewise, "a mimeograph machine may turn out to be more useful than a machine gun, a soldier trained as a pediatrician more important than a mortar expert, cement more wanted than barbed wire, clerks more in demand than riflemen."

Even when this kind of war required fighting, the rules were different. In conventional war, a soldier under attack must return fire with the maximum possible force. In counterinsurgency warfare, the reverse was sometimes true, especially if civilians were nearby, as, after all, the ultimate goal of the war was less to kill insurgents than to protect the civilian population.

All of this would have been heady, if disorienting, stuff for any American Army officer coming up through the ranks at a time when the top brass was focusing exclusively on big wars and concentrated firepower. But the book had added luster for young Lieutenant Petraeus. First, in this kind of war, a soldier had to *think* and to act *creatively,* an appealing notion to a West Point star man. Second, this kind of war was, as Galula wrote, "primarily a war of infantry," especially of "highly mobile and lightly armed" infantry. Its key elements were foot soldiers out on patrol, not heavy tanks rolling through the countryside or pilots dropping bombs. It was, in other words, a type of warfare ideally suited for the branch of the Army that Petraeus had chosen and to which he was feeling increasingly attached. It was an idea that might give his career path and passion new meaning.

Seven years passed before Petraeus saw this promise fulfilled. Meanwhile, at the end of 1978, as his four-year tour in Italy drew to a close, he lobbied hard for a slot commanding a rifle company in the 24th Infantry Division at Fort Stewart, Georgia, an audacious move for an officer who had just been promoted to captain a few months earlier. The 24th didn't match his interests completely, especially since the Army chiefs were beefing it up to a *mechanized* infantry division, meaning that it would take on a large complement of tanks. But Petraeus's real sights were on a Ranger unit located at the same base; he figured that if he did well as a company commander, he'd be allowed to try out for the elite squad down the road. In any case, his superiors, impressed with his record, gave him the rifle company.

The company, in fact the entire division, was in dreadful shape. It was the era of the "hollow" army. Post-Vietnam budget cuts had emptied out the supply bins of ammo and spare parts; repair depots were backlogged; serious training took a dive; and the quality of recruits, in those early years of the all-volunteer Army, had plummeted. Petraeus pushed his men with his merrily frantic enthusiasm, and they responded in surprisingly good cheer. They won first place in the base's basketball tournament. They won a foot race against the vaunted Rangers. And—what really grabbed his superiors' notice—they won Expert Infantryman Badges for excelling at a dozen combat tasks, in which Petraeus had drilled them incessantly.

Very quickly, Petraeus was promoted to operations officer for the entire battalion, a job usually assigned to a major. It was unclear whether this marked an advance toward or a detour from his dream of a posting with the Rangers. But then, all of a sudden, that ambition was rendered moot.

Officials in Washington had decided to convert the 24th Infantry into the lead element of a new "Rapid Deployment Force" designed to stave off a hypothetical Soviet invasion of the Middle East's oil fields, an emerging scenario in the Pentagon's catalogue of threats. So they assigned Major General John Galvin, one of the Army's top officers in Europe, to come take command of the division.

Galvin needed an aide-de-camp. One of the senior officers at the 24th recommended Petraeus. Galvin gave him a try. At their first meeting, he told the young captain that he didn't want a flunky who would carry his valise and light his cigarette; he wanted someone to go with him everywhere, see what he saw, take notes on what was going well and going badly, discuss how to improve matters, and compose a weekly report card on the progress. Galvin had mentored six aides-de-camp before coming to Fort Stewart, but none leapt into the job as eagerly as Petraeus, who used the opportunity to learn every aspect, large and small, of how a division operated—getting a crash course, on how to command a division, that few officers received so early in their careers. Even during his trial period, Petraeus offered one suggestion after another, many of them unsolicited, on how to solve this problem, fix that glitch, clarify that procedure. Some generals would have been annoyed; Galvin was impressed. He made Petraeus his aide.

Jack Galvin was an unusual Army general. The son of a Massachusetts bricklayer, he'd gone to art school with hopes of becoming a cartoonist, joined the National Guard to earn some money, then, at the suggestion of his sergeant, applied to West Point. To his surprise, he got in, entered its gates in the fall of 1950, and took his life in a different direction.

He was twenty-one when he enrolled, a bit older than most of his classmates and more intellectually inclined. Much later, when he went back to West Point for three years as an assistant professor, he taught in the English Department. Over the years, while an active-duty officer, he would write at least one journal article about the issues facing him at each assignment—almost fifty articles in all—as well as two scholarly books about the American Revolution and one about the origins of airborne infantry.

In the mid-1960s, Galvin was sent to Vietnam as operations officer in the 1st Infantry Division, the legendary "Big Red One." After a particularly grueling firefight, his superior officer ordered him to add forty-five to the tally of Viet Cong dead—the official "body count," which the Pentagon masters loved to tabulate as a self-deceiving indicator of an impending American victory. Galvin, then a rising major, refused to falsify the count. The next thing he knew, he was relieved of his duties and told that he had no future in the 1st Infantry. Shunted off to a public-affairs office, where he compiled the daily press clippings about the war, he got into trouble for including too many critical news articles.

Luckily, Galvin had a friend in high places: a colonel named Paul Gorman, who'd been his battalion commander during the body-count incident and sympathized with his position. Gorman got him a Pentagon job helping to write the secret history of the Vietnam War (which, after it was leaked by military analyst Daniel Ellsberg in 1971, became known as the Pentagon Papers). Galvin discovered, to a greater extent than he'd known, how badly the war had been bungled all along, how hopeless the whole venture really was. He felt further vindicated in his refusal to jack up the body count. And the experience steeled his courage a year later, when, as the commander of a cavalry battalion, he refused a superior's order to send his men into a nighttime frontal assault on a Viet Cong enclave outside the range of US artillery fire. It would have been a suicide mission, for no purpose whatever. The colonel who'd given the order put a disciplinary notation—a mark just short of a reprimand—in Galvin's personnel file. Galvin regarded it as a badge of honor.

Gorman was looking out for him again, and, despite this latest act of insubordination, he got Galvin transferred to Europe, where he earned plaudits at various command positions and eventually won his stars.

By the time Galvin came to Fort Stewart and met Petraeus, he was one of the most highly respected generals in the Army. But he was also still the student and teacher of literature who valued the written word. After a few days of making the rounds on the base, Galvin remarked that there were several young officers doing very creative work; they should be urged to write articles for one of the military journals, so that their ideas could spread across the Army's entire ranks.

Within a few weeks, Petraeus had thirty officers writing articles. He then helped the officers tighten their prose and submit their pieces to what he figured would be the most receptive editors. Many of them were eventually published.

Galvin called the campaign the "War of Information." It was an idea that Petraeus would take with him and build on for years to come.

Knowing full well the value of a mentor's protection, Galvin gave his young aide-de-camp—twenty-three years his junior—a pivotal piece of advice. There was more to the job of general, Galvin told him, than scoring high at Ranger School or winning an Expert Infantryman Badge, laudable as those achievements were. It was important to have a *strategic* outlook, a broader vision of the *world.* He encouraged Petraeus to go back to school. First, Galvin got him assigned to the Command and General Staff College at Fort Leavenworth, where the top tier of junior officers—most of them majors, one rank higher than Petraeus—took off a year to study strategy and play war games, making the kinds of assessments and decisions that generals made in real battles. After that, Galvin urged him to go earn a graduate degree at a top-notch university, which would give him a more sophisticated perspective on politics and policy than any military academy could. Finally, Galvin told him, he should return to West Point to teach for a few years before resuming his climb up the command ladder.

Petraeus took his advice. At Leavenworth, he not only scored first in his class, out of nearly one thousand officers, he also took part in a war game that deepened his understanding of counterinsurgency. The game replayed one of the Army's largest search-and-destroy missions in the Vietnam War. Petraeus and his teammates concluded that simply chasing and killing guerrillas, even with heavy firepower, had little effect on the battle; the Viet Cong simply went into hiding and came out again after the big guns were gone. It was the most concrete vindication of Galula's ideas—if not what should be done, then at least what should not be—that Petraeus had seen yet.

Afterward, he won a fellowship at Princeton University's Woodrow Wilson School of Public and International Affairs and, early on, experienced the comeuppance that Galvin knew he needed before he could develop much further. Petraeus, who'd always earned straight As, got a D on his first economics test and a B on his first political science paper. He suddenly realized that he was on a higher intellectual playing field. He studied harder; the As soon resumed.

He finished the coursework for a PhD in two years. Then, in the summer of 1985, he took an open faculty slot in the Social Science Department at West Point, teaching international relations and economics. "Abe" Lincoln, the Sosh founder, had died a decade earlier, but his tradition of critical inquiry—and exploiting connections in high places—lived on. Petraeus spent much of the time holed up in his basement office, writing his doctoral dissertation. His subject was the Vietnam War and its impact on the US military's attitude toward using force. The thesis was a bit obvious at first glance. By this time, it was common knowledge that the Vietnam debacle had left the Army averse to fighting small wars. Caspar Weinberger, President Reagan's secretary of defense, and General Colin Powell, the chairman of the Joint Chiefs of Staff, had each articulated a list of rules for when to wage combat. The rules became known as the Weinberger Doctrine and the Powell Doctrine, though actually they were restatements, to some degree refinements, of the Army's long-standing outlook on whether and how to fight. American interests had to be *vital,* the political objectives had to be clear, the level of force had to be overwhelming, the ability to win had to be plausible, the support from the public had to be manifest. Under these guidelines, the chances of going to war—short of some cataclysmic shock, such as a Soviet invasion of Europe or a Chinese attack on Taiwan—seemed slim. It was widely joked, and wasn't far off the truth, that some of the most dovish officials in Washington were the generals in the Pentagon.

But Petraeus was trying to go beyond this observation and to work it into an argument that was radical, at least in the context of Army culture. He wanted to make a case for building up light infantry and preparing to fight the sorts of wars that he'd been studying informally for nearly a decade now: the sorts of wars that Powell and Weinberger were rejecting but that he believed the Army was most likely to confront in the near future.

Toward the end of his first year on the West Point faculty, Petraeus learned that General Galvin had been awarded his fourth star and was about to take charge of US Southern Command in Panama, with responsibility for all military forces stationed in Latin America. Throughout the region, communist-backed insurgents were rebelling against US-backed regimes. Petraeus sent his old mentor a note, asking if he could come work for the summer as his assistant. Galvin accepted the offer gladly.

The morning after his arrival, Petraeus went to the daily intelligence briefing. He knew the command's area of operations was rife with turmoil; the troubles in El Salvador were particularly prominent in American newspapers. But he'd had no idea of the fierceness or scope of the violence. The Farabundo Martí National Liberation Front was waging an insurgency war in El Salvador, the Revolutionary Armed Forces of Colombia were doing the same in that country, the Shining Path guerrillas were fomenting chaos in Peru, and, all the while, Cuba and Nicaragua were supplying weapons through harbors and airstrips in Costa Rica and Honduras. General Galvin's briefer rattled off the latest updates on the numbers of firefights, casualties, rocket attacks, ambushes, assassinations, and incidents of sabotage.

"Holy cow!" Petraeus thought to himself. "These guys are at *war*!"

Petraeus had been an Army officer for twelve years now, but this was his first exposure to anything remotely resembling combat. He accompanied Galvin on trips to El Salvador twice, and both times were harrowing.

The fighting had diminished somewhat since the civil war's start five years earlier, but it was still intense, both in the cities and in the countryside. (By the time the war ended in 1992, in a stalemate followed by a political settlement, more than 75,000 Salvadorans—about 1.5 percent of the population—would be killed.) The US embassy in the capital resembled a fortress, with thick bars blocking entry to all the windows and entrances. When Galvin was driven from one place to another in the capital, armed guards surrounded his car in escort vehicles. If an unknown vehicle tried to pass them, the guards raised their long rifles, with standing orders to blow out its tires if the pursuer didn't slow down, though no incident ever came to that.

Technically, American soldiers weren't "fighting" in this war. Congress, fearing a replay of Vietnam, had limited US involvement to 55 military personnel, none of whom could engage directly in combat. (However, through bookkeeping tricks, the actual number rose at times to 150 or so, and a few of the covert personnel sometimes did more with weapons than merely wield them.) Congress further insisted that these military personnel be called "trainers," not "advisers," because the escalation in Vietnam had started with advisers.

The Joint Chiefs hadn't objected to these restrictions because they had no desire to get involved in this conflict to begin with. By the definitions laid down in Army field manuals, this wasn't even a "war." It was a "low-intensity conflict," or LIC (a deliberately unappealing acronym), and the only American armed forces to play any role in LICs were Special Forces, not regular Army soldiers. The 55 "trainers" in El Salvador were all from the 7th Special Forces Group. They were fired on repeatedly, and some of them carried weapons—even Petraeus stashed a submachine gun in a map case when he went out on the road—but they were not officially considered to be at war.

Petraeus had read books about the Special Forces. He knew that they were the legacy of President John F. Kennedy, who entered the White House in 1961 deeply concerned about Soviet Premier Nikita Khrushchev's support for "national liberation movements" throughout the third world. Kennedy set up a secret panel in the National Security Council called "Special Group (Counterinsurgency)" and authorized the creation of a base at Fort Bragg, North Carolina, to recruit and train the Special

Forces. In a speech to West Point graduates in June 1962, Kennedy made a pitch for these forces, telling the cadets about the emergence of "another type of warfare, new in its intensity, ancient in its origin—war by guerrillas, subversives, insurgents, assassins"—requiring the American military to devise "a whole new kind of strategy, a wholly different kind of force, and therefore a new and wholly different kind of military training."

Vietnam was seen, initially, as the laboratory for this different kind of war. Early on, a mix of Special Forces, CIA agents, and action officers from the Agency for International Development pursued classic counterinsurgency methods to isolate the South Vietnamese people from the Viet Cong insurgents.

Petraeus's father-in-law, William Knowlton, had been involved in the most ambitious of these programs, known as CORDS (Civil Operations and Revolutionary Development Support), which created "strategic hamlets"—distinct areas where the population could be separated (in some cases, physically resettled) from the insurgents—and then trained local self-defense units to stave off the insurgents' return. CORDS was led by a brilliant but wild-eyed White House official named Robert Komer, known to those who worked with him as "Blowtorch." (He didn't mind the nickname.) Knowlton had served as Komer's military deputy, and after Petraeus married Knowlton's daughter, the two talked at length about CORDS: how it operated and its similarities to other counterinsurgency campaigns that Petraeus had been studying.

CORDS was a mixed success at best. After a brief experiment with the program under Kennedy's successor, Lyndon Johnson, the Joint Chiefs shifted to a more conventional strategy based on large concentrations of troops and massive firepower. By the end of the war, Special Forces had lost its élan. The whole branch was seen as a career dead-ender; its dismantlement seemed all but inevitable.

Reprieve came in 1977, when commandos from a secret West German counterterrorism squad, called GSG-9, landed stealthily on a runway in Mogadishu, Somalia, and stormed a Lufthansa jetliner that had been hijacked by a group of Palestinians in support of a German terrorist group called the Red Army Faction. The only people killed in the raid were three of the four hijackers. All eighty-six passengers survived without injury.

Several congressional leaders started asking what kind of capabilities the US military had to pull off an operation like this. The answer, it turned out, was none. So the Army created Delta Force, a secret unit within the 5th Special Forces Group. In 1980, President Jimmy Carter called on Delta Force to rescue US embassy personnel who'd been taken hostage by the Islamist revolutionaries in Iran. The planning was inept, the resources were insufficient; the result was a fiasco. In the last months of the Carter administration, Special Forces received a budget boost. In the early months of Ronald Reagan's presidency, which followed, it got a bigger boost still.

In 1981, in their first months in office, President Reagan and his secretary of state, Alexander Haig, decided to "draw a line in the sand" in El Salvador. Two years earlier, the communist-backed Sandinista rebels had overthrown the reactionary US-backed regime in Nicaragua. Reagan and his aides feared that a replay in El Salvador would spark revolutions across the hemisphere.

Brigadier General Fred Woerner, who led the US Military Strategy Assistance Team in El Salvador, conducted a review of the local military and found it riddled with corruption, incompetence, appalling human rights violations (including "death squads" that murdered critics at whim), and an utter cluelessness of how to deal with shrewd insurgents. This combination, if left alone, would soon lead to military defeat and the collapse of the ruling regime: in short, another victory for left-wing insurgents in the Western Hemisphere.

Woerner drafted a National Campaign Plan that addressed what he called "the root causes" of the insurgency. It laid out a program of rural land reform, urban jobs, humanitarian assistance, and basic services for a wider segment of the population. Fighting the insurgents directly was part of the plan, but only part of it—and, even then, only in tandem with a reorganization and reform of the Salvadoran military. The idea behind this approach was that the insurgents were fueled by the country's terrible poverty, its inequitable land-distribution policies, and its murderous repression. If the Sandinistas hadn't triumphed a few years earlier, if Fidel Castro's Cuba wasn't aiding the Salvadoran rebels—in short, if the Salvadoran civil war wasn't seen as a proxy battle in the Soviet-American Cold War—the United States would not have been aiding the regime at all. Certainly Congress wouldn't have tolerated even a minimal presence of US military forces, especially since, in 1980, a Salvadoran death squad had murdered four American churchwomen who'd been aiding victims of the army's violence. On a number of levels—strategic, tactical, and moral—the regime could not (and, even many of the US officers in the region believed, should not) survive unless it underwent drastic political, economic, and social reforms.

A widely read sixty-three-page Army War College paper by John Waghelstein, a Special Forces colonel who'd fought insurgencies all through the 1960s, in Panama, Bolivia, the Dominican Republic, and Vietnam—and who'd been commander of the US Military Group in El Salvador when Woerner wrote his plan—concluded with this sentence: "Simply killing guerrillas will not solve El Salvador's problems."

Woerner's National Campaign Plan, at this point, was still a work in progress; sizable pockets of resistance remained in the military and the ruling elite. Still, Petraeus was stunned when he read the plan and Waghelstein's paper on the document's origins. Here was an insurgency war, and here were US Special Forces—some of them old hands from the Vietnam CORDS program—trying to rescue another deeply flawed regime by reviving the classic principles of counterinsurgency.

Petraeus was ebullient about his discovery. When a *Wall Street Journal* reporter came to Southern Command to write about this new kind of war, Petraeus, who'd been assigned to escort him, exclaimed (and was quoted as saying, in his first of many appearances on the front page of a national newspaper), "LIC is a growth industry."

But Petraeus also recognized that, for the moment, anyway, LIC was confined to *Special* Forces, which had been created to perform missions that the regular Army could not or would not touch.

Galvin was frustrated by this marginalization. Not that he wanted thousands of US combat troops to fight El Salvador's war; in fact, he and several of the Special Forces officers, including Waghelstein, saw an advantage in keeping America's footprint small. But he thought it was dangerous to pretend that this wasn't a war. Galvin had recently given a speech in London about the failure of Western military institutions to come to grips with the world's new dangers—terrorism, guerrilla wars, international drug trafficking, the alarmingly swift collapse of suddenly unstable regimes—and he decided to expand the ideas into an article for *Parameters,* the journal of the US Army War College.

Petraeus was spending much of his time that summer writing papers, or coordinating the assignment of papers to others, on various issues in the region. He'd typed up a list of these ideas under the heading, "War of Information Status Report," invoking the term that Galvin had coined back in their days together at the 24th Infantry Division. Topics on the list included the links between drug traffickers and insurgents, the historical context of Latin America's growing instability, a broad strategy for SouthCom, and why El Salvador was not like Vietnam, among others.

Galvin gave Petraeus the task of ghostwriting the article for *Parameters.* There was no transcript of the London speech, nor had Galvin written out a text ahead of time. As usual on such occasions, he'd only scribbled some ideas and a rough outline on a small stack of three-by-five-inch note cards. He handed Petraeus the cards and told him to expand on them as he saw fit.

The article, published in *Parameters'* Winter 1986 issue, was called "Uncomfortable Wars: Toward a New Paradigm." It was widely, and correctly, read as an assault on the Army establishment: an assault so direct and piercing that only a four-star general—and an unusually self-contained four-star general, at that—would have dared put his name on it. And only the most confident and nurtured young major would have dared go along for the ride, much less take control of the wheel, even anonymously.

The article began:

> We in the military . . . tend to invent for ourselves a comfortable vision of war . . . one that fits our plans, our assumptions, our hopes, and our preconceived ideas. We arrange in our minds a war we can comprehend on our own terms, usually with an enemy who looks like us and acts like us. This comfortable conceptualization becomes the accepted way of seeing things and, as such, ceases to be an object for further investigation unless it comes under serious challenge as a result of some major event—usually a military disaster.

Galvin's warning, via Petraeus's pen, was that the West was skating on the brink of that disaster. New kinds of conflict were coming to dominate the landscape: subversion, terrorism, guerrilla wars. "They do not fit into our image of war," so we tend "to view them as being on the periphery." We call them low-intensity conflicts, to suggest that they're "a kind of appendage, an add-on, a lesser thing." We are accustomed "to thinking about defeating our enemy by bringing combat power, primarily firepower, to bear on him." Yet in these kinds of "revolutionary wars," firepower was no longer so relevant. In these kinds of wars, the article went on—drawing on Galula and CORDS and the National Campaign Plan for El Salvador—the two sides "compete principally for the support of the national population." And the government must not only fight the insurgents on the battlefield but also "reestablish its political legitimacy" by addressing "contentious, long-ignored, but popular issues tied to key facets of national life—sociopolitical, economic, educational, juridical." In this kind of war, a doctrine based principally on firepower and body-counts may be not merely futile but disastrous. "If, for example, the military's actions in killing 50 guerrillas cause 200 previously uncommitted citizens to join the insurgent cause," the article argued, "the use of force will have been counterproductive."

It was an idea that Petraeus would repeat often years later.

At this point in the article, Petraeus quoted his favorite passage from Larteguy's *The Centurions,* about the two sides in the French Indochina War playing two different games with two different decks of cards. He then noted that, like the officers in that novel, "we are experiencing something new in warfare, something that requires us to restudy our doctrine, tactics, organization, and training."

The key problem lay in the ethos of the modern officer corps itself. "One reason we have accepted the comfortable vision of war," the article continued, "is that we keep our noses to the grindstone of bureaucratic business and don't look up very often." The article concluded, in words reminiscent of Colonel Lincoln's statement of purpose for West Point's Sosh department, "Let us get our young leaders away from the grindstone now and then, and encourage them to reflect on developments outside the fortress-cloister. Only then will they develop into leaders capable of adapting to the changed environment of warfare and able to fashion a new paradigm that addresses all the dimensions of the conflicts that may lie ahead."

Twenty years later, after his first tour in the Iraq War as commander of the 101st Airborne Division, Petraeus wrote an article in the Army journal *Military Review,* under his own name, on how he learned to apply the principles of counterinsurgency during his occupation of Mosul. In it, he quoted those last passages from "Uncomfortable Wars," and added, "General Galvin's words were relevant then, but they are even more applicable today"—never noting that he was the one who'd written those words.

At the end of the summer of 1986, after his brief posting at SouthCom was over, Petraeus returned to the "fortress-cloister" at West Point with a clearer vision of a plausible career path for himself in the Army—and a living example, in General Jack Galvin, of an officer who'd managed to rise through the ranks while prodding change from within.

First, though, Petraeus had to earn his PhD, and the summer with Galvin also gave him some ideas on how to do that. He turned the final third of his 328-page dissertation into an open appeal for the US military, especially his Army, to get over its post-Vietnam aversion to low-intensity conflicts and to take a deeper interest in counterinsurgency doctrine.

The "reluctance to get involved in Central America with US troops," he wrote, "was translated into military reluctance to develop plans for such potential operations, based apparently on the theory that if one has no plans, they cannot be executed." However, he went on, reciting the argument that he'd ghostwritten for General Galvin in *Parameters,* small wars affecting US interests were not only more likely to take place than large wars, they were already upon us—and the military should "come to grips" with that fact by changing its doctrine, tactics, and personnel policies so that new officers could devise effective plans.

"Lessons of history" can be "misleading," he went on. It was well understood that the Cold Warriors of the early 1960s had distorted history when they likened the communist assault on South Vietnam to Adolf Hitler's invasion of Poland or Czechoslovakia. Now, he wrote, the military chiefs of the mid-1980s were similarly "myopic" in seeing every third-world crisis as another Vietnam. He quoted Mark Twain on the broad issue of lessons:

"We should be careful to get out of an experience only the wisdom that is in it—and stop there; lest we be like the cat that sits down on a hot stove-lid. She will never sit down on a hot stove-lid again—and that is well; but also she will never sit down on a cold one anymore."

Which way the Army would go—whether it continued to avoid all stove lids or came to realize that it might sometimes be necessary to sit on one—

"will depend," Petraeus concluded, "on forthcoming generations of military leaders" and "the lessons *they* take from Vietnam."

Petraeus was determined to be one of those new military leaders who sat on stove lids—and carried forth the forgotten, age-old lessons on how to do that.

But not just yet.

Petraeus's adviser at Princeton, Richard Ullman, a prominent scholar of international relations, urged him to publish his dissertation as a book. The young officer was reluctant.

Recently, an Army major named Andrew Krepinevich Jr., a former instructor in the Sosh department who graduated West Point in 1972, two years before Petraeus, had turned his dissertation, which he'd written at Harvard, into a book called *The Army and Vietnam.* In it, he argued that the United States lost the war not because of the news media or because politicians forced the generals to fight with one hand tied behind their backs (the military's standard excuses), but rather because the Army's commanders didn't understand the kind of war they were fighting: they fought the kind of war they knew—a war waged with large units and heavy firepower, as they had in Korea and World War II—but the Viet Cong were fighting an insurgency war, which required a different approach.

Krepinevich and Petraeus, it turned out, had read the same books on counterinsurgency, Malaya, and the Philippines. Shortly before his book was published, Krepinevich came to West Point to give a lecture about it. Petraeus, who had just started to teach in the Sosh department, attended the talk and approached the speaker afterward, practically bouncing with energy, eager to get a copy of his work, which seemed to reinforce and expand on some of the conclusions that he was gleaning from his own research.

When Krepinevich's book came out, the backlash was severe. Bruce Palmer Jr., a retired Army general and former Vietnam commander, wrote a scathing review in *Parameters,* condemning the author for his "crippling naivete," his "lack of historical breadth and objectivity," and his "abrasive" tone. Palmer was no lightweight. He had once been the Army's acting chief of staff and was still on close terms with many active-duty generals. A four-star general like Jack Galvin might get away with broad swipes against the institutional culture, but not a major, not one writing under his own name, anyway. Palmer's review was widely—and correctly—interpreted as a death-sentence for the upstart's career. Krepinevich went on to a few staff jobs in the Pentagon as a military adviser to high-ranking civilians. But the notion that he might ever command a combat unit was out of the question. He was barred even from speaking again at West Point. (A few years later, he would retire from the Army as a lieutenant colonel and head up a defense-policy think tank.)

Petraeus, too, was a mere major when he finished his dissertation. He may have been assertive, but he wasn't crazy. Toward the end of his paper, he wrote, "Those who criticize the conventional wisdom do so at their own risk." He then summarized the case of Major Krepinevich, but only in a footnote, ending it with the observation that a book review as harsh as the one in *Parameters,* written by a retired general with the cachet of Bruce Palmer, "can be unsettling to say the least." Petraeus knew that he needed a star or two on his shoulders before he could openly wage his own War of Information on the Army itself—especially the sort of assault that he was advocating behind the scenes, first as General Galvin's ghostwriter, then as the author of a dissertation that he was intent on ensuring almost no one would read.

The task of publishing, promoting, and proselytizing a dissertation that pressured the Army to abandon its traditional ways, and embrace the doctrine of COIN, was left to Petraeus's protégé, John Nagl.

3.

"Eating Soup with a Knife"

When John Nagl and David Petraeus first met in the spring of 1987, they were both about to go to Europe for a close-up view of the Cold War's climax.

Nagl, finishing his third year at West Point, was the highest-ranking cadet in the Sosh department's international relations section, a distinction rewarded with a summer internship at SHAPE—Supreme Headquarters Allied Powers Europe—the military-operations branch of the Atlantic Alliance, situated on the outskirts of Mons, Belgium.

Petraeus was wrapping up his second year as a Sosh professor. By contract, he was supposed to stay for a third year, but General Jack Galvin was on his way to SHAPE to take over as supreme allied commander, and Petraeus again asked his mentor if he could tag along as his speechwriter, not just for the summer but full-time. A phone call from a four-star could override all other obligations; Galvin made the call, and Petraeus's days at the academy were over.

Nagl had seen Petraeus in the Sosh corridors but had never taken a class with him. Since they would both soon be at SHAPE, another professor in the department introduced them to each other. Petraeus had just finished his dissertation and proudly showed Nagl a copy. Nagl gave it a glance but nothing more. He still saw his future in the armor corps along the East–West German border. Like most of his fellow cadets, like most Army officers, he regarded the Vietnam War as ancient history, to the extent that he thought about it at all.

Though he was cutting out early, Petraeus had been on the Sosh faculty long enough to absorb the ethos and traditions of the Lincoln Brigade: the sense of fraternity, the value of networking, and the admonition by the department's founder, Colonel "Abe" Lincoln, to "pick good people, pick them young, help them to grow, keep in touch." Petraeus figured that Nagl must be smart, given his class ranking. He noticed the same gleam in the eye that he'd possessed at Nagl's age, thirteen years earlier. So when Nagl dropped by Petraeus's office that summer to say hello, the major cleared a corner of his desk where the cadet could work and invited him to stay.

The two didn't talk much about counterinsurgency or El Salvador, though the civil war there was still going on. Petraeus had enough SHAPE business to keep him busy: the startling phenomenon of Mikhail Gorbachev, the Soviet Union's new reformist leader; the Reagan-Gorbachev nuclear arms talks to remove all medium-range missiles from Europe; the prospect of unilateral Soviet troop cuts from East Germany and Czechoslovakia; and, at the same time as all this, discussions within the NATO alliance on continuing to "modernize" tanks, planes, and other major weapons, in case Gorbachev was ousted in a coup or turned out to be a fake.

Nagl too was immersed that summer in classic Cold War issues, spending much of his time at the corner of Petraeus's desk, writing a senior thesis on interoperability, the nuts-and-bolts issue of ensuring that NATO's sixteen nations were able to use one another's weapons, bases, and supply lines in case they had to fight a war together. In between his own projects for Galvin, Petraeus supervised Nagl's thesis as if he were conducting a tutorial back at West Point, peppering him with questions, suggesting research material, and copyediting his drafts. Petraeus thought it was one of the best papers by a cadet that he'd ever read, maybe the best paper on the topic by anybody.

Petraeus knew that Nagl was angling to win a Rhodes Scholarship after graduating the following year. He wrote a letter of recommendation and got General Galvin to sign it.

Nagl went back to West Point in the fall, graduated in the top 2 percent of his class, won the Rhodes, and studied international relations at Oxford for the next two years. While he was there, the Berlin Wall crumbled. Soon after he got back to the States, Saddam Hussein invaded Kuwait, and Nagl was sent to Saudi Arabia with the 1st Cavalry Division as part of Operation Desert Shield. Then came the American counterattack known as Desert Storm, the rapid crushing of Iraq's crack forces, and Nagl's realization that there were no longer any countries in the world capable of confronting the US Army in tank-on-tank warfare—the sort of warfare for which Nagl had been preparing.

Still, Nagl's crisis at this point was merely a personal matter: what was he going to do with the rest of his life? The shift in global politics didn't seem to pose a threat to national security. The United States might face different kinds of challenges—from guerrillas, terrorists, shadow warriors of various sorts—but, at first glance, they didn't seem very formidable. In southern Iraq, his tank platoon had come across Iraqi foot soldiers hiding in the dunes—not the sorts of targets that he and his men were trained to fight, but taking them out had been no problem.

Then, almost exactly a year later, on February 14, 1992, Nagl fought a second conflict. This one took place at the National Training Center in Fort Irwin, California, a vast stretch of the Mojave Desert—nearly one thousand square miles of uncluttered terrain—that the Army had turned into a complex of mock battlefields a dozen years earlier to give soldiers a round of fairly realistic training. The center's scenarios were nearly always the same: the "Krasnovian" army—a stand-in for the Soviets, played by an American unit whose entire mission was to play the "Red Team" in these war games—has invaded an ally; the US combat unit rotating through the training center that week must defend the territory and defeat the enemy.

Nagl's tank company, equipped with brand-new M-1 tanks, had no problem blowing away the Krasnovians, who were using slightly older American tanks, modified to resemble Russian T-72s and T-80s. But at one point in the mock battle, some of the Krasnovian soldiers dismounted from their tanks, maneuvered on foot, and managed to surround and obliterate Nagl's unit. One of the most up-to-date tank companies in the US Army was, as Nagl later put it in an article about the exercise, "decimated by a light-infantry company of approximately 150 men."

The main difference, it seemed, between the real enemies in Iraq and the pretend ones in California was that the former fought badly and the latter fought well. What if the next real enemies were more skilled than the Iraqis had been? Ever since Desert Storm, Nagl had thought that his nation might soon have to face new, more furtive kinds of foes. Now, after the war game at Fort Irwin, he had a more disturbing thought: his Army didn't know how to fight them.

Not long after the battle at Fort Irwin, Nagl went back to Oxford. He was about to marry the British girlfriend he'd left there, Susanne Varga, a student of French and German literature whose parents had fled Hungary in 1956 during the Soviet crackdown. Nagl's official rationale for returning, though, was to earn a doctorate degree and, in the process, to write a dissertation that somehow came to grips with this new face of warfare.

Nagl never read Petraeus's dissertation, nor had he ever come across David Galula's work, which was out of print. But now, back at Oxford, he did read the British counterinsurgency classics, which made similar points, including some of the books that Petraeus had perused a decade earlier: Kitson, Thompson, Colonel C. E. Callwell's *Small Wars: Their Principles and Practice.* From there, he embarked on a research project about Britain's colonial war in Malaya. On a trip to the National Army Museum in the Chelsea section of London, he came upon the papers—thirty boxes' worth—of Field Marshal Sir Gerald Templer, the British commander who defeated the Malayan insurgency. Only two other scholars before Nagl had ever checked out this cache of documents. Nagl's friends were telling him that he was crazy to write his dissertation on such a thoroughly discarded topic. The dust gathered on Templer's papers seemed to confirm that he was headed down a lonely alleyway.

While pursuing this odd new interest, he was also taking graduate-level courses, and in one of them, a theoretical class on international relations, he found himself particularly drawn to some essays by Alexander George. A political scientist at Stanford University and the RAND Corporation, George had pioneered the "case studies" approach, premised on the idea that a nation's decisions in wars and crises are shaped by the cognitive and intellectual styles of its leaders: how they view the workings of the world, how they think through problems, how they deal with stress, and how swiftly they learn lessons from the histories they've read or the events in which they've participated.

Nagl's research project was evolving into a sort of case study as well, examining why, after a few years of failure, the British succeeded in crushing the Malayan insurgency in the 1950s—and why, despite a decade of trying, the United States failed to defeat the Viet Cong in the 1960s. Reading George, he wondered if a key factor might have been the two empires' military leaders and the contrasting ways in which they *learned.*

The conclusion Nagl wound up reaching confirmed his suspicion: the difference between the victory in Malaya and the defeat in Vietnam, he wrote, was "best explained by the differing organizational cultures of the two armies; in short, that the British army was a learning institution and the American army was not."

The Malayan peninsula, in Southeast Asia, formed one of several colonies where communist rebellions stirred in the wake of the Second World War, some motivated by nationalism, others by ideology, most by a mix or convergence of both. In Malaya, the insurgents were mostly ethnic Chinese who emulated Mao's guerrilla-war doctrine and rallied popular support through a battle cry for independence from Britain's colonial rule.

Initially, the British commanders fought back with the sorts of large-scale sweeps and battlefield set pieces that they'd mounted against the Japanese a few years earlier. The strategy changed in 1950, when Lieutenant General Harold Briggs, a veteran of an earlier campaign in Burma, took over as director of operations and, through a massive intelligence effort, discovered that the insurgents were getting the bulk of their support—food, supplies, and information about British military movements—from the Malayan people. In short, Briggs realized (and Nagl discovered through his research) that this was a political as well as a military campaign, fought for the allegiance or control of the people. So Briggs embarked on a campaign of separating the population from the insurgents, then supplying the people with a slew of basic services to help earn their trust and allegiance—or at least to slacken their opposition.

Briggs's strategy wasn't an example of what would later be called "soft power" or "winning hearts and minds"; it had a more brutal dimension than those phrases implied. The people, nearly a half million of them, were *forcibly* separated from the insurgency, relocated from their homes to a string of 450 "new villages," many of them fenced off and guarded, at least until the areas could be "pacified." And amid this process, the insurgents—cut off from their supplies—were literally starved to death. Those who didn't die either surrendered or wandered out of their hiding places to gather food, at which point British soldiers, who by this time had gathered intelligence on the insurgents' locations, were standing by to kill them.

In that sense, war was still war. But the operations of fighting and killing were very different from conventional practices. There was little of the indiscriminate bombing, shelling, or wholesale slaughtering that often came with strategies built on massive concentrations of troops and firepower.

In a campaign centered on winning over the population, those techniques would have been not just futile but counterproductive.

Nagl unearthed a book by Harry Miller, a journalist reporting on the Malayan Emergency, as the war was euphemistically called. In one chapter, Miller quoted Briggs as saying about his war plan, "You know, some brigadiers and battalion commanders aren't going to like what I'm going to tell them—that they won't be able to use battalions or companies in sweeping movements anymore." To the extent that combat forces were used at all, they would operate in "small patrols" led by junior officers, sometimes lance corporals, who would have to "make decisions on the spot."

Templer, the hero of Nagl's book (and of many popular British accounts as well), stepped up these small-scale military patrols when he took over in 1952, covering an ever-wider area of the country, one province at a time. He also promised independence for Malaya, a pledge that co-opted the insurgents' most potent slogan and thus undercut the main source of their appeal.

The British army may have been more open to this sort of warfare, Nagl surmised, because of its colonial traditions, which required cultivating "an understanding of the nature of the peoples and politics" in a specific area—and learning from experience "that a military solution stands or falls as the people affected decide to support or oppose it."

More important still, from Nagl's perspective, Templer institutionalized the lessons learned from the Malaya campaign. Digging through the British army's archives, he found a memo that Templer had written at the outset of his command:

"I have been impressed by the wealth of jungle fighting experience available on different levels in Malaya and among different categories of persons. At the same time, I have been disturbed by the fact that this great mass of detailed knowledge has not been properly collated or presented to those whose knowledge and experience is not so great. This vast store of knowledge must be pooled."

And so Templer commissioned the writing of a book, which would lay out this knowledge for colonial soldiers and police. The book was titled *The Conduct of Anti-Terrorist Operations in Malaya*. Designed to fit inside a pocket of jungle-green uniforms, it became known as "the soldier's bible."

By contrast, the US Army, from the nation's origins, had seen its mission as "the eradication of threats to national survival." As a result, Nagl wrote, quoting the military historian Russell Weigley, "the strategy of annihilation became characteristically the American way in war." The irony was that, throughout the twentieth century, American presidents had frequently sent troops (usually marines) to fight small wars in colonies or third-world countries: Cuba, the Philippines, Honduras, Mexico, Nicaragua, and the Dominican Republic. But any lessons of these conflicts, Nagl wrote, "were quickly lost to the belief that such wars were not the Army's true business."

Nagl recounted President Kennedy's brief fling with counterinsurgency doctrine—the recognition that this was "another type of warfare," requiring another type of strategy, training, and soldier—and its still briefer revival in the Johnson administration, with Robert Komer's creation of CORDS and the "strategic hamlets" (similar to Malaya's "new villages") to separate the South Vietnamese people from the Viet Cong's insurgents. General Creighton Abrams, who took command of the US Army in Vietnam in 1968, rather late in the war, had a go at steering his troops away from "search and destroy" toward "protect the population." But the attempts didn't take hold; the top brass resisted them.

More typical was Abrams's predecessor, General William Westmoreland, who when asked at a press conference how he planned to deal with an insurgency, replied, *"Firepower."* In the spring of 1965, in response to repeated requests for British assistance in the war, Sir Robert Thompson himself led an advisory mission to US headquarters in Saigon. Thompson concluded that the American focus on heavy firepower was counterproductive and suggested a switch to smaller patrols and a strategy of protecting the population. His advice was ignored.

Westmoreland's operations chief, General William DePuy, who was widely regarded as one of the Army's most intellectual officers, later told an official historian, "I guess I should have studied human nature and the history of Vietnam and of revolutions, and should have known it, but I didn't."

DePuy's admission was more a shrug than a lament. After the war, he was put in charge of writing the new edition of the Army's *Operations* field manual. Not only was it silent on the matter of small wars, it envisioned even the big war—NATO versus the Warsaw Pact on the plains of

Europe—as little more than a clash of frontal assaults, with the question of victory or defeat settled by a calculation of which side had amassed the most firepower.

It was the contrast between DePuy's field manual and Templer's handbook on antiterrorist operations that Nagl found most telling and alarming. A book of army doctrine was no small matter. It conveyed to everyone, from the chiefs and the officer corps on down, basic instructions on their missions and objectives. It determined how they would fight under certain circumstances and what kind of training they would receive in the meantime. It shaped what kinds of weapons would be developed and built. In other words, doctrine could nudge a large organization like the Army into recognizing, and adapting to, new challenges. It was essential to learning, and as Nagl understood from his studies, learning was the key to everything. Templer ordered up a doctrinal handbook, precisely so that the entire British army could learn the lessons he was learning in Malaya. A big problem with the US Army in Vietnam, to Nagl's mind, was that it had no doctrine on how to fight these kinds of wars.

In his research, Nagl found an eye-opening passage in Westmoreland's 1976 memoir, *A Soldier Reports:* "Like most Americans who served in Vietnam," the general had written, "I had at first only vicarious experience in counterinsurgency warfare," as "no earlier assignment had involved such an intricate relationship between the military and the political . . . There was no book to tell us how to do the job."

Nagl then recited the contemporary lesson that he'd been mulling for some time: that Operation Desert Storm, his one experience in combat, "may well have been an aberration, the last of the conventional industrial age conflicts; it was certainly a lesson to the states and non-state actors of the developing world not to confront the West in conventional combat." But, he went on, those foes could draw on "many other ways to use force to achieve political goals: terrorism, subversion, insurgency." And so the "end of the Cold War has returned to the front pages the small wars of the nineteenth century that were so critical an element in shaping the culture of the British army," including the wars in such places as Afghanistan and, later, Malaya. "In these dirty little wars," Nagl continued, "political and military tasks intertwine and the objective is more often 'nation-building' than the destruction of an enemy army." The US Army's leaders "will have to make the ability to learn to deal with messy, uncomfortable situations"—an unwitting echo of his mentor Petraeus's ghostwritten article on "uncomfortable wars"—"an integral part of their organizational culture."

In short, someone would have to write the book of US Army doctrine that Westmoreland acknowledged didn't exist, the book that would tell everyone else "how to do the job" and that, as a result, would change the Army's "organizational culture." Nagl made it his mission to be the one who wrote that book. In the meantime, his dissertation would serve as his calling card.

One afternoon in the spring of 1996, soon after he'd started writing the first draft of his dissertation, Nagl was reading T. E. Lawrence's *Seven Pillars of Wisdom* while taking a bath in his married-students' residence at St. Antony's College, Oxford. Lawrence was the renegade British officer who helped lead the "Arab revolt" against Ottoman occupiers during the First World War, and his classic, if somewhat flamboyant, memoir was among the very few volumes written in English from an insurgent's vantage point. Nagl was about a quarter of the way into the thick volume when one sentence raised his eyebrows:

"War upon rebellion was messy and slow, like eating soup with a knife."

He jolted out of the tub, shouted "Eureka!" and dashed, dripping wet, into the living room, where he announced to his wife, "I've found the title of my dissertation!"

Nagl wound up altering Lawrence of Arabia's vivid metaphor just slightly to highlight his main theme, which involved how armies learn, and don't learn, to adapt to change. The title he emblazoned on his own book's cover was *Learning to Eat Soup with a Knife.*

The phrase would catch on as a slogan and a mandate among like-minded officers and military analysts. But in their enthusiasm for the COIN cause, many of them, including sometimes Nagl himself, would tend to downplay, even ignore, the other half of Lawrence's sentence: that eating soup this way—that making war on insurgents as a general proposition—was "messy and slow," perhaps messier and slower than Americans in the early twenty-first century would tolerate, regardless of how well the Army had learned to do it.

4.

Revolutions

Late in the summer of 1997, John Nagl returned to West Point to teach in the Social Science Department, as he'd committed to do when he went off to grad school at the Army's expense. As a cadet a decade earlier, Nagl had loved hanging out with the officer-PhDs on the Sosh faculty, all of them fast runners and voracious readers who'd fought the pretend wars in the California desert and could hold forth on the relative merits of German beers and quaint villages, which they assumed they'd be exploring through the coming best years of their lives. Now he was one of them, and while the banter about things German had faded along with the Cold War, the cultish swagger still swayed.

Sosh had always fostered a climate of critical inquiry, even benign insubordination. But the air of scrutiny and rebellion was thickening in the years of Nagl's return. He and his new colleagues had spent the past few years in real firefights, and Nagl was far from the only one who came back with doubts about the judgment of his superiors.

Nagl had fought in Desert Storm, which the Army chiefs regarded as a "major combat operation," however brief. But some of his colleagues had fought, or faced hostile fire, in Haiti, Somalia, Central America, or the Balkans, in the sorts of small wars that Nagl foresaw as dominating the coming post-Soviet era.

One of Nagl's closest colleagues, Isaiah "Ike" Wilson, who'd graduated West Point a year behind Nagl and now cotaught a course with him on American foreign policy, had been company commander of an Apache helicopter unit, flying missions in support of civilian-evacuation operations in the Balkans. He'd faced daily threats from shoulder-mounted Stinger antiaircraft missiles, at least a thousand of which were circulating in the world, many of them in the hands of hostile militias and terrorists; but the Army's chiefs didn't define what he'd been doing as "war." A soldier whose career-sheet showed a check mark next to "combat experience" had a good chance of steady promotion. But since these kinds of wars weren't regarded as combat, there was no such check mark for Wilson or for the other soldiers who'd risked their lives in similar settings.

The Army had a new term for these kinds of armed engagements, a term that made LIC, for low-intensity conflicts, seem macho by comparison. It was "military operations other than war," or MOOTW, widely and derisively pronounced "*moot*-wah." There were signs that a few high-ranking officers were taking these operations seriously. A new Army field manual stated that regular soldiers—not just Special Forces and CIA agents—might sometimes be allowed to participate. A few especially imaginative officers also managed to set up a Peacekeeping Institute at the Army War College, in recognition that the soldiers who'd been sent to Somalia in the early nineties had no idea how to deal with humanitarian crises in the heat of a civil war. The Army also created the Joint Readiness Training Center at Fort Chaffee, Arkansas, a complex modeled after the National Training Center at Fort Irwin, California, except that, instead of big head-on battles against the Krasnovians, the scenarios involved dirty little wars in which US forces were deployed to support the fictitious third-world nation of Cortina against the Cortina Liberation Front, an insurgent group assisted from across the eastern border by the People's Democratic Republic of Atlantica. And instead of driving tanks on a vast desert plain, the troops sent to the JRTC—light infantry, Special Forces, and occasionally marines—went out on foot patrols in mock villages, where they had to distinguish bad guys from innocent bystanders (all played by hired actors), defeating the former while protecting the latter.

Nonetheless, the signals from the top made clear that the official attitude toward these kinds of conflicts had barely changed. Army General John Shalikashvili, the chairman of the Joint Chiefs of Staff and thus the highest-ranking officer in the entire US military, was widely known to have muttered, "Real men don't do *moot*-wah." The Peacekeeping Institute was funded at less than $1 million a year, and, in the five years of its existence, only congressional support had kept the Pentagon from shutting it down. Even the field manual that allowed regular soldiers to fight in these operations contained a caveat—which top generals had demanded—that no Army units could be trained for these missions unless and until they were expressly ordered to go take part in one. Which meant that if they ever did receive such an order, they'd have almost no time to learn what they needed to do. This, of course, was not an oversight; it was deliberate; the higher-ups didn't want the Army to "do *moot*-wah," and the best way to ensure it never did was to keep soldiers from learning how.

These were the issues that Nagl, Wilson, and other Sosh professors discussed with cadets in their classes and, more intensely, with one another afterward in their offices or nearby bars. They, too, uttered "*moot*-wah" with a smirk, but their sarcasm was directed at the absurdity of the term, not at the seriousness of the conflicts it described. These were soul-searching discussions about their personal experiences in "the 'other-than-war' wars of the nineties" (another snarky phrase they'd coined to describe the conflicts that felt like wars to *them*) and what these wars meant, both for national security and for their own prospects in the Army.

They strode the cusp of a generational shift, and they saw themselves as the elite of their generation, the new centurions manning the vanguard, plotting the course of change from within.

Change was coming, and sooner than they anticipated: in less than a decade, ushered in—as agents of change often are—by the widening awareness of a looming disaster.

Meanwhile, a competing vision of future warfare was taking hold in high-level policy circles, a vision that would push the American military in a very different direction. Its enthusiasts called it a "revolution in military affairs," even turning the phrase into an acronym, RMA, as if to make it official. It foresaw, and advocated, a style of warfare that relied not on human contact or ground troops but on high-tech sensors and "smart bombs," thus relegating the Army's budding COIN factions to still more distant sidelines.

The revolution in military affairs began with a model airplane and a lawn-mower engine.

John Foster, a nuclear physicist, the Pentagon's chief scientist, and a former director of the Lawrence Livermore weapons laboratory, was a devotee of model airplanes. In 1971 he proposed adapting the stuff of his hobby into a new type of weapons system. The idea was to develop an inexpensive, unmanned aircraft and to equip it with a camera pointed down toward the ground. The plane would fly reconnaissance missions over enemy targets;

if a bomb could fit inside the plane's belly, the same plane could be used to destroy those targets, too. Within two years, DARPA, the Defense Advanced Research Projects Agency, the Pentagon's experimental weapons center, built a prototype. Weighing seventy-five pounds and powered by a modified lawn-mower engine, it could stay aloft for two hours while carrying a twenty-eight-pound payload.

Around this time, the Vietnam War was grinding to its grim conclusion, and the military was refocusing on the balance of power in Europe, where it seemed that the Soviet Union and its Warsaw Pact allies outnumbered the United States and NATO. If the Soviets invaded West Germany, and if NATO couldn't hold the line with conventional forces, America was treaty-bound to respond with nuclear weapons. Yet that would be suicide: over the previous decade, the Soviets had built up a nuclear arsenal of their own; if America nuked them, they could nuke America.

So DARPA commissioned a secret study to "identify and characterize" new military technologies that might give the president "a variety of response options"—including "alternatives to massive nuclear destruction"—in the event of a NATO–Warsaw Pact war. An unstated purpose of the study (as anyone who had ever done Pentagon contracting would intuit) was to make a case for throwing a lot more money at some of DARPA's own high-tech projects.

DARPA's drawing boards held several programs that fit the bill, including Foster's unmanned plane, which could conceivably be fitted with high-tech bombs and missiles capable of hitting a target with uncanny accuracy. The idea, as laid out in the study, was that these weapons could destroy military targets deep behind enemy lines—air bases, supply depots, follow-on echelons of tank formations—and thus disrupt and delay the Soviet offensive, giving NATO a chance to reinforce, regroup, and fight back.

In 1978, as a direct result of this study, DARPA and the Army conducted the first tests of a weapon called Assault Breaker, which was modeled after the study's concept almost exactly.

One year later, a Pentagon official named Andrew Marshall—who had worked on the DARPA study—started noticing signs that the Soviets were in a panic. Marshall was director of the Office of Net Assessment, where one of his jobs was to monitor Soviet military journals. In several of these journals, a number of prominent Soviet generals were portraying

Assault Breaker as a serious threat—the harbinger of a "military-technical revolution," as they called it, which their own scientists might be unable to match.

It was a bit strange. Assault Breaker wasn't in production yet; its early tests were uneven. But if it worried the Russians, if *they* believed it not only worked but revolutionized warfare, Marshall took that as an argument for the Pentagon to speed up its development, and, when it was ready, to build lots of them, in order to reinforce the Russians' worries, to persuade them that they couldn't win a war in Europe and therefore shouldn't start one.

By the mid-1980s, as microprocessing technologies advanced, all the branches of the US armed forces were developing new weapons along these lines: laser-guided bombs, radar-guided missiles, high-resolution surveillance gear, and high-speed communications networks to link them together.

In the summer of 1986, Marshall began work on a follow-on report, this one unclassified and eventually presented with fanfare at a Pentagon press conference. The result of a fifteen-month study, it concluded that the Russians were right: that, over the next two decades, these new American weapons really would change the face of warfare. Marshall was loath to copy a Russian term, the "military-technical revolution," so he came up with one of his own: the "revolution in military affairs."

A shrewd, gnomish intellectual, Marshall carried far more weight in the defense world than his obscure title suggested. He used his office—which he'd managed to continue directing since its creation in 1973—to build a network, funding small projects that intrigued him, cultivating smart staff assistants and installing them in influential places afterward, talking behind the scenes with powerful legislators who felt smart when they talked with someone as smart as Marshall, and sponsoring conferences to which all these increasingly important people were invited. As a result of Andy Marshall's mere utterances, RMA—the term, the concept underlying it, and the weapons systems needed to turn it into reality—rose to the top of the agenda in congressional committees, party caucuses, private think tanks, and blue-ribbon policy panels.

On November 9, 1989, the Berlin Wall fell. Five days later, Don Rice, the secretary of the Air Force, called a meeting of his staff. The US military had been focused for decades on the threat of a war in Europe; now the continent's great divide seemed on the verge of mending. What would this new world look like? What threats would America face? These were the same questions that creative officers in the Army were asking. But to Rice, the most important question was how the new world would affect the United States Air Force.

Rice's job was a civilian post, and usually a decorative one; most of its occupants had done little more than kowtow to the generals. But Rice was more engaged and knew more about the subject. Through most of the seventies and eighties, he had been president of the RAND Corporation. He'd since kept in touch with Andy Marshall, who'd been a RAND analyst in the fifties and sixties, and knew about his study on the revolution in military affairs.

What Rice was really asking in his staff meeting was what role these revolutionary new weapons would play in the new world, keeping in mind the fact that the most potentially impressive of these weapons—the super-accurate "smart bombs"—were Air Force weapons.

Rice assigned a like-minded and extremely energetic major named Dave Deptula to write the staff paper. The final version was finished the following June, under the title "Global Reach—Global Power." It argued that as the Cold War wound down, new threats would emerge from as-yet-unknown quarters; that America might have to respond to these threats on short notice with massive force; and that the modern Air Force uniquely possessed the required traits: "speed, range, flexibility, precision, and lethality." The last traits, "precision and lethality," fit the RMA template. Rice circulated Deptula's paper widely. The Air Force public-affairs office adopted the title as the service's new slogan. Commanders scheduled a military exercise in August 1990 to demonstrate the concept.

On August 2, Saddam Hussein invaded Kuwait. President George H. W. Bush decided to fight back. The Air Force demonstration would be a real war.

Operation Desert Storm, the US and allied war against Saddam's Iraq, marked the high-profile debut of the new laser-guided bombs. A few had been dropped toward the end of the Vietnam War, with impressive but isolated results. In Desert Storm, they were used in far greater numbers, against targets not only on the battlefield but also in the heart of Baghdad, and the most spectacular effects were televised—and rerun over and over—on the worldwide Cable News Network.

Deptula had drawn up a chart before the war started, to illustrate the new weapons' potential impact. In World War II, the average bomb missed its target by more than a half mile, so a B-17 airplane had to drop 9,000 of them to score a direct hit on something like a factory. In Vietnam, when the first laser-guided bombs entered the arsenal, an F-104 or F-105 still had to drop 176 bombs to hit a specific target. By contrast, he predicted, an F-16 in Desert Storm would have to drop a mere 30 bombs, and the brand-new F-117 Stealth fighter-bomber could hit a target with just one.

The actual upshot turned out to be less revolutionary than the numbers had implied. First, these weapons were still scarce; of the thousands of bombs dropped in the Gulf War, only 9 percent were smart bombs. Second, they homed in on their targets by tracking laser beams, and since laser beams tended to reflect or refract in the face of dust and smoke (common conditions on a battlefield), an untold number of them went astray. Third and most significant, the war didn't end until Saddam's elite Republican Guards were pushed back the old-fashioned way: by American troops, a half million of them, on the ground.

Still, on January 24, 1991, a mere week after the air war began, Andy Marshall called a staff meeting to wonder aloud whether the revolution in military affairs was now a reality; whether the Gulf War's opening air strikes marked a fundamental change in the nature of warfare, similar to the Germans' blitzkrieg tactics at the start of World War II.

Marshall asked his military assistant, Andrew Krepinevich, to write a paper. This was the same officer who'd landed in trouble with his Army bosses a few years earlier for suggesting that they'd lost in Vietnam because they were fighting an insurgency war with conventional tactics. Now he was assessing whether the brass needed to change the way they fought conventional wars, too.

Krepinevich's report agreed with Marshall, concluding, "Quality is becoming far more important than quantity, revolutionizing the nature of warfare." It would soon be possible, he wrote, to identify an enemy's "center of gravity": the small number of targets that, if successfully hit, would destroy its ability to resist; and the new technologies made it possible to hit these nerve centers with a small number of bombs or missiles. The Gulf War had been a "sequential war": five weeks of air strikes followed by four days of fighting on the ground. The new weapons would make possible "near-simultaneous operations" in the air and on land. And the land operations could be carried out by far fewer troops and much smaller numbers of traditional armaments such as tanks and artillery—heavy weapons that required cumbersome supply lines to function. The emphasis would now be on speed, not mass, as the smart bombs and missiles could destroy troop formations—even specific targets, like an individual tank—from the air.

The paper was finished in July 1992. Few in high office, civilian or military, paid much attention. Desert Storm was seen as a glorious victory for the American military. Why fix something that wasn't broken? The Cold War was over, and we'd won that, too. Why think much about military affairs at all, revolutionary or otherwise? Some of Marshall's friends on Capitol Hill began to worry that nobody in power cared.

In 1996, Senators Joe Lieberman, Democrat of Connecticut, and Dan Coats, Republican of Indiana, coauthored a bill to create a National Defense Panel, which they saw as a forum to advance what they called—in an explicit nod to Marshall—the "revolution in military affairs."

The panel had nine members: seven selected by the Pentagon, one by the Senate Armed Services Committee's Democrats, and one by its Republicans. The Democrats picked Krepinevich. The Republicans picked a former Pentagon official named Richard Armitage. The final report stated up front: "We are on the cusp of a military revolution, stimulated by rapid advances" in information technologies. The report, released in December 1997, was titled *Transforming Defense: National Security in the 21st Century*, and prompted another addition to the lexicon. If the revolution in military affairs was the new situation, "transformation" was what was needed to exploit its possibilities.

Not long afterward, Armitage went to work on the presidential campaign of Texas governor George W. Bush. On September 23, 1999, Bush gave a speech at the Citadel, the military college in Charleston, South Carolina. The speech, written primarily by Armitage, heralded a "revolution in the technology of war," in which battles would be won not by an army's "mass or size" but by its "mobility and swiftness," assisted by extremely accurate bombs and missiles.

Two days before that speech, Donald Rumsfeld was chairing a panel assembled by James Wade, a physicist, former Pentagon official, and Andy Marshall acolyte, who had formed the panel to discuss and promote a book he'd recently cowritten called *Shock and Awe: Achieving Rapid Dominance.* It was an endorsement of Marshall's RMA with an emphasis on the primacy of speed. The aim of shock-and-awe warfare, he wrote, was "to stun, and then rapidly defeat the enemy through a series of carefully orchestrated" strikes from land, sea, and air, launched "nearly simultaneously," with the aim of throwing the enemy into "immediate paralysis" and "capitulation." (Three years later, as Rumsfeld prepared for another Iraq war, he sent a copy of Wade's book to the US commander, General Tommy Franks. Soon after the war began, Franks said at a press conference that the bombing campaign would "shock and awe" the enemy.)

Andy Marshall was a member of the Wade-Rumsfeld panel, as was John Foster, the former Pentagon scientist who'd conceived the idea of remote-control attack airplanes.

Rumsfeld had spent the last decade making a fortune in the corporate world and was ready to move back to Washington. When he read Bush's Citadel speech, he knew, from having just chaired Wade's panel, where its ideas came from—and their central place in the modern Republican agenda. When Bush interviewed Rumsfeld for the job of defense secretary (at the suggestion of his running mate, Dick Cheney, who'd been friends with Rumsfeld since their time together, a quarter century earlier, in the Nixon White House), he was impressed with his knowledge and enthusiasm.

Two weeks after Bush's inauguration, Secretary Rumsfeld invited Andy Marshall—who was still director of net assessment—to lunch. He'd known Marshall from his first tenure in the Pentagon, renewed the acquaintance at Wade's shock-and-awe conference, and now wanted him to write a paper on the ideas of RMA and transformation, a paper that would help him shape new US policy. Marshall was nearly eighty, but this was the paper that he'd wanted to write for well over a decade. He wrote the first draft in a few days.

Every four years, by congressional mandate, the secretary of defense had to submit a "Quadrennial Defense Review," a document outlining the nation's military strategy and how it related to the Pentagon's programs and budgets. The next QDR was due in the fall of 2001. Rumsfeld decided to make Marshall's paper the basis of that document. He brought back Andy Krepinevich as a consultant to write much of it and asked Dave Deptula, now a two-star general, to contribute sections.

Its themes were familiar to many of the document's readers, but now they were spelled out as official policy: "the ongoing revolution in military affairs" and the need for an "ambitious transformation of U.S. military forces," including a "transition to network-centric warfare" emphasizing "long-range precision-strike" weapons and "rapidly deployable" forces, which could deal with threats "swiftly wherever they might arise."

On September 11, 2001, al Qaeda hijackers smashed two passenger jetliners into the World Trade Center and another one into the Pentagon, killing nearly three thousand Americans in the largest terrorist incident in the nation's history. Bush decided to strike back at the Taliban regime in Afghanistan, al Qaeda's base of operations. Four weeks later, the bombing began.

By this time, the first armed unmanned aircraft, the culmination of thirty years of dreams and engineering, was entering production. The Predator, as it was called, could fly for twenty-four hours at an altitude of twenty-five thousand feet, carrying a 450-pound payload. An early version of Predator, which President Bill Clinton had deployed over Bosnia, was fitted with only a digital video camera; the images were beamed to a satellite, then transmitted to a ground station thousands of miles away, where an operator, who controlled the Predator's flight path with a joystick, could watch its video stream on a monitor in real time.

By the end of Clinton's presidency, the Pentagon and the CIA had developed a modified version of the Predator that could carry a laser-guided Hellfire antitank missile in addition to a camera. A newer weapon still, developed by the Air Force and the Navy, was just coming off the production lines in the fall of 2001: the Joint Direct Attack Munition, or JDAM (pronounced "Jay-dam"), which was guided not by laser or radar but by more accurate signals from the Global Positioning System's satellites.

The fusion of these technologies had three huge implications. First, a smart bomb would no longer have to follow a quirky laser beam to the target. Rather, the ground operator would punch a target's coordinates into a computer and upload the instructions to a satellite, which would beam the data to the JDAM's GPS receiver. The JDAM, in turn, would plunge to that specific point on earth—a designated latitude and longitude—and explode precisely on target, regardless of the weather or the environment. Second, JDAMs were cheap. The laser-guided bombs used in Desert Storm had cost as much as $250,000 each; one JDAM cost just $20,000, less than one-tenth the price. Finally, the JDAM was a kit, consisting of a GPS receiver and other electronic gear, which could be attached to the tail of almost any bomb in the US military's inventory. In other words, JDAMs turned dumb bombs into smart ones for almost no money.

In the opening days of the Afghan War, JDAMs destroyed the Taliban's handful of bases and runways, putting the regime's air force out of commission. For the next two weeks, the bombing had little effect; there were few remaining targets of consequence to hit. Then, on October 15, US Special Forces met up with Afghan warlords from the Northern Alliance, the main anti-Taliban resistance group. And that's when the revolution in military affairs revealed the extent of its possibilities.

A few miles outside Mazar-i-Sharif, Afghanistan's fourth-largest city, an American Special Forces officer, wearing native garb and a thick beard, rode along a trail on horseback. Spotting a regiment of Taliban fighters a few hundred yards away, he pulled out a laptop computer, typed out the regiment's coordinates, and pushed the SEND button. A Predator drone, hovering twenty thousand feet overhead, received the message and beamed it to the Prince Sultan Air Base in Saudi Arabia. There, an American officer sent back a signal to the Predator, directing it to fly over the regiment. The drone's video camera scanned the terrain and streamed the images back to the base. The officer then ordered a B-52 pilot, who was patrolling the skies, to attack the target. The pilot flew to the area, punched the target's coordinates into the GPS receiver on one of his JDAMs, and fired the weapon, which darted toward the regiment, exploded, and killed the Taliban.

The total time that elapsed—from the officer punching in the data to the pilot dropping the bomb—was *nineteen minutes.* A decade earlier, in Desert Storm, the sequence would have taken three *days.* A few years before then, the whole idea would have been dismissed as science fiction.

Over the next few weeks, the pattern was replicated all across Afghanistan: spot-on air strikes by American bombers, followed by offensives on the ground by anti-Taliban rebels, sometimes along with small teams of American Special Forces or CIA agents. In mid-November, just five weeks after the war began, the Taliban were driven out of Kabul, the country's capital. Osama bin Laden, al Qaeda's leader, no longer had a base of operations. On December 22, an interim government, led by Hamid Karzai and backed by an international coalition, took office.

On January 31, Donald Rumsfeld delivered a triumphant speech at the National Defense University in Washington, recounting the air strikes at Mazar-i-Sharif as the turning point of the war—and as the vindication of transformation. "This is precisely what transformation is about," he exclaimed. "Here we are in the year 2002, fighting the first war of the twenty-first century, and the horse cavalry was back . . . being used in previously unimaginable ways. It showed that a revolution in military affairs"—Marshall's phrase again—"is about more than building new high-tech weapons, though that is certainly part of it. It's also about new ways of thinking and new ways of fighting."

Rumsfeld was overstating the case. Air strikes had no effect on the Taliban's hold until ground forces were in place to follow through. Even then, the Taliban and al Qaeda fighters not only put up fierce resistance but gradually adapted to the new technology, smearing mud on their vehicles, camouflaging their movements, and taking cover along the mountainous terrain so that the cameras in the sky couldn't spot them. By early December, they'd mastered cover and concealment so well that US Special Forces couldn't find them and thus couldn't beam their positions to the Predators overhead.

When Rumsfeld gave his victory speech, Kabul had fallen, but the Taliban and al Qaeda were still fighting. The war's fiercest battle, Operation Anaconda, wouldn't be waged until March. As a run-up to the operation, Predators and spy satellites took aerial photos of the entire Shah-i-Kot Valley, a fairly confined space of roughly fifty square miles, in order to locate every al Qaeda position. It turned out, according to postwar analyses, that the drones and satellites detected fewer than half of these positions. At the start of the battle, when American infantry troops dismounted from their assault helicopters, they found themselves almost on top of dug-in al Qaeda fighters. A battle raged all day, with the Americans pinned down until they could be airlifted out of the area that night. For the next week, US bombers pounded al Qaeda's positions. Yet when the soldiers went back in, they still met al Qaeda fire. The Americans won eventually, but only after overrunning and killing the enemy on the ground. The feat was harder than it might have been because, after Kabul fell, Rumsfeld—thinking the war was over—ordered that not a single extra soldier or marine could be sent to Afghanistan without his personal authorization.

Meanwhile, airpower hadn't stopped Osama bin Laden from escaping into the mountains of Tora Bora along the Pakistani border. Nor were the Taliban fighters defeated. They maintained an armed resistance against Karzai's government and stepped it up after Bush and Rumsfeld, basking in apparent victory, moved on to their next war in Iraq.

Rumsfeld's ideas about fighting in Iraq were heavily influenced by what he thought were the lessons of Afghanistan. General Franks and the Joint Chiefs came in with a first-draft plan that involved four hundred thousand American troops. Rumsfeld scoffed at the numbers as another case of "old thinking." The Army's plan for Afghanistan had figured that two divisions, sent in through Pakistan, would be needed to oust the Taliban. The generals had been wrong about that, so Rumsfeld thought they must also be wrong that a few hundred thousand troops were needed for regime change in Iraq.

Rumsfeld, though harsh, was a sharp, inquisitive executive, while Tommy Franks was seen, even in Army circles, as a dim bulb, the opposite of a strategic thinker, an artillery officer whose concept of war was shelling targets. Rumsfeld asked Franks lots of questions about the Iraq invasion plan: Why did each brigade need so much heavy artillery, when smart bombs dropped from the sky could smash up enemy defenses more efficiently? And if the artillery were cut back, wouldn't the brigades need much less support gear? In transformational warfare, as he saw it, ground forces should be light, lithe, and fast. Artillery cannons and the long supply lines that went with them were heavy, cumbersome, and slow. Franks had no ready reply, so Rumsfeld plunged into the guts of the war plan and sliced away.

The invasion got under way on March 19, 2003. As some soldiers complained about the lack of adequate armor and the shortfall of supplies, Rumsfeld replied, with either cynicism or a lack of self-awareness, "You go to war with the army you have; they're not the army you might want or wish to have at a later time."

Still, on one level, the first phase of the war proved Rumsfeld right and the generals wrong. The Army, it turned out, did not need a few hundred thousand troops to crush the Iraqi military and topple Saddam's regime.

Nor did its brigades need as much artillery as the Army's initial plan provided. Precision bombing and shelling from the air blasted and scattered Iraqi defenses, so that the M-1 tanks and Bradley Fighting Vehicles could punch on through.

Two factors were at play here. First was the technology, especially the smart weapons. Second (and Rumsfeld knew little if anything about this), the US Army had gone through its own transformation of sorts in the previous decade.

In the early-to-mid-1980s, a small group of creative officers, led by a colonel named Huba Wass de Czege, had revised the Army's field manual on operations, realizing that the 1976 edition by General DePuy was too static for the fast-moving modern battlefield. Wass de Czege's revision emphasized speed, maneuver, and taking the offensive, not just to outgun the enemy forces but to envelop them from the flanks and the rear. While preparing to write the manual, Wass de Czege had read the classics of military strategy: Carl von Clausewitz's *On War,* Sun Tzu's *The Art of War,* J. F. C. Fuller's *The Conduct of War,* and B. H. Liddell Hart's *Strategy: The Indirect Approach.* All of them stressed the importance of surprise, shock, and maneuver on the battlefield. Wass de Czege had never read any of these works as a cadet at West Point or as a junior officer at the Command and General Staff College in Fort Leavenworth. Yet in the course of his research, he'd come across an Army field manual written in 1940, on the eve of the Second World War, that read remarkably like the books he'd just been reading—the books that the Army had neglected in the decades since. Those earlier American officers had studied up on how to wage war after decades of neglect. Wass de Czege saw himself as doing the same.

There was another new element in his revised field manual: it integrated operations on the ground with those in the air. The Army and the Air Force would remain separate services with their own budgets and cultures, but they would fight jointly in a "combined-arms campaign." The new manual reflected this fact even in its title: *AirLand Battle.*

After completing the manual, Wass de Czege was promoted to brigadier general and assigned to create a new department at the Command and General Staff College, called the School of Advanced Military Studies, or SAMS. Its purpose would be to instill these ideas in the elite tier of the junior officer corps—and to train these officers not to command battalions or brigades but rather to serve as *planning* chiefs, to devise the actual battle plans. The first group of SAMS graduates called themselves "Jedi Knights," after the maneuver warriors in the movie *Star Wars: Return of the Jedi,* which was released in 1983, the year the school opened. In the early 1990s, several of these Jedi Knights served on General Schwarzkopf's staff, planning the ground-war offensive for Operation Desert Storm. By the time of the second Iraq war, in 2003, the ideas of *AirLand Battle* had pervaded not just the Army but the entire armed forces. And so, for all its shortcomings and oversights, the US invasion force—ground troops and airpower, working in tandem—dashed up the Iraqi desert roads with amazing speed, roaring into Baghdad and toppling the regime in just over a month.

On May Day, President Bush, flying in the copilot's seat of a Navy S-3B Viking jet, swooped onto the deck of the aircraft carrier *USS Abraham Lincoln,* leapt out of the plane wearing a tight padded flight suit, and, standing before a crowd of cheering sailors, beneath a huge banner blaring MISSION ACCOMPLISHED, proclaimed, "Major combat operations in Iraq have ended. In the battle of Iraq, the United States and our allies have prevailed."

But, of course, the war was just beginning.

Donald Rumsfeld embraced transformation not out of an infatuation with high tech but because it fit his thinking about geostrategy in the post–Cold War era: a time when budgets were shrinking, military bases were closing, and allies were drifting away, no longer joined to American interests by fear of a common enemy. As Rumsfeld saw it, the weapons of transformation—the revolution in military affairs—would allow the United States to continue projecting global power and toppling rogue regimes, unilaterally, with a small number of troops (aided by long-range aircraft firing accurate missiles and bombs), and that, therefore, it could do so repeatedly, anytime, anywhere, at low cost and with little effort.

Rumsfeld wasn't interested in postwar Iraq because it couldn't be shaped by transformation and had nothing to do with his broader vision of American power. Over the next several months, as Iraqi society plunged into chaos, split into sectarian factions, and sired an insurgency opposed to both the nascent Iraqi government and the American occupiers, Rumsfeld refused to call this enemy an "insurgency"; he prohibited even the utterance of the word. Rumsfeld was seventy, old enough to remember the entire course of the Vietnam War; he'd been a congressman at its start, a White House aide at its conclusion. If the enemy in Iraq was an insurgency, he'd need to fight it with a counterinsurgency, which he knew would require lots of troops to stay on the ground for a long time, at great cost. And doing that would nullify the whole point of transformation; it would sharply limit America's ability to project power and threaten enemies elsewhere.

And so, at the outset of the war, Rumsfeld followed an age-old formula, familiar to generals and politicians wishing to avoid a specific course of action. He didn't want to get bogged down in securing and stabilizing Iraq after Baghdad had fallen—so he didn't make any plans to do so, and he didn't approve any proposals for such plans from his top officers. He didn't plan for the postwar because he didn't want a postwar. It wasn't an oversight; it was deliberate.

Rumsfeld was far from alone in this failure.

During the Second World War, the Army had an enormous civil-affairs apparatus, which started planning the occupation of Germany two years before the war ended. Over the next few decades, postwar planning dwindled to a lost art. There was no chance to practice it: Korea was a stalemate, Vietnam a rout; wars in the Western Hemisphere were minor and manageable.

But this lapse was also deliberate. During the Cold War, officers were promoted on the basis of their performance in combat training exercises or their success at managing big-ticket weapons programs. Joining a civil-affairs battalion or the military police was no way to get ahead, so the best officers steered clear.

By the time of the Iraq invasion, the topic of postwar stability had diminished to the point where few senior officers even saw it as a topic. When Baghdad fell in early April, General Franks proclaimed that most of the troops would go home by summer and that the occupation would be down to thirty thousand troops—about one-fifth the size of the invasion force—by the fall.

A year earlier, in the spring of 2002, the Army had held a weeklong war game called "Vigilant Warrior" at the Army War College in Carlisle, Pennsylvania. The game started on a Monday morning, with several officers, active-duty and retired, paired off into a Blue Team (representing the US side) and a Red Team (playing the enemy); the game's managers set the scenario and refereed the moves. Like most of these games, it was scheduled to end on Friday, when senior officers would show up and get debriefed. Though billed as a game to help the Army set its requirements over the next two decades, it was, in fact, a rough rehearsal for the coming war in Iraq. In its scenario, Blue was invading a fictitious country called "Nair" (an anagram of Iran), the terrain of which resembled a composite of Iran and Iraq.

Wass de Czege had retired from the Army in 1993, but he'd kept in touch with old colleagues and frequently took part in these games. In Vigilant Warrior, he played a Blue Team officer. The United States won, as usual. But Wass de Czege was disturbed because, to his mind, the game skirted the main issue.

In a memo that he wrote and widely circulated afterward, he noted that these games "tend to devote more attention to successful campaign-beginnings than to successful conclusions." They "usually conclude when victory seems inevitable to us (not necessarily to the enemy)." But winning a *war*, he went on, didn't mean simply defeating the enemy on the battlefield; it meant—as Clausewitz had observed in his classic tome—achieving the strategic goals for which the war was fought in the first place. In the game he'd just played, the Clausewitzian question—how to achieve those strategic goals—hadn't been addressed, much less answered, because the game ended too soon. Winning battles is important, Wass de Czege allowed, but "it is just as important to know how to follow through to the resolution of such conflicts." If the game's managers had followed through and kept playing after the enemy's army had been defeated, they might have realized that they—and, by extension, the commanders getting ready to fight a real war—were underestimating "the difficulties of 'regime change' and the magnitude of the effort required to achieve strategic objectives."

Grasping these difficulties, and overcoming them, would require a change in strategy and the ascension of a different type of strategist. The first step in this change would be an acknowledgment that just because the tyrant had fallen, the war wasn't necessarily over; that it might now evolve into an insurgency war; and that, therefore, the new strategists should know something about *counter*insurgency.

5.

The Insurgent at War

With the invasion of Iraq, David Petraeus finally went to war. He was fifty years old, a two-star general, and commander of the 101st Airborne Division. But unlike many of the younger, lower-ranking officers around him, he'd never fought in combat. During Desert Storm, a decade earlier, he was stuck in the Pentagon as the assistant executive officer to the Army chief of staff, General Carl Vuono, who kept saying he'd cut him loose and get him a battle assignment, but never did.

Petraeus, then a major, was frustrated. Soldiers spent their whole careers preparing for war; Desert Storm looked to be the war of his generation, and he was missing it. Petraeus had reason to fear that getting left behind could stall his career more than most. He was aware of his reputation in certain circles as a schemer, a self-promoter, and, worst of all, an intellectual. The Army as an institution tended to scorn officers who stood out or were too bookish, and Petraeus fit both descriptions. Even taking off a few years to get a PhD, followed by a teaching stint at West Point, was seen by some generals as frivolous. That was why Petraeus had rushed through both—and why he now wanted to stay out in the field, deployed with combat units, as much as possible.

At least his Pentagon staff job had involved working with generals. Dan Kaufman, the West Point Sosh department's director of national-security studies, had urged Petraeus to take an assignment as a junior military assistant in the office of the secretary of defense. Kaufman had gone to some trouble lining up the position for him. But Petraeus refused to take it and launched into a screaming match with Kaufman right in the Sosh department's main corridor. Spending a year or two as an analyst or speechwriter for *civilians* would only solidify his egghead stereotype and seriously damage his career.

His saving grace, in a near-tragic sense, came in the fall of 1991. General

Vuono finally did get Petraeus a slot as a battalion commander, in the 101st Airborne Division. It was too late to see combat—Desert Storm had ended six months earlier—but he saw action in another way. During a live-fire training exercise, one of Petraeus's men accidentally pulled the trigger on his machine gun when he took a fall, and one of the high-velocity bullets pierced Petraeus's chest. Flown to a hospital, he underwent more than five hours of surgery; the bullet had severed an artery and damaged a lung. The doctors said that recovery would take ten weeks of rest, but within a few days, Petraeus was insisting he was fine, at one point dropping to the floor to do fifty push-ups. The doctors let him go. A month later, he was back in the field, leading his battalion in a major training exercise.

The Army had settled into a peacetime mode for several years. With no wars to test a soldier's valor, the top brass judged—and promoted—officers partly on the basis of their strength and stamina, and Petraeus's recovery was an impressive display of both. He would later joke that getting shot overcame the stigma of missing Desert Storm, but it was no joke. Petraeus had always stayed fit, running faster and farther and doing more push-ups than any of his fellow officers, partly as a product of his competitive streak but also because he knew that in the eyes of his superiors, speed and strength would compensate for his bookishness.

His brawny side's reputation received a further boost in 2000, during a yearlong stint as assistant commander of the 82nd Airborne Division. In the course of a routine jump, Petraeus's parachute collapsed, and he free-fell sixty feet to the ground, breaking his pelvis. That accident was more painful than the bullet wound and led to months of physical therapy. But again he recovered fully; if anything, he seemed to run faster still afterward.

And now here he was, nearly three years and another star later, finally preparing for a big-time war, as the commanding general of the 101st Airborne, the "Screaming Eagles," heir to the paratroopers who in 1944 had landed at Utah Beach, led the Ardennes offensive in Belgium, and chased the German army through the Ruhr Valley into Bavaria. The 101st was now an "air assault" division: four thousand soldiers, no longer packing parachutes but instead hurtled across the battlefield in 256 helicopters, 72 of them Apaches armed with heavy ammunition and antitank missiles.

The invasion plan called for those Apaches to break up Saddam's defenses along the southwestern approaches to Baghdad, clearing the way for the 3rd Infantry Division to smash through with its M-1 tanks and Bradley Fighting Vehicles. But as the offensive bogged down in sandstorms, shortages, and the completely unexpected threat posed by Iraqi militiamen driving around the desert in pickup trucks, ambushing American troops and disrupting supply lines (the first sign, to some, that the war might be followed by an insurgency), Petraeus and his men wound up getting in the fight more deeply than anticipated. They exchanged fire with militias, regular soldiers, and Saddam's elite Republican Guard—from the air and, as infantry soldiers, on the ground—in Najaf, Hillah, Karbalā', and finally on the outskirts of Baghdad itself.

But it was in the postbattle phase of the war, as the 101st was deployed in northern Iraq to pacify the city of Mosul, that Petraeus drew on the lessons he'd learned, and fulfilled the ambitions he'd harbored, through the previous two decades.

A crucial experience in this preparation had come eight years earlier, in January 1995, when Petraeus was made chief of operations in the US-led multinational peacekeeping mission in Haiti.

This was his first exposure to full-fledged "nation-building," a term and a concept that most senior Army officers detested. It was, after all, an extreme case of *moot*-wah, "military operations other than war"—but for the same reason, it was everything that Petraeus had long hoped to get involved in. The soldiers performing the mission were from the few Army units that had a taste, and some training, for these kinds of operations: paratroopers from the 82nd Airborne, light infantry from the 10th Mountain Division, and a fair-sized complement of Special Forces.

The mission, mandated by a UN resolution, was called Operation Uphold Democracy. It had started the previous fall, with a multipronged military assault designed to topple Haiti's brutal dictatorship, which had taken power in a 1991 military coup, and to return to office the lawfully elected president, Jean-Bertrand Aristide. As it happened, a team of emissaries, sent in advance by President Bill Clinton with an ultimatum to step down or soon face a storm of fire, had its effect. When the American troops landed, they managed to restore Aristide's regime with no resistance. Then came the twist. The twenty thousand American troops, joined by about five thousand from other nations, pivoted from their original mission—

storming the palace and shooting bad guys—to a different set of tasks: setting up security enclaves for the local people, training the police, reforming the judiciary, training the government's administrative apparatus, and setting up free elections, all with an eye toward handing over control to UN peacekeepers by the end of March.

When the troops landed, Petraeus was in Washington, having just been assigned, with some disgruntlement, to another year in academia, this time as part of the Army Fellows program at Georgetown University's graduate school in international relations. Intrigued by what was going on in Haiti, he decided to write a research paper on the operation. He traveled around the capital, interviewing officials in the Pentagon, the State Department, and the White House, and found himself invited to sit in on a few high-level policy meetings. After one of these sessions, an Army colonel named Bob Killebrew approached him. The two had worked together on General Vuono's staff and held similar views on modern warfare. Killebrew had come through the ranks in the Army's airborne branch, dating back to Vietnam, and was now putting together the team to do nation-building in Haiti. He was having a hard time finding good people to take part (this was around the time when General Shalikashvili, the nation's top general, said, "Real men don't do *moot*-wah") and asked Petraeus if he was interested. In part because he wanted to get out of the classroom, in part because this was the sort of operation that had long riveted his attention, Petraeus signed up without hesitation.

He came on the scene four months into the operation, and he would stay for only six months more, leaving soon after the UN peacekeepers arrived. Meanwhile, he found himself having to improvise just about everything. He arranged for engineers to renovate the operations center, which lacked a floor and a ceiling. The peacekeeping troops would need bases out in the countryside, among the people. So Petraeus and a few aides surveyed the island by helicopter. When they spotted a suitable base site, they'd touch down, find the owner, and negotiate a rental fee. Then, after getting back to headquarters, they lobbied various embassies for the money to build a base, as the operation's budget had no such funds.

Petraeus also helped coordinate the intelligence effort that tracked down the missing war criminals and mounted the raids on their hideouts. He came to deal routinely with diplomats, aid agencies, local officials, police, soldiers, Special Ops officers, and spies. During his summer nine years earlier at Southern Command with General Galvin, Petraeus had observed these sorts of missions—multinational, interagency operations that were as much about economic aid and government reform as about killing the enemy—but this was the first time he was in the thick of the action as a player.

Six years later, the action and his involvement in it would thicken considerably.

In the summer of 2001, after a series of assignments with the 82nd Airborne and as executive assistant to the chairman of the Joint Chiefs of Staff, Petraeus was posted to NATO's Stabilization Force in Sarajevo, Bosnia and Herzegovina, and that was where his future course was charted.

SFOR, as the organization was abbreviated, had been created to enforce the Dayton peace accord, which ended the war between Serbian president Slobodan Milošević (who had since been ousted and arrested) and the area's Muslims and Croats. The effort involved thirty-two thousand troops from NATO and eleven other nations outside the alliance. The Dayton accord allowed them to use "robust" force, if necessary, to support political and economic reconstruction, keep ethnic militias separated, and prevent hostilities from resuming—although hostilities did resume, and had to be suppressed, with intense regularity. The US Army refused to regard an assignment with SFOR as "combat duty." Still, the chief of staff, General Eric Shinseki, told Petraeus, upon giving him his orders, that the mission was as close to combat as he'd likely ever get.

Petraeus wore two hats in Sarajevo. One was as NATO's assistant chief of staff for operations; the other was as deputy commander of a clandestine unit called the Joint Interagency Counterterrorism Task Force. When Petraeus first arrived, the main business of this task force was hunting down Serbian war criminals in a secret mission called Operation Justice Assured, which was carried out almost entirely by US Special Forces.

But a few months into his deployment, the attacks of September 11 occurred, and the mission, like much else, changed drastically. Stepped-up intelligence operations by global agencies and on-the-scene spies uncovered a presence of al Qaeda fighters and other Islamic jihadists inside Bosnia. Some had entered the country years earlier to help their fellow Muslims do battle against the Serbs; others had infiltrated legitimate Muslim charity groups, or set up wholly illegal ones, to funnel money and weapons or to provide safe harbor for extremists, including several from Pakistan and Afghanistan, who, once inside Bosnia, could move freely throughout Europe.

The task force continued the hunt for Serbian war criminals. But it also expanded its mandate—and received more resources from the Pentagon—to capture jihadists and take down the phony charities. Because it was a clandestine unit, the task force set up liaisons with local police chiefs, who would conduct the raids and make the arrests. And it sanitized top-secret intelligence into evidence that Bosnian authorities could submit to the courts or to Western law-enforcement agencies.

In the early stages of both operations—hunting Serbian war criminals and international terrorists—the chain of command was at best inefficient and at times disruptive. NATO soldiers and military police would patrol neighborhoods, trying to earn the trust of local residents, in order to pick up bits of intelligence about where bad guys were hanging out and to help the new government deliver basic services. Then, in the middle of the night, an elite squad of black-hooded Special Ops officers would smash down doors and haul away a few men whom their own intel had identified as bad guys—leaving the grunts to handle the angry wives, or the rioting brothers and cousins, the next morning.

Petraeus and SFOR's commander, Lieutenant General John Sylvester, proposed integrating the conventional forces with the Special Ops forces—to make it a truly "joint" task force. The Pentagon gave them the green light. In the months that followed, their work led to the arrest of several jihadists, most notably in a highly publicized raid at the fashionable Hotel Hollywood in Sarajevo, and to the takedown of several corrupt charities, including the Benevolence International Foundation, the Saudi High Commission for Relief, the al Haramain Foundation, and the Red Crescent (the Bosnian equivalent of the Red Cross, a thin slice of which was financing terrorists' travel into Europe).

Petraeus personally came along on some of the less risky raids, most of them involving the delivery of letters to known associates of war criminals. He wouldn't wear a helmet on these raids, just a baseball cap with the insignia SOF (for Special Operations Forces), though he'd be surrounded by a pack of heavily armed soldiers. He'd knock on the door, then do what he and the guys called "the Eddie Murphy routine": flash a wide, toothy smile, as Murphy had done in the movie *Beverly Hills Cop,* and say with mock innocence, "Hi! Can I come in?" He'd give the resident the letter, which had been written in a very polite tone, alerting the addressee that he'd been seen consorting with certain war criminals, requesting his cooperation, and suggesting that he please contact the following official. The task force would then covertly monitor what the suspect did afterward—whom he called, where he went—which, a remarkable number of times, led them straight to the criminal they'd been pursuing.

Through all this, Petraeus continued to wear his NATO hat as the operations chief of the thirty-two-thousand-man mission to enforce the Dayton peace accords. And in that capacity, he put in place something close to a classic counterinsurgency plan. He didn't use the word "counterinsurgency" (which was still, in effect, banned from the Army lexicon), but that's what it amounted to.

Key to his plan was the idea that the military should not only fight bad guys but also deal with the social, political, and economic sources of conflict. It was no secret why jihadists had flocked to Bosnia as a haven: the government's legitimacy was shaky, the police force was feeble, the economy was weak, and all authorities—from border guards to judges on up—were easily bribed.

Petraeus was a big believer in PowerPoint briefings. The entire military was shifting into that mode, to the dismay of many officers, who felt that it too often oversimplified the problem at hand. But Petraeus was determined to avoid that pitfall. He would spend hours, days, sometimes weeks preparing his slides, compressing dozens of interrelated ideas into a single geometric diagram; and yet his script, which he'd narrate while flashing the slides, was clear, even simple. His briefings took on legendary status as objects of derision, admiration, puzzlement, or all three.

In December 2001 Petraeus delivered a PowerPoint briefing summarizing his quarterly assessment of the operations in Bosnia. One of his slides displayed two columns, labeled "Conditions That Support Terrorism" and "Conditions That Counter Terrorism." Under the first, he listed "Extreme ideologies," "Unemployment," and "Sanctuaries"; under the second, "Moderate ideologies," "Employment," and "Deny sanctuaries." Other slides stressed the need for NATO to "leverage all assets"—military, economic, diplomatic, and so forth—to make the local government seem more effective and legitimate in the eyes of its people, so that it could plausibly claim credit for successes.

These ideas were the product of Petraeus's experiences to date in the Army: a mix of what he'd done a few years earlier in Haiti, what he'd observed a decade before then in El Salvador, and what he'd been reading since his days as a young paratrooper in Italy and France. And the ideas in turn inspired his style of operations a year later, when he set up a task force to stabilize northern Iraq.

Another practice that Petraeus picked up in Bosnia and continued for the rest of his military career drew on his still-deeper past, a legacy created by the founder of the West Point Social Science Department. It was the idea of the Lincoln Brigade, or, as its newer members sometimes called it, the "Sosh network" or "Sosh mafia."

Bosnia wasn't considered a "real war," after all, so the mission ranked far down on the list for getting money or manpower. Overburdened with work and short on resources, Petraeus did what West Point cadets-turned-generals had done for nearly a half century: he called the chairman of the Sosh department and asked him to send help. The chairman at the time, Colonel Russ Howard, knew just the man: his deputy chair, Lieutenant Colonel Mike Meese, who happened to be on leave the following semester. So, at the start of 2002, Meese went off to Sarajevo to be Petraeus's executive officer.

In 1999 Meese had spent two weeks in South Africa as a consultant, hired by the Clinton administration to help Nelson Mandela's postapartheid government integrate the country's formerly white-led army with what had been the African National Congress's black militias into a unified National Defence Force. The effort was not going smoothly: the black officers were pushing for faster change; the white officers seemed obstructionist; both sides saw the tension as racial in nature and were, therefore, resistant to a peaceful solution. But after talking with all the generals, black and white, Meese concluded that the real issue was cultural. It wasn't that the regular army officers were white; it was that they had been trained in an Anglo-American bureaucratic style. And it wasn't that the ANC officers were black; it was that they'd been guerrilla fighters in the Maoist tradition, trained to appeal to the people and to make decisions in a lean, decentralized manner. Integrating the two wasn't so different from integrating regular soldiers and Special Operations forces in the American Army—which is what Petraeus was doing in Bosnia when Meese came to help.

Meese proved so helpful that Petraeus would call him again from Iraq and, later still (after Meese himself had been promoted to full colonel and Sosh chairman), in Afghanistan.

At the start of 2003, when war with Iraq seemed all but certain, Petraeus traveled to Fort Leavenworth, Kansas, with his 101st Airborne Division's staff officers and brigade commanders to take part in a high-level refresher course called the Battle Command Training Program. He also needed to recruit a chief of plans, and he'd heard good things about a major named Isaiah Wilson, who was studying at Leavenworth's Command and General Staff College.

Ike Wilson had been one of the Sosh faculty members who, in the late 1990s, spent long hours talking with John Nagl about the future of the Army in the post–Cold War era. The year before Petraeus came to see him, he'd won the George C. Marshall Award for having been the Staff College's top-scoring student. Now he was in SAMS, the School of Advanced Military Studies, the small enclave within the college that had been created in the mid-eighties to train an elite corps of war planners.

Wilson was in a SAMS seminar one afternoon when a captain wearing a 101st Airborne badge entered the room and called out, "Is there a Major Wilson here?" Wilson raised his hand. The captain, who turned out to be Petraeus's aide-de-camp, informed him that the general would like to have dinner with him that evening at seven o'clock at the High Noon Saloon & Brewery in downtown Fort Leavenworth. Wilson showed up on time—Petraeus and the aide were already there—and soon realized that the dinner conversation was a job interview, which lasted for nearly two hours.

Early on, Petraeus asked Wilson where he'd earned his PhD. When he replied "Cornell," Petraeus asked, "Why not Princeton?" Knowing that was where Petraeus had gone to grad school, Wilson allowed, with a self-deprecating grin, that he might have committed "a strategic error" in his selection.

Petraeus asked about his dissertation. Wilson explained that it dealt with the politics and security implications of US foreign arms sales, and then outlined its main conclusions. Petraeus challenged each point, one by one. Wilson was surprised by how much Petraeus seemed to know about arms sales, but he figured that this part of the interview was a test to see whether he'd stand up for his ideas, so he argued back, conceding no quarter.

Petraeus then asked what books Wilson was reading, besides those in the SAMS course curriculum (which, he knew, amounted to nearly 150 books over the school year). Wilson mentioned Joseph Campbell's *The Power of Myth* and *The Hero with a Thousand Faces,* Daniel Quinn's *Ishmael,* and several works about Sitting Bull and the frontier Indian wars. Petraeus seemed impressed.

The next question took Wilson aback: Who are your favorite poets? Wilson, figuring it was best not to fake it, replied, "I do not read poetry." Petraeus looked shocked, said the answer was "unacceptable," and launched into a seminar-style lecture on the *importance* of reading poetry, its insights into the human condition, and its value as a balm for suffering. He proceeded to discuss, in striking directness and detail, how Siegfried Sassoon's poems from just after the First World War, especially those describing the brutality of the trenches, had eased the process of recovery from his own injuries.

Toward the end of the evening, Petraeus asked Wilson if he was a runner or a weight lifter. Wilson replied without hesitation, "Weight lifter," knowing that if he picked the other option, he would have been challenged to a legendary "Petraeus Death Run" early the next morning or possibly that very night. (Petraeus often interviewed candidates for jobs *while* running. "You can learn a lot about someone at the fifth mile," he often said.)

After dinner, out in the parking lot, Petraeus shook Wilson's hand and congratulated him for his fine work at SAMS and for having won the Marshall Award the previous year. Wilson knew that Petraeus had won the award in the early 1980s.

Less than a month after his strange dinner-interview, Wilson was informed that he would be graduated early from SAMS to go to Iraq. In May he got a call from Petraeus himself to come join him in Mosul as his division's chief of plans.

Wilson had spent the three weeks of the invasion as one of the Army historians assigned to chronicle the war from the battle's front lines. He'd enjoyed access to all the military planning documents and all the field reports submitted by the units involved in the fighting.

His job in Mosul would be to help refine and execute the plan to stabilize Iraq. From his studies of military history at every level, he knew that war plans by nature contained four phases. Phase I: Set the conditions. Phase II: Initial operations. Phase III: Decisive operations. Phase IV: Post-conflict stability operations. This was elementary. By the time President Bush made his May Day victory speech on the deck of the *USS Abraham Lincoln,* the US military had accomplished Phases I through III, but Phase IV had yet to begin.

Looking over the cache of documents, Wilson realized—at first slowly, because he couldn't quite believe this was possible—that there *was* no plan for Phase IV. He and Petraeus would have to devise one on their own.

It was a fluke that Petraeus was sent to Mosul. The war plan had called for the 101st to wind up in southern Baghdad; the 4th Infantry Division, which was to have invaded Iraq from the north through Turkey, would occupy Nineveh Province, of which Mosul was the capital. But on March 1, less than three weeks before the war began, the Turkish parliament voted to bar the United States from using its country as a staging ground for the invasion. Bush, Cheney, and Rumsfeld were eager to get the war under way. (One reason was to get it over with by summer, so the troops wouldn't have to fight in Iraq's blazing heat. They, of course, ended up fighting in its heat for the next nine summers.) So Bush gave the GO order without the 4th Infantry; its troops and equipment were still en route to Kuwait by ship when Saddam fled Baghdad on April 9.

Nine days later, Petraeus was ordered to change plans and redeploy his division—more than 18,000 soldiers, 5,000 vehicles, and 256 helicopters—from Baghdad to Mosul as quickly as possible. Within three days, he assembled the largest air assault in history, his entire 2nd brigade—1,600 soldiers, crammed into every functioning helicopter—making the 250-mile trip in a single lift, while the rest of the division followed on the ground.

The 2nd brigade commander, Colonel Joseph Anderson, was a veteran of joint civil-military operations in Kosovo and Panama. He was also a graduate of West Point, class of 1981, with a concentration in the Sosh department. Petraeus's brother-in-law, a West Point instructor, had said good things about Anderson. In the mid-1990s, when Petraeus was operations director of the 101st Airborne, he'd tried to recruit Anderson to be one of his battalion commanders, but Anderson was locked into an assignment at the Command and General Staff College. The two had never met until just before they plowed into Iraq.

When Anderson hit the ground in Mosul, he had to make a judgment: would the division have to fight its way in, or could it simply occupy the city in one swoop with little resistance? He and some of his staff drove around on a reconnaissance mission. Unlike in every other town they'd entered in the fight up through Iraq to Baghdad, nobody in Mosul shot at them. At one point, Anderson even stopped at a bakery and bought some bread without incident. So he called Petraeus with the good news: there was probably no need to fight his way in.

Petraeus arrived the next day, amid further reports from Anderson that the city was in shambles, without water, electricity, or sanitation services. The civil administration had crumbled along with the regime, as was the case, it turned out, all across Iraq. To make matters worse, a week earlier, a small unit of US marines, which was called in to Mosul to quell riots and looting, had shot and killed seventeen civilians.

From his experiences and studies over the years, Petraeus knew what had to be done. Right away, he called a meeting of his brigade and battalion commanders and told them, "We're going to do nation-building."

He could hear the intake of breath. The *n* word was still forbidden in military circles, and the idea behind it was unpopular not just in Washington but also among many rank-and-file soldiers, who hadn't joined the Army to "play social worker." Petraeus understood the attitude, but there was no choice. The US reconstruction officials in northern Iraq, only a handful in any case, were far away in the relative safety of Kurdistan; they weren't coming to Mosul and lacked the resources to do much if they did. The dozen or so civil-affairs officers in his division had been trained to set up liaison between the military command and the local government. But there *was* no local government, so the 101st Airborne would have to create one.

Anderson's brigade would be situated in Mosul. (The 1st brigade would be based a bit to the south, the 3rd a bit to the west.) On his first full day on the job, Petraeus had him contact local tribal chiefs, ex-military officers, and business leaders who might be cooperative. Three days later, the two officers met with seven citizens who'd agreed to help find suitable candidates to run in elections for district governor and the provincial council. Four days after that, on May Day, Petraeus personally chaired a six-hour meeting with a few dozen emerging leaders to work out an election plan that would ensure a slate of candidates evenly divided among the various districts, tribes, and ethnic groups. For nearly a week, he spent a few hours each day interviewing and vetting each prospective candidate, rejecting those who didn't meet the agreed-upon criteria or who still seemed loyal to Saddam's regime. On May 5, the elections took place. On May 10, Petraeus congratulated the victors and opened the new city council in a grand ribbon-cutting ceremony.

Meanwhile, Petraeus's staff officers were setting up a civil-military operations center to restore basic services and institutions. Few civilians were available for this sort of work, so Petraeus sought out specialists within his own ranks. He assigned the commander of his signals battalion to help rebuild the city's communications infrastructure. It turned out that a warrant officer in his aviation battalion had been a network-systems technician, so he was tasked to help local engineers rewrite the computer programs at Mosul University. An assistant division commander happened to speak Arabic, so he was put in charge of organizing the city's merchants. Language was a big problem all around—none of the divisions in Iraq had been allotted enough translators—so Petraeus recruited some English-speaking students from the local university to fill the gaps.

By the end of April, truck deliveries had resumed at the city's gas stations, where American soldiers were standing guard and, in some cases, pumping gas. By the end of May, water, electricity, and sanitation services were 90 percent restored. And the university was up and running: the class of 2003 graduated with only a few weeks' delay.

The operation was straight out of Galula's book on counterinsurgency, which Petraeus had brought with him and frequently consulted.

Petraeus had posters put up all around the base: "What Have You Done to Win Iraqi Hearts and Minds Today?" and "We Are in a Race to Win Over the People. What Have You and Your Element Done Today to Contribute to Victory?" But the slogans only reinforced a tone that was already clear. When sergeants and captains saw a one-star general spending part of each day coordinating fuel convoys from Turkey, and especially when they saw the division commander attending city council meetings twice a week, they got the message about the mission's priorities.

Knowing the value of what his old mentor General Galvin called the War of Information, Petraeus also restarted the local television station, funded twenty-four newspapers, and invited reporters and cameramen to follow him and his officers as they met with sheikhs, opened schools, and performed ribbon-cutting ceremonies.

Petraeus, Anderson, and the others were doing all this entirely on their own. Invoking the power and obligations of an occupying army, Petraeus had full authority over his area of operation, and he assumed it to the maximum extent, at one point even opening up the border to Syria after realizing that Mosul's economic recovery would spark inflation unless new goods could flow in. Petraeus informed his superiors in Baghdad what he was up to, but he never asked permission and certainly didn't await instructions (knowing there wouldn't be any).

The idea, he made clear to his staff many times, was not to get the people of northern Iraq to love America; rather, it was to get a critical mass of these people to develop a vested interest—to feel a stake of ownership—in the new Iraq, because unless that happened, the country would spin out of control.

His plan was nearly wrecked in mid-May, just as things were starting to get off the ground, when the new American proconsul, L. Paul Bremer, known to his friends as Jerry, arrived in Baghdad. Bremer was a former diplomat—he'd once been an aide to Henry Kissinger—who possessed a martinet's manner and far too much confidence in his instincts and abilities. Barely a week into his tenure as head of the Coalition Provisional Authority, the formal title of his office, Bremer promulgated two directives (at whose behest is still unclear) that all but guaranteed disaster.

CPA Order No. 1, issued May 16, banned all but the lowliest members of Saddam's Baath Party from holding any government job. CPA Order No. 2, released a week later, disbanded the Iraqi army.

The orders stunned nearly every American officer and senior official, in Iraq and back in Washington. Bremer explained in a public statement that the intent was to "show the Iraqi people that the Saddam regime is gone and will never return." He seemed unaware that the first order would also throw fifty thousand suddenly angry Iraqis out of their jobs—including the civil-service elite, most of whom had joined the Baath Party only because membership had been required. The second order was still more calamitous, as the hundreds of thousands of men who would be thrown out of the Iraqi army possessed weapons and knew the locations of arsenals where they could get more. Petraeus would reflect later, as did many officers, that if Bremer's orders didn't create the insurgency, they certainly inflamed and accelerated its rise.

In the short term, strict enforcement of Order No. 1 would mean the shutdown of Mosul University, which Petraeus had worked hard to reopen, and the suspension of the provincial councils, which he'd done so much to create. (Two-thirds of the college faculty and several of the elected officials had been Baath Party members.)

Bremer visited Mosul on May 18, having heard that things were going well there. Petraeus put on his usual grand show, taking him around to the city council, the working gas stations, the busy merchants, capped by a PowerPoint briefing on how it all came to be. In the end, he persuaded Bremer to exempt Nineveh Province from the order banning Baathists from government positions. Bremer demanded only that their deal be kept secret. As Petraeus learned later, a few other division commanders had also asked for exemptions, to no avail—and thus with catastrophic results.

As a gesture to Bremer's largesse, Petraeus staged a massive "renunciation ceremony," attended by thousands of townspeople, in which senior Baath Party members signed an oath of allegiance to the new Iraq and received an official-looking certificate denoting their loyalty. (In one of his earlier ceremonies, Petraeus had learned that Iraqis didn't quite believe an agreement was real unless it was stamped with an official seal. So he had some of his men design a seal, sending them into the local bazaar to find popular emblems and symbols with which to embroider it.)

Much of this was financed by the treasure trove of Saddam's cash, which American soldiers had discovered in his various palaces. It amounted to hundreds of millions of dollars—piled together into a discretionary fund called CERP, the Commander's Emergency Response Program—which Petraeus and several other American generals used, with varying degrees of creativity and effectiveness, to subsidize neighborhood services, bribe local officials, and pay compensation to people whose houses had been destroyed or family members killed needlessly. By the early fall, Petraeus and his aides had spent $28 million on over 3,600 CERP projects. "Money is ammunition," he liked to say, reciting one of Galula's dictums.

Not that the 101st engaged exclusively in "social work." From the outset, thousands of its soldiers performed conventional military operations: patrolling the streets to enforce law and order (the first principle in any counterinsurgency guide was to make the local people feel secure), gathering intelligence, raiding weapons caches, and sometimes shooting and killing (as well as getting shot at and killed by) bad guys. But even then, Petraeus insisted on restraints. The troops on patrol were not to fly American flags on their vehicles. Raids were to be mounted only on specific homes and buildings that intelligence had firmly identified as harboring insurgents; there was to be no cordoning off whole neighborhoods on the strength of mere rumors.

By the summer, the insurgency, which had started to grip other provinces with alarming force, crept into Mosul, too, or, rather, emerged from the back rooms of Mosul, as the city was home to at least forty retired Iraqi generals and hundreds of ex-soldiers, many of them instinctively suspicious of foreign occupiers and made all the more so by the crushing effect of Bremer's directives.

In mid-June, Iraqi police shot four protesters, sparking a riot that resulted in the wounding of eighteen American soldiers. Petraeus stepped up the aggressive side of his operation, forming a Joint Interagency Counterterrorism Task Force, modeled after the one he'd helped direct in Bosnia, bringing in agents from the CIA, Defense Intelligence Agency, and National Security Agency. He and Mike Meese prepared the PowerPoint briefings, which included several of the exact same slides that they'd made for the briefings in Sarajevo.

But then the American soldiers were ordered home, and not just Petraeus's division. Between December 2003 and April 2004, one of the largest troop rotations in modern military history took place, the result of a Pentagon order that no unit should spend more than twelve successive months on the ground in Iraq. All of the US armed forces who'd taken part in the invasion—120,000 in total—returned to their home bases, while roughly the same number of fresh faces took their place. This period coincided with the rise of the insurgency, and the turnover—with the arrival of inexperienced replacements—may have given the militias a freer ride than they otherwise would have had at a crucial juncture.

The switch was particularly devastating for Mosul and its environs. Two months before they left, Petraeus and Ike Wilson prepared a PowerPoint briefing with twenty-six slides spelling out why more troops were needed to sustain what they'd accomplished. Yet the eighteen thousand troops of the 101st Division were replaced by a single infantry brigade, known as the Arrowhead Brigade, augmented by some headquarters staff—just nine thousand troops in all. More than that, the new brigade's commanders had no idea of what Petraeus's team had been doing, and no training or background in those kinds of operations. Nor had the war's political or military leaders yet devised a coherent Phase IV plan or any guidance of what to do.

Wilson told his successors that he was leaving behind four thousand gigabits of data and memoranda—a comprehensive record of everything the 101st had been doing, the status of its operations, a guide to the district's key players—but the new officers ignored it. Instead, they focused exclusively on what most of the American brigades in Iraq were doing: killing suspected insurgents, surrounding whole neighborhoods, pounding down doors in the middle of the night. As any reader of Galula could have predicted, this was bound to make things worse in an insurgency war, alienating the local people and breeding more insurgents than it neutralized.

In 2004 the violence intensified and the militias spread, to the point where, finally, most senior Bush officials had to admit that they were indeed facing an insurgency. Even so, nobody put in place a coherent *counter*insurgency strategy; nor were those who had been right about the war all along promoted or otherwise rewarded. Quite the contrary.

The troops of the 101st Airborne spent the year after Mosul back at their base in Fort Campbell, Kentucky. On October 14, Ike Wilson, still the division's chief of plans, delivered a speech called "Thinking Beyond War" at Cornell University, his grad school alma mater.

Regarding the US occupation in Iraq, Wilson stated bluntly, "There was no Phase IV plan." He blamed America's senior civilian and military leaders, who, as he put it, had "conceived of the war far too narrowly," failed to "recognize a war of rebellion, a people's war, even when they were fighting it," and suffered generally from "stunted learning and a reluctance to adapt."

Tom Ricks, a war reporter for the *Washington Post,* obtained a copy of Wilson's speech and wrote it up in a story that appeared Christmas Day on the newspaper's front page. A friend called Wilson at home and told him to turn on the TV, any of the news channels, because all of them were reporting on the *Post* story about his speech.

Wilson had been slated to start work soon as head of the Iraq desk at the National Security Council in the White House. The assignment was suddenly revoked. Several senior officers—from colonels to a few three-star generals—phoned him to say that his analysis was spot-on but that they couldn't do anything to support him. Instead, Wilson spent the next year as an Army Fellow at the Council on Foreign Relations, the long-standing private think tank, then returned to West Point to teach in the Social Science Department. Mike Meese, who was now the Sosh chairman, told Wilson that it was a good thing Ricks had identified him as an "Army historian" instead of an active-duty officer; otherwise, certain people in the Pentagon would have ended his career.

6.

The Irregulars

The Iraq war gave Major John Nagl an opportunity not merely to study an insurgency but to fight one. The odds of such an encounter had seemed remote a decade earlier, when he was writing his dissertation on Malaya and Vietnam. Most of his fellow officers had considered those kinds of wars ancient artifacts. He joked to friends that he'd written the decade's best and worst dissertation on the subject, which was to say he'd written the only one.

His thesis was published as a book in September 2002, on the eve of the war, by Praeger Publishers, which specialized in scholarly books on military issues. But even among the interested, few read it because its retail price was $81.

Now, a year later, Nagl was off to Iraq with his old armor battalion, this time as its third in command. The unit hadn't been called up for the March invasion, but it was among the first rotation of replacement troops, arriving on September 24, 2003, in the town of Khaldiya, in al Anbar Province, a hundred miles west of Baghdad, in the heart of the so-called Sunni Triangle, the emerging locus of the insurgency.

Nagl was usually the smartest guy in the room and made no effort to hide that he knew it. He wasn't overbearing in his arrogance; he could joke about it in a way that some of his men found winning. One of them drew a parody of a *Dilbert* comic strip, in which a caricature of Nagl is pictured saying, "At Oxford I learned to use my huge brain. But I try not to frighten ordinary people with any gratuitous displays of mental superiority." Nagl taped the drawing up on the wall above his desk.

When Nagl first landed in Khaldiya, he figured he'd have the place cracked in no time. He'd read the counterinsurgency classics; he knew the histories. He had "something of a blithe sense," he would later admit, that once Briggs and Templer showed the British army what to do in Malaya, defeating the communist insurgents was a sure thing; he thought that defeating the Sunni insurgents in Iraq would be no harder.

He learned fairly quickly that real war was more complicated. The British colonialists had been in Malaya for well over a century; they'd long acquired what the counterinsurgency theorists called "cultural awareness" and had formed tight relationships with several local leaders. By contrast, the Americans in Iraq knew next to nothing about the local culture, the social networks, not even the language—and Nagl's unit, like every US Army unit in the area, had far too few translators to overcome that most basic obstacle.

Nagl remembered a line from one of the books he'd read on the subject, Colonel Charles E. Callwell's *Small Wars: Their Principles and Practice,* published in Great Britain back in 1896: "In a guerrilla situation, the guerrilla is the professional, the newcomer the amateur." Nagl was experiencing the unfamiliar sensation of being very much the amateur.

Over time, things improved a bit. Nagl was surprised by how much his academic studies helped him grasp the nature of the conflict and was pleased at how quickly his battalion adapted to the *tactical* challenges. Within a couple of weeks, two of its three companies had abandoned their tanks and were patrolling in Humvees or on foot. They'd been trained to shoot at an enemy fighting in plain sight; now they were spending most of their time trying to *find* an enemy that was *hiding* in plain sight. It was a different kind of war, requiring a different style of thinking. At times, it seemed more like cracking a mafia crime ring than fighting a conventional battle; then, all of a sudden, it was like fighting a conventional battle, too.

Nagl had based his book's title on T. E. Lawrence's line "War upon rebellion was messy and slow, like eating soup with a knife." He now realized that he hadn't fully appreciated just how messy and slow. His battalion departed Iraq on September 10, 2004, after a tour that lasted two weeks short of a year, way short of what was needed. At best, they were just getting started.

One of Nagl's captains printed up souvenir coffee mugs that read, "Iraq 2003–2004: We Were Winning When I Left." But most of the soldiers, very much including Nagl, knew they weren't.

By this time, it was clear to a small but growing number of officials inside the Pentagon that the war was not going well. To a few, this had been clear almost from the outset. One of them was a deputy assistant secretary of defense named Jim Thomas.

As far back as April 2, 2003, one week before American troops rolled into Baghdad and Saddam Hussein's regime imploded, the *Washington Post* published an op-ed piece by a retired Marine colonel named Gary Anderson predicting that, after Saddam's inevitable defeat in the conventional war, the dictator would shift to a "protracted guerrilla war against the 'occupation,'" in the hopes that the Americans would grow fatigued and leave.

Thomas had met Anderson in the mid-1990s, when the colonel was stationed at the US Marine Corps's main base in Quantico, Virginia, thirty-five miles southwest of Washington. Anderson had a long history with low-intensity conflicts, having served as a UN observer in southern Lebanon and a marine in Somalia at the height of its insurgency. Now he was a war-game consultant, designing and conducting simulations of conflict under Defense Department contracts.

The previous January, he'd been part of a war game at the Institute for Defense Analyses, a think tank in Alexandria, Virginia. It wasn't billed as a war game about Iraq, but that's clearly what it was. Anderson headed the "Red Team"—that is, he was commander of the bad guys, the Iraqi army under Saddam's regime. The point of a Red Team in a war game is to give American officers a taste of some unanticipated challenges that a real war might throw at them. Early in the game, Anderson realized that he couldn't beat the invaders, so he decided to go underground, telling his fellow Red Team players not to resist the Americans but instead to stand by and re-emerge afterward as an insurgency.

Anderson's op-ed piece was inspired by this game. It was based not on any intelligence about Saddam's actual intentions but only on what Anderson had figured *he* would do if he were an Iraqi commander. As it happened, whether planned or spontaneous, this was what many Saddam loyalists actually did.

Thomas knew little about insurgencies. In the 1990s he'd studied defense strategy as a graduate student at SAIS, the School of Advanced International Studies, in Washington, DC. But the only thing he'd read about insurgencies was a single chapter on the French experience of "Revolutionary War" in one of his textbooks, *Makers of Modern Strategy,* and Thomas remembered finding the topic "quaint." Now, if Anderson was right, it was on the verge of staging a comeback.

So Thomas read every book he could find on the subject: Galula's *Counterinsurgency Warfare,* T. E. Lawrence's *Seven Pillars of Wisdom,* the Marine Corps's seventy-year-old *Small Wars Manual,* Bing West's *The Village,* and Nagl's *Learning to Eat Soup with a Knife* (though that one, he borrowed from the Pentagon's library).

Paul Wolfowitz, the deputy secretary of defense and Thomas's boss a couple notches up the chain of civilian command, read Anderson's op-ed piece, too. By mid-April, after Saddam's regime was ousted, Donald Rumsfeld had lost interest in the war; this was clear to everyone around him. The Iraq beat fell to Wolfowitz, who was beginning to wonder whether the war might really be devolving into an insurgency. He called Gary Anderson and asked him to come by.

Anderson worked up a briefing and presented it to Wolfowitz in early May. One of his proposals was to train the Iraqi army not so much in border defense but in counterinsurgency techniques. Another was to organize local police and citizens into "neighborhood watch" groups, similar to the Revolutionary Development teams that Robert Komer had devised as part of the CORDS program in Vietnam. To Anderson's thinking, not only was this a way to stabilize Iraq, it was America's only responsible way out of Iraq. Thomas, who sat in on the briefing, agreed.

Wolfowitz asked Anderson and Thomas to go to Baghdad and present the briefing together to Jerry Bremer.

The briefing took place on July 3 in Bremer's office. It was a disaster. The moment Anderson mentioned CORDS and Vietnam, Bremer stopped him short. Already critics were calling the Iraq War a "quagmire" and comparing it to Vietnam. "Iraq is not Vietnam!" Bremer shouted, pounding the table.

Yes, Anderson replied, but not everything went wrong in Vietnam; there were some lessons to be learned from that war.

"I don't want to hear the word *Vietnam* in my office," Bremer said angrily. "This meeting is over."

And it was.

The following January, Wolfowitz sent Thomas and Anderson back to Iraq, this time to travel around the country, on their own if Bremer wouldn't meet with them (he didn't), and to come back with a written assessment of overall security.

American troops had found Saddam Hussein in his spider hole the month before, and many hoped that his arrest would demoralize the insurgents. (By this time, even most officials in the White House and Pentagon had acknowledged that they were fighting an insurgency.) But Thomas and Anderson's report to Wolfowitz was grim. They noted a few bright spots, especially Mosul, where Major General David Petraeus was achieving remarkable things; he clearly understood what counterinsurgency was about, as did a few brigade commanders here and there. But their main finding was that the American forces had *no* overall strategy. Lacking guidance, most of the brigades did what they'd been trained to do by default: shoot first and ask questions later, with no vision of the desired end-state. Thomas and Anderson also found the program to train the Iraqi security forces—the foundation for a clean exit strategy—ill conceived. The American trainers, most of them artillery soldiers with nothing better to do, were teaching the Iraqi army how to defend the border from an Iranian invasion; they'd been given no instructions on how to teach the army or the police about countering an insurgency.

As a short-term measure, the pair recommended that Petraeus, whose tour in Mosul was almost up, be put in charge of the program to train Iraqi security forces. That idea was approved. In the longer run, they called for an overhaul of the American war strategy. That one would take more time and more pushing.

That summer, Anderson introduced Thomas to a former colleague from his days at Quantico, a Marine one-star general named Robert "Rooster" Schmidle. It was natural, at this point, for the Marines to take a greater interest in counterinsurgency than most Army officers. The Marine Corps had a longer tradition in these kinds of conflicts; its *Small Wars Manual,* published back in 1940, had noted that they "represent the normal and frequent operations of the Marine Corps," which, from 1800 to 1934, had landed 187 times in 37 countries "to suppress lawlessness or insurrection," mainly in Latin America but also as far away as the shores of Tripoli, as the "Marines' Hymn" put it.

After the First World War, the Marines split in two factions: one continued to stress these banana wars; the other pushed for evolving the corps into a "naval infantry," the main mission of which would be to mount amphibious assaults on an enemy's beachhead, then to fight on land alongside the Army. In both missions, the Marines relied less on heavy armor (which was too destructive for the banana wars and too heavy for the amphibious boats) and more on foot infantry, wheeled vehicles, and (starting in the 1950s) helicopters. In this sense, the Marines were cousins—albeit from rival clans—of the Army's light-infantry and airborne-assault brigades.

Schmidle and Anderson had both been directors of the "experimental unit" at Quantico's Warfighting Laboratory, created in the mid-1990s to develop new tactics and technologies for warfare in the twenty-first century, which the Marine Corps's commandant, General Charles Krulak, thought would be dominated by urban conflicts. One of Krulak's ideas was that a modern marine should be trained and equipped for a "three-block war"—in which he might be called on to wage combat on one block, conduct peacekeeping operations on the next block, and distribute humanitarian aid on the block after that. (There was family lineage here: during the Kennedy administration, Krulak's father, Victor "Brute" Krulak, also a Marine general, was the military's representative on the NSC's top-secret Special Group on counterinsurgency.)

Like Thomas, Anderson, and a growing number of officials and officers in the fall of 2004, Schmidle worried that Iraq was unraveling and that the main problem was the American military's lack of training on how to fight an urban insurgency. He wanted to organize a conference on the subject at Quantico and to invite more than the usual crowd of marines, expanding the guest list to Army, Air Force, Navy, and Special Forces officers, as well as high-ranking Pentagon civilians, a few think-tank types, and some officers from foreign governments that had joined the US-led coalition in Iraq. Thomas said that his office would cosponsor the event and defray some of the expenses.

The session was called the Irregular Warfare Conference, in part because "counterinsurgency" was still a frowned-upon term inside the Bush administration. It took place on October 6, in the officers' club at Quantico, with fifty-five officers, officials, and like-minded defense analysts attending, including Schmidle, Thomas, and Anderson. But the unexpected star of the show turned out to be a thirty-seven-year-old lieutenant colonel from the Australian army named David Kilcullen.

Kilcullen was born in Canada while his parents were on Commonwealth Scholarships, teaching at the University of Toronto and completing their PhDs, his father's in medieval political philosophy, his mother's in English literature. The family returned to Australia in 1971, after his father got a job at the national university in Canberra, just in time to march in the frequent campus protests against the Vietnam War. Dave, who was four at the time, often joined in on his father's shoulders, although he had more fun (so he was told later) playing war in his living room, crouching behind a chair, pretending to dodge American bombs, while watching the nightly TV newscasts. A few years later, he took a youthful interest in the grit of warfare, reading Ernest Hemingway's *For Whom the Bell Tolls* at age eleven and T. E. Lawrence's insurgent memoir at seventeen.

In January 1985, several months before turning eighteen, he enrolled at the Royal Military College in Duntroon, the Australian equivalent of West Point, although, unlike American cadets, Kilcullen and his classmates studied irregular warfare routinely in their courses. The Australian army, after all, had fought almost nothing but irregular wars, from the Second Boer War around the turn of the twentieth century on through the campaigns in Malaya, Borneo, and East Timor, among others, sometimes fighting irregulars, sometimes "fighting irregular"—that is, sometimes as counterinsurgents helping to uphold a foreign government, sometimes as insurgents helping to overthrow it. And after Vietnam, where it deployed a counterinsurgency unit for several years, the Australian army—unlike the Americans—incorporated the war's lessons into its curricula and doctrines.

Kilcullen took his first-year politics class from a civilian professor named William Maley, who happened to be one of the world's leading scholars on Afghanistan. The Soviets were waging war in Afghanistan at the time, an unusual twist in the annals of insurgencies: an Islamist rebel force fighting to topple a regime backed by communist occupiers. Maley steered his precocious student to take an interest, getting him a pass to the National University's library, so he could read articles on the war in English translations of Soviet military journals. Remarkably freewheeling discussions were going on in these journals: critical analyses of military operations, letters from company commanders debating tactics, detailed descriptions of battles in the eastern hills along the Pakistani border and in the southern green belt around Kandahar. Kilcullen found these articles riveting.

His final year at Duntroon was devoted almost entirely to cultivating skills in jungle warfare, parachuting, demolitions, and tactical leadership. Meanwhile, all cadets had to learn an Asian language; Kilcullen chose Indonesian and scored first in his class. He joined the infantry and was sent to advise Indonesia's special forces, who were fighting insurgents in East Timor.

He moved on to West Java for advanced language training. One day, in a military museum, he came across an exhibition about Indonesia's counterinsurgency campaign in the 1950s and '60s against a separatist movement called the Darul Islam. Kilcullen had never heard of this war and, in his subsequent hunts, could find almost no books about it, even though the conflict had apparently been much larger than Britain's famous and much-documented Malayan Emergency. Kilcullen, who had entered graduate school in political anthropology at the University of New South Wales (while still on active duty in the army), decided to write a dissertation on the Darul Islam. He went to live in a West Javan village and sought out former members of the movement for chats over tea. During his stay, he also witnessed the rise—and, in tense sittings, interviewed a few members—of a new, more extremist Islamist insurgency called Jemaah Islamiya, which had a loose affiliation with al Qaeda.

Kilcullen would later reflect that if he were a Muslim, he'd probably have joined a jihadist militia. "The thing that drives these guys—a sense of adventure, wanting to be part of the moment, wanting to be in the big movement of history that's happening now—that's the same thing that drives me," he told a magazine reporter.

Most of his friends thought that he was a bit daft, spending so much time researching some long-forgotten Muslim rebel group, just as John Nagl's friends had clucked at him for obsessing over the ancient cult of counterinsurgency. Kilcullen finished his dissertation in March 2001. Six months later, al Qaeda attacked the World Trade Center and the Pentagon. His dual expertise in counterinsurgency and Islamist insurgencies was suddenly in demand.

In June 2002, by now a major, he was sent as the Australian army's delegate to a conference on Afghanistan at the Royal Military College of Canada. The Americans at the conference, mainly Special Forces officers, gave a briefing on their invasion the previous year, specifically on the tactical aspects of their campaign to help the Northern Alliance defeat the Taliban.

Kilcullen responded with what he hoped would be a sobering blow. Yeah, yeah, very impressive analysis of the operation, brilliant, really, as far as it goes, he told them, *but,* he added, the war isn't over. The *invasion* is over, he went on, but the next *phase* of the *war,* the *counterinsurgency* phase, is just beginning, and you need to start thinking about what happens next and how to follow through.

To Kilcullen, this was basic stuff, not even advanced Galula, more Clausewitz 101 (war as politics through other means). After the panel, he discussed his point further with the Americans over several beers at the bar, and he was struck that they'd never considered the distinction. They really did think that toppling the regime was the same as winning the war. It was Kilcullen's first exposure to what he later realized was the classic American way of thinking about—as well as planning and waging—warfare.

Stunned as he was by the Yanks' apolitical concept of war, he was flabbergasted when, nine months later, President George W. Bush invaded Iraq. Rumors of an invasion had been in the air at the conference in Canada, but nobody Kilcullen talked with—not even the guys from US Special Forces—believed it would really happen. He found the notion mindless beyond belief, not because he was antiwar or regarded Saddam Hussein as harmless, but because it would be a distraction of resources, manpower, and attention from the more important war in Afghanistan, which, as he'd argued, wasn't nearly over. He regarded invading Iraq as a serious *strategic* error, along the lines of Hitler invading Russia in 1941 without having defeated Great Britain first.

At the time of the invasion, Kilcullen was a colonel stationed at army headquarters in Canberra. Australia had a Special Ops contingent in Iraq, so Kilcullen was tasked to watch the development of the war as a counterterrorism analyst. By late April, just a few weeks after Saddam's ouster, he and his staff concluded that an insurgency was in the making; and, based on what he knew about patterns of insurgency, he knew it had to be nipped before it bloomed.

Kilcullen wrote a paper, sounding the alarms. It went up the chain of the

Australian army command, then across the waters to the Pentagon, where it circulated in certain circles. The official response, sent via the two countries' military liaisons, was polite but dismissive: interesting, but don't worry, there's no insurgency.

Over the next month or so, Kilcullen heard from a number of American colonels and one-star generals at Quantico, the Army War College, and the military's various analytical branches. They all confided that they agreed with his analysis, or at least found it worth exploring, but they couldn't pursue it because they weren't allowed to discuss insurgencies or counterinsurgency, not even to utter the words.

As a result of these exchanges, when Bob Schmidle and a few other marines at Quantico were organizing the Irregular Warfare Conference in the fall of 2004, they invited Kilcullen to give a briefing as the Australian army's delegate.

Kilcullen's briefing was nothing remarkable, as far as he was concerned: a standard PowerPoint show, twenty-one slides in all, less a bold statement of his own ideas than a textbook recitation of the Australian army's common wisdom. He even titled the briefing "United States Counterinsurgency: An Australian View."

But Kilcullen had a fine sense of theater, and he'd discovered in Canada, as many Brits had learned about Americans long ago, that a droll accent and a dry wit could go a long way toward making banal ideas seem brilliant and uncomfortable ones seem palatable.

He opened with a slide asking the question that he figured many in the audience must be wondering: "Who cares what we Aussies think?" Then he answered it by listing several of the COIN wars that his country had fought through the decades. From an Aussie's perspective, he went on, the name of this conference was all wrong: there was nothing "irregular" about the kinds of wars under discussion; the vast majority of wars in history had fit the definition, so they should be called "regular wars"; the only reason they were called "irregular" was that the establishment army didn't want to fight them.

Then he went off on the themes, flashing the slides and narrating with a purposefully rowdy insouciance. The problem, he began, was that the American military saw COIN as a specialty when it should be mainstream. US commanders tend to attack the *insurgents,* when they should attack the insurgents' *strategy*. They lean toward purely military solutions, but COIN is 75 percent hearts and minds, just 25 percent combat. They also favor technological solutions, but COIN was about controlling, influencing, and winning over *the people;* therefore, soldiers have to fight and live not in big, heavily protected, remote bases but *among* the people. The metrics of success aren't how many enemy troops you kill but how many townspeople or villagers are spontaneously providing intelligence about where the enemy is (an indication of how much less they're fearing the enemy and how much more they're trusting you), how many community leaders openly support the government (and how long such leaders continue to live before the insurgents threaten or kill them), and how much spontaneous economic activity is going on in a town (reflecting the sense that it's safe to go out on the streets).

Kilcullen's final slide was labeled "Questions to Consider." He recited some of them: "What are our key capability gaps and what should we be doing about them? Are there institutional obstacles to success? Is American military culture conducive to effective COIN? Who has overall responsibility for COIN within DoD?" Most people in the audience knew the answer to that last question: nobody. That was one of the big problems.

After the briefing, Jim Thomas came up to Kilcullen, introduced himself, and asked, slightly dumbstruck, "Who *are* you?"

Kilcullen responded with a puzzled chuckle. Thomas explained that he was in charge of the shop in the Pentagon that produced the QDR, the Quadrennial Defense Review, a congressionally mandated report that outlines the nation's strategy and links it to the Defense Department's budget and programs. The last QDR, published in the fall of 2001, had reflected Rumsfeld's enthusiasm for the "revolution in military affairs," although it triggered few actual changes in the way the Pentagon did business. Thomas was determined that the upcoming QDR, to be published in 2005, would advocate a big boost in resources for, and revive strategic thinking about, irregular warfare.

Thomas then popped the question: Would Kilcullen be interested in coming to work for him in the Pentagon? "You're the guy from Central Casting that we need on the QDR," he said.

Kilcullen was very interested. He was growing weary of the Australian army; his commanders hadn't been giving him choice assignments; a change would be good, and a change placing him closer to the action better still.

The next day, Kilcullen went to see Thomas in his office. He noticed, with a raised eyebrow, two dog-eared books on his desk, both COIN classics: Lawrence's *Seven Pillars of Wisdom* and John Hersey's *A Bell for Adano*. They talked a bit more about the job. Kilcullen warned of a potential hitch. Thomas (or, since he was a mere deputy assistant secretary of defense, someone higher up) would have to write the Australian defense minister a letter requesting the transfer.

Thomas didn't think that would be a problem. He wrote a letter for Wolfowitz's signature. Wolfowitz signed it, and off it went.

Officials in the Australian defense ministry didn't like the idea at all. This Kilcullen, they replied, is just a lieutenant colonel. Let us send you a one-star general. Thomas was also hearing through back channels that in senior circles back home, Kilcullen wasn't much liked, was regarded as a showboat. Clearly Thomas needed to take the pressure up a notch. He wrote back more firmly, again for Wolfowitz's signature: We're not asking for an Australian *liaison;* we want someone embedded in the project, as if he were an American, and Kilcullen is specifically the man we want. A compromise was finally reached: the Yanks could have Kilcullen, but they'd also have to take a colonel from the Australian army's force-planning bureau, as a formal liaison.

In the first week of December, Kilcullen started work in the Pentagon, settling into a cubicle in a small office in a remote basement, where Thomas and the rest of his staff hoped to change the American way of war, preferably in time to affect the course of the war in Iraq.

By this time, John Nagl was working in the Pentagon, too.

He'd returned to the States a month and a half earlier, planning to take a breather and apply for an Army fellowship at the Council on Foreign Relations. But he got a phone call from a one-star general named Frank Helmick, a former assistant division commander to David Petraeus and now the senior military assistant to Paul Wolfowitz. The deputy secretary was looking for a new junior military assistant; Helmick had asked Petraeus if he knew of any suitable candidates. Petraeus recommended Nagl.

Nagl had taken on an unusually high profile for a junior officer. While he was in Anbar Province, a reporter for the *New York Times Magazine* named Peter Maass had come through looking for a story. The battalion commander hated dealing with the press, so he directed Maass to Nagl. Maass stayed for two weeks and wrote a nine-thousand-word article that focused specifically on Nagl, this Army historian of counterinsurgency who was now fighting a real insurgency. The article was published in the January 11, 2004, issue, under the headline "Professor Nagl's War."

In the months leading up to Helmick's call, Wolfowitz was spending a growing share of his time on Iraq, initially by default but over time with real interest. He would phone several of the American commanders in Iraq at least once a week for updates. He spoke with Petraeus, who by now was a three-star general commanding the Iraqi training program, every Saturday night at seven o'clock East Coast time. Wolfowitz had read the *Times Magazine* profile of Nagl and, since the briefings by Thomas and Anderson, had been dipping into some of the literature on counterinsurgency. He interviewed Nagl, was impressed, and hired him.

Nagl started work on November 1. It was a hectic time in the Pentagon. A week into the job, the second battle of Fallujah got under way, with ten thousand US soldiers and marines mounting an offensive to clear the city of insurgents in what turned out to be the fiercest fighting any Americans had faced since the battle of Hué in Vietnam. Even the optimists in the building realized the war was getting dicey; the interim Iraqi government had, at best, a tenuous grip on its country; the US military strategy seemed, to say the least, inadequate. Meanwhile, President Bush was immersed in a tough reelection campaign, which most people figured he would lose, due in part to the war's unpopularity.

The work schedule was brutal: thirteen-hour days, six days a week, and this with almost no downtime after a nonstop year at war. Nagl was exhausted. But in his meager spare time, he roamed the Pentagon's corridors with a gaunt, hungry look on his face, seeking someone, anyone, who might take the slightest interest in counterinsurgency. Initially, to his shock and distress, he couldn't find a soul. The United States was fighting an insurgency war, yet no one in the Pentagon seemed aware of the fact or knew how to deal with it.

Nagl met Jim Thomas early on in his tenure. They had mutual friends; Thomas said he'd read his book. But it wasn't until March that Thomas told him about Kilcullen, who was about to give a briefing to the QDR group; Nagl should come down and see it. So Nagl followed the labyrinthine path to the group's basement office. Kilcullen's briefing was pretty much the same slide show that he'd given at the Irregular Warfare Conference at Quantico. Nagl sat transfixed. Here was the guy he'd been looking for, the guy who thought about war the same way he did. He leapt to his feet after the speech, dashed over to Kilcullen, and introduced himself.

Nagl was scheduled to speak on a panel the following month at the annual strategy conference of the Army War College in Carlisle, Pennsylvania. Its organizer, a civilian professor named Steve Metz, had been studying low-intensity conflict, and trying to put the subject on the Army's radar screen, for nearly a decade. He'd clearly decided the time was ripe, for the title of this year's conference was "Defeating America's Irregular Enemies." Nagl was asked to present a summary of his book, which, he'd learned since getting back from Iraq, was going to be published in a paperback edition later in the year by the University of Chicago Press, whose board members had looked into acquiring the rights from Praeger after reading his profile in the *New York Times Magazine*.

Nagl told Kilcullen that he should come speak at the conference, too. Kilcullen said he was interested but hadn't been invited. When Nagl got back to his office, he phoned Metz and urged him to add this guy to the panel; he was incredible; Nagl would even be willing to give Kilcullen half of his own time. Metz had no objections.

The two made the 115-mile road trip up to Carlisle together, Nagl driving while talking at a rapid clip, Kilcullen navigating with MapQuest, a service he'd never used, across terrain he'd never seen. They got lost a couple of times. As a result, the car ride turned into a long voyage, and the pair bonded, telling their life stories, talking family (they both had sons the same age), comparing West Point with Duntroon, teasing each other over which of them, Nagl the tank leader or Kilcullen the foot soldier, had the more authentic combat experience—all of this banter rooted in their mutual delight at finding someone with the same interest in COIN and the same commitment to changing the conventional thinking and the official policy.

About two hundred people—mainly officers, faculty, think-tank denizens, and a few congressional aides—showed up for the conference. During the panels before theirs, Nagl and Kilcullen sat in the back of the room, whispering commentary back and forth, finally taking their conversation out in the lobby when those around them grew visibly annoyed by their chatter and giggling.

The next day, during their own time on the stage, Nagl delivered what was essentially a replay of his dissertation defense from back at Oxford, with PowerPoint slides tacked on to satisfy standard Army form, while Kilcullen gave a slightly shortened version of his Quantico briefing.

They both raised a stir. Nagl learned, upon arrival, that he was already regarded in some circles as a folk hero, photocopies of key chapters from his (still prohibitively expensive) book circulating as a sort of samizdat critique of the Pentagon's policies in Iraq. Soon after the conference, summaries of both their talks, apparently jotted down by someone in the audience, started appearing on a few online forums that dealt with military matters.

And so began what some of their friends, and a few disparagers, called "The John & Dave Show," a tight friendship but also a joint venture, the two of them appearing at the same conferences, sharing notes on books and articles, talking regularly on the phone or in each other's offices at the Pentagon, all with the aim of refining and spreading their ideas. To Nagl, it stirred fond memories of the heady bull sessions in the faculty bar and dining hall back at West Point. Only this time, he and his new comrade in arms were in the thick of things.

7.

"Where's My Counterinsurgency Plan?"

In May 2004, as the insurgency's existence could no longer be denied, General George Casey, the newly appointed commander of US forces in Iraq, went to see General Peter Schoomaker, the Army chief of staff, to discuss the changing nature of the war.

Early on in the conversation, Schoomaker gave Casey a book and urged him to read it right away. It was John Nagl's *Learning to Eat Soup with a Knife*. Casey noticed a dozen or so copies of this book on a table behind the chief's desk. Schoomaker said that he'd been handing them out to all the four-star generals, that it offered the clearest analysis he'd read of how to think about counterinsurgency.

One year earlier, Donald Rumsfeld had called Schoomaker out of retirement—which he'd been enjoying for the previous three years—to come back and serve as the Army's top officer. To Rumsfeld's mind, there were no active-duty four-star generals qualified for the job. More than that, Schoomaker seemed ideally suited for steering the Army in the direction Rumsfeld wanted it to go.

The two had met briefly in the weeks after the September 11 attacks. Schoomaker was part of a small team of retired generals assembled by the Army War College to write a transition plan to help the Army shift from a peacetime establishment to a wartime expeditionary force. Afterward, Rumsfeld pulled him aside to talk about how Special Forces might be used in the impending invasion of Afghanistan.

Schoomaker had risen through the Army's ranks primarily as a Special Forces officer; his final posting, before retiring in 2000, was commander of the US Special Operations Command. Rumsfeld liked the Special Ops branch; it exemplified what he thought the entire Army ought to be in the transformation age: fast, agile, and, above all, small.

Special Forces had also long been in the business of irregular warfare.

Schoomaker had done time in Grenada, Panama, Haiti, and northern Iraq, where, in the wake of Desert Storm, he helped quell rioting among Kurdish refugees along the Iraqi-Turkish border, then organized a program of humanitarian assistance. Two years before retiring, he'd written an article arguing that the Army as a whole should "become more like" Special Forces.

But the general's reasoning on this point was different from that of the defense secretary. Schoomaker thought that in the future the United States would face fewer big wars but many more small conflicts, and so American soldiers should be trained as "warrior-diplomats," ready for combat and nation-building. (In the year Schoomaker wrote that article, Special Forces teams were deployed in 152 countries and foreign territories, to deal with everything from clearing land mines, to capturing drug lords, to distributing food, to fighting insurgents—though, of course, the chiefs of the day regarded none of those deployments as "combat.")

George Casey was a more conventional Army officer. He'd grown up in an Army family; his father, also named George Casey, was one of a dozen American generals killed in the Vietnam War: in his case, the casualty of a helicopter crash in 1970, when George Jr. was not quite twenty-two. Thirty years later, he took command of the 1st Armored Division, matching the career peak of his father, who was commander of the 1st Cavalry at the time of his death. Then came three consecutive assignments in the Pentagon—as director of strategic plans and policy, then director of the Joint Staff, and finally vice chief of staff—a pattern that usually denoted a prelude to retirement.

And so it came as a complete surprise when President Bush awarded him a fourth star and named him commander of multinational forces in Iraq. Casey had never been in combat and had scant experience of any sort in the Middle East.

Nor had he ever been interested in any kind of war except the big kind. In 1974 he'd gone to Ranger School and scored first in his class. (Dave Petraeus would do the same in the following session.) But Casey put himself through its rigors mainly as a personal test; he had little desire to follow up and even turned down an offer to join the elite Delta Force.

His only deployment in a low-intensity conflict had been as an assistant division commander of peacekeeping forces in Bosnia, and it left him with a sour taste for the whole idea. Unlike Schoomaker or Petraeus, who regarded Bosnia as a model for future conflicts, Casey saw it as a case study in what to avoid. The observation he took away was that when American soldiers were sent abroad to do good or to help settle conflicts, they had a tendency to do everything themselves. In some ways, this was commendable; it reflected the Army's can-do spirit. But ultimately it was a trap: the more the Americans did, the less the native soldiers did, and so the Americans wound up staying longer; and the longer they stayed, the more the local people resented them. It seemed a losing game.

Casey left Schoomaker's office with Nagl's book in tow, and he read it over the weekend. It was the first book he'd ever read about counterinsurgency. He found it interesting, but not interesting enough to seek out a second book.

Still, it did acquaint him with the subject, and he knew that Schoomaker's interest meant he had to take an interest, too. So, upon arriving at Baghdad headquarters on July 1, one of the first questions Casey asked at his first staff meeting was, "Where is my counterinsurgency plan?"

No answer. Clearly, there wasn't a plan.

Casey's second question: "Who is my counterinsurgency expert?"

The nominal chief strategist, an Air Force brigadier general named Stephen Sargeant, perhaps embarrassed by the silence that greeted the new boss on his first day, piped up that he was the COIN expert.

Casey, a bit doubtful, asked for his qualifications. Sargeant replied that he'd read Mao Zedong. Casey knew that didn't quite cut it. But since Sargeant had been bold enough to take the bait, Casey put him in charge of finding a team of experts to do better.

It took Casey little time, and no prompting from experts, to figure out that Iraq was in shambles and so was the war. His predecessor, Ricardo Sanchez, a three-star general who'd apparently spent his year as commander in a constant state of cluelessness, had left him nothing to build on. Not only was there no counterinsurgency plan, there was no plan of any sort: no strategy, no mission statement, no criteria or benchmarks for how to measure, or even define, success or failure.

"George Bush has given me a pile of shit," Casey mumbled more than once.

Meanwhile, Sargeant riffled through the military's personnel records, looking for officers with some experience at planning strategy for this kind of war. Then, on August 5, a month and a few days into Casey's command, strictly by chance, a colonel named William Hix walked into his office. Sargeant's title was director of strategy, plans, and assessment. He already had two colonels working as deputies, one on plans, the other on assessment; Hix was reporting for duty as the deputy in charge of strategy.

The son of a career CIA agent, Hix had graduated from West Point in the class of 1981 with a concentration in the Social Science Department. He joined the 82nd Airborne Division right out of the academy, then segued into Special Forces, where he advised counterinsurgents in the Philippines, trained peacekeepers in the Sinai, and fought in the shadows of Desert Storm.

He was unlike any Army colonel Casey or Sargeant had ever met. His demeanor was intense, single-mindedly professional, but also casually brazen. He took delight in saying whatever he felt like, with no apparent worry about the consequences for his career. In short, Bill Hix was just the guy Sargeant was looking for. And since Sargeant was confident enough in his own position to delegate authority without feeling threatened, he gave his new strategist direct and unlimited access to Casey.

Unfortunately, the day Hix arrived, Casey had just signed off on a twenty-eight-page campaign plan for the next phase of the occupation. To Casey's astonishment, Sanchez had never written a campaign plan—the basic outline of a commander's strategy and how he intended to achieve it with the available resources—so he was under pressure from the White House and the Pentagon to come up with *something*, and *quickly*. More flustering still, Casey was dealing with contradictory mandates. Rumsfeld had told him, in a conversation before he left, not to do too much, to focus on setting the stage for withdrawal—a sentiment that Casey shared, given his own experience in Bosnia. But Schoomaker wanted a counterinsurgency plan, which, Casey knew from reading Nagl, would require doing quite a lot and staying for quite a while ("messy and slow," as Nagl quoted Lawrence, "like eating soup with a knife").

With no time for outside experts to materialize, Casey put together a team of personnel within reach of headquarters—officials from the State Department and the CIA, as well as a few military officers—to write an assessment of the situation. From that, he and Sargeant cobbled together a campaign plan on their own, even though Casey had barely unpacked and could claim only the slightest grasp of counterinsurgency concepts, while Sargeant, a former A-10 attack plane pilot, had a looser grip still.

Hix read the Casey-Sargeant campaign plan, titled "Partnership: From Occupation to Constitutional Elections." At least it *was* a plan; there hadn't been one before. It acknowledged the threat of an insurgency, which hadn't been accepted universally. But beyond that, the paper was a mess. Any brigade commander who read it would have only a vague idea of what to do. In some passages, the plan defined the mission as "full-spectrum counter-insurgency operations" to isolate the people from "former regime extremists and foreign terrorists" and to "enhance the legitimacy" of the new Iraqi government. But there was no guidance on how to do this. It was all boilerplate, pidgin-COIN talk: the right words, bereft of meaning. The plan listed "key strategic tasks," which included protecting Iraqi leaders, the local UN mission, and the occupation authority's credibility—but it said nothing, anywhere, about protecting the Iraqi *population,* the centerpiece of any real counterinsurgency strategy.

In other passages, the plan more crisply defined the mission as maintaining offensive operations against the insurgents and accelerating the training of Iraqi security forces, so that, after the upcoming elections, the United States and its multinational coalition could hand off authority to the new Iraqi government and start moving out. The plan estimated that the transfer would take place in "key cities" by the end of the year and throughout Iraq by July 2005, at which point the "liberation/occupation" phase would wrap up and the "transition" phase would be well under way.

Hix knew that wars of this sort just didn't go so smoothly or quickly, especially in a country like Iraq, which had no democratic traditions and, at the moment, no functioning government. And, in any case, if miracles did somehow occur, the plan's two themes—full-spectrum COIN and speedy transition—were contradictory; you couldn't do both at the same time.

The whole plan would have to be rewritten, reconceived.

At their first meeting, Casey gave Hix carte blanche to do just that. Sargeant had put together a group of PhDs, mainly from the RAND Corporation, to help with advice. (They soon became known as the "doctors without orders," a play on the international health group Doctors Without Borders.) But Hix knew that there was someone else he needed to call:

a former fellow Special Forces colonel and Harvard PhD named Kalev "Gunner" Sepp.

Kalev Sepp was no longer in the Army; he'd retired in frustration five years earlier. But it was only slight exaggeration to say that he was born for this assignment.

His father, Sulev Sepp, was born and raised in Estonia. In the winter of 1940–41, at age sixteen, Sulev joined a resistance movement against the Soviet occupation. After World War II, he went west, settling in Southern California, first picking oranges with Mexican migrants, then working at a lock factory. Amid the region's Cold War prosperity, and as his English improved, he joined the Air National Guard and, in 1950, signed up to fight in Korea, happy to do battle once more against communists, this time as a member of the American armed forces. After that war, Sulev got a job as a paratrooper with a Special Ops unit based in Marin County. His mission: in the event of a nuclear war, he would be flown over the area where a Soviet bomber had been shot down, parachute near the wreckage, and retrieve whatever materials were still extant.

As a boy, Kalev watched his father and the other men of the unit practice their parachute jumps onto nearby farm fields. The men were all lean, sunburned, and happy. Kalev thought, "I want to be like that."

Sulev Sepp had never finished high school, but he spoke five languages and was a voracious reader of history. Kalev grew up listening to stories about the Estonian resistance. Much later, he discovered that, in 1960, when Kalev was seven years old and living with his family in West Germany, his father had run agents across the East German border. After that (this part was known at the time), he'd served two tours in Vietnam as an intelligence specialist.

For as long as he could remember, Kalev wanted to join the military. His poor eyesight ruled out the Air Force; he was too tall for the submarine Navy; so that left the Army. He graduated high school in 1971. A guidance counselor who knew nothing about military academies had told him that West Point was an engineering school (strictly speaking true, as all its students got degrees in engineering); Kalev had no interest in that, so he applied to the Citadel and got in. From there, following in his father's footsteps, he signed up for jump school, where he scored fourth in a districtwide summer class of 1,600, and that landed him a Ranger's slot in the 82nd Airborne Division.

The Vietnam War had recently ended. Sepp's instructors were all captains and majors who'd fought in the war and, in an attempt to prolong the experience, pushed hard to turn their new crop of trainees into *combat* leaders. Sepp and the other paratroopers found themselves jumping out of airplanes all the time. And because the division had tons of ammunition, stockpiled for Vietnam but not shipped in time, their infantry training on the ground included lots of *live-fire* exercises—artillery shells whizzing over their heads and jet fighters dropping napalm at their feet. A few young officers were killed amid this derring-do. For the others, it became a point of pride, a sign of experience and fearlessness, to walk around the base, their pant legs and boot cleats streaked with the white stripes of dry napalm, which, it was well known, would never wash out.

This was in the late 1970s, not long after the West German commandos rescued the Lufthansa airline hostages at Mogadishu airport. Special Forces were suddenly fashionable again. Sepp was aching to join up, but his superior officers told him that he'd ruin his career if he went in that direction. They also invoked a technical restriction: Sepp was an artillery officer at the time (it was during a training exercise that he picked up the nickname Gunner), and Special Forces had no need for artillery. He was reassigned to South Korea, where he started petitioning again for a transfer and finally found a general to sign the paperwork. In December 1986, nearly a decade after he'd put in his first request, Sepp was transferred to the Green Berets at Fort Bragg, North Carolina, and from there to Honduras, as a team leader training local paratroopers, infantry soldiers, and military police.

Then it was on to El Salvador as one of the fifty-five US military personnel, training a battalion in 1989–90, during the final offensives of the civil war. This was Sepp's first direct exposure to counterinsurgency operations. He was a lowly captain, but he came under attack almost constantly—from mortar shells, ambushes, and machine gun fire—while also immersing himself in civil affairs, psychological operations, training local police, trying to reform district governments, and analyzing how the cycle of the coffee harvest affected popular support for the guerrillas. He and the other Special Forces officers had to do all of this, in part because there were so few of them to go around.

Sepp found the whole scene thrilling but also chastening. Back when he was a Ranger in the 82nd Airborne, he'd undertaken a study of counterterrorism, poring over classified reports on operations by Israeli commando teams. The Israelis had done more hostage rescues than anyone and were most celebrated for their boldness and skill. Yet it turned out, to Sepp's surprise, that even they'd racked up almost exactly as many failures as successes; plenty of their missions had ended with the hostages killed or the terrorists escaping. Sepp began to realize this was a dicey business.

The impression was reinforced when he went through the rigorous training exercises in the Carolina sandhills west of Fort Bragg. When he'd gone through the conventional Army's training regimens—the schools for infantry, armor, and artillery—every scenario had a "school solution": if you followed the right procedure, you succeeded. The Special Forces' regimen was murkier. There were no set solutions: you could do everything right, and things still wound up wrong; the best you could do was wreak the least amount of havoc.

The difference, Sepp concluded, had a lot to do with the trainers running the schools. The conventional Army's trainers hadn't fought a war lately—not a big war, tank on tank, major power versus major power. The Special Forces' trainers were retired officers who'd served with the Green Berets in Vietnam or with the Office of Strategic Services, the forerunner of the CIA, in World War II. They knew what it took to raise guerrilla armies in contested terrain, and they'd learned, from hard experience, the deep grayness of these sorts of fights, the infiltrators in your midst, the vast unknowns all around you.

Sepp wanted to be deployed with Special Forces in Operation Desert Storm, but the brass sent him to the Command and General Staff College at Leavenworth, then urged him to get an advanced degree at an Ivy League grad school, at the Army's expense, followed by a teaching stint at West Point.

He studied history at Harvard, got his degree (minus the dissertation, which he started but didn't complete until later), then at West Point created a course in the History Department called Revolution, Insurgencies, and Civil Wars.

The West Point History Department had once been a part of the Sosh department, but it splintered off a few years before Sepp's arrival, and a good-natured rivalry hardened the divide. The history professors saw themselves as the serious scholars and the Sosh crew as the go-go policy elite, polishing their CVs for the impending inside-track job arranged by a fellow star man from the Lincoln Brigade. Sepp liked to sum up the cultural difference this way: at lunch, the history profs would be discussing a new book on the politico-military impact of the longbow, while the Sosh profs debated the merits of the new BMW and the Saab.

Sepp was more a midcareer man than most of the faculty in either department. He'd already seen a fair bit of action, so he used his time at West Point to settle in and deepen his knowledge, reading voraciously about the subject of his teaching, insurgency wars throughout history.

After his three years at West Point, Sepp was assigned to TRADOC, the Training and Doctrine Command, where he was put to work in an adventurous think tank called Army After Next, which was set up after the end of the Cold War to explore ideas and scenarios, without restriction, about the nature of warfare and the requirements of security twenty years in the future. Sepp loved this job. But a year into it, TRADOC got a new commander who saw no point in long-range thinking and twisted Army After Next into a rubber stamp for the Army's most cherished weapons programs. No longer were there free discussions about the possibilities and implications of an antisatellite war with China; instead, there were studies on whether the Army's new fighting vehicle should have six wheels or eight. One part of Sepp's new job involved writing thank-you letters to the study's participants.

He was rescued by a phone call from a housemaster he'd befriended at Harvard, offering him a job as a resident scholar. Sepp retired from the Army, took the job at Harvard, and finished his dissertation. (He reached some of the same conclusions that Petraeus had reached in his thesis about the Army's disinclination to take small wars seriously. But Sepp, who didn't know Petraeus at the time and hadn't read his dissertation, was a bit more jaundiced: after interviewing all the senior officers, whom he'd never seen while stationed in El Salvador, he realized that the *real* mission, which had been highly classified at the time, was to build regional support for the contra guerrillas' struggle to overthrow the Sandinista government in neighboring Nicaragua.)

After the September 11 terrorist attacks, Sepp was recruited by the historian's office at Fort Bragg to write an analysis of the Special Forces' role in the invasion of Afghanistan and the ouster of the Taliban. The charter was to pull no punches. Sepp interviewed dozens of officers and examined all the documents. Midway through, the charter changed. It became a puff job: all the screwups, miscommunications, and near-disasters were expunged; the final version, published by the Command and General Staff College Press under the title *Weapon of Choice: U.S. Army Special Operations in Afghanistan,* read like a Tom Clancy novel and was nearly as fictitious. Still, Sepp had done the real research; it gave him insight into how these things worked, and it hooked him into a network of senior Special Forces officers. Soon after, he got a job teaching at the Naval Postgraduate School in Monterey, California, where Special Forces captains and majors went for a yearlong academic respite.

While in Monterey, Sepp got the phone call from Bill Hix. The two had met while working on long-range analysis at Army After Next during its heyday. They'd become friends, talked often about their common backgrounds in the shadow Army, left at around the same time (after the new commander wrecked the place), and stayed in touch. When Hix got approval to form a team to write a new campaign plan for Casey, it was only logical that he'd ask Sepp to come join him.

Sepp arrived in Iraq in early November 2004. Not long after, he sat in on a meeting with Hix and Casey, and he was stunned by the dynamics. Casey was leaning back in a big red leatherette easy chair; Hix sat on a nearby couch, leaning forward, explaining some concept in the new campaign plan that he was working on. Casey would try to summarize one of the points, and Hix would say, in an annoyed tone, "No, that's not it at all!"

In all his years in the Army, Sepp had never seen a colonel sitting in a room with a four-star general, just the two of them, talking as if equals. But this was an odder scene still. It played out like a teacher tutoring a student, or Aristotle instructing the prince, with Hix in the role of the philosopher-mentor. Sepp didn't know which was more dizzying: Hix's assertiveness or

Casey's indifference to the decorum of rank for the sake of getting something done.

One day, early on in Sepp's tenure, Hix leaned into his office and said he needed a research paper, something like what they do in the business world to explore how different companies perform a certain task or sell a particular product, how they analyze which techniques work, which techniques don't—you know, what do they call it (he snapped his fingers to speed up his thinking), a "best practices" paper, that was it. "I need a paper," Hix said, "on 'best practices' for counterinsurgency."

Then he turned around and left Sepp alone to get started.

Sepp spent the next thirty-six hours working on the paper: thirty hours of thinking and writing, six hours of sleeping in one- to two-hour breaks. He drew on everything that he'd taught at West Point and Monterey, studied at Harvard, done in Honduras and El Salvador, and learned from his father. It was a summation of his entire professional life and a good bit of his personal life, too.

As a first step, he wrote out a list of all the insurgency wars in the twentieth century. He came up with fifty-three: the Anglo-Boer war, the Philippine insurrection, the Arab revolt against the Turks, the Nicaragua interventions (in the 1920s and the 1980s), the Greek civil war, and on and on through Malaya, Kenya, Algeria, Cuba, Vietnam, Northern Ireland, the Soviet-Afghan war, Somalia, and, of course, the ongoing struggles in Afghanistan and Iraq.

Then, jotting down the factors that led to victory or defeat in each conflict (some of the data pulled from memory, some from files of class notes or the internet), he spelled out in detail roughly a dozen common denominators of victory and nine common elements of defeat.

After writing the paper, Sepp summarized its conclusions in a chart labeled "Successful and Unsuccessful Counterinsurgency Practices." The list of "Successful" practices included "Focus on population, their needs and security . . . Insurgents isolated from population . . . Emphasis on intelligence . . . Amnesty and rehabilitation for insurgents . . . Conventional military forces reoriented for counterinsurgency . . . Special Forces, advisers embedded with indigenous forces . . . Insurgent sanctuaries denied."

The "Unsuccessful" practices included "Priority to 'kill-capture' enemy, not on engaging population . . . Military units concentrated on large bases . . .

Building, training indigenous army in image of US Army . . . Special Forces focused on raiding . . . Open borders, airspace, coastlines."

None of this was new. The ideas were straight out of the basic COIN curriculum: Galula, Nagl, Lawrence, Kitson, the Marine Corps's *Small Wars Manual*, and the rest. But the novelty of Sepp's paper was its empirical grounding. Nobody had tested, and confirmed, the theories against the expanse of modern history, the accumulated data of the entire past century.

But the paper also cut deep in an immediate way. Those reading it inside Casey's headquarters couldn't possibly miss its implications: the list of unsuccessful practices matched precisely what most US military forces were doing in Iraq; and the successful practices were being followed by very few, especially after Petraeus's departure from Mosul nine months earlier.

Sepp's paper amounted, in short, to a sweeping critique of US war strategy—and, as he and Hix intended, the foundation for a new counterinsurgency campaign plan in Iraq.

Hix was enthusiastic about Sepp's paper and, after some minor editing, brought the paper into Casey's office along with a proposal. He wanted to append it as an unclassified annex to the next campaign plan—a novel notion in itself, since everything about campaign plans was usually secret—and, in the meantime, to submit the paper to *Military Review*, the US Army's leading professional journal, so that officers and soldiers throughout the chain of command could understand the war and their role in it, since they hadn't been told up till then.

Casey gave the go-ahead to both proposals.

To the extent that there was any discussion about these kinds of wars in Army circles, it was taking place in the pages of *Military Review*. The journal, published bimonthly by the Combined Arms Center at Fort Leavenworth, had been around since 1922. In the decade after Vietnam, it served as a widely read forum for the intense debate over the new Army doctrines on conventional combat: the field manual on *Operations* authored by General DePuy in the 1970s and the revision on *AirLand Battle* by General Wass de Czege in the 1980s. But in the decade since Desert Storm, the magazine had gone steeply downhill, turning into a notepad for senior officers who wanted to beef up their CVs and for academics seeking outlets for theoretical treatises on the dynamics of conflict. In the wake of the victories in the Cold War and the Persian Gulf, the Army's journal of ideas had become irrelevant.

When Lieutenant General William Scott Wallace took over as Leavenworth's commander in June 2003, he was determined to change that, among many other things. Wallace had been the deputy commander of US forces in the invasion of Iraq. One week into the war, when the American advance was thwarted by Iraqi militiamen firing bazookas from the back of Toyota pickup trucks, Wallace told a reporter, "The enemy we're fighting is a bit different than the one we war-gamed against." The remark put the general on the outs with Donald Rumsfeld, and his assignment to Leavenworth, Kansas, was widely seen as an act of exile.

Wallace came into the job full of fire, wanting to turn Leavenworth into a pertinent player in the war, even if from halfway around the globe, and he saw the renovation of *Military Review* as a big part of this upheaval. His first act on that front was to hire a new editor, and his choice was a public affairs officer he'd known in Iraq named William Darley.

Darley, a career staff officer in the Army's Special Forces, had spent the previous decade in the public-affairs branches of US Special Operations Command in Tampa, Florida, and the Office of the Assistant Secretary of Defense for Special Operations in the Pentagon. When Wallace called him, he was in Iraq, handling public affairs for Lieutenant General Ricardo Sanchez. Darley saw clearly that an insurgency was bubbling up, and he was angered, not just professionally but personally, that the higher-ups were refusing to acknowledge it.

He came to Leavenworth for his new job in mid-March 2004. At their first meeting, Wallace laid down three rules for the journal's new incarnation. First, its articles had to be relevant to the war. Second, it would no longer publish articles by and for academics; anyone could write for it, and if an academic had something interesting to say, that was fine, but this was a journal for soldiers. Third, he shouldn't be afraid of controversy, although he shouldn't be outrageous for its own sake. As long as Darley followed those guidelines, Wallace would give him editorial free reign.

When Darley walked into the journal's office, he was appalled. There was a stack of 190 articles, all approved but not yet published, some dating as far back as four years. He skimmed through them and instantly threw out more than 100. Over the next few weeks, he pored over official documents and conference reports, looking for specialists who seemed to have insight on the war, then sought them out to write for him.

In the year before Darley's arrival, the journal had published only nine articles having the slightest connection to counterinsurgency. In Darley's first year, he published twenty-nine—an average of nearly five per issue—many of them by officers or consultants who'd recently been on the ground in Iraq or Afghanistan.

When Sepp's essay on best practices came through the mill, Darley knew he had a classic on his hands. He emailed Sepp, saying that he wanted to publish it as soon as possible but that it needed footnotes. After all, most readers had never heard of Kalev Sepp; the article made a lot of provocative claims, and he needed to back them up.

Sepp spent the better part of the next four days double-checking all the facts and jotting down the exact page numbers where they appeared in various books. (By this time, he'd returned to Monterey, so had access to his personal library; he would go back to Iraq the following summer.)

The footnoted essay appeared in the May–June 2005 issue, along with eight other articles on COIN-related themes (out of sixteen articles altogether), written by an assortment of scholars and officers who hadn't previously known of one another's existence. The articles included an anthropologist's analysis of the "social context" of the Iraqi insurgents' roadside bombs, arguing that US forces should track down the bomb-makers through contacts with tribal sheikhs; a review of the British army's experience with counterinsurgency; an essay on the US pacification campaign in the Philippines from 1899 to 1913 and the lessons it held for today's commanders in Iraq; and a historical survey by an Army War College historian titled "Phase IV Operations: Where Wars Are Really Won."

It was with articles like these, in issue after issue, that *Military Review* was reemerging as a must-read journal for Army officers and defense intellectuals. A community was forming; a conversation about the Army's policy and culture was under way.

8.

The Basin Harbor Gang

Every summer since the start of the decade, Eliot Cohen had organized a weeklong national-security workshop at the Basin Harbor Club along the sparkling shores and verdant hills of Lake Champlain, Vermont. Cohen was director of the Strategic Studies Program at Johns Hopkins University's School of Advanced International Studies in Washington, DC. The point of the workshops was to bring together a couple dozen professors in national-security programs from universities around the country and discuss better ways to teach and research the subject. But early in 2005, Cohen decided to do something different, more urgent, in the coming summer: he would assemble a group of counterinsurgency specialists—a few academics, but mainly military officers, government officials, and veterans of past COIN operations—to discuss how to fight a better war in Iraq.

Cohen had given a talk at the Irregular Warfare Conference at Quantico in October 2004. (Its cosponsor, Jim Thomas, had been one of his graduate students at SAIS a decade earlier.) More pertinent, the previous May, as a member of the Pentagon's Defense Policy Board, an outside advisory council appointed by the secretary of defense, Cohen had traveled to Iraq. The only board member to make such a trip, he'd stayed for eight days, visited several Army and Marine bases, talked with commanders, junior officers, and grunts, as well as some Iraqis—and came away with the grim sense that the United States was losing the war and that the failings were entirely those of its own political and military leadership.

At age forty-nine, Cohen was one of the country's most respected military scholars and, from appearances, the least likely. A bit dweebish in appearance, he wore glasses, a patrician's trim moustache, and—always—a bow tie. Officers who disparaged academic advisers on principle referred to him behind his back as "Professor Bow Tie." But many others, especially younger officers, were respectful, even admiring.

For one thing, Cohen was an Army Reserve officer himself. Born and raised in Boston, he'd immersed himself as a boy in the region's history, especially the landmarks of the Revolutionary War, which sparked a fascination with military matters generally. He'd also grown up in a devoutly Jewish family, learning early about the Holocaust—an aunt had been liberated from the German concentration camps—which imbued him with an awareness of evil in the world and the occasional need to fight it. In the late 1960s, when Vietnam made much of his generation viscerally hostile to all things military, Cohen was affected more by Israel's triumph in the Six-Day War.

As a graduate student at Harvard (where he'd also been an undergrad in the class of 1977), he felt guilty that he'd probably spend his life studying the military without being in some way a part of it. So he signed up for ROTC and, twice a week, took the subway to the other side of Cambridge for Reserve officers' training exercises on the campus of the Massachusetts Institute of Technology. (The program didn't exist at Harvard.)

In 1982, after earning his PhD, he taught at Harvard for three years, moved to the Naval War College for four more, then spent a year in the Pentagon as a lieutenant in the Army Reserve, working for Andy Marshall in the Office of Net Assessment. From watching Marshall, Cohen learned not only the enterprise of defense analysis but also the craft and benefits of professional networking. Through the 1990s, as a tenured professor at SAIS, Cohen proved to be a popular teacher (twice winning awards for excellence) as well as an agile practitioner of the Marshallian art, creating a program in "executive education"—basically an advanced course in military history and strategy—for general officers and senior Defense Department officials.

Over the next few years, Cohen emerged as a prominent member of the neoconservative movement, and was among the first to sign petitions and write op-ed columns calling for the ouster of Saddam Hussein through American military force. But Cohen possessed an independent streak that most of his fellow neocons lacked: he had looser ties to the Republican Party and harbored less overt ambition for public office;* he was more a scholar, and sometimes a critical one.

In 1991, after Desert Storm, Don Rice, the secretary of the Air Force, commissioned Cohen to conduct a detailed study of how the air campaign

* Cohen changed in the 2012 presidential election, not only advising Republican candidate Mitt Romney, but appearing as one of his spokesmen.

had affected the war. Rice anticipated that the study, which he called *The Gulf War Air Power Survey,* would vindicate the revolution in military affairs and thus make a case for Air Force dominance in future defense plans and budgets. But Cohen's multivolume report concluded that the new smart bombs and high-tech computer systems had not been as crucial as many had assumed. He turned the study's executive summary into a book, published by the US Naval Institute Press under the title *Revolution in Warfare?* (The question mark was significant.)

The year before, Cohen had coauthored a book called *Military Misfortunes: The Anatomy of Failure in War*. In it, he examined three failures—the disaster at Gallipoli in 1915–16, the fall of France in 1940, and the rout of the US 3rd Army at the start of the Korean War in 1950—and attributed them not to the performance of the troops but rather to the incompetence of the commanding officers: specifically their failure to learn, to anticipate the enemy's moves, and to react to those moves when they happened.

Coming back from his trip to Iraq in May 2004, Cohen worried that the American commanders and officials he'd just seen in action were making the same mistakes. They displayed no insight, or even much curiosity, about the enemy's motives, goals, or organizational structure; the program to train Iraqi security forces was ill conceived and poorly resourced. More to the point, the US military command was in total disarray: the general officers at headquarters had formulated no strategy, issued no guidance, and were out of touch with the fight on the ground. The civilian authorities, in both the embassy and Jerry Bremer's Coalition Provisional Authority, were useless. The officers out in the field were left to their own devices in a war for which they hadn't been trained: a few were doing well nonetheless; most weren't.

Cohen was not a COINdinista, but his knowledge of military history ran broad and deep. He knew what an insurgency looked like, and he knew what a counterinsurgency had to do. Back in 1984, when he wasn't quite thirty, he wrote an article for the journal *International Security* called "Constraints on America's Conduct of Small Wars," in which he decried "two dominant characteristics" of the American military's institutional culture: "the preference for massing a large number of men and machines and the predilection for direct and violent assault." It was the same syndrome—

the same belief that firepower, and more of it, could solve every strategic problem—that Galvin, Petraeus, Nagl, Krepinevich, and others observed in their critiques of America's failure in Vietnam. And now Cohen was seeing it again, not in books but before his own eyes, in Iraq.

There was another factor deepening Cohen's worries: his oldest son, also a Harvard graduate, had joined the Army a year earlier and was now about to be deployed as an infantry platoon leader in Iraq. Cohen was proud of his son's decision, but he was angry that the administration's bungling of the war—its failure to plan for the aftermath of Saddam's ouster, its refusal even now to change strategies or so much as acknowledge the rise of an insurgency—was putting his son's life at greater risk than necessary. And this was an administration that he'd been advising; it was a war that he'd not only supported but long urged. He felt embittered by his own complicity. His feelings didn't turn Cohen against the war, but they did rouse a sense of responsibility for its consequences and for doing what he could to forestall the impending disaster.

And so, he decided that the Strategic Studies Conference for the summer of 2005 would be devoted to a workshop on irregular warfare. He consulted his Rolodex and his library in deciding on the list of participants. David Kilcullen was a natural: Cohen had met him at the Quantico conference and knew that he was now working on the irregular-warfare chapters of the Pentagon's QDR. Another one was John Nagl: he'd read the *New York Times Magazine* profile, which led him to read *Learning to Eat Soup with a Knife*. When Nagl started working for his friend Paul Wolfowitz at the Pentagon, Cohen invited him a couple of times for lunch.

Others on Cohen's list included John Waghelstein, the former US MilGroup commander in El Salvador, still teaching at the Naval War College; Frank Hoffman, a Marine colonel who'd helped organize the Quantico conference; T. X. Hammes, a retired colonel, former CIA officer, and now a professor at the National Defense University, whose writings on "fourth-generation warfare" (his term for counterinsurgency) were gaining adherents; Robert Killebrew, another retired but still influential colonel (he was the one who'd brought Dave Petraeus to Haiti); Henry "Hank" Crumpton, a CIA officer who was about to be named the State Department's special adviser on counterterrorism; Steve Metz, the longtime scholar of low-intensity conflicts at the Army War College; and Janine Davidson, a former Air Force pilot who'd flown humanitarian supply missions into Bosnia and would soon be working in the Pentagon's Office for Stability Operations.

And, at the last minute, Cohen invited Kalev Sepp. The two had never met; Cohen had never heard of him. But his article on counterinsurgency's best practices in the May–June issue of *Military Review* made him, in one stroke, a major figure in this still somewhat underground field.

The group, numbering thirty altogether, assembled at Basin Harbor on Monday evening, June 6, and stayed until noon on Friday, June 10. They met twice a day in the sun-soaked Terrace Room, with its grand view of the lake and the woods—once in the morning, again in the afternoon, each session lasting two and a half hours—for panel discussions on the comparisons between Iraq and Afghanistan, the relevance of counterinsurgency theory, the problem of dealing with "failed states," the best techniques for advising and training indigenous armies, and the impact of globalization on irregular warfare.

Some of the participants recited arguments they'd been formulating for a while in books, articles, or their own thoughts: the importance of human intelligence to build support among the local people and to isolate them from the insurgents; the need for nation-building, so that the host government can sustain this popular support; the need for more civilian personnel from the State Department and the Agency for International Development (AID); the need somehow to overcome the Army's institutional hostility toward small wars (the *moot*-wah syndrome); and the need to cultivate senior officers with the agility to command such wars, since a general who was comfortable at leading the thunder run to Baghdad might be unsuitable for conducting Phase IV operations once the invasion was over.

Some of the discussions were contentious. What was the definition of victory in these sorts of wars? Should foreign armies confine themselves to a small footprint, as US Special Forces had done in El Salvador? Or did some situations—for instance, a host government with almost no capacity to govern—require a larger intervention, and, if so, could such a thing succeed in a country that distrusted outsiders? Beyond these questions, *could* the American military change its cultural stripes? Was it institutionally capable of absorbing and adapting to the best practices of counterinsurgency? And what about support on the home front? John Nagl pointed out that it had taken twelve years for the British to put down the insurgents in Malaya; no US war had gone on nearly that long before exhausting the American people's patience and will. Finally, were historical precedents relevant? The insurgencies in Malaya, the Philippines, Vietnam, and El Salvador—the examples usually discussed—were ideological in nature, inspired by the writings of Marx, Lenin, and Mao. Did they hold any wisdom for fighting the sectarian insurgencies in Iraq or Afghanistan? And if not, were the broader theories of counterinsurgency irrelevant, too?

But Basin Harbor's larger impact flowed not so much from the substance of the discussions as from the fact of the meeting itself: the meals in between the panels, the hikes through the woods, the evening strolls along the lake, the cigars and brandies on the veranda, the personal chats, the exchanges of phone numbers and email addresses—the dawning realization among these scholars and officers and officials, many of whom were meeting one another for the first time, that they formed a community; that their ideas and interests had common grounding and intellectual heft; and that, in the context of the country's two floundering wars, which the current political and military leaders seemed to have no idea how to handle, they—this insurgency of counterinsurgency thinkers—might be of use, might have impact.

This self-awareness as an emergent counter-elite, imbued with deeply relevant but uncommon knowledge, received a major jolt the last night of the conference when Lieutenant General Ray Odierno delivered the after-dinner speech.

Odierno was the assistant to the chairman of the Joint Chiefs of Staff. More to the point, he had been commander of the 4th Infantry Division during the first year of the Iraqi occupation, patrolling the heart of the Sunni Triangle, the country's most violent sector, which included Saddam's hometown of Tikrit. Odierno had graduated from West Point, class of 1976, but hadn't taken more than the required courses in the Sosh department. Afterward, he got a master's degree in nuclear engineering at North Carolina State University. He'd risen through the Army's ranks as an artillery officer. An artillery unit's task was to fire rockets at targets, and so the Army's cultural disposition to view war as little more than a clash of firepower resonated with him instinctively.

The 4th Infantry had entered the war late. It was supposed to have been a part of the invasion, rolling into northern Iraq from Turkey. When the Turkish parliament blocked that plan, its soldiers and equipment traveled by boat to Kuwait and, like the units before it, moved into Iraq from the south. By this time, Saddam's army had collapsed and his regime had fled; Petraeus's 101st Airborne Division, already as far north as Baghdad, was sent to occupy the northern districts, including Mosul. So Odierno's 4th Infantry was sent to the central districts, including Tikrit. Possessing no strategic guidance from headquarters, frustrated at having missed the fight, and facing violent resistance from Saddam's holdouts, much more so than Petraeus faced in Mosul, Odierno and his men did what they'd been trained to do: assume the enemy was all around them, capture and kill as many of them as possible, and if some innocent civilians got caught in the crossfire, well, war is hell.

Some of Odierno's brigade and battalion commanders had some background in counterinsurgency, having served in Bosnia or one of the other *moot*-wah wars of the previous decade. Odierno, too, understood, in a vague way, that part of his mission should include political and economic reconstruction, but he didn't know how to integrate those pieces with the military strands. Like Petraeus, he'd asked Jerry Bremer for an exemption to the order banning Baathist Party members from holding government office in the new Iraq. But his request was turned down. So Tikrit fell apart, spurring Odierno to step up the pressure, compelling many previously neutral Iraqis to aid or join the insurgency, which threw Tikrit into deeper chaos, spurring Odierno to escalate still further, and on and upward the cycle of violence spiraled.

By the time the 4th ID left Iraq in April 2004, Odierno knew that he hadn't handled things well. He would educate himself over the next two years before going back. But when he was asked to come speak at Basin Harbor, this learning process was in the early stages. The invitation had come through one of his brigade commanders in Iraq, Colonel Jim Hickey, who'd studied with Eliot Cohen as a graduate student at SAIS. So, on the afternoon of Thursday, June 9, Odierno took a military plane from Washington to Vermont.

Dave Kilcullen was apprehensive when he saw Odierno's name on the program. As part of his work on the Pentagon's Quadrennial Defense Review, Kilcullen had analyzed the operations of all the US Army and Marine units in Iraq. The 4th Infantry Division was among the worst, a textbook case of how not to deal with an insurgency.

Odierno cut an imposing figure. He even looked a bit like an artillery rocket: six-foot-five with an iron physique and a gleaming shaved head in the shape of a bullet. Yet he failed to get a lock on his target that evening at Basin Harbor. In his opening line, he congratulated his audience for holding such an "interesting" conference, adding, "We in the Army don't think much about counterinsurgency." Some of those listening looked around, slightly jaw-gaped. Was this an admission of guilt, a dismissive shrug at the topic, an attempt at a joke?

The remainder of the talk was no more assuring. It was a string of banalities, a stock after-dinner speech that a visiting general might deliver to a Kiwanis Club. Halfway through, Odierno himself seemed aware of the mismatch: he was clearly uncomfortable, borderline nervous, and confused. It was a cool evening, a breeze wafted through the windows in the hall, yet Odierno's head glistened with beads of sweat.

During the question-answer period, Kalev Sepp asked the general to define the American mission in Iraq. Odierno replied that his first priority was to get the best equipment into the hands of his soldiers, so they can protect themselves as much as possible. Sepp was dumbstruck. He thought to himself, "If the main objective is protecting our soldiers, then take them back to Fort Carson." Others in the audience rolled their eyes, too. Obviously, many of them reflected, commanders should do what they can to minimize *unnecessary* deaths, but what's the point of the *war,* what are the troops who've been sent there supposed to *do*?

Odierno flew back to Washington that night. The next morning at Basin Harbor, over breakfast, his speech was all anyone could talk about. John Nagl tried to shout down the grumblings of how appalling it was, how shocking, how demoralizing. Look, Nagl told his colleagues, the Army still needs war fighters, and Odierno's a good one. Besides, you have to recognize his constraints: he's working in the Pentagon, under a defense secretary who still won't allow anyone in his presence to utter the word "counterinsurgency." In fact, Nagl went on, we should see his speech as *positive:* Odierno at least *mentioned* the *C* word, said its ideas were "interesting"; it may not seem like much, but a year ago, he couldn't have done even *that*. It may be the best that the Army, at this point, can offer.

His pleas didn't quiet the grumblers, who recognized that Nagl, too, was speaking under constraints: the obligation of a lieutenant *colonel* to stand up for a lieutenant *general*. Still, if Odierno did represent the Army at its best, then the Army had to change. And it seemed to the assembled discontents that they would have to be the ones to prod the changing.

9.

The Directive

Nagl and Kilcullen got back to the Pentagon from Basin Harbor with an overwhelming sense of urgency and mission. Nagl's boss, Paul Wolfowitz, had resigned the week before to become president of the World Bank. His replacement, Gordon England, had a background in management, not policy, in keeping with the style and responsibilities of most deputy secretaries of defense. (He'd been an executive vice president at General Dynamics, followed by a stint as secretary of the Navy.) This left Nagl with a little more time for roaming the corridors, seeking allies for his cause, and helping Kilcullen with the latest drafts of the Quadrennial Defense Review's irregular-warfare section, which was meeting resistance from the uniformed services and from some of Rumsfeld's civilian aides.

Late that summer, Nagl's book, *Learning to Eat Soup with a Knife,* came out in paperback, opening up new pathways of influence. For one thing, it retailed for just $17, one-fifth the price of the Praeger hardcover. For another, it included a new foreword by General Peter Schoomaker, the Army chief of staff.

How Schoomaker came to write the foreword was a typical tale of Nagl's brazenness. While in Iraq, Nagl had heard from friends in the Pentagon that Schoomaker kept a stack of the books in his office—the hardcover edition—and that he was handing them out to every four-star who dropped by. One day, not long after Nagl started working in the Pentagon himself, he saw Schoomaker sitting outside Wolfowitz's office, waiting for a meeting to begin. The lieutenant colonel approached the four-star general, introduced himself, said that his book was coming out in paperback soon, and asked if he would be so gracious as to write the foreword. Schoomaker, who always liked bold young officers, said he'd be happy to.

The general went all out, hailing Nagl's book as "especially relevant today, and one that military leaders and interested citizens at all levels should read"—an endorsement that gave it an air of credibility in national-security circles and a guaranteed place on bookshelves throughout the Pentagon.

One official who kept a copy prominently on his shelf was Eric Edelman, a career diplomat who, in early August, had replaced Doug Feith, a key member of Rumsfeld's inner circle (many had called him Rumsfeld's henchman), as undersecretary of defense for policy. Edelman was no less hawkish than Feith—he'd signed the neocon petitions calling for regime-change in Iraq, and he'd been Vice President Cheney's deputy national security adviser in the first two years of the Bush administration—but he was a more critical thinker. He was a friend of Eliot Cohen and Andrew Krepinevich (he'd later go work for both) and, like them, was well versed in the history of the Vietnam War. In his new job, he read up on counter-insurgency, and, after Nagl's paperback came out, he, too, bought a stack of copies and handed them out to everyone he worked with in the Pentagon and the White House.

Edelman had once been a Rumsfeld-admirer but soon realized that the secretary had lost all interest in Iraq—a lapse, he felt, that both reflected and accentuated the aimlessness of US strategy and the looming collapse of the whole war effort.

A few weeks into his new job, Edelman handed Rumsfeld a copy of Nagl's book and told him that its author happened to be working just a few steps down the hall; he should call him in for a chat.

Yes, I've heard that, Rumsfeld replied.

Rumsfeld never called Nagl. The two never exchanged a word.

Edelman, however, did have Nagl into his office, several times, and Kil-cullen, too.

For much of the previous year, a handful of Pentagon officials had been drafting, and trying to rally support for, a directive ordering the military to spend more money, train more personnel, and develop new doctrine on "stability operations"—the phase of the war after the tanks and artillery have defeated the enemy's army and overthrown the dictator, the phase that involved reconstruction, governance, and nation-building: the phase, in other words, that the American commanders were fumbling at the moment in Iraq.

The effort had begun in August 2004, when a task force of the Defense Science Board, one of several Pentagon advisory panels, completed a 199-page report titled *Transition to and from Hostilities*. It concluded, "Stability and reconstruction missions must become a core competency of both the Departments of Defense and State," and training for those missions must be treated "as seriously as we treat learning combat skills." The report concluded with an unusually blunt coda: "We urge greater than usual speed in implementing the recommendations of our study. The nation's security demands it."

The chairman of the task force was Craig Fields, a former director of the Pentagon's Defense Advanced Research Projects Agency and a friend of Rumsfeld's for twenty years. Fields briefed the report to Rumsfeld personally. Its premise and conclusion cut against Rumsfeld's grain, but he was reluctantly coming to realize that wars like the one in Iraq had an unavoidable political dimension, which needed to be addressed with political as well as military means. After the briefing, Rumsfeld told his staff to work up a Defense Department directive that put the report's recommendations into effect.

The task was turned over to Jeffrey "Jeb" Nadaner, the deputy assistant secretary of defense for stability operations. But Rumsfeld never got actively behind it, resistance throughout the Pentagon mounted, and soon the effort stalled.

A lawyer and former State Department official who'd worked on issues related to Iraq and counterterrorism, Nadaner knew something about counterinsurgency. He'd studied the Vietnam War as a student at Duke University and had interviewed Robert Komer for a research paper about the CORDS project. Like Edelman, he delved more deeply into the COIN literature once he arrived at the Pentagon, discovered Nagl's book when it came out in paperback, realized that the author was working in the building, and sought him out. Nagl, in turn, introduced him to Kilcullen.

Nadaner was relieved to find them both. Like Nagl in his first few months on the job, he had roamed the Pentagon's corridors in search of possible allies outside the handful of analysts on his staff. To his astonishment, Nagl and Kilcullen were the only ones he found who knew much of anything about the subject.

It also turned out that Nagl and Kilcullen had already met most of his staff. Janine Davidson had been at the Basin Harbor conference. (She and

Kilcullen became especially close friends and eventually got married.) Another staffer, Lieutenant Colonel Richard Lacquement Jr., who'd recently worked as special assistant to David Petraeus in Mosul, had been, several years earlier, one of Nagl's faculty colleagues in the Sosh department at West Point.

Rumsfeld had said, after Fields's briefing, that he wanted a directive written within sixty days. But nearly a year had passed, nothing had come of it, and no one at the top, least of all Rumsfeld, was complaining. The project was plagued with delays from the outset. Not until midfall of 2004, two months after Fields's briefing, did the order to write a directive land on Nadaner's desk, along with instructions to get endorsements from the Joint Chiefs of Staff and the relevant assistant secretaries—always a recipe for gridlock.

Nadaner's staff wrote and circulated a rough ten-page draft capturing the study's main recommendations. At subsequent meetings, senior officers, ranging in rank from colonel to three-star general, filed adamant objections to every point. The draft noted that in stability operations, intelligence agencies should acquire information about not just the enemy's military order of battle but also the country's social structure and culture—a key point in Fields's study. The officer representing the Army's intelligence command crossed out that line, saying the task didn't fall under his statutory responsibilities. Similarly, the draft stated that stability operations should be given the same priority as combat operations—the Fields study's central conclusion. An officer from the vice chief of staff's office objected that this notion violated the fundamentals of Army doctrine going back to the Second World War. Indeed it did. That was the premise of the report: that the military hadn't been paying enough attention to a war's post-battlefield phase.

When Rumsfeld heard about the stalling, he called his old friend Martin Hoffman, who had been secretary of the Army in the mid-1970s during Rumsfeld's first tour as defense secretary in the Ford administration. Hoffman had set up an office in the Pentagon to persuade retired business executives to come help out in Iraq and Afghanistan. It was a volunteer effort, and Hoffman had recruited some distinguished citizens. He also knew something about counterinsurgency, having been an Army officer in Vietnam.

At first Nadaner took Hoffman's involvement as a hopeful sign, but soon realized he'd been mistaken. Hoffman rewrote the document completely, undoing some compromises that had been hammered out with the services, putting the Army in charge of all operations and insisting on policy changes that far exceeded the scope and purview of any DoD directive ever issued. Because Hoffman was Rumsfeld's friend, everyone involved assumed he was reflecting the secretary's views, and this stiffened resistance still further.

Rumsfeld was brought in to break the deadlock, an unusual step at this stage of a draft, but there was no choice. The meeting took place on July 25, a few weeks short of a year since he'd ordered the directive to be written within sixty days. Rumsfeld spoke via videoconference from his Pentagon plane, seated next to General Peter Pace, the chairman of the Joint Chiefs of Staff. Rumsfeld skimmed through Hoffman's revised draft and agreed with Nadaner: it was unacceptable; the Army couldn't be left in control of this policy; that was the job of the secretary of defense or his undersecretary for policy, working with all the services, to ensure civil-military cohesion. He threw out his friend's work.

Nadaner, watching Rumsfeld on a video monitor in a Pentagon office, suggested that an outside commission review the pre-Hoffman draft and report on how to go forward. Rumsfeld gave his go-ahead.

To make sure that this outside commission had authority, Nadaner asked Nagl to get his boss, Gordon England, the deputy secretary of defense, to issue the formal document creating it. England did that on August 10. Craig Fields, who'd signed the original Defense Science Board report, agreed to chair the panel. Fields held hearings, with testimony from some of the experts who'd worked on the original study. On September 15, he signed a follow-on report, affirming the urgency of the problem and endorsing the draft that Nadaner and his staff had written just before the Hoffman fiasco, with only a few minor changes.

Then another obstacle dropped from the sky. Admiral Edmund Giambastiani Jr. had just been named vice chairman of the Joint Chiefs of Staff. His previous job was head of Joint Forces Command, where he'd written several essays and memos about stability operations and reconstruction. He decided to take a crack at the draft and rewrote it still again, with an emphasis on enlarging the State Department's role in these matters so that the

Pentagon wouldn't have to do much at all. Nadaner, who'd worked in the State Department, disagreed, not on principle but because State simply lacked the capacity and resources to take the lead, especially in a country like Iraq or Afghanistan, where a war was still going on.

Finally, in mid-October, a compromise was fashioned. The title of the directive would be changed to "Military Support for Stability, Security, Transition, and Reconstruction (SSTR) Operations." SSTR was a phrase that came out of the State Department's handbook on this subject; one could, therefore, infer that State would be involved, although nothing in the document said so explicitly. It was a finesse, which everyone was willing to accept.

In this brief window of bureaucratic harmony, Nagl brought the draft to his boss (DoD directives were generally signed by the deputy secretary of defense). England signed it on November 28, 2005, fifteen months after Rumsfeld had nudged the process into motion.

On paper, Defense Department Directive 3000.05 was a remarkable document, more radical in its implications than even the Defense Science Board had recommended. The key passage read:

> Stability operations are a core US military mission that the Department of Defense shall be prepared to conduct and support. They shall be given priority comparable to combat operations and be explicitly addressed and integrated across all DoD activities including doctrine, organization, training, education, exercises, materiel, leadership, personnel, facilities, and planning.

The definitions and elaborations were straight out of classic counterinsurgency literature. The immediate goal of stability operations, the document noted, "is to provide the local populace with security, restore essential services, and meet humanitarian needs," adding, "US military forces shall be prepared to perform all tasks necessary to establish or maintain order when civilians cannot do so." These tasks might include "ensuring security, developing local governance structures, promoting bottom-up economic activity, rebuilding infrastructure, and building indigenous capacity for such tasks."

If put into effect, this would be a very big deal, not just for the war strategy in Iraq and Afghanistan, but for the way the Pentagon did business generally. It could mean a *real* transformation in the American way of war, a declaration—with changes in the budget, organization, and institutional culture to match—that Phase IV, nation-building, COIN, call it what you will, was just as much a "core US military mission" as combat. It would mean that the kinds of conflicts once derided as Military Operations Other Than War ("Real men don't do *moot*-wah") were, in fact, wars after all.

The trick, of course, was putting the directive into effect. Far-reaching as its guidelines seemed, they were mere guidelines. The document put forth no timetables, targets, or benchmarks for progress, no specific goals, no express authority for officials to *take* many of the recommended actions—only orders that certain officials should *consider* whether and how to do so. It would take an active and committed secretary of defense to push his subordinates to ensure that decisions were made and actions were taken. Rumsfeld was not that secretary of defense.

If Rumsfeld were that secretary, the Quadrennial Defense Review would have been the forum in which to do those things. But Rumsfeld resisted all such pressures and traps there as well.

Kilcullen, Nagl, and the rest of Jim Thomas's crew were crafting and polishing the QDR at the same time that Nadaner and Nagl were pushing Directive 3000.05 through its final obstacles. The QDR had four sections—on beefing up homeland defense, countering weapons of mass destruction (especially those that might be built by Iran and North Korea), dealing with the potentially emerging threat from China, and rebuilding a capability for irregular warfare—but only the last was a new element, the section that set this QDR apart from earlier editions.

Irregular warfare was the topic that Thomas highlighted in the document's introduction, knowing that it would be the only part of the ninety-eight-page booklet that many officials would read. His opening sentence stressed that the context of this year's QDR was the "long war"—the war on terrorism—"a war that is irregular in its nature." A major purpose of the review, he asserted, had been to place "greater emphasis" on "irregular warfare activities," including "counterinsurgency and military support for stabilization and reconstruction efforts."

The body of the report, too, stressed repeatedly the need for more resources to "conduct a large-scale potentially long-duration irregular warfare campaign," such as those that the United States was presently waging in Iraq and Afghanistan. And it emphasized the need to recruit, train, and equip "a new breed of warrior" who was "as proficient in irregular operations, including counterinsurgency and stabilization operations," as in high-intensity combat.

In this sense, the introduction stressed, this QDR was prescribing a "new direction" for the entire US armed forces.

But Rumsfeld blunted this theme by writing a "preface," which, in the published document, appeared before Thomas's "introduction," and which said, up front: "There is a tendency to want to suggest that documents such as this represent a 'new beginning.' Manifestly, this document is not a 'new beginning.'"

Rather, Rumsfeld emphasized at the end of his five-page preemption: "it is important to note" that this QDR "is part of the continuum of transformation" laid out in the edition four-and-a-half years earlier—the edition that had touted the revolution in military affairs.

There was no indication that the preface and the introduction had been written by two different people with two different agendas. (Rumsfeld's was the only signature that appeared in the document.) But word got around the building that this was the case—that Rumsfeld was in effect nullifying the more radical sections of the report. This came as reassurance to many uniformed officers, who had no desire to go down the road that Thomas, Kilcullen, and their comrades were trying to pave. For those who didn't get the message, the effect was merely confusing; the secretary's intent, what it was that he wanted the military to *do,* came off as muddled. And that was just how Rumsfeld wanted it to be.

Still, the QDR and Directive 3000.05 were useful as tools of bureaucratic politics. Both documents contained enough verbal endorsement of COIN principles to provide cover for officials and commanders who, in the absence of an overriding strategy, wanted to pursue that approach. They could now do so without prompting accusations of violating Army doctrine or flaunting the secretary's orders; they could cite chapter and verse of these two policy statements, which had been signed by the Defense Department's top civilian authorities.

The commander who invoked this cover most shrewdly was Lieutenant General David Petraeus, who, in October 2005, just as both documents were nearing completion, came home from Iraq with the firm intention of fulfilling a thirty-year ambition to push COIN into the mainstream of Army doctrine and culture.

In a brief conversation with Petraeus soon after his return, Nadaner told him about the directive and all the obstacles he was navigating to get the language just right.

Petraeus told him not to worry so much about the details. The important thing was to get the basic principles up front and the directive signed. That, he said, would serve as his "sword and shield." The rest, leave to him.

10.

The Insurgent in the Engine Room of Change

Had it been up to a handful of generals, David Petraeus's Army career might have sputtered to an end soon after his second tour in Iraq.

In the spring of 2005, Colonel Mike Meese, the West Point Sosh professor who had been Petraeus's executive officer in Bosnia and his special assistant in Mosul, was working on loan in the Pentagon as head of the transition team for Francis Harvey, the newly confirmed Army secretary. Harvey mentioned casually that the higher-ups were thinking about making Petraeus the academy's next superintendent.

Meese was appalled. "Sir," he said, "that is the stupidest thing I have ever heard." The West Point "supe," he explained, was a terminal assignment; if that was Petraeus's next posting, it would mean that one of the Army's most creative strategists would end his service days as a three-star general stuck with administrative duties, far from the battlefield or planning rooms, while two wars were raging.

Petraeus's second tour in Iraq hadn't been as stellar as his first. In May 2004, just a few months after leaving Mosul with the 101st Airborne Division, he was brought back to take charge of the mission to train the new Iraqi security forces. It was a thankless task: Jerry Bremer's CPA order from the year before, disbanding the Iraqi army, meant that Petraeus had to start pretty much from scratch, and the Army was sending him second-rate soldiers to do the training—understandable, since too few first-raters were available for the higher-priority combat missions, thanks in good measure to Donald Rumsfeld's decision at the start of the war to send half as many troops as the generals had requested. Petraeus had felt the additional pangs of watching from the sidelines as his successor in Mosul—with half the number of soldiers, no feel for counterinsurgency, and no strategic guidance of any sort—let northern Iraq, his legacy, collapse into chaos, along with much of the rest of the country.

Relations with General Casey had also been tense, as had those with Donald Rumsfeld. Petraeus had first encountered Rumsfeld back in Bosnia. The secretary had came through for a briefing on counterterrorist operations. At one point, Petraeus was listing the various jihadist front organizations, noting that they included the Red Crescent, when Rumsfeld interrupted him with a dismissive snicker.

The Red Crescent is like our Red Cross, Rumsfeld said in a tone half condescending, half bullying.

Petraeus had no patience for either attitude, and he smacked back hard. That's very good, he replied in a slow, singsong voice, as if he were teaching math to a slow third-grader. But, he went on, we have *very* firm intelligence that a *slice* of Red Crescent is supporting terrorist operations.

Rumsfeld respected a certain amount of pushback; he'd been puzzled why so many generals cowered at his criticism. (Most of these generals, in turn, wondered if Rumsfeld didn't grasp the American officer corps's post-MacArthur allegiance to the principle of civilian control, which made them disinclined to talk back to a secretary of defense.) After their exchange, Rumsfeld never gave Petraeus a hard time again; he would even call him in Iraq now and then to ask how things were going. But Petraeus had gone further in his pushback—he'd been more overtly scathing—than Rumsfeld liked. Nor was the secretary a big fan of what the major general had done in Mosul: Petraeus's penchant for nation-building and his tendency to go rogue, to exercise more autonomy than his rank allowed, rubbed against Rumsfeld's views on military strategy and hierarchy of command.

But Petraeus's biggest problem lay with some of his fellow generals, who'd never liked him, who regarded him as a showboat, a self-aggrandizer, and who bad-mouthed him to one another—and to Rumsfeld, reinforcing his own suspicions—at every chance.

Ricardo Sanchez, the three-star general who commanded US forces in Iraq during the first year of the occupation, found Petraeus particularly annoying. Sanchez was an incompetent commander, he half knew that he was in over his head, and he was known to feel bitter about the swooning press coverage that Petraeus had elicited and received for his work in Mosul. Just before he returned to Iraq in the spring of 2004, Petraeus had appeared on the cover of *Newsweek* along with the headline: "Can This Man Save Iraq?" Sanchez called a meeting of the headquarters staff in Baghdad to meet him. During the question-answer period, Petraeus took all the questions, as if Sanchez—his superior—weren't in the room.

Finally, one of the staff officers directed a question specifically at Sanchez.

"I don't know," Sanchez dryly replied. "Why don't we let the messiah take that one."

Every staffer in the room looked down at the floor in shock and embarrassment. Petraeus answered the question without flinching.

At Mike Meese's urgings, Francis Harvey implored Rumsfeld to keep Petraeus out of West Point. Rumsfeld agreed, though not with enthusiasm. Ordinarily, the next assignment for a rising three-star with Petraeus's record would be director of the Joint Staff or assistant to the chairman. But Petraeus was notified in the summer of 2005 that his next job, after leaving Iraq in September, would be commander of the Combined Arms Center in Fort Leavenworth, Kansas.

Petraeus's detractors were fine with the appointment; they took it as a sign that the fair-haired boy was being sent, literally, out to pasture. The general he'd be replacing, William Scott Wallace, had been the corps commander in Iraq who told a reporter during the invasion that the enemy was different from the one he'd war-gamed against—a remark that ticked off Rumsfeld and several other senior administration officials. At first Wallace, too, had viewed his assignment to Leavenworth as punishment, the purgatory before retirement. Petraeus's outlook on his own status wasn't quite that bleak, though when he first got the notice, he did wonder what there was to *do* out there, what the job was *about*.

In early October, Petraeus stopped off at the Pentagon before heading out west. One of the first officers he visited was General Schoomaker, the former Special Forces commander who'd been called out of retirement to be the Army chief of staff. The two had met in the mid-1990s, when they were both stationed at Fort Bragg, Petraeus as a brigade commander with the 82nd Airborne Division, Schoomaker as a Special Forces officer. Five days after Schoomaker took over as chief of staff, he flew to Iraq for a fact-finding mission. Petraeus met him at Baghdad airport and promptly took him on a two-hour helicopter ride to Mosul, briefing him (replete with PowerPoint slides) the entire way, then, once they landed, walked him through the city streets, introducing him to the mayor, the police chief, the provincial governor, taking him to the market, the town hall. It was exhausting but impressive—and a contrast to the bleakness Schoomaker found elsewhere in Iraq.

Schoomaker now confided to Petraeus that he planned to send him back to Iraq as commander after Casey's term expired. Meanwhile, he further assured him, Fort Leavenworth was far from a diversion or demotion. A lot went on out there. Schoomaker had grown up in Leavenworth, when his father, who'd fought in World War II, Korea, and Vietnam, studied there in the late 1950s. Schoomaker himself had been stationed there in the early eighties, when Huba Wass de Czege was writing the *AirLand Battle* field manual. He'd returned there again right after retiring from the Army, to teach a course called Leading Change at its School of Advanced Military Studies.

He told Petraeus that, at this very moment, Leavenworth's Combined Arms Center was putting together a new field manual on counterinsurgency, the Army's first in twenty years. It was just an interim manual, and it had problems. But that meant Petraeus could throw it out and write his own, and then instill its principles into the curriculum of the Command and General Staff College. He could reshape not only the strategy of the war but also the future of the Army.

Petraeus was relieved that he had Schoomaker's backing for a return to Iraq as top commander. But he was also now intrigued with the implications of running Leavenworth. During his most recent stint in Iraq, training the country's new security forces, he hadn't focused much on American counterinsurgency policy, or the lack of it. But COIN had always been his passion, and now he felt it reigniting.

As the two parted, Schoomaker said, "Go out there and shake up the Army, Dave!" Petraeus marched out, determined to do just that.

Later that day, Petraeus dropped in on Brigadier General Frank Helmick, an old friend who'd been one of his assistant division commanders in Mosul and who was now the senior military assistant to Gordon England, the deputy secretary of defense. In the course of that reunion, he ran into England's junior military assistant, John Nagl.

The two had kept in touch since their summer in Europe two decades earlier. They'd seen each other a few times: at West Point, when Petraeus made visits while Nagl was on the faculty, and in Iraq just the year before, when their tours overlapped. More recently, they'd talked on the phone several times during Nagl's present tenure in the Pentagon.

Nagl asked Petraeus if he could have a word in private, then took him into England's office. (England was away at the time.) Still full of missionary steam from the Basin Harbor conference a few months earlier, Nagl lectured his old mentor on all the things he could do as commander at Leavenworth. Above all, he could rewrite the field manual on counterinsurgency, pulling together contributions from officers—including fellow members of the Sosh mafia—who had studied COIN and fought in Iraq; Nagl already had a list of suitable names in mind, and could pass it along. He also suggested that Petraeus hold a workshop where experts would vet the new manual; friendly members of the press could be invited to sit in, too, and, afterward, promote it.

Petraeus had been thinking along the same lines since his meeting with Schoomaker, but Nagl's urgings quickened his newborn excitement about the job. It had been Petraeus's ambition for a quarter century to change the Army, to maneuver the outlaw ideas of irregular warfare and counterinsurgency into the mainstream of Army doctrine and culture. Could he be on the verge of making this happen?

It was a long drive from Washington to Leavenworth, and, at one point, to fill the time, Petraeus played a CD of the "end-of-tour interview" that General Wallace had recently given to an Army historian. What Petraeus heard so astonished him that he would play the disc twice more before the trip was over.

Wallace told the historian that at the start of his assignment, he'd figured his main job would be supervising the Command and General Staff College, so he'd probably play golf most afternoons. As it happened, though, he spent almost no time with the college, which pretty much ran itself. His main job turned out to be running all the other things that the Combined Arms Center controlled. He quickly discovered, for instance, that the CAC commander was also deputy head of the Army's Training and Doctrine Command, which gave him power over all the combat schools (including their curricula), the National Training Center and the Joint Readiness Training Center (where soldiers between deployments played war games and held live-fire exercises), the Battle Command Training Program (where troops received their final preparation before heading off to combat), and the Center for Army Lessons Learned (where military historians analyzed the combat operations of all the units in Iraq and Afghanistan).

Wallace recalled looking over all of these billets of authority and realizing that Leavenworth wasn't the backwater it seemed—that, in fact, if you wanted to make big changes in the Army, it was, at least potentially, *the* place to be. The whole cycle of change took place at Leavenworth or at places that Leavenworth controlled. The Combined Arms Center wrote new doctrine; the Command and General Staff College taught the doctrine; the National Training Center tried it out in exercises; the Center for Army Lessons Learned evaluated the results on the battlefield and noted areas for improvement. And then the cycle began all over again: the doctrine was altered to reflect the lessons, the teaching and training shifted to adjust for that, and on it went—or on it could go, if the commander wanted to make it so—in a continuous loop of learning, adaptation, action, learning, adaptation, action.

Petraeus's new job began on October 20. He arrived at the base a few days early, met with Wallace—the first time they'd seen each other since the early days of the Iraq War—and discussed these issues in greater detail. Toward the end of their conversation, Wallace highlighted the point about the command's multiple domains and the way they interconnected by recalling a phrase that his chief of staff, Colonel Dave Buckley, had coined to capture Leavenworth's possibilities: it was, he said, the Army's "engine of change."

Petraeus sat in what was soon to be his office, feeling a shiver of amazement. "Holy cow," he thought to himself. "They're putting an insurgent in control of the engine of change."

A few days into the job, Petraeus discovered that Wallace had already laid a fair stretch of the path to be paved. He'd beefed up the Center for Army Lessons Learned; reports were pouring in on how units in Iraq were performing and how future units could be trained in advance to do better. He'd opened up the curriculum at the college to comments from the students, many of whom had just come from Iraq and thus, in some senses, knew more than their instructors about that kind of warfare. More impressive still, Wallace had initiated a complete overhaul of the National Training Center, the vast war-game complex in the California desert. Not only had he changed the nature of the games, from Cold War tank-on-tank combat to modern-day urban stability operations, he'd also erected mock Iraqi villages, devised a range of tense scenarios (involving political rivalries and street riots, as well as guerrilla assaults), and hired Iraqi émigrés to play the various figures (mayors, tribal elders, jihadists, even ordinary citizens complaining about the lack of services or the unjust shooting of a cousin) that American soldiers were having to deal with in the real Iraq.

But there were still gaps. Early on, Petraeus visited Fort Sill, Oklahoma, to observe the training of field artillery officers who were about to be promoted to captain. The room simulating a command center was impressively up to date, with digital controls and high-def screens displaying interactive video animation of a firefight in Baghdad. In the scenario for the exercise, intelligence reports cited the coordinates of an insurgent hideout; the artillery officer in the field called for a mortar strike; the mortar shell was fired; it hit the target in one shot. The officers in the room shouted, "Hoo-ah!"

Petraeus was alarmed. He asked the staff sergeant running the game if he'd been in Baghdad.

Yes, sir, the staff sergeant replied.

Did you ever use mortars in Baghdad? Petraeus asked.

Hell, no, sir, he answered. Mortars would miss the target and kill a lot of civilians.

Who's training on this simulator? Petraeus asked.

Every lieutenant going to Iraq, he replied.

So, Petraeus pressed, you are telling every lieutenant that they should call in mortar fire in Baghdad, even though you know that's a stupid thing to do?

Petraeus told the staff sergeant to shut down the simulator until the program had been changed. Back at Leavenworth, he called around to the captains' training courses for the other branches of the Army—armor, infantry, and so forth—and discovered that, in some cases, the captains themselves were rewriting the scenarios after returning from Iraq. Petraeus thought that was a great idea and ordered the whole network of courses to shut down until the revisions were complete.

One day, Petraeus took an Army training manual that he'd been going through, crossing out lines or whole paragraphs and scribbling in new ones, and asked a staff officer to print out a legible version of the changes.

Sir, the staffer told him, it's impermissible to change more than 10 percent of a field manual on your own.

Where does it say that? Petraeus asked.

The staff officer looked into the matter. It turned out that there was no such rule; it apparently was a myth passed down over time. Petraeus kept crossing out old ideas and scribbling in new ones.

There was still a lot of changing to do.

One big challenge was coordinating the changes from one realm of his new estate to another, making sure that a reform in the college was followed through at the combat training centers and followed through from there to tactics and operations. The key to synchronizing all this was getting the "big ideas" right and carving them in the stone of doctrine. And that was where Petraeus's top priority came into the picture: writing a new Army field manual on counterinsurgency and using that as the wedge, the scripture from on high, to lock in place a new strategy for the present war and a new way of thinking about and fighting wars generally.

Scott Wallace had tried to launch a new COIN field manual back in February 2004, a little over a half year after his stint at Leavenworth began. The officers of the Army's III Corps had just come through the base for their Battle Command Training Program's "mission-readiness exercise," the final stage of preparation before heading out to Iraq. Wallace noted a mismatch between what the officers were doing in the exercises and the kinds of things they'd really have to do in Iraq. The official "after-action review" confirmed his impression: the corps's leaders had come away from the exercise with little understanding of counterinsurgency. The training program, Wallace realized, was dangerously out of date, and the main reason was that the Army's doctrine was out of date.

Wallace ordered the director of Leavenworth's doctrine division, Colonel Clinton Ancker, to produce a new COIN field manual within the next six months. Field manuals usually took two years to prepare, write, edit, send up the chain, elicit comments, debate revisions, and hammer out a consensus. But a war was on, there was no doctrine on how to fight it, so the essential task was to get *something* out there *quickly*.

Ancker had been waiting a long time for a commander to say this. As a cadet at West Point, class of 1970, he'd taken the Revolutionary Warfare course. The Vietnam War was at its peak; counterinsurgency hadn't yet been barred from the Army's lexicon; the books by Galula, Thompson, and Larteguy were still in print—and Ancker imbibed it all. A decade later, when he returned to West Point as an instructor, he put in a request to teach the Revolutionary Warfare course for all three years of his tenure.

He'd taken over Leavenworth's doctrine office in February 1996. Two weeks later, an Army civilian came into his office a bit panicked: he'd been writing a new field manual on low-intensity conflicts; he hadn't finished, and he was about to retire. Ancker was keen to take it over and sought permission from the deputy commandant of the base.

"Don't bother," the deputy told him. "The Army will never again commit conventional forces to counterinsurgency, so go focus on something we *will* do."

Now with Wallace's order, the tide was rolling back in.

Ancker passed on the assignment to Lieutenant Colonel Jan Horvath, the new doctrine writer in his office. Horvath had never been in Iraq or studied counterinsurgency. But he had been through Special Forces training, he'd planned joint operations in Korea, and he'd been a doctrine officer at Fort Hood. That made him the best man available for the job.

Horvath was smart enough to know what he didn't know, so the first thing he did was fly to Fort Bragg, North Carolina, the Special Forces' headquarters, with the intent of riffling through its library for old field manuals, operational plans, whatever documents on the topic were on file. To his astonishment, the library had nothing of the sort; it had all been thrown out years before.

Upon his return to Leavenworth, he asked Ancker for a reading list and holed himself up in the Combined Arms Center's research library for the next week, poring over a stack of books on the theory and history of counterinsurgency. After reading Galula, he grasped the concepts and the terminology but still needed a model for how to write a field manual on the subject. He went through all the Army field manuals that might have some relevance, but found nothing.

So he called some of his old friends from Special Forces days, asking them to recommend a consultant. A few of them mentioned Tom Marks.

Marks was a self-styled throwback to the romantic era of shadow soldiers' derring-do. As a cadet at West Point, class of 1972, he'd taken the course on Revolutionary Warfare and read the COIN classics, but he was quicker than most to extend his studies into action. His father was a Navy doctor stationed at a Marine base in Thailand. During school breaks, Tom would visit him and finagle a way to go out on patrols with some marines in Vietnam across the border. He left the Army soon after his five-year commitment expired, bored with his prospective assignments, and got a job as chief correspondent for *Soldier of Fortune* magazine. Marks traveled with spies, mercenaries, and foreign armies' Special Ops commandos through wars across jungles, swamps, and mountains worldwide, and, when his editors let him, he wrote serious analyses of these conflicts as well.

When Horvath called him, Marks was just finishing up twenty years as lead instructor at the Joint Special Operations University, the last academic holdover from President Kennedy's COIN creations. He said he'd be happy to help with the project.

"They've got a tiger by the tail," Marks said of the American commanders in Iraq, "and they don't know it's a tiger."

Horvath flew back to Fort Bragg, enjoyed several hours talking with Marks about old times and new plans, and persuaded him to write the first chapter, which, in the format of field manuals, would set the tone and define the terms: the nature of an insurgency, the nature of a counterinsurgency, their respective goals, dynamics, and historical origins. This stuff was second nature to Marks; he dashed it off in a single day.

The language came right out of the classic COIN literature. An insurgency, Marks wrote, "is a protracted politico-military struggle designed to weaken government control and legitimacy while increasing insurgent control . . . Political power is the central issue in an insurgency . . . The support of the people is the center of gravity." The counterinsurgency's goals were to "protect the population, establish local political institutions," and "eliminate insurgent capabilities," in part by exploiting intelligence "from local sources."

Horvath took Marks's contribution as the conceptual base and found specialists in the relevant branches of the Army to write or at least outline subsequent chapters on rules of engagement, command and control, civil-military relations, intelligence procedures, psychological operations, legal issues, and the like.

He made the deadline, finishing the manual in August, but he wasn't happy with it. Some sections were too abstract, some too detailed. Civilian officials and sergeants might get something out of it, but not the commanders and junior officers who turned to field manuals for strategic and tactical guidance.

Ancker sent the draft around to the various Army commands for comment. On his own, Horvath sent it informally to some of the friends and colleagues he'd consulted over the months. One of them suggested that he contact Kalev Sepp.

Sepp hadn't yet been to Iraq; his work with Bill Hix on General Casey's staff wouldn't start for another couple of months. Meanwhile, the fall semester had just begun at the Naval Postgraduate School. Several of Sepp's students were Special Forces captains and majors who'd just returned from, or were about to go to, Iraq; he made copies of Horvath's draft and had them write comments as a class assignment.

The students were brutal. One noted that the manual assumed that once a society was stabilized, insurgents couldn't thrive, when, in fact, they could. Another criticized the manual for referring to the insurgency's followers as a "mass," when they often consisted of disparate factions; a COIN manual, the student wrote, should direct Army intelligence to help weaken the insurgents by identifying the factions' interests and exploiting their fissures. Others complained that in discussing a local "culture," the manual made no mention of tribes, clans, religious or ethnic groups, or ideological parties; soldiers who read the manual wouldn't know what cultural indicators to look for. Even the fundamental idea of "winning hearts and minds" was presented in the manual as mainly a PR gambit, not as a COIN campaign's central goal. There was no recognition of the links between military tactics and political strategy, or the principle of building trust among the people, so that they, in turn, would provide intelligence about the insurgents. In short, the students' common critique was that the manual didn't really get what "counterinsurgency operations"—the manual's title—were about.

Horvath agreed with everything the students wrote—the manual *was* a rush job—and inserted some revisions that dealt with their concerns to some extent. Ancker and Wallace thought the effort was good enough for now: it was better than any other manual out there; and the title alone would make clear to commanders and soldiers in the field, as well as to officials in the Pentagon, that the Iraq War *was* an insurgency war and that *counterinsurgency* was now an element of official Army doctrine—notions that were still far from universally accepted. They ordered a print run of five hundred copies and had them distributed to all relevant Army commanders, including those in Iraq.

The manual was published in October 2004 as *FMI 3-07.22.* "FM*I*" stood for Field Manual *Interim,* a very unusual designation. The cover stated explicitly that the manual would expire in two years, a sign that Wallace and Ancker weren't completely pleased with it, either. They knew they had to come up with something better.

When Petraeus took over Leavenworth in October 2005, Horvath had started work on a follow-up manual, but what Petraeus had seen of it struck him as falling short; the project required officers with more experience and higher academic caliber. Petraeus knew where to find these sorts of people: among the officer-PhDs of the Lincoln Brigade, the Sosh mafia. That's where he'd found them in earlier crises, and he was working with some of them still.

First, though, the project needed a set of overarching principles—"big ideas," Petraeus liked to call them—from which the tactical minutiae would follow logically. Even before he arrived at Leavenworth, he'd started putting together a PowerPoint briefing called "Thirteen Observations from Soldiering in Iraq," drawn mainly from his experiences in Mosul. He finished the slide show during his first couple of weeks on the new job, presented it to a packed hall of students and officers, and, at Bill Darley's urging, turned it into an essay for *Military Review* under the title "Learning Counterinsurgency: Observations from Soldiering in Iraq." (The first word—"learning"—was meant as a nod to his once and future acolyte John Nagl.)

In early November, Petraeus flew to Washington for some meetings in the Pentagon and the first of many public speeches on the war in Iraq. He made two appearances. The first, on Monday the 7th, was a wrap-up of old business: a PowerPoint briefing to the think-tank conservatives of the Center for Strategic and International Studies on what he called the "great strides" made by the Iraqi army under his recent tenure as commander of its training program (an assessment that would soon prove premature, to say the least).

The second appearance, the next day, marked something pivotal: Petraeus's debut as a public promoter for the cause of COIN. The event was a conference called "Counterinsurgency in Iraq: Implications of Irregular Warfare for the United States Government," cosponsored by the Army War College and Harvard University's Carr Center for Human Rights Policy. The two institutions may have seemed strange bedfellows, but they'd been quietly holding joint conferences like this every year or so for much of the past decade, a result of the peculiar proclivities of the Carr Center's director, Sarah Sewall.

Sewall had developed an interest in military matters as a Harvard undergraduate in the early 1980s. It was a time when critics of US defense policy had to master the gritty details of strategy and weapons systems to be credible, and Sewall plunged in deeply. Her first job was at the Federation of American Scientists, calculating the ellipses of military-satellite orbits for a critique of President Ronald Reagan's space-based missile-defense program, nicknamed "Star Wars." But around this time, real wars were erupting in Central America, and Sewall found them more compelling. She went off to grad school at Oxford from 1984 to 1986 and spent endless hours on the floor of Blackwell's bookstore, reading the tomes it stocked on guerrilla warfare. She earned a master's degree, writing a thesis on the Vietnam War, came back to Washington, worked on Capitol Hill, then landed an appointment, in the early years of Bill Clinton's presidency, as the Pentagon's first-ever deputy assistant secretary of defense for peacekeeping operations and humanitarian assistance.

When her husband found a job in Boston, Sewall moved with him but commuted to Washington during the week, until she gave birth to triplets and realized that she couldn't spend many days away from home again. After maternity leave, her friend Samantha Power, who taught at Harvard's John F. Kennedy School of Government, persuaded her to come work at the school's Carr Center for Human Rights Policy.

Sewall wasn't interested in human rights per se, but she had been troubled by the debate over the US intervention in Kosovo. She supported the intervention and was annoyed that many human-rights activists didn't—or, worse still, that they'd supported American military action until some people started getting killed as a result, at which point they grew horrified and turned against it. She found their stance naïve, their conversations uninformed. Yet at the same time, she was disturbed by the cavalier way in which so many US military officers dismissed the topic of civilian casualties. "Collateral damage," they called it: a ghastly phrase from the Vietnam War, dreadful enough when it referred to a conventional war but simply fatuous—contrary to the nation's political goals—when applied to a war like Kosovo, which was supposedly fought to *protect* civilians from repressive tyrants.

Sewall decided that she'd use her new position at the Carr Center to organize a forum for dialogue between the two communities—human-rights advocates and military officers (she had plenty of contacts among both)—about the moral and strategic issues surrounding civilian casualties in modern warfare.

The forums started out small and low-key, with a dozen or so people from each of the two worlds talking off the record. Sewall tried to frame the discussions so that the human-rights advocates felt comfortable talking about war without opposing it on principle and the officers felt comfortable talking about casualties without coming off as pacifists.

After Desert Storm, attendance at these meetings swelled. The human-rights people saw more clearly that wars were sometimes justified; the officers saw that the new emphasis on air strikes raised strategic and ethical questions that could no longer be evaded.

Conrad Crane, the chief military historian at the Army War College, heard about the conferences, understood their importance, and drew in a wider circle of officers. After the September 11 terrorist attacks, the range of interested parties expanded further. Sewall was scheduling four or five conferences a year, some of them in conjunction with the war college, attracting as many as a hundred people.

In the summer of 2003, it was clear to many that Iraq was devolving into an insurgency war. So Sewall decided to plan some conferences on Iraq and counterinsurgency. It was a logical connection: not only did Sewall have a long-standing interest in COIN, but one of the doctrine's central tenets—protecting the population—converged with her present passion of finding ways to fight wars while minimizing civilian casualties.

One conference, hosted by the Kennedy School in June, dealt with the ethical dilemmas of special operations, and she brought in several Special Forces officers, who were about to deploy to Iraq, to discuss hypothetical scenarios with regional specialists: What do you do if you're stuck in traffic, and a local man gets out of his car with a gun? Do you have the right, and is it a good idea anyway, to shoot him without hesitation? Are there signs to watch for, or facts about the local culture, that might provide clues to the man's intentions?

By mid-2005, Sewall sensed it was the right time to hold a broader conference on the topic. She knew about the community taking hold: the articles in *Military Review,* the impending Quadrennial Defense Review with its section on irregular warfare, Eliot Cohen's recent workshop at Basin Harbor, and the news that David Petraeus, the COIN hero of Mosul, was about to come home to Leavenworth.

She'd met Petraeus once before, back when she worked in the Pentagon and Haiti was the big US peacekeeping operation. Petraeus, a lieutenant colonel at the time, had sat in on some of the interagency policy meetings before heading down to Haiti himself. She remembered his surprise (it *seemed* to be a delighted surprise) that the three administration officials most closely involved in running the operation were women: Susan Rice at the National Security Council, and Sewall and Michèle Flournoy in the Pentagon. He said that he'd never seen that before.

Sewall wanted Petraeus to come speak at this conference. Conrad Crane, the Army War College historian with whom she'd organized earlier workshops, helped on this; it turned out that the two had been classmates at West Point. Sewall phoned Petraeus and introduced herself.

"Sarah, it's so good to hear from you again!" he exclaimed.

She hadn't expected him to remember her. (She would soon realize that Petraeus remembered everybody who might advance his ambitions.) She asked him to speak at the conference; again to her surprise, he consented without hesitating.

Sewall also called John Nagl. She'd read the article about him in the *New York Times Magazine*. Nagl, too, was eager to take part and helped her organize the attendance list.

And so, among the ninety speakers and observers who gathered for two days in the large conference room at the Carnegie Endowment for International Peace in Washington—mostly Sewall's usual mix of officers, think-tank analysts, and human-rights activists—several of them were beginning to recognize one another.

Besides Crane and Nagl (who gave his usual talk about Malaya and Vietnam), there were Kalev Sepp (much in demand since the publication of his article on COIN's best practices), Bill Hix (who'd worked with Sepp under General Casey in Iraq), Bruce Hoffman of the RAND Corporation (who'd served on Hix's advisory team of "doctors without orders"), Richard Lacquement (Nagl's former faculty colleague at West Point) and his office mates in the Pentagon's Office for Stability Operations, Jeb Nadaner and Janine Davidson (who, at the time, were putting the final touches on Directive 3000.05), Frank Hoffman of the Marines' Warfighting Lab (who'd organized the Irregular Warfare Conference at Quantico a year earlier), Steve Metz from the Army War College (who'd invited Nagl and Kilcullen to speak in the spring), as well as such emerging regulars as T. X. Hammes (author of *The Sling and the Stone*) and Michèle Flournoy, who was writing studies of COIN at a nearby think tank and who, a few years later, would become an undersecretary of defense. (Dave Kilcullen was invited, but he'd been called back to Australia to help with counterterrorism policy after a bombing in Bali.)

Petraeus was the lunchtime keynote speaker on the conference's second day. His article, "Learning Counterinsurgency," wouldn't be published in *Military Review* for another couple of months, so he decided to deliver a précis of the original briefing, condensing its "thirteen observations" to ten and delivering them without PowerPoint slides (so uncharacteristic of Petraeus that he cracked a joke about it).

"Observation number one," Petraeus began. "T. E. Lawrence, 'Lawrence of Arabia,' had it right: 'Do not try to do too much with your own hands . . . Better the Arabs do it tolerably than that you do it perfectly. It is their war . . . and you are there to help them, not win it for them.'"

This was one of the few principles derived less from Mosul than from Petraeus's latest stint training the Iraqi military, and in the coming years, some would invoke it to highlight a contradiction, or at least a tension, in COIN doctrine: the need to do the job quickly, as Lawrence urged, versus the reality that insurgency wars were protracted by nature and can thus rage on for many years.

Observation number two was related and similarly paradoxical: "Every army of liberation has a half-life, beyond which it turns into an army of occupation." This half-life, Petraeus said, can be extended through humanitarian projects, but it's still a race against time. At some point, the people come to see the checkpoints as too inconvenient, the helicopters as too noisy, the accidental killings and mistaken detentions as too appalling—and the bloom wears off.

Number three, like all the subsequent points, harked back to Petraeus's time in Mosul: "Money is ammunition." Sometimes it can be even more important than ammunition. The trick, though, was not just to scatter money around (as, Petraeus thought but didn't say out loud, most of the other commanders had done with Saddam's stash of cash in the summer of 2003) but rather to focus on the most urgent needs and on agents who can spend it most shrewdly.

Fourth: The point of "winning hearts and minds" is not to make the Iraqi people love or thank us but rather to ensure that they *have a stake* in the success of the new Iraq.

Fifth: Before carrying out a *military* operation, an officer should ask, "Will this operation take more bad guys off the street than it creates by the way it's conducted?" That is, will the violence tick off so many Iraqis that they join the insurgency in their outrage? (Again, Petraeus didn't say so, but that's what was happening all over Iraq.) If the answer is "No," if it looks like the operation will spawn more bad guys than it kills . . . well, we might have to start shooting anyway. No one, he stressed, should think that he and his men had been "reticent" about "going after the Saddamists, terrorists, or insurgents." One night in Mosul, they had to attack thirty-five bad guys simultaneously and took down twenty-three of them. Still, the *point* was, you should think very hard about whether you really *had* to go that route.

Sixth: The key thing in these kinds of operations is to have good intelligence, most of it from human sources on the ground. That night in Mosul, he said, his men fired no more than one or two shots per target—sometimes they didn't need to shoot at all—and they *knocked* on doors; they didn't break them down or cordon off whole neighborhoods.

Seventh (and back to the main point): "Defeating insurgents requires more than just military operations." A COIN strategy also involves "efforts to establish a political environment that helps reduce support for the insurgents and undermines the attraction of whatever ideology they may espouse." These efforts include economic recovery, education, and supplying basic services.

Eighth: It's important to cultivate Iraqi leaders who are seen by their people as legitimate at all levels.

Ninth: In COIN campaigns, lieutenants, sergeants, and even corporals have to make *strategic* decisions, so they must be trained how to think strategically ahead of time.

Finally, tenth: The critical job for a commander is to "set the right tone." If he's seen to be more enthusiastic about shooting bad guys than handing out aid or negotiating with tribal leaders, his men will take that as a cue to do the same. In Mosul, Petraeus said, he had to make clear to some of his battalion commanders that helping with reconstruction wasn't an option; it was crucial, and had to be treated with the same priority as firefights and raids.

These were the basic guidelines that Jan Horvath's interim field manual hadn't quite articulated and that Petraeus would keep hammering away at over the next six years—first at Leavenworth, then back in Iraq, and finally on to Afghanistan—with uneven degrees of success.

After the speech, Petraeus sat down at the head table for lunch. In the course of multiple conversations, someone sitting near him asked how well the Army was adapting to counterinsurgency.

"Not as well as it should," he replied, "and that's why John Nagl is going to write the Army's new COIN field manual."

As he said this, Petraeus nodded toward Nagl, who was sitting at the same table and heard every word. Nagl kept a straight face, but, in fact, he was flabbergasted. This was the first he'd heard of such an assignment. He'd urged Petraeus to commission a new field manual when the two ran into each other in the Pentagon a few weeks earlier; but Petraeus hadn't contacted him since about actually getting the project going, much less letting him lead it.

This, of course, had been Nagl's fantasy for years. He'd described in his dissertation how Sir Gerald Templer defeated the insurgency in Malaya in part by commissioning a handbook for colonial soldiers that codified his ideas into official British army doctrine. Now, it seemed, Nagl would be writing the book that might do the same thing for his fellow American soldiers in Iraq.

Nagl couldn't wait to get started. Early that evening, after the conference wrapped up, he grabbed a few like-minded friends—Lacquement, Davidson, and Erin Simpson, a Harvard graduate student in her twenties who was teaching a course on counterinsurgency at Quantico's Marine Corps University—and took them to the Front Page, a nearby restaurant. On the way, they ran into Kyle Teamey, who had been Nagl's intelligence officer in Iraq and was now, thanks to a recommendation from Nagl, an analyst on an Iraq task force at the Defense Intelligence Agency in the Pentagon. Teamey, who was also attending grad school, studying under Eliot Cohen at SAIS, happened to be walking toward the Dupont Circle subway station after a class when he heard someone call out his name.

It was Nagl. "Come with us to the Front Page," he said. "I'm writing the Army's new counterinsurgency field manual."

The five of them sat at a table in the back of the restaurant, discussing the project, Nagl scribbling a rough outline of the manual on a large napkin. His notes closely anticipated the published document's actual outline. Chapter 1: Insurgency and counterinsurgency—definitions, overview, Mao, Philippines case study. Chapter 2: Unity of command—political/military integration. Chapter 3: Intelligence as the element that drives military activities. Chapter 4: Operations—population support as the key. Chapter 5: Information operations—the importance of message and public opinion, with Malaya as a possible case study . . . And on it went through Chapter 10: Leadership and ethics, followed by an annotated bibliography.

Nagl was still the junior military assistant to the deputy secretary of defense. The next morning, he asked his boss, the senior assistant, Brigadier General Frank Helmick, for permission to take on the task. Helmick was amazed that Nagl could even ask such a question. No Army officer doing staff work for a top-level Pentagon civilian could get involved in such a sensitive matter of policy. Helmick said he'd let him take brief leaves and as much personal time as he wanted to help out on the manual, but no way could he be the guy in charge.

Nagl was disappointed, but he would take Helmick's words on what he could do informally as a mandate to do a lot—and wound up being, in effect, the project's deputy, coauthor, cheerleader, and, once it was published, chief promoter. Petraeus would refer to him, soon after the project took off, as "the ubiquitous John Nagl."

Eliot Cohen had been in Leavenworth giving a lecture soon after Petraeus took command of the Combined Arms Center. The two had met at various academic conferences in the 1980s, when Petraeus was an instructor at West Point and Cohen was teaching at Harvard. Cohen had seen a draft of Jan Horvath's interim field manual and found it wanting. He dropped in on Petraeus after his lecture, to say hello and to urge him to take control of the project and start all over. Petraeus assured him that doing so was his top priority.

The two met again at Sarah Sewall's COIN conference in Washington. Five days before then, on November 2, Cohen had held a workshop at SAIS called "US Military Operations in Iraq: Planning, Combat, and Occupation." One of the speakers was Conrad Crane. Cohen was very impressed with Crane's talk and advised Petraeus to get him to write the new field manual.

Cohen didn't know that Petraeus and Crane were already acquainted from West Point, first as classmates and, a dozen years later, as fellow faculty members, Petraeus in the Sosh department, Crane in History.

In any case, Crane was a good match for the job. Back in early 2001, soon after retiring from the Army and joining the war college staff as a civilian historian, Crane had been recruited by the Pentagon to conduct a study on the roles that the various military services had played in crises. As part of his research, he drew a timeline marking the four phases of conflict. He saw that in almost every war that America had entered in the post-WWII era, the Air Force and the Navy had thrown in their peak forces during the most intense fighting, then left the scene in the "post-combat" phase. The Army, it turned out, had been the only service whose troops stayed in the war zone after—in some cases, long after—the shooting had stopped, the period known as Phase IV or stability operations. Crane wrote a paper, concluding that since the Army had spent so much time doing stability operations, it ought to take a closer look at what it takes to do them well, something it hadn't done in decades. Bill Darley, the editor of *Military Review,* read the paper and published a shortened version in the May–June

2005 issue—the same issue that carried Kalev Sepp's "Best Practices in Counterinsurgency"—under the title "Phase IV Operations: Where Wars Are Really Won."

From that paper, Crane acquired a reputation in Army planning circles as "the stability-operations guy" or "the COIN guy." In October 2002, as the Bush administration geared up to invade Iraq, some of the top officers in the Pentagon, knowing that the Army would get stuck with the aftermath's dirty work, asked the war college to set up a team to examine the issue. Crane led the team and wrote the resulting monograph, called *Reconstructing Iraq*. Published in January 2003, two months before the war started, it concluded that the post-combat phase would be the hardest of all—that the US occupation might trigger resistance, in which case it would take more troops to win the peace than it had to win the war.

The monograph was circulated widely after it proved prescient. As its author, Crane started receiving invitations to lecture or sit on panels from a wide assortment of national-security centers and think tanks—which was how he came to speak at Eliot Cohen's workshop, which led to Cohen's chat with Petraeus at Sarah Sewall's conference.

After that chat, Petraeus approached his old classmate and said he'd like to talk with him sometime about a COIN field manual that he was putting in the works. Eight days later, he emailed Crane from Leavenworth, asking if he would be interested in heading up the project. Crane was surprised, but after clearing it with his boss the next day, he accepted the offer. "It is an imposing task, but an important one," he replied.

Petraeus wrote back, "Super news, Conrad . . . I think this is a unique opportunity to be the 'Wass de Czege' of our generation," a reference to Huba Wass de Czege, the general who'd written the Army's *AirLand Battle* field manual in the mid-1980s. Petraeus added that he hoped a draft could be finished around the Christmas holidays, followed by a two-day conference in late January or early February that would "pull together 25 or so great minds to comment on the draft and then help nail down the final version in the subsequent months."

Crane expressed just one caveat: he'd recently undergone a medical exam, and one of the lab results was ambiguous; he was scheduled for a follow-up in December. If it turned out badly, he noted, he might have "some major distractions," so it would "probably be a good idea to have a strong coauthor for the project, somebody like John Nagl, if he is available."

Nagl certainly was available, and Petraeus had already decided to make him a big part of the project, regardless of Helmick's hesitation or Crane's health (which turned out to be fine).

Petraeus sent Crane his "super news" email at 11:03 p.m. on November 17. At 7:57 the next morning, Nagl sent Crane an email expressing "congratulations . . . and sincere concern for your health as well." He explained that Petraeus had cc'd him their correspondence about the COIN field manual. "I want to help with this as much as I can from this desk," Nagl wrote. "In furtherance of that effort, I attach my proposed outline for the manual and my suggestions for the folks who should attend the COIN conference"—the one that Petraeus had proposed in his email to Crane the night before—"to work it and to roll it out."

The outline Nagl attached was an elaboration of the one he'd scrawled on the napkin at the Front Page ten days earlier, along with suggestions of who might be assigned to write each chapter. Nagl also attached a list of thirty-two people who should be invited to the conference: most of them the officer-scholars and civilian analysts who'd formed the nascent COIN community at Eliot Cohen's Basin Harbor conference and renewed it at Sarah Sewall's Carr Center conference.

By the time Petraeus's two-day COIN conference took place—in late February, as it happened, and in front of 106 invited guests and speakers, not the mere 32 on Nagl's list—an all but final draft of a new field manual had already been written.

Two months earlier, on December 15, Nagl and Crane had flown to Leavenworth, in part to attend a conference on a related topic but, more important, to write a detailed outline of the manual and to decide which of their friends they should ask to draft which chapters.

As a fitting coincidence, the conference taking place during their visit was on the subject of "information operations," or IO, the Army's term for any activity that enhanced combat power by influencing, disrupting, or manipulating perceptions of the battlefield. These activities could include electronic jamming, deception, psychological operations, and counterintelligence. They could also include dealing with the news media, molding public opinion, and shaping the views of elite decision-makers—the enemy's in the war zone or one's own back home.

In Petraeus's mind, IO—the very term—harked back to the War of Information that he and General Galvin had plotted all those years ago at the 24th Infantry Division and again at US Southern Command. It was a key element of counterinsurgency (the French COIN strategists called it, less euphemistically, "propaganda"), and it was a key element of Petraeus's upcoming conference on the COIN field manual.

Hundreds of Army field manuals had been published without fanfare; they were meant as instruction booklets for commanders and their troops, covering specific aspects of tactics or training for specific kinds of battles. But this field manual would be something different: a how-to book for a kind of war that the Army's leaders had decided long ago to stop fighting, yet here they were fighting precisely this kind of war and doing it badly. By its very existence, the manual would burst forth as a manifesto, an urgent assault on the Army as an institution.

This was a serious, risky business: the mounting of an intellectual insurgency from within the Army itself.

And so Petraeus and his emerging circle knew that getting the field manual accepted, and acted upon, would require some information operations of their own. They needed endorsements—"buy-in," as Petraeus liked to call it—from all the branches of the Army, from other military services if possible, from civilian agencies experienced in overseas reconstruction, and, not least, from critical segments of the public, which needed to see a change in policy, a chance for victory, a reason for not giving up on the war just yet. Petraeus had to "win hearts and minds" on the home front. Winning hearts and minds in Mosul had meant making the Iraqi people feel invested in the success of the new Iraq. Now, when it came to this field manual (and this war), he knew that he needed to make the American people—which, as a first step, meant American politicians and opinion leaders—feel invested in the success of counterinsurgency.

The core of the conference would consist of the COIN stalwarts on Nagl's list. But Petraeus also invited his counterpart in the Marine Corps, Lieutenant General Jim Mattis, whom he knew from Iraq, to take part and, in the end, cosign the manual. He brought in officials from the CIA, the

State Department, and AID. He called up the older generation of spies and Special Forces who'd done counterinsurgency in El Salvador and Vietnam. He invited everyone who'd written an interesting article about COIN or the war in *Military Review*. He urged a few critics to attend: maybe they'd be converted; if not, their dissent would be noted; they couldn't complain that they'd been excluded.

And he invited a few members of the mainstream press. Petraeus liked to talk with reporters. It was one reason many of his fellow officers considered him a showboat, though he was baffled by this disdain. He would frequently tell his fellow officers that reporters were going to find out things, they were going to write critical articles; better to cooperate with them, to help them understand your perspective, than to leave them to their own devices. Treat them well, they'll treat you well; they might even adopt your viewpoint. This wasn't just Information Operations 101; it was basic human nature.

Finally, Conrad Crane told Petraeus that he'd mentioned the COIN conference to Sarah Sewall, who expressed interest in cosponsoring it and even getting the Carr Center to kick in some money, if she could use it to defray the expenses for a dozen of "her people"—human-rights activists and aid-group executives—to attend. Petraeus thought this was a great idea: what better way to signal to everyone that this project constituted something new!

Not long after Crane took the assignment of chairing the effort, he had a long discussion with Petraeus about what the manual should emphasize. Petraeus gave him a copy of his forthcoming *Military Review* article, "Learning Counterinsurgency," with its thirteen (in his final draft, he'd expanded it to fourteen) observations from soldiering in Iraq.

Make sure these observations get into the manual, Petraeus stressed. They should form its basic principles.

On the first day of the IO conference in December, Nagl gave his usual lecture on learning counterinsurgency in Malaya and Vietnam. On the second day, he and Crane skipped the proceedings and went off to a nearby room with Jan Horvath and some other members of Leavenworth's doctrine-writing team to work on their main project.

Crane had prepared a list that he labeled "COIN Principles, Imperatives and Paradoxes." It was inspired by several sources: Petraeus's fourteen observations, Kalev Sepp's "Best Practices" article, his own essay on Phase IV operations, certain sections of Nagl's book, and a rereading of Galula.

He wrote out the list on a whiteboard, which had been set up on an easel, and talked his colleagues through the points:

"Legitimacy is the main objective" (building popular support for the host nation's government is crucial).

"Unity of effort is essential" (military operations must be geared to the political goals).

"Understand the environment" (you can't appeal to the people, or know what they want, without understanding their society and the culture).

"Security under the rule of law is essential" (the main focus is not so much killing the bad guys as protecting the population).

"Insurgents must be isolated from their cause and support" (they must be cut off from the people, and their ideas must be co-opted or discredited).

"Intelligence drives operations."

"Use *measured* force" (massive firepower kills innocent civilians, and killing five insurgents is futile if "collateral damage" sires the recruitment of fifty).

"Prepare for a long-term commitment" (the people won't support the counterinsurgent unless they're convinced he's staying till he wins).

Some of these principles Crane then reworded into paradoxes, a literary form that he'd always enjoyed:

"The more you protect your forces, the less secure you are" (retreating to remote bases, as the US military was doing in Iraq, means you can't engage with the people or build their trust, meaning the insurgents grow stronger in the vacuum).

"The more force you use, the less effective you are" (the collateral damage problem).

"Sometimes doing nothing is the best reaction to a provocation."
"The best weapons for COIN don't fire bullets."
"Sometimes it's better for the local people to do something poorly than for us to do it well."
"If a tactic works this week, it won't work next week; if it works in one province, it won't work in the next province" (the insurgent learns and adapts, so the counterinsurgent needs to do the same).
"Tactical success guarantees nothing" (America won every head-on battle in Vietnam, but that had no effect on the war).
"Most important decisions are not made by generals" (this is a block-by-block war; lieutenants and even corporals must make "strategic" decisions—hence the importance of this manual).

The group discussed these concepts for the rest of the day. The paradoxes in particular would unleash enormous controversy; Crane knew they would, and acknowledged that some were probably overstated. He meant for them to dramatize how different this kind of war was from the wars the Army was accustomed to fighting—and how differently commanders and soldiers would have to *think* in order to meet its challenges. After all, it was called *irregular* warfare.

Nagl, meanwhile, had refined the outline that he'd sent Crane a month earlier and jotted down a list of candidates to write each section, figuring correctly that Petraeus himself would have a hand in writing and rewriting a good deal of it, too.

Chapter 1. "Insurgency and Counterinsurgency"—Crane and Nagl.
Chapter 2. "Unity of Effort"—Rich Lacquement.
Chapter 3. "Intelligence"—Kyle Teamey.
Chapter 4. "Operations"—Horvath and Nagl.

. . . and so forth, capped with:

Bibliography—Nagl.

The bibliography—the very act of including a bibliography—was, in some ways, Nagl's favorite part of the project. It would send out the word that this was not just a how-to manual, that this kind of war was intellectual as well as physical, that it required further study, deep thinking, imagination, and creativity at every echelon of command, from general officer down to corporal.

During his oral presentation at the COIN conference two months later, Nagl would say he was "proud" that this was the first Army field manual to contain an annotated bibliography. In the published version of the manual, as an epigraph at the top of chapter 1, he quoted a remark by a friend who was a Special Forces officer in Iraq:

"Counterinsurgency is not just thinking man's warfare—it is the graduate level of war."

11.

The Workshop at Tatoine

Thursday, February 23, 2006, was an unusually warm winter morning on the banks of the Missouri River. The hundred-plus guests at Hoge Barracks, the quaint hotel inside the gates of Fort Leavenworth, assembled in the parking lot and boarded the vans waiting to take them to Tice Hall, a squat building on a far corner of the base. There, in a large classroom with tiered rows of desks and chairs, normally used by the Battle Command Training Program, Lieutenant General David Petraeus welcomed them to the Counterinsurgency Field Manual Workshop.

Many of the guests knew one another by now from similar conferences or from COIN campaigns of yore. There were the officers and scholars who'd been at Eliot Cohen's Basin Harbor workshop and Sarah Sewall's Carr Center conference: Dave Kilcullen, Kalev Sepp, Bill Hix, Steve Metz, Janine Davidson, Michèle Flournoy, and, of course, the sponsors themselves. There were Special Forces vets who'd worked the trenches of El Salvador—Tom Marks, who'd written the first chapter of Jan Horvath's interim field manual, John Waghelstein, T. X. Hammes, and a half dozen more. There were a handful of midlevel CIA officers who were working similar trenches at the moment. There were Sewall's associates. And there were a few journalists, some of whom had written critical articles about the war and had been invited not to report on the workshop's proceedings (which were off the record) but to participate in them: the *Atlantic*'s James Fallows, the *New Yorker*'s George Packer, the *Wall Street Journal*'s Greg Jaffe, and *U.S. News & World Report*'s Linda Robinson (who was also writing a book about Petraeus in Iraq).

No one in the Army had ever gathered such an eclectic crew in one place for any purpose, certainly not to vet a field manual. On the night between the two sessions, when several dozen of them went to the bar in the basement of the officers' club to chat, argue, reminisce, tell dirty jokes, and, above all, to drink, Michèle Flournoy, looking around, couldn't help but recall the scene in *Star Wars* where the motley monsters from the far corners of the galaxy get plastered and break into fistfights at the Mos Eisley Cantina on the planet Tatooine.

It had been a hectic two months pulling the conference together. Nagl's team of writers had churned out their manuscripts over the holidays. Crane and Horvath had spent the subsequent weeks editing and refining the drafts. They'd all met the day before the conference began to go over the results. The latest issue of *Military Review*, containing Petraeus's article, "Learning Counterinsurgency: Observations from Soldiering in Iraq," had just come off the presses. He made sure that all the guests received a copy as they checked into the hotel.

Meanwhile, to prep himself, Petraeus was rereading the classics—Galula, Kitson, a bit of Nagl, and, several times, the article on "Uncomfortable Wars" that he'd ghostwritten for General Galvin twenty years earlier—to pound the themes and arguments into his head.

Finally, on the first morning, Petraeus brought the meeting to order. Standing at the podium, he recited the litany of changes that had transformed Leavenworth into the Army's "engine of change": the new curriculum at the college (including two hundred hours of instruction in COIN), the shift in training brought on by reports of lessons learned from the battlefield, the radical revamping of the National Training Center from a vast terrain for tank-on-tank war games ("a big-time thing of the past!" Petraeus exclaimed) to a vast complex of mock Iraqi villages, with foot soldiers facing real Iraqi role players and insurgents ("lessons learned on steroids!" he extolled).

The Army was now "a learning organization" (invoking Nagl's term), and Leavenworth was the "catalyst" of the learning. These innovations, Petraeus said, formed the backdrop of this conference. The new field manual, which they were about to discuss, would codify the results of this learning, ushering it into the military mainstream.

Sarah Sewall got up to speak. Some in the audience couldn't help but squint or squirm. In one of the vans on the way over from the hotel, several men had asked her what a human-rights advocate from an Ivy League college was doing there, much less cosponsoring the event.

"We don't take a purely legalistic or critical approach to war," she now explained. The principles of COIN converged with the principles of human rights: both had as their central aim the protection of civilians caught up in war. The military had perfected high-intensity, quick-fix warfare. Now it was trying to deal with the slowest, messiest kind of war there was. The two groups had a lot to say to each other about the complexities.

Petraeus made a point of sitting next to Sewall, front row center, and staying there at her side throughout both days of the conference, thus signaling to those present that this liberal woman from Harvard was a co-sponsor of the event in more than mere name, that he took what she said very seriously, and that they should, too.

After Sewall finished speaking, Conrad Crane stepped to the podium. Crane would be running the show from here on out, introducing the speakers, moderating the discussions, organizing the backroom revisions that took place after hours, and forwarding them to Petraeus for his final edit.

Crane flicked on a slide, which read, "Why Are We Here?" He flicked on a second slide: a photo of the grave of Lieutenant David Bernstein, above a caption reading, "To Minimize This." Bernstein, West Point class of 2001, had been killed in Iraq on October 18, 2003, early on in the insurgency, before the political and military leaders admitted that there *was* an insurgency—in short, as Crane put it, "while we were flailing around."

He didn't say so, but this was a personal matter to Crane. Bernstein had been a friend of his niece's, the valedictorian of her high school class in Phoenixville, Pennsylvania. Crane got to know the boy and came to regard him as the best that West Point had to offer: a natural leader, venerated by his classmates. On the day he died in Iraq, Bernstein's convoy had come under rocket fire. His gunner was killed, and his driver was thrown from the vehicle, trapped under the wheels as it rolled to an embankment. Bernstein jumped out, firing; the insurgents fired back, hitting him in the thigh, severing his femoral artery. He managed to climb back in and steer the Humvee off his driver. Then he limped out and pulled him to safety. The driver lived; Bernstein collapsed from a loss of blood and never regained consciousness.

Bernstein had once joked to Crane that he was miffed over graduating fifth in his class at West Point. The top four cadets won gold medals; number five got nothing. At the prompting of his family, the academy remedied this after his death. Each year since, the fifth-ranking cadet has been presented with the 1st Lt. David R. Bernstein Memorial Award.

"Why are we here?" Crane repeated, pointing to the picture of the gravesite. "To minimize this." He paused.

"You are the best and brightest of COIN," he went on, with none of the irony that the phrase had implied in the Vietnam era. "That's why you're here."

Over the course of the next two days, the manual's writers would step to the podium and summarize their various chapters. Someone who'd been sent the draft ahead of time would comment. Then the floor would open for discussion.

Crane started with chapter 1. There was nothing new here, he stressed. Its themes drew on Galula, Kitson, Thompson, Lawrence, the Marine Corps's *Small Wars Manual*, "the Marx Brothers (Lenin, Mao, Ché, and Giap)," the RAND Corporation's studies from the early sixties, the West Point course on Revolutionary Warfare from the seventies, Leavenworth's latest lessons-learned reports, Petraeus's "Observations from Soldiering in Iraq," and the book by "the ubiquitous John Nagl, the project's designated gadfly."

But, of course, in the context of official current thinking, this was all very new.

Crane rattled off the "principles, imperatives, and paradoxes" that he, Nagl, Horvath, and Cohen had jotted down and refined a couple of months earlier. "Some of it is exaggerated a little bit," he acknowledged. "The idea is to get people to think differently."

Finally, he raised some questions that the group should debate: Was the chapter's concept of an insurgency based too much on Mao? The goal of a counterinsurgency campaign is to build the people's loyalty to a legitimate government, but how do we measure "legitimacy," how do we determine what it *is*? What should we call the appropriate level of force: "measured force," "minimal force," "discriminate action"? Is the manual broad enough to cover all insurgencies but specific enough to cover the wars we're currently fighting?

Most of what followed was, to the core group, familiar stuff. Tom Marks stressed that COIN was "a battle for legitimacy," likening it to a political campaign that "has violence as one of its means," and noting that "winning hearts and minds" doesn't mean the people have to like you, "but they have to respect you; they have to accept that the system works for them." Rich Lacquement, in his summary of chapter 2 ("Unity of Effort"), quoted Galula to the effect that the elements of COIN are a matter of multiplication, not addition—it's "military *times* civilian government *times* judicial," and "if one of those factors is zero, the whole is zero." Kyle Teamey, talking about chapter 3 ("Intelligence"), noted that, in conventional war, the most important intelligence concerns the enemy army's order of battle, but in COIN it concerns "cultural awareness" of social networks, such as tribes. His chapter's coauthor, Montgomery "Mitzy" McFate, an anthropologist with an interest in the military, stressed the need to understand a culture's rituals and narratives, its core motivations, in order to devise incentives that might lure the people away from an insurgency. Another officer, James Corum, who'd written the chapter on training indigenous security forces, said that while Special Forces had done a good job of doing this in the past, the regular Army had to get involved now.

Most of those in attendance agreed with the premise, but their discussions and disagreements went beyond mere details.

Several raised the urgent need for more translators. (Nagl agreed, saying that some of his biggest problems in Anbar Province had stemmed from a shortage of interpreters, not of bullets or armored vehicles.) A few wondered how to calculate the number of troops that were needed for a given insurgency. Another, more complicated matter: given that COIN is often a shifting mosaic of offensive, defensive, and stability operations (a "three-block war," as General Charles Krulak had put it, where a unit might fight on one block, keep the peace on the next block, and hand out humanitarian aid on the block after that), how do soldiers determine which phase they're in, and how should they change their behavior, their perception of the mission, accordingly? (Michèle Flournoy ended up drawing an elaborate chart that spelled out the elements of the transitions and provided guidance on what to do in each phase.)

But there were some comments that challenged, or at least raised serious questions about, the doctrine's fundamental tenets.

Steve Metz, Con Crane's colleague from the Army War College and a longtime scholar of small wars, opened up the discussion. He knew that Crane had consulted a fellow faculty member, Max Manwaring, on the question of "legitimacy." Back in the 1980s, as a Special Forces officer in El Salvador, Manwaring had conducted a quantitative study of the variables that determined (or at least were correlated with) success or failure in COIN campaigns since World War II. He concluded that the most significant factor was whether the local population viewed its government as legitimate. But Manwaring had imposed a Western definition of legitimacy, involving democratic governance, rule of law, and a pluralistic society. Metz warned that this standard set the bar too high and that, in any case, people in other cultures might have different values, a different level of tolerance for corruption, different ideas about what makes a regime worthy of their loyalty—which is to say, what makes it legitimate.

(In the manual's final draft, Crane, taking these comments into account, would write that troops in a COIN campaign "should strive to avoid imposing their ideals of normalcy on a foreign cultural problem." He also inserted, in a list denoting indicators of legitimacy, that one such sign might be "a culturally acceptable level of corruption.")

Françoise Hampson, a human-rights activist and professor of law at the University of Essex in England, raised the stakes on the question of legitimacy. In many places in the world, if a government has to call in foreign armies to help maintain its power, that fact alone makes it illegitimate. Once your army is there, she said, it's fine to figure out ways to reduce the people's opposition to your presence; but the issue is what *they* want and *their* view of power, not what some Western power thinks they *should* want. "There are a lot of Americans," she said, "who don't think government should be responsible for health care. Is *that* legitimate?" A few people around her chuckled; a few others gasped.

Some of the Special Forces veterans in the room had a problem with the idea of running a *large-scale* counterinsurgency campaign in the first place. James Steele, who'd been in El Salvador and had briefly advised Petraeus in Iraq, said that any American intervention should be kept to a "small footprint" and that the advisers should build up the host country's security forces as quickly as possible.

"It's about the host country," he said. "It's *really* about the host country." Every day in Salvador he'd cursed the congressional mandate that limited the number of American advisers to fifty-five, but in retrospect he saw it as a blessing: it had forced him and his fellow officers to focus on advising the host country and kept them from doing too much themselves. "A protracted war for us," he said, "is a bad thing." And for any ally, the presence of foreign troops—including American troops—"is almost always a liability."

John Waghelstein, who had been the MilGroup commander in Salvador and the author of the study that inspired the country's National Campaign Plan agreed. "I see too much gringo in this," he said of the field manual's first draft. "It took ten years to do this in Salvador, a country the size of Massachusetts with five million people. To assume we're going to produce a document with a road map that solves the career problems of the people in this room—I think you're smoking little green cigarettes."

Colonel John Martin, a professor in the Counterinsurgency Center that Petraeus had recently set up at Leavenworth, wondered about the relevance of historical examples, or at least of those chosen by the manual's authors, especially the British in Malaya. In that case study, the counterinsurgents *were* the sovereign power; they set the national policy, and could appoint and fire commanders and ministers at will. By contrast, in Iraq and Afghanistan, we may have vetted or selected the provisional leaders, and they may remain dependent on our largesse. But their countries were nominally independent; they had to answer to their own constituents and power groups, whose interests may differ from ours.

Molly Phee, a Foreign Service Officer who'd recently spent seven months as a provincial governor in southern Iraq, took that point further, noting that some of the power groups that a nation's leader needs to placate may be the insurgents themselves. She questioned some of the manual's premises about a COIN campaign's goals, especially the "isolation of the insurgency from the population" and "the destruction of the insurgency political organization." The problem was that in some cases (Hezbollah in Lebanon, Hamas in the Palestinian territories, and, very much to the point, certain militias in Iraq), the insurgency *was* the population or an important segment of it. If, as the manual stated, a purely military solution isn't possible, if these kinds of wars usually end with a political negotiation, this poses a problem. "You can't just pick people up and move them out," she said (though that was precisely what the British and Americans had done, in an earlier era, in Malaya and the Philippines). "And I don't know if you want to *destroy* their organizations," not if you might need to negotiate with them in the endgame.

The chapter on leadership and ethics had been farmed out to Colonel Richard Swain, who taught a course on the subject at West Point. "You have to remember," he told the group, "not all Iraqi people are insurgents." Swain was upset that one draft chapter had cited Algeria as a COIN case study. "This was a colonial war to impose foreign authority," he said. "Do we want to cast our doctrine in that kind of situation?" We have to get over this romance of colonialism, he stressed, adding, "We have to get over *The Centurions.*"

Petraeus agreed. "Let me assure you," he said, not only addressing Swain but turning now and then to face the rest of the group, "this section of the field manual is wrong and will be fixed. The Algiers example is *not* appropriate. You can't sacrifice your principles as an American service person." He added, "I have a 'Front Page of the *Washington Post* Rule': If you don't want to see something on the front page of the *Washington Post,* then don't do it, don't say it."

This was a bold statement on Petraeus's part. He was taking a *policy* stance that went beyond his station, and many of those in the room knew it. He had been the one to insist on an ethics chapter from the outset. The news stories about torture at the Abu Ghraib prison had broken not long before the field manual was planned; the damage inflicted not only on America's moral position but also on its strategic interests in Iraq, the entire region, and the global war on terror were too obvious to overlook. The Army was, at the same time, drafting a new field manual on interrogation; whether to inflict torture and under what circumstances was a live issue all through the Army. Petraeus, on his own authority, was settling the matter; he was saying, Don't do it, period.

His statement also marked a step of personal independence: he was carving out a separate path, in certain crucial ways, from his elders. General Bruno Bigeard, the model for the protagonist of *The Centurions,* and long a hero to Petraeus, as well as a correspondent and friend, had been tainted by the practice of torture in Algeria. Even Galula, his other model, had allowed his men on occasion to place detainees in a brick oven and threaten to light it up as a way of getting them to talk. Petraeus decided he wouldn't go there. The notion of "a culturally acceptable level of corruption" would have its limits.

The most hostile comments on the manual came from Francis "Bing" West. This was expected. Petraeus had invited him as one of the likely stock critics. West was a legendary figure, a retired marine, gruff but also something of a policy intellectual; he'd spent a few years as an analyst at the RAND Corporation and in the Pentagon as an assistant secretary of defense. He was also a prominent writer. His book *The Village,* published in 1972, about a squad of marines who took back a string of South Vietnamese hamlets from the Viet Cong, was still regarded as a classic in counterinsurgency literature. West had been one of the marines in that book, and even now, at age sixty-five, he craved the action. When the United States invaded Iraq, West embedded with the 1st Marine Division as a journalist, stayed with them all the way from Kuwait to Baghdad, and coauthored a book about the adventure, called *The March Up*.

West had read the draft field manual's first two chapters, and now sat listening to the authors recite their conclusions, with growing dismay and occasional disgust. He disliked Crane's "paradoxes" most of all, the notion that the best weapons didn't shoot bullets. This was crap. At bottom, West didn't believe in nation-building, didn't think Americans knew how to do it. "Population protection"—what did that mean to a soldier with a rifle who didn't speak the local language? Yes, West and his squad had protected the Vietnamese villagers, but they did it by going out on patrol every night and killing every Viet Cong they could find.

"An insurgency—it's war!" West bellowed. "The weapons we have, the reason people want us there, is *we kill people*!" The manual had to address this fact. There needed to be a section on the *fighting* that goes on in an insurgency war: when soldiers do apply firepower, as well as when they do not.

Petraeus took up the challenge. "We do need to address the *balance* of kinetic and nonkinetic," he acknowledged ("kinetic" being the Army word for shooting people), "and we may have gone too far in one direction." But that was because soldiers were predisposed to go the other direction. You didn't need to *tell* a nineteen-year-old soldier with a rifle that sometimes he had to shoot bad guys. You needed to emphasize that sometimes shooting bad guys caused more problems than it solved. "But," he conceded, not wanting to make waves and, more than that, knowing that West had a valid point, "you have to require balance, you still have to do war-fighting, it's still a big part of the picture."

West was alone in his views on this issue. Most of those in the room, including the ones who weren't COIN enthusiasts or human-rights activists, understood that killing was a large part of war, even this kind of war; the manual's draft noted explicitly and repeatedly that *irreconcilable* foes had to be captured or killed.

Still, some agreed with one of West's criticisms: How *do* you make the distinction between when, and whom, you fight and don't fight? How *do* you resolve the host of ambiguities posed by an insurgency war? The field manual didn't offer a clue.

This was a problem that Huba Wass de Czege had with the whole project: not so much the issue of killing or not killing, but whether the dilemmas and ambiguities ever-present in these kinds of wars might simply be too hard to untangle. Wass de Czege was something of a legend as well: the founder of the School of Advanced Military Studies, the author of the mid-1980s' *AirLand Battle* field manual, the general most responsible for turning Leavenworth into the Army's intellectual center. He'd retired from the Army long ago, as a one-star general, but he'd kept his hand in war games and conferences such as this one, and he still lived on the outskirts of town.

Wass de Czege worried that the manual was taking "an engineering approach" to insurgencies. "You're underrepresenting the *difficulty* of doing this," he said. "It needs more practical advice about how to do the difficult things." This is an art, and it's a mosaic; each local setting, even within a single theater of war, is different, requiring a different approach. "This fact doesn't come through." And, most important, he said, you need to know how difficult it is *ahead* of time, because if what you can bring to the conflict—in the way of troops, intelligence, time, or whatever—isn't enough to win the battles, then it's better to stay out.

Some of the manual's authors knew there was plenty of truth here. Before, after, and in between the sessions of the Leavenworth conference, they held a number of informal conversations on whether counterinsurgency was even possible. The question had two parts. Was the US Army up to the task? And, at least as uncertain, were the American people?

The field manual's first chapter stated that successful counterinsurgency campaigns required soldiers and marines "at every echelon" to possess a daunting set of traits, including "a clear, nuanced, and empathetic appreciation of the essential nature and nuances of the conflict" and an "understanding of the motivation, strengths, and weaknesses of the insurgent," as well as a rudimentary knowledge of the host country's culture, behavioral norms, and leadership structure.

It was a logical requirement, given what this kind of war entailed, but was it a reasonable expectation? Could any nation's military—not just its officers but the "soldiers and marines *at every echelon*"—be recruited and trained to such a high standard? (In the manual's final draft, the phrase "a clear, nuanced, and empathetic appreciation" was toned down to "a clear appreciation," but the question still held.)

As for the American people, the manual noted that these kinds of wars were "protracted by nature," requiring "firm political will and substantial patience," along with "considerable expenditures of time and resources." Phrases to this effect were repeated several times. The emphasis was deliberate. This was an Army field manual, not a policy statement. It would have been out of place for the authors to pass judgment on whether the country *should* get involved in these kinds of wars. The manual's mandate was to say: *If* the Army is ordered to wage counterinsurgency warfare, here is the official guide on how to do it. But the cautionary passages about firm will and patience were *intended* as warnings. Conrad Crane had been against the idea of invading Iraq, precisely because he figured the aftermath would be a slog. Some of the manual's authors, especially Kalev Sepp (whose list of COIN best practices was reproduced in one of its chapters), wished that they could spell out the corollary of those cautionary passages, something like: "If the nation and its leaders are unprepared for the long, hard fight that counterinsurgency entails, they should not begin one in the first place." But they couldn't say that explicitly; they could only hope that the message came through between the lines.

There was another fine line that the manual finessed: the paradox, or perhaps contradiction, between Petraeus's warning that "every army of liberation has a half-life before it becomes an army of occupation" and the field manual's observation that counterinsurgency requires "a long-term commitment." Petraeus qualified his warning, noting that you could extend the half-life—sway people to tolerate the stifling burdens of occupation—by providing them with security, basic services, and good governance. The trick was striking the right balance. As he would tell skeptics, that was a big reason why it was so important to focus on the nonkinetic side of the war: why COIN was "20 percent military, 80 percent political." The people needed rewards to put up with the checkpoints, the low-flying helicopters, the occasional miscreants and misfires; that was the only way they'd extend the half-life. It was also why, Petraeus and Nagl would say, they called COIN "graduate-level warfare." It wasn't for amateurs.

Petraeus sometimes talked about an army of "pentathlete" soldiers and counterinsurgency as one piece in a broader doctrine of "full-spectrum operations": the art of conducting offense, defense, and stability operations not just over a three-block span, as General Krulak had envisioned, but *simultaneously* across an entire province or country.

But this raised Wass de Czege's question all over: Was the concept realistic? Not all students were graduate students; not all athletes were pentathletes. Could *all* soldiers be three-block warriors and full-spectrum operators? Was this, as Wass de Czege insisted, a lot *harder* than the manual implied—a lot harder than the Army and the nation could manage?

Over the next few weeks, the draft chapters were revised to tie up loose ends, tone down exaggerations, and fill gaps that the discussions had uncovered. A few bureaucratic battles would persist for several months over a handful of these issues. But the larger critiques—whether historical parallels were valid, how to balance the three-block war, how to define "legitimacy," and whether COIN was a feasible goal for the American Army in the modern world—were left unresolved, for the most part unaddressed.

On the second morning of the conference, before the discussions resumed, Crane, Nagl, Horvath, and Eliot Cohen woke up early and met at the Santa Fe Depot Diner in downtown Leavenworth to discuss writing an article for *Military Review:* a précis of the first two chapters that would serve as a bit of "advertising and marketing," as they called it, for the full field manual to come. They dashed off an outline over breakfast; Nagl and Crane tweaked the prose. Bill Darley, the journal's editor, published the article in the next issue under the title "Principles, Imperatives, and Paradoxes of Counterinsurgency."

Petraeus had suggested the idea. His goals in this whole enterprise were twofold. First, he wanted to have an Army doctrine on counterinsurgency in place by the time he went back to Iraq, so that he'd have official cover for the new strategy he was intent on imposing. (The finished manual would be published as *FM 3-24: Counterinsurgency* in December 2006, two months before his return.)

Second, over the long haul, he wanted to force a change in mind-set, to drive a wedge into mainstream Army thinking, to broaden and overhaul the official definition of war in a way that he'd been thinking about and advocating for over twenty years.

This was what the two days in Leavenworth were ultimately about: giving Petraeus the chance to lay out his "big ideas" to a broad range of professionals who would be needed, in one way or another, to join or support the two wars: the fighting war going on now in Iraq and the political war that would go on inside the Pentagon, perhaps for years to come.

Some of the old hands knew what was up. As the session came to a close, Tom Marks turned to one of his Special Forces mates and said, "This cake was already baked. We were the icing."

For the most part, Marks had no problem with that. In fact, he admired Petraeus's craft. This was classic information operations, this was what insurgents do—and Marks saw very clearly that Petraeus was staging an insurgency against "big Army."

In that sense, the conference was a success. In his concluding remarks, Petraeus told the group, "I want to keep the dialogue going. We have a community now." It started, he said, with Sarah Sewall's conference in Washington. Actually, it had started well before then. But now it had a leader who wore stars on his epaulets.

12.

Hearts & Minds

Meanwhile, all hell was breaking loose in Iraq.

David Kilcullen showed up for the COIN Field Manual Workshop at Fort Leavenworth, but he had to leave on the first day, after news came over the wire that Sunni insurgents had bombed the Golden Mosque, a major Shiite shrine in Samarra, signaling a new, more intensive phase in the bourgeoning sectarian civil war.

Two months earlier, Kilcullen had gone to work for Henry Crumpton, the State Department's new adviser on counterterrorism. They'd met at Eliot Cohen's Basin Harbor conference the summer before and struck up a friendship. Kilcullen's work on the Pentagon's Quadrennial Defense Review was coming to a close. He was scheduled to go back to Australia, where he was still a lieutenant colonel in the army, but his superiors told him that in his absence he'd missed an opening to command a battalion. He took the message as an act of spite. He wanted out of the Army anyway, preferring to stay in the States and play some part in the war. His marriage was crumbling, too; his wife had already left for home. So Crumpton arranged—through another request to the Australian government, this one signed by his boss, Secretary of State Condoleezza Rice—for Kilcullen to stay on as his chief strategist.

Kilcullen was already scheduled to go to Iraq in a few days on a classified mission for Crumpton. When he heard about the bombing of the mosque, he moved up his schedule.

Once in Baghdad, Kilcullen spent some time with American soldiers working the streets, as well as with diplomats in the embassy, and the contrast alarmed him. The soldiers were panicked by the escalating violence; the diplomats exuded their usual nonchalance. The occupation had been going on for nearly three years, an insurgency had been mounting almost from the outset, yet the American authorities still seemed in denial over the nature and scope of the problem.

There were signs of recognition here and there, most notably a COIN Academy at the US military base in Taji, about twenty miles north of Baghdad, which every soldier coming into Iraq was now required to attend for five days to get briefed on the rudiments of counterinsurgency. General Casey had set up the academy in November 2005, just three months earlier, and it was still in a primitive state. But Kilcullen was encouraged that such a thing existed.

The project had been Bill Hix's brainchild; Casey himself referred to it as "the Hix Academy." It grew out of a project that Hix and Kalev Sepp had initiated the previous August, soon after they returned to Iraq. Sepp in particular felt a sense of mission in the wake of the Basin Harbor workshop and the warm reception he'd received for his "Best Practices" article in *Military Review*. The campaign plan that Casey had signed a year earlier, vague and inadequate as it was, did mention counterinsurgency. Hix used that fact as an opening to propose a "COIN Survey," in which he and Sepp would visit the various US military units in Iraq to assess whether and how well they were following COIN principles. Casey gave his assent and let them use his personal helicopter to travel around the country.

Over the next few weeks, Hix and Sepp visited thirty-one American brigades, battalions, and regiments. About 20 percent of the commanders appeared to get the idea of COIN and were doing at least fairly well at applying it in the field. Another 60 percent were struggling: they understood the doctrine's elements but didn't quite see how they added up to a plan of action, and they felt uncomfortable with the notion of delegating authority to their own junior officers, much less to Iraqi security forces. They were for the most part good officers, but they'd learned all too well the lessons of the conventional battles at the National Training Center, and they'd absorbed all too thoroughly the dictates of a rigid command structure.

Finally, there were the other 20 percent of the commanders, who were not only ignoring the COIN sections of the campaign plan but unwittingly fueling the insurgency. Sepp was most shaken by a warrant officer in the 2nd Marine Regiment, who openly took pride in killing people. "We see ourselves as a motorcycle gang," he told Hix and Sepp. "We drive around, beat up the bad guys, and move on to the next town." An intelligence officer with another unit told them, "We secure a town, but after we leave, some of our informants are killed by the insurgents; that's a problem." He at least perceived the problem, but didn't grasp that one of his responsibilities was to solve it—to stick around for a while after the bad guys had been chased away.

What struck Hix and Sepp most of all as they traveled around the country was the creativity of the top 20 percent, those few officers who were dealing with the challenges and improvising solutions on their own, despite the lack of guidance from the top. The most creative of them, they agreed, was the commander of the 3rd Armored Cavalry Regiment, an Army colonel named Herbert Raymond McMaster.

H. R. McMaster had made his mark as an Army rebel a decade earlier, when his PhD dissertation was published as a book, provocatively titled *Dereliction of Duty: Lyndon Johnson, Robert McNamara, the Joint Chiefs of Staff, and the Lies That Led to Vietnam*.

Based on extensive research into declassified files, the book argued that in the mid-to-late-1960s, the Pentagon's top generals betrayed their constitutional duties by failing to express their honest military judgments to the president and the secretary of defense as the nation plunged into the quagmire of Vietnam.

It was a far more devastating critique than Andrew Krepinevich's *The Army and Vietnam,* which derailed the author's prospects for promotion, or David Petraeus's dissertation, which he decided not to publish after witnessing Krepinevich's fate. All three had been majors when they wrote their works, a delicate point in an ambitious officer's career.

But a decade had passed. The generals who lambasted Krepinevich had been commanders in Vietnam; they took his book as a personal insult. By the time McMaster came along, they had long ago retired or died. The new crop of generals had slogged through the mud and rice paddies of Vietnam as lieutenants or captains; they could appreciate the book without self-abasement. General Hugh Shelton, the chairman of the Joint Chiefs of Staff soon after McMaster's book was published, had been one of those lieutenants. Not only did he admire the book, he ordered all his service chiefs and commanders to read it and follow its lessons to the letter: to express disagreements to their superiors, even if it risked getting yelled at. President Bill Clinton's secretary of defense, William Cohen, echoed the sentiment.

David Petraeus, then a colonel, was General Shelton's executive assistant at the time. Petraeus called McMaster, gave him his phone number, and said that he should contact him personally if he ever caught trouble for what he'd written.

Like John Nagl, McMaster had risen through the ranks as a tank officer. At the time of Desert Storm, he was a captain in the 2nd Armored Cavalry Regiment, commanding a small unit called Eagle Troop. During the massive assault into Iraq from Saudi Arabia, his unit unexpectedly came across a Republican Guard formation. McMaster and his men, with just nine M-1 tanks at their disposal, wiped out all of the Guard's vehicles—nearly eighty, including twenty-eight tanks and sixteen armored personnel carriers—without suffering a single casualty of their own. It was one of the war's few classic tank-on-tank battles, something straight out of a scenario from the National Training Center.

But McMaster had also studied history when he was a cadet at West Point, class of 1984. (Conrad Crane had been one of his professors.) He'd gone on to grad school at the University of North Carolina, then, after writing his dissertation, spent three years back at West Point, teaching the department's core course on military history as well as an elective on the Korean and Vietnam Wars.

So he was well attuned to the emerging trend of low-intensity conflicts, the wars that most Army generals in the 1990s refused to call "wars." When his teaching obligations at West Point's History Department were complete, McMaster went to the Command and General Staff College at Fort Leavenworth, where he team-taught a course that took a critical look at the National Training Center and recommended changes in its scenarios, to allow for more flexible tactics against an unpredictable, guerrilla-like enemy. Afterward, he was assigned to the 11th Armored Cavalry Regiment, which played the part of the Krasnovians—the fictitious enemy army—in the NTC war games. There, along with some of his like-minded colleagues, he pushed the games into less rigid scripts, even free play.

It was no surprise, then, that in the late spring of 2003, as the second war in Iraq began to segue from liberation to occupation, McMaster was among the first officers on the ground to detect the glimmerings of an insurgency.

At the time, he was executive officer to General John Abizaid, the deputy commander of Central Command, which had responsibility for all US military forces throughout the Persian Gulf and Southwest Asia, including in Iraq. McMaster was ill suited to the job, and he knew it. His organizational skills were paltry, his distaste for paperwork all too undisguised, his instinct for fawning nonexistent. The two kept up a banter: Abizaid would tell McMaster that he was the worst XO he'd ever had; McMaster would reply that Abizaid displayed poor judgment for hiring him in the first place.

General Tommy Franks, who had been CentCom commander up through the invasion, retired from the Army in July, just as the occupation started to sour. Abizaid was promoted to replace him, and he named McMaster the head of his advisory group. The first thing McMaster did at his new, far more appropriate job was to write Abizaid a memo recommending that CentCom start calling the resistance an "insurgency," so that the staff could draw on the vast historical records of counterinsurgency as a guide for what to do.

McMaster assembled a commander's library at headquarters, ordering all the classic books still in print. He also tracked down a long-forgotten document: the proceedings of a weeklong symposium on counterinsurgency held at the RAND Corporation in April 1962, just as JFK's advise-and-assist mission in Vietnam was taking off. The participants had included Galula himself (who happened to be spending the year on a fellowship at Harvard), Kitson, General Edward Lansdale, and a dozen other officers, active or retired, American or (mainly) foreign, who'd led COIN campaigns in Malaya, Kenya, the Philippines, Algiers, or Southeast Asia. Here in a single 170-page volume were the theorists and practitioners of the art, sitting around a table, telling war stories and discussing lessons learned.

Over the next several months, McMaster traveled with Abizaid to visit every American brigade in Iraq. On the trip to Mosul, he saw Petraeus for the first time since the controversy over *Dereliction of Duty* six years earlier. Not knowing his background in COIN, he was surprised by how thoroughly Petraeus grasped the nature of the conflict and how shrewdly he was translating the theory into action. The two talked at length about the Mosul campaign, and afterward stayed in touch.

In December 2003, McMaster wrote Abizaid a thirteen-page memo titled "Assessment of the Counterinsurgency Effort in Iraq," based on their travels around the country. To prepare the memo, he drew up a checklist of criteria for success, drawing on a similar list in the 1962 RAND report and inspired to do so by the living example he'd seen in Mosul.

The memo's opening lines, which came right out of Galula, read:

"Military operations alone cannot defeat an insurgency because only economic development and political action can address most sources of disaffection. If military operations are not conducted consistent with political objectives or occur without economic development, they are certain to alienate the population further, reduce the amount of intelligence available to US and Iraqi security forces, and strengthen rather than weaken the enemy."

By this standard, almost every American unit in Iraq was failing badly. McMaster's recommendations: coordinate civil and military policy; allow former Baathists who had not engaged in criminal activity to work in the new Iraqi government ("This is a *precondition* for success," he wrote, not long after Jerry Bremer issued his CPA order barring Baathists from official jobs); increase the commanders' discretionary funds and make sure the money is directed at projects in stable neighborhoods; "enhance political legitimacy" of the new government by developing "a peaceful path for political reconciliation" of the warring sectarian factions; and, above all, "control [American] troop behavior and firepower."

It was still early in the war for these ideas to circulate widely, much less to be enacted. At a recent Pentagon press conference, which most senior officers in Iraq watched or later heard about, General Peter Pace, the chairman of the Joint Chiefs of Staff, had referred to the enemy as an insurgency, and Secretary Rumsfeld, standing at his side, brusquely admonished him, insisting that the resisters in Iraq were too disorganized to merit the *i*-word. Abizaid had once made the same mistake, prompting a similar scolding. He chose not to push the matter.

But McMaster was determined to push it, on his own authority if necessary, the first chance he could get.

His chance came in June 2004, when he was placed in command of the 3rd Armored Cavalry Regiment. The unit of 5,200 soldiers was scheduled for deployment to Iraq the following February. In the meantime, they were set to train at Fort Carson, Colorado, and McMaster had his own ideas of how to do that.

The National Training Center had just begun setting up mock Iraqi villages to prepare the soldiers for some of the situations they'd soon encounter. McMaster did the same thing at Fort Carson, but with more intense and realistic scenarios, matching those that he'd seen played out in the real Iraq. He also distributed hundreds of copies of the COIN classics—Lawrence, Nagl, Galula—as well as Phebe Marr's seminal book *The Modern History of Iraq*. He had a few of his troops, those with the aptitude and the rank to make use of it, take a rudimentary Arabic language course.

The regiment headed to Iraq in February 2005, assigned initially to South Baghdad Province. But McMaster soon received orders to redeploy to Tal Afar, a city of a quarter million people in Nineveh Province in northwestern Iraq. Tal Afar had been under Petraeus's purview when he commanded the 101st Airborne Division; his troops had cleared the town of insurgents the previous November. But after the division left—replaced by a single brigade that was untrained and inexperienced for the task at hand—the insurgents returned and Tal Afar fell apart. The city emerged with alarming speed as a guerrilla training center for the most militant Sunni insurgents, a staging ground for attacks throughout northern Iraq, and a transit point for foreign fighters entering the country through Syria. By the time McMaster arrived, it was home to between five hundred and a thousand armed insurgents who controlled every local institution and terrorized the population.

In early July, with help from a brigade of the nearby 82nd Airborne and some Special Forces units, whose officers had gathered intelligence in advance, McMaster's regiment launched an assault on the insurgent strongholds in Tal Afar. The fighting stretched into several pitched battles. By the end of September, the insurgents were defeated or in retreat.

Then came the hard part of the operation. Even while the fight was raging, McMaster and his top aides had contacted town leaders and tribal elders, gradually persuading them to provide intelligence on the insurgents and offering them assurances—in the face of much suspicion and doubt—that they would stick around until the town was secure.

McMaster also ordered the construction of an eight-foot-high wall around the city to keep insurgents from moving in and out. He spent lavish sums of money, from the commander's discretionary fund, to restore basic services, to recruit and train local security forces, and to pay returning city workers. And, from the beginning, when it was extremely dangerous to do so, his troops worked, ate, and slept not in massive, fenced-in bases on the outskirts but in outposts that he'd set up alongside the people. That would be the only way to learn the people's needs, earn their trust, fight the war the way McMaster had learned it needed to be fought.

It was the first classic multistaged counterinsurgency operation in the Iraq War, conducted with total independence from headquarters (as was every operation across the country, good, bad, or otherwise). And it was a model success, at least for the year that McMaster's regiment remained.

Bill Hix and Kalev Sepp came through Tal Afar on their COIN Survey less than two months into the operation. They could tell even then that McMaster grasped the concept more deeply, and had figured out how to apply it more practically, than any other commander they'd met. Just as Petraeus in Mosul had convinced McMaster that counterinsurgency could work in Iraq, so McMaster in Tal Afar convinced Hix and Sepp that their agenda—getting General Casey to lay down a COIN strategy for all Iraq—was worth pressing.

During their travels for the COIN Survey, Sepp filled a dozen notebooks with his summaries and observations. From these notes and his own mental whirrings, Hix wrote a report, much of it while being flown in Casey's helicopter from one locale to another. Back at headquarters, he packaged it into a ninety-minute briefing with PowerPoint slides and delivered it—first to Casey, then to Abizaid, along with their respective staff officers—without pause, never uttering so much as the same adjective twice.

His main conclusion was that most officers in the field weren't getting any training back in the States for the kind of war that awaited them, so they should get at least a dose of preparation upon arriving in Iraq. Hence, the COIN Academy.

Hix and Sepp drew up the curriculum, basing it on the classic COIN literature (including Sepp's "Best Practices" article), their experiences as Special Forces officers, the ideas bandied about at the workshops and conferences they'd recently attended (the academy was created before Petraeus's conclave at Leavenworth but after Eliot Cohen's at Basin Harbor and Sarah Sewall's in Washington, DC), and, not least, the further lessons they'd learned about what worked and what didn't from their COIN Survey.

Casey took the idea seriously. When each new rotation of troops arrived in Taji for the academy's weeklong session, he made a personal appearance and delivered the opening talk in the form of a twelve-slide PowerPoint briefing that Hix and Sepp had written. The briefing constituted a new security strategy, titled "*Iltizam Mushtarak*—United Commitment."

In tone and substance, the new strategy marked a stark contrast from Casey's campaign plan of August 2004. The earlier plan's guiding principle had been to provide security for the Iraqi elections, then turn over authority to the new government and get the American troops home as quickly as possible. In the new plan, the ultimate objective was still "transition to self-reliance" for the Iraqis, but the path laid out to get there was at once less fanciful and more ambitious.

The earlier plan had ticked off seven "key strategic tasks," including "Protection of key Iraqi *leaders*" and "Protection of the *political process,* both Iraqi and UN, including support to the elections." The new plan also cited seven tasks, but they fell under the heading "To Defeat an Insurgency"—which had not been a goal in the earlier plan—and they were very different in their particulars. They included the COIN benchmarks: "Deny the enemy sanctuary and freedom of movement," "Build effective, legitimate governance," "Meet population's basic needs," and—core to all the other tasks—"Protect *the population.*"

It was a barebones briefing book, not a detailed operational guide. But it aimed an arrow, it nudged the new crop of soldiers coming into Iraq, in a different direction from the Army's traditional path.

When Dave Kilcullen came to Iraq in late February 2006, he spent several hours talking with some of these newly arrived junior officers: the American lieutenants, captains, and majors who were suddenly supposed to take the initiative and make the sorts of decisions that in a conventional war would be made by colonels. They'd read Casey's new COIN strategy and understood its drift, but they were having trouble translating it into specifics.

"I get what we're supposed to *achieve*," one of them said, "but what are we supposed to *do*?"

When he got back to Washington, Kilcullen mulled over these conversations. He'd offered a few answers to the young officers, drawing on his experiences both as a COIN scholar and as a company commander in the Australian infantry. But the chats were too short and informal to delve deeply into the issues. Petraeus's field manual would help a lot, but it was still in draft stages and wending its way through the Army bureaucracy; several months, possibly a year or more, would pass before the soldiers in Iraq could take a look. Meanwhile, they should have something with more detail than Casey's latest guidance provided.

On Tuesday afternoon, March 28, Kilcullen went to the Pentagon for a scheduled meeting about Iraq with Mario Mancuso, the deputy assistant secretary of defense for special operations and counterterrorism. When he got to the office, he was told that Mancuso had been called away and the meeting would have to be rescheduled. It was four thirty, too late to go back across the river to the State Department. So Kilcullen settled into the Starbucks in Pentagon City, Virginia, pulled out the little black Moleskine notebook that he always carried with him, and, over the next forty-five minutes, jotted down some key points about COIN *technique* that the junior officers he'd met should know. It was a sketchy outline, filling just a couple of pages. Then he went home, spent some time with his son, put him to bed, cracked open a bottle of Laphroaig scotch, and typed up his notes, expanding them into a full-blown essay.

He kept his audience in mind: young lieutenants and captains who might be smart but had never heard of, much less perused, Galula, Kitson, or Lawrence; who, judging from his conversations with them, probably weren't quite sure what "counterinsurgency" *meant*. Casey's latest security strategy hadn't defined the term. So, high up in the piece, Kilcullen filled this gap:

> If you have not studied counterinsurgency theory, here it is in a nutshell: Counterinsurgency is a competition with the insurgent for the right to win the hearts, minds, and acquiescence of the

> population. You are being sent in because the insurgents, at their strongest, can defeat anything with less strength than you. But you have more combat power than you can or should use in most situations. Injudicious use of firepower creates blood feuds, homeless people, and societal disruption that fuels and perpetuates the insurgency . . . For your side to win, the people don't have to like you, but they must respect you, accept that your actions benefit them, and trust your integrity and ability to deliver on promises, particularly regarding their security.

Then he ticked off his list of principles, "expressed as commandments, for clarity," he wrote, adding that they were "really more like folklore," so "apply them judiciously and skeptically."

His first commandment: "Know your turf. Know the people, the topography, economy, history, religion, and culture. Know every village, road, field, population group, tribal leader, and ancient grievance."

The second: "Diagnose the problem. Who are the insurgents? What drives them?" COIN is "a competition between each side to mobilize the population in support of its agenda. So you must understand what motivates the people and how to mobilize them." The most dangerous opponent "is not the psychopathic terrorist of Hollywood; it is the charismatic follow-me warrior who would make your best platoon leader. His followers are not misled or naïve; much of his success may be due to bad government policies or security forces that alienate the population."

The third: "Organize for intelligence. In counterinsurgency, killing the enemy is easy. Finding him is often nearly impossible."

And on the commandments went: form networks of alliances with local people one neighborhood at a time, avoid knee-jerk responses to provocations, follow your plan ("only attack the enemy when he gets in the way")—each illustrated with specific steps that junior officers, *company* commanders, could take at their own initiative: precisely how to patrol, how to find a cultural adviser among your troops, how to approach local families, tribal chiefs, or community leaders.

Kilcullen finished writing at two thirty in the morning. He counted up the number of his commandments, saw that they totaled twenty-eight, so whimsically titled the piece "Twenty-eight Articles: Fundamentals of

Company-level Counterinsurgency"—a play on the "Twenty-Seven Articles" that T. E. Lawrence had famously written for British officers helping Arab insurgents fend off the Ottoman occupiers in 1917.

He emailed the draft, along with a request for feedback, to some like-minded friends, among them John Nagl, Eliot Cohen, Janine Davidson, Hank Crumpton, T. X. Hammes, Frank Hoffman—the usual crowd, by this point. As the comments trickled in over the next two days, he modified a few of his points accordingly. On Sunday, April 2, he emailed the final draft—a compact essay, just short of three thousand words—to a wider set of colleagues, including some of the officers he'd met in Iraq, who, he was sure, would circulate it widely on the internet.

The memo went viral, and well beyond his circle of acquaintances, almost instantly. The editors of *Small Wars Journal,* an online magazine read mainly by soldiers and marines who were interested in this sort of thing, posted it on their site. So did the managers at CompanyCommand.com, a restricted forum, set up at the start of the decade by a couple of West Point graduates, to let junior officers exchange tips and ideas, mainly about leadership techniques. Hundreds of comments poured in to each site, some expressing agreement, others dissent or caveats, still others posing further questions.

On Monday, David Petraeus, who wasn't on Kilcullen's email list, wrote him a note saying that he'd read the essay and liked it a lot. Nagl sent a note to Crane, urging him to reprint the essay as an appendix to the field manual. (It appeared, somewhat rewritten, under the heading "A Guide for Action.") Bill Darley, the editor of *Military Review,* came across it as well and told Kilcullen he'd like to publish it in the next issue. A couple of days later, the editor of *Marine Corps Gazette* asked if he could print it, too. Darley, who wanted as many American armed forces as possible to read it, regardless of their service, granted permission, as long as the Marines credited the Army journal; the *Gazette*'s editor complied.

The same week that Kilcullen circulated "Twenty-eight Articles," *Military Review* published the essay by Nagl, Crane, Cohen, and Horvath on COIN's "principles, imperatives, and paradoxes," giving Army readers a taste of the field manual to come; George Packer, one of the journalists who'd attended Petraeus's workshop in February, published a long piece in the *New Yorker* about H. R. McMaster's strategy at Tal Afar; the RAND Corporation republished the report on its 1962 COIN symposium, with the roundtable discussion by Galula, Kitson, Lansdale, and the rest; and, not least, Praeger's paperback division reissued Galula's long-out-of-print *Counterinsurgency Warfare* (with a new foreword by John Nagl), prompting Petraeus to order 1,500 copies and to make the book required reading for every officer-student at Fort Leavenworth's Command and General Staff College.

For the first time in decades, counterinsurgency was coming into vogue.

Back in Iraq, the scene was rapidly deteriorating. Sectarian violence between Sunnis and Shiites was spiraling out of control. Attacks on American troops by insurgents of all stripes were soaring, mainly through the use of roadside bombs, which were exploding at the rate of six hundred per week. Al Qaeda fighters were flowing freely into the country across the Syrian border. The new US-backed Iraqi government had yet to pass serious laws or make an imprint on society. And, notwithstanding the pockets of success like McMaster's or the doctrinal maneuverings of Hix and Sepp, the top American commanders couldn't get a handle on the chaos.

General George Casey thought he had a good idea why. Casey probably knew as much as anyone about the intricate workings of the US Army. He could mobilize troops and array them on a conventional battlefield, at least a simulated one, with impressive proficiency. But he was, as a few of his aides put it, an "iterative thinker." Faced with a tactical challenge, he would study all the relevant facts and materials very carefully and, more often than not, come up with a solid judgment—if the situation allowed for such a thing, the *right* decision—on what step to take next. But he wasn't so adept at seeing how the game played out a few moves ahead or how his assessment and decision fit into a broader strategic context.

That spring, traveling around Iraq, reading the various commanders' memos and intelligence reports, Casey had an epiphany: the war had degenerated into a battle for political and economic power among many ethnic and sectarian factions; in other words, *the enemy was no longer an "insurgency."* That being the case, he inferred that it no longer made sense to pursue a *counterinsurgency* strategy.

And so, Casey reverted to the only alternative he knew: his original campaign plan, which called for turning over authority to the Iraqi government and getting American troops out as quickly as possible. In fact, since there was little he thought he could do in this increasingly complex setting, it was best to accelerate the withdrawal.

He wrote a briefing for a new security strategy. It had the same title as the previous one, "*Iltizam Mushtarak*—United Commitment—," but nearly all references to counterinsurgency—the word or the concept—were deleted. On a page headlined "Strategy," the key passage read:

"This strategy is shaped by a central tenet: *enduring strategic success in Iraq will be achieved by Iraqis.* Our approach will increasingly place the GOI [Government of Iraq] and its institutions in the lead across all lines of operation, first with Coalition monitoring and support, and then with progressively less support until they can govern effectively without our assistance."

A timetable of "projections and goals" envisioned the Iraqi army taking the lead in all military operations, and the Iraqi government taking political control in every provincial district, by the end of the year, an astonishingly short time period.

The briefing's final slide listed eleven "Commanding General's FARs" (the Army's slang acronym for "Flat-Ass Rules"). The first: "Make security and safety your first priorities"—meaning *your,* the *American soldier*'s, security and safety. If there was any doubt on this point, the last rule on the list cleared it up: "Take care of yourself and take care of each other." The rules mentioned nothing about protecting the Iraqi population, providing basic services, or enhancing the Iraqi government's legitimacy.

Hix and Sepp might have challenged this list and the strategic shift it reflected, but they'd left Iraq soon after the COIN Academy started up. Sepp had resumed teaching in Monterey; Hix had been rotated to a year-long national-security fellowship at Stanford University's Hoover Institution. The whole group of outside COIN consultants, the "doctors without orders," had been disbanded with their departures.

So Casey did his own analysis, and he fell back on his tendency toward "iterative thinking." He took the word "counterinsurgency" too literally. Someone like Hix or Sepp might have pointed out that COIN was closely related to the concept of stability operations. In some manuals, COIN was a subset of stability ops; in any case, their principles and methods were similar. There may not have been a monolithic insurgency to counter; in fact, there never had been. But Iraq in the spring of 2006 was the very picture of instability, which a large foreign army, like the one the United States had in place, might be able to help stabilize, if its commanders were so inclined and its soldiers properly instructed.

Casey's move away from COIN, stability operations, peacekeeping, or whatever anyone wanted to call it, wasn't entirely a misunderstanding or an oversight. It was clear to those around him that Casey had never been comfortable with the COIN doctrine's full implications. From the beginning of his command, he'd been, and still was, under constant pressure from Rumsfeld to *lower* America's profile in Iraq, to ease the troops *out* of the fight and pave the way for their complete withdrawal. By contrast, COIN demanded, at least in its initial phases, a higher profile, an immersion in the area where the fighting was most intense, and a prolonged presence in the country. Casey was not the type of general to buck orders from Washington. More to the point, though, his instincts in these matters—stemming from his traditional training and reinforced by his unhappy time in Bosnia—were in tune with Rumsfeld's inclinations.

Finally, Casey was above all an Army man, and the Iraq War was draining the Army: recruitment and reenlistment rates were declining; the budget was getting eaten away by the demand for repairs and spare parts. Doubling down on the commitment to Iraq would carry too many risks. Even those who wanted to go that route acknowledged that it might not work, and in the short run, it would just drain the Army further.

Some of Casey's staff officers found his switch, and its logic, bewildering. True, the insurgents had splintered and proliferated into several warring groups. But the big gap in Casey's analysis—the big, developing story in Iraq that he somehow seemed to miss—was that the Shiite-dominated Iraqi government was one of these warring groups. The interior ministry's police forces weren't guardians of public order; they were death squads whose officers were kidnapping and assassinating Sunnis in broad daylight. The health ministry's guards were refusing to treat—in some cases, they were murdering—wounded Sunnis in their emergency wards. The American soldiers and marines were the only forces, if there were any at all, that could prevent Iraq from plunging into full-blown ethnic cleansing or cataclysmic civil war.

This crisis also had a regional dimension. If the violence did escalate to civil war, the Shiite regime in Iran might feel compelled to come to the aid of its Iraqi neighbors. The Saudis were already threatening to come in on the side of the Sunnis; if they did, Turkey would find it hard to resist clamping down on the Kurds in northern Iraq to keep them from fomenting rebellion among its own fledgling Kurdish militias.

An Army major named Joel Rayburn was the most outspoken of the officers waving a red flag. A strategic analyst in General Abizaid's advisory group at Central Command's headquarters, Rayburn had been H. R. McMaster's political adviser in Tal Afar, where he saw firsthand how the shrewd application of American military power could suppress an insurgency, restore order, and alter the politics of an entire city or district. The methods that McMaster used in Tal Afar, he thought, could alter the dynamics, or at least tamp down the violence, throughout Iraq. In any case, he was certain that accelerating an American troop withdrawal amid such rampant violence would unleash disaster.

McMaster had met Rayburn during a brief visit to West Point just as the Iraq War was starting. Rayburn was an instructor in the History Department. A former cadet himself, class of 1992, he'd gone to graduate school at Texas A&M University and written his dissertation on British policy in the Middle East. His study of Iraqi culture and history was what prompted McMaster to offer him the job as his political adviser.

Once Rayburn left Tal Afar and moved on to CentCom headquarters, this background informed his critique of Casey's new policy. Both Casey and Abizaid held the view that *they*—the American occupiers—were the main source of the violence in Iraq; that once they withdrew, the insurgents would be without a cause and would thus eventually fade away. Casey would often trot out a joke for the long string of senators, congressmen, and diplomats who came through Baghdad for a fact-finding tour. "You know, houseguests are like fish," he'd say. "They stink after two or three days. We've been in Iraq for three years now, and we're starting to stink."

To Rayburn's mind, there was some truth to this. At its beginnings, the insurgency was aimed primarily at the American occupiers, and if the uprisings had been nipped in the bud (an action that would have required the American commanders to recognize it as an insurgency), things might have gone very differently. But at this point, it was unrealistic to expect the Iraqis to take responsibility for their own security. They lacked the capacity and—since the government itself was a faction in the emerging civil war—the desire to do so. If the American troops departed, only militias and criminals would fill the vacuum.

A handful of staff officers felt the same way Rayburn did, but they saw their jobs as executing the commander's policies, not as offering their own opinion, unless someone higher up asked them to express it, and no one did. Which made Rayburn all the more impassioned and insistent.

Abizaid agreed with some of Rayburn's analysis, but not with his conclusions. Like Casey, with whom he spoke on the phone almost every day from CentCom headquarters, he felt the same pressures from Rumsfeld—and he also harbored the same skepticism about COIN. He, too, had graduated from West Point, class of 1973, with a concentration in Sosh, history, and English literature; he then signed up with Ranger units and fought the small wars in Grenada and Bosnia. Unlike Casey, he didn't come away from Bosnia with a distaste for stability operations. But unlike Petraeus, he didn't think Bosnia's lessons were relevant to Iraq.

The son of Lebanese immigrants, Abizaid had earned a master's in Middle Eastern studies from Harvard, studied Arabic at Jordan University in Amman, and traveled extensively in the region. In the aftermath of Operation Desert Storm, he was deployed not to the south in Kuwait but to northern Iraq, where he helped protect Kurdish rebels from the wrath of Saddam's henchmen; he witnessed the seething hatred between the Kurds and Arabs. Before then, he'd spent a tour as an operations officer for the UN peacekeeping mission in Lebanon, just as Hezbollah's militants were beginning to attack Israeli occupiers with suicide bombs; much later, he talked with Israeli officers who, at the end of their eighteen-year adventure in southern Lebanon, wondered why they'd stayed so long.

At CentCom, first as deputy commander, then as the top man, Abizaid recognized the sectarian conflict earlier than most; he just didn't think that Americans could do much to settle it. The peacekeepers in Bosnia had deployed there with the warring parties' consent, under NATO auspices in Central Europe, where NATO had legitimacy. Nothing of the sort was true in Iraq, where the people, like many Muslims in the region, deeply distrusted foreign occupiers.

Abizaid read Rayburn's memos, some of them, anyway, and passed them on to Casey. But neither general felt the inclination or the need to pay much attention. Rayburn was just a major after all.

• • •

Casey had a harder time ignoring Peter Chiarelli, an Army three-star general who happened to be his deputy.

Chiarelli had come to the job on January 17, 2006, brimming with enthusiasm for the adventure ahead. Five weeks later, Sunni militants blew up the Golden Mosque in Samarra, Shia militants struck back, chaos erupted everywhere, and Chiarelli's life turned into a ceaseless barrage of frustration and failure.

Until then, he thought that he'd found the magic formula for fighting this kind of war, the same formula that other members of the West Point Sosh mafia had come upon. Chiarelli had taught in the Social Science Department in the 1980s and loved it so much that he stayed an extra year beyond the mandatory three. He hadn't been to the Point as a cadet; he'd been an ROTC student at Seattle University. His time at Sosh marked his first exposure to a cadre of officers who were also thinkers, who valued and debated ideas about history and political theory and their relevance to national security.

Later he studied for a year at the National War College in an interagency program where he discussed these issues with civilians from the State Department and the Agency for International Development. He hadn't thought much before about the role that aid and development played in security policy; he was intrigued with the notion and impressed with the technical knowledge of the officials he met.

Chiarelli was and always had been a tank officer. He'd spent several years in Germany preparing for the titanic battle between NATO and the Warsaw Pact, with its sweeping formations, synchronized maneuvers, and decisive breakthroughs across the enemy lines. Once, when he was a junior officer, during an exercise in northern Africa, he gazed across the plains and exclaimed, "God, this is such great tank territory!"

But when he took command of the 1st Cavalry Division in the spring of 2004, just as the insurgency was gaining strength, Chiarelli quickly realized that the lessons he'd learned at Sosh and the National War College would be the most relevant.

On his first trip to Iraq that March, the standard ten-day "predeployment survey" for general officers, he met a colonel named Kurt Fuller, a no-nonsense infantryman's infantryman, the sort of guy, Chiarelli reflected, that you'd like to put in a glass box with a sign that read "Break in case of war." Yet the point that Colonel Fuller impressed upon him most emphatically was the need to start up and maintain the main power plant in Dora, a neighborhood in southern Baghdad that was rife with Sunni militants. Fuller, a brigade commander with the 82nd Airborne, had gone to the trouble of arranging for a West Point engineer, a lieutenant from another unit, to be transferred to Dora precisely for that purpose. He told Chiarelli that he wished he had ten of those guys.

Chiarelli was struck that a tough soldier like Fuller thought that one of his most important tasks was getting a power plant up and running, that one of the key indicators of his success was how many of its four smokestacks were blowing steam. Fuller's point was that the way to win over the Iraqi people, to lure them away from the insurgents, was to provide basic services—and electricity was one of the services they most sorely lacked.

The 1st Cav would be stationed in Baghdad, where the biggest challenge was dealing with Muqtada al-Sadr, the Shiite cleric whose Mahdi Army militia had taken over a teeming slum of two-and-a-half million people, called Sadr City, after his father, the Grand Ayatollah Mohammad Sadiq al-Sadr, who'd been murdered five years earlier by gunmen of Saddam's Baath Party. Chiarelli noticed that one way the son held on to power was to keep electricity pumping in Sadr City twenty-four hours a day. It was the only place in Baghdad, one of the few places in all Iraq, where this was the case, and he did it in part by draining electricity from other stations. It seemed that Fuller was right. If Sadr could gain favor, or at least submission, from the people this way, maybe Chiarelli could, too.

Chiarelli went back to Fort Hood, Texas, where the twenty thousand troops in his division were getting set to deploy. He told his staff what he'd learned during his visit, then took them on a five-day tour of nearby Austin for briefings on how to run a city from the managers of the municipal power and sanitation companies. The managers agreed to keep open a line of communication 24/7 to help the troops deal with any technical problems they confronted.

Meanwhile, Chiarelli read all the counterinsurgency books he could get hold of, and he studied carefully the reports on what Petraeus had done in Mosul. The two hadn't known each other at West Point; Petraeus had come back to teach just as Chiarelli went off to Germany. But they shared the

Sosh connection—the Lincoln Brigade was still very much functioning—so Chiarelli would frequently call Petraeus to discuss the issues, too.

Several months into his command, Chiarelli and his aide-de-camp, Major Patrick Michaelis, conducted an analysis pinpointing the locations of all the violent incidents in the 1st Cav's area of operation: roadside bombs, rocket-propelled grenade attacks, sniper shootings, murders. It turned out that the neighborhoods with the heaviest violence were also those with the gravest shortfalls in services—not just electricity but also water, sewage, sanitation, trash pickup: the basic elements of civilized life.

To illustrate the connection, Michaelis and the staff drew a map and overlaid it with two transparencies: one with dots showing the density of attacks, the other with dots showing where services were most lacking. The first set of dots lined up with the second set almost precisely.

Chiarelli came up with a concept: SWET, standing for sewage, water, electricity, and trash-collection. Provide those services, he believed, and the insurgency will wobble.

When he first arrived in Baghdad, the Bush administration had allocated $18.6 billion for Iraqi reconstruction, but Chiarelli soon realized that the program was disastrously ill conceived. The first few contracts had gone to large American corporations, mainly Bechtel Group, which constructed or refurbished gigantic power plants and sewage treatment centers—but it neglected to string the wires or lay the pipes to get the electricity or clean water from the plant to the cities' neighborhoods.

Small scale seemed a better way to go, with local labor and integrated civil-military teams supplying security. Chairelli realized that he and his staff would have to organize these projects themselves.

On August 3, Chiarelli put his plan into motion. With a mere $100 million that he'd managed to wrest from the American embassy, he and his men moved into Sadr City and hired eighteen thousand men to build a landfill and lay PVC pipe to remove the ankle-high sewage from the streets.

It was a risky move. Four months earlier, on April 4, nineteen of his soldiers had been ambushed while on patrol in Sadr City. They'd called in support, but so did the Mahdi Army's black-clad snipers. In the ensuing two-hour firefight, seven of Chiarelli's men were killed, more than sixty wounded. The fact that five hundred of Sadr's militants died in the battle did little to buoy his spirits. This time, Chiarelli assembled plenty of backup armor, ready to move in if the militants tried to disrupt his SWET campaign. But, for whatever reason, they didn't. The eighteen thousand workers seemed happy to be earning some money. Services improved. The slum stayed calm.

The calm lasted for a few weeks. Then General Casey and the US ambassador, John Negroponte, decided that the money would be better spent on training the new Iraqi army. Embassy officials had promised Chiarelli several hundred million more dollars to rebuild Sadr City if the first installment proved worthwhile. But that was before Negroponte arrived. He'd been in Iraq for only a couple of weeks when he made the decision to reroute the funds, and there was nothing anyone could do about it. Casey, too, had only recently arrived as commander of US forces in Iraq, so he was inclined to support Negroponte.

With the money gone, the workers laid off, and the cleanup projects left half-finished, the Mahdi Army resumed its attacks. The 1st Cav responded in kind and repelled the militias with force. But Chiarelli knew they'd be back, probably with new fighters recruited from the families and friends of the ones his men had killed.

It was unclear whether Chiarelli's methods would have produced results much more enduring. James "Spike" Stephenson, an AID official in Baghdad whom he frequently consulted on the nuts and bolts of reconstruction, was supportive of the SWET campaign but also skeptical. What would happen, he'd ask Chiarelli, when the workers in Sadr City finished laying the pipes and cleaning the streets? These were temp jobs, useful as far as they went, but they had no spin-off effect, nothing to sustain long-term employment.

In the spring of 2005, the 1st Cav rotated back to Fort Hood. Chiarelli was frustrated that his experiment had been thwarted at a crucial moment. He and his aide-de-camp, Major Michaelis, worked up a PowerPoint briefing, with the overlays displaying the correlation between violence and the absence of services. Chiarelli delivered it during a commander's session at Fort Leavenworth. General Wallace was in charge, and he'd already instituted some of the reforms that Petraeus would build on in the coming months, one of which was the revitalization of *Military Review*. Bill Darley, the magazine's editor, attended Chiarelli's briefing and approached him afterward.

"You have to write this up," Darley told him. "This could be the most important article we've ever published." Chiarelli put Darley in touch with Michaelis, who reshaped the briefing into an article. It was published in the July–August issue and, along with Kalev Sepp's piece on best practices from the issue before, bolstered the sense inside the still nascent COIN community that these ideas might have real value in this war.

When Chiarelli returned to Iraq with a third star as Casey's deputy, he was determined to use his new powers to give SWET another chance. But the resistance proved overwhelming—from Casey, from a few subordinate commanders, and especially from the Iraqis.

The Samarra bombing in February was discouraging enough; Chiarelli sensed that it would set off a steep spiral of sectarian bloodshed. But compounding this funk was the American response. Many of his fellow officers dealt with the violence the only way they knew how: by storming the city and killing or capturing everyone who might be an insurgent, which usually meant all Iraqi men of military age.

The brigade commander in Samarra, Colonel Michael Steele of the 101st Airborne (Petraeus's old division, which, in his absence, had changed), was particularly aggressive, having lectured his men before they came to Iraq, "Anytime you fight—*anytime* you fight—you always kill the other son of a bitch! You are the hunter, the predator; you are looking for the prey."

Once when Chiarelli came to see Steele, he brought with him the leader of the local police commando squad, an Iraqi two-star general named Adnan Thabit. Steele refused to let Thabit have a seat, until Chiarelli ordered him to. (Steele was later given a written reprimand after soldiers in his brigade killed four Iraqi men on an island in the Tigris River. The soldiers testified that Steele had told them to make no distinction between combatants and civilians. He denied the charge, but it was clear that he'd sown a toxic climate.)

The Steeles of the Army might have reassessed their instincts had there been orders from the top to do so. But Casey issued no such orders, despite the opening of the COIN Academy just a few months earlier and the revised security strategy that went with it.

Chiarelli was most flustered, though, by the Iraqi government. He'd order a raid on an insurgent safe house in Sadr City, and, by the time his men got there, the insurgents were gone. He'd authorize money for a hospital in western Baghdad, then discover that the money had gone unspent. He'd give money to the ministry of finance for reconstruction projects, then see the projects grind to a halt, half-completed. He'd find out that some interior ministry police were torturing Sunni detainees, order the police to be fired and the torture to stop, then hear that the miscreants had been rehired and the practice resumed.

At first he blamed the problems on miscommunication and incompetence, another instance of weak governance, which American money and expert training could help cure. Gradually, though, he concluded that, at least in these matters, the Iraqi government was performing quite capably: the problem was that its leaders *wanted* all these bad things to happen; they were responsible for *making* them happen.

Wiretaps revealed that Muqtada Sadr's lieutenants had been tipped off just before an American raid got under way—not by double agents inside the Iraqi security forces but by top aides to the Shiite prime minister, Nouri Kamal al-Maliki, perhaps by Maliki himself. Maliki's power base rested in part on Sadr, so, regardless of what the Americans wanted, Maliki's administration would protect him. Leaders in the ministry of health were deliberately withholding money from hospitals in Sunni neighborhoods because ethnic cleansing was their *policy*. Finance ministry officials weren't *mismanaging* construction money; they were pocketing it. It wasn't a few bad cops who were torturing Sunnis; it was senior officials in the interior ministry. Worse still, when ballistics experts tracked the arc of rockets or mortars fired on US troop positions, it turned out on several occasions that the weapons had been launched from inside some of those ministries' compounds.

By the late spring, the violence was out of control. Some mornings, the streets were littered with dead bodies, most of them young men who had been abducted and murdered the night before, many executed in the same fashion: shot in the head, their hands tied behind their backs. This, it was soon too clear, was the signature of Shia police—the government's official, uniformed police—on their rampage to murder Sunnis.

Chiarelli's staff marked the locations of these killings on a map. He then took the evidence to Maliki and demanded that the culprits be punished. The prime minister looked at the map and said calmly, "This isn't so bad. It was much worse under Saddam."

That was the last straw. Chiarelli was set to crack down on the ministries and use the punishment as leverage against Maliki. But Casey wouldn't let him. The next time Chiarelli tried to move a company into Sadr City to storm a safe house where roadside bombs were reportedly being assembled, a checkpoint guard ordered him to retreat. Chiarelli called Casey, who insisted that he obey the order.

Casey's mantras were "We can't want democracy more than the Iraqis do" and "Iraqi problems demand Iraqi solutions." Reasonable principles, up to a point; but in the meantime, American troops were getting killed, Iraqi civilians were getting massacred, the country was falling apart, and, if it collapsed completely, the region might well follow.

The war was also going badly in a strictly military way. As part of his new post-COIN strategy, Casey was ordering US battalions and brigades that had cleared a neighborhood or village of insurgents to turn over the area to Iraqi battalions and brigades as quickly as possible. As the commander in charge of day-to-day military operations, Chiarelli was responsible for executing the order, and the results were almost always disastrous. The Iraqi forces weren't yet up to the task. In many cases, they would surrender their ground at the first sign of a fight. When an Iraqi unit was ordered to relocate from one region to another (say, from Mosul to Baghdad), many of the soldiers would simply stay home; the unit would arrive on the scene with as little as half its original troop strength. And so the insurgents would return and take back their old patch of turf almost instantly.

Chiarelli considered resigning, a permissible, even honorable course of action under the circumstances. He'd won his current assignment as the result of a resignation. Major General John Batiste had been slated to be Casey's deputy at the start of January, but he quit the Army in protest of the way the war was being handled broadly. Three months later, he joined a group of five other retired generals who were publicly calling on Rumsfeld to resign, citing in particular the secretary's refusal to send as many troops as his generals had advised and Jerry Bremer's order to disband the Iraqi army after Saddam's ouster. There was no way the American military could complete its mission under those crippling conditions, the retired generals were saying. Chiarelli was now feeling similar pangs.

In the end, though, Chiarelli stayed on. First, he noticed that the "revolt of the generals," as some news stories called the petition by Batiste and the others, had no effect on policy; in fact, it aroused anger from many junior officers, who wondered why the generals had held their tongues for so long, why they hadn't made their case to the politicians more fervently or resigned in protest at the time, when their dissent might have mattered. Many of these officers had read H. R. McMaster's *Dereliction of Duty*, and they felt that they were witnessing a replay of the Joint Chiefs' passivity on Vietnam.

More to the point, Chiarelli wasn't the protesting or resigning type. He'd signed on to this assignment, to this war. He valued the Army's hierarchy and its ethos of loyalty. He gnashed his teeth over Casey nearly every day, but he always spoke up on his behalf and never—at least at the time—spoke out against him.

Friends of Chiarelli's regarded him that summer as a tragic figure: an officer who was trying to do the right thing but was shackled by association to a stubborn commander and a misguided policy.

How stubborn and misguided was beginning to be noticed even in Washington.

13.

"Clear, Hold, and Build"

At the beginning of May 2006, David Petraeus called Meghan O'Sullivan, President Bush's deputy national security adviser on Iraq and Afghanistan, and asked her to fly down with him to Fort Benning, Georgia, to watch the graduation ceremony of the Army's Ranger School. The first Iraqi officer to go through the school would be among those receiving their Ranger badges. This was a big deal. She should see it.

Petraeus really did think O'Sullivan would find the ceremony interesting, maybe even moving. And he enjoyed her company, found her intelligent, her views enlightening. But he also wanted an opportunity—and there were few more captivating opportunities than an airplane ride—to talk with her about the crisis in Iraq and the need, as he saw it, for a new strategy, one that would require more troops, not fewer, as Casey's plan envisioned.

The two had met in 2003 in Iraq, when O'Sullivan was working eighteen-hour days for Jerry Bremer's Coalition Provisional Authority and Petraeus was commander of the 101st Airborne. They ran across each other again two years later, when she was making frequent trips to Iraq as a senior White House aide and he was running the training program for the new Iraqi army. Ever since returning to take command at Fort Leavenworth, Petraeus had been keeping in touch with all his high-level contacts—an important element of information operations—and O'Sullivan was in the top tier of his list.

O'Sullivan was in her midthirties, trim, with blazing red hair, all of which signaled to most military men that she probably wasn't worth taking seriously. But, like many civilians with whom Petraeus enjoyed talking, she also had a PhD. More pertinent still, her dissertation, which she'd completed at Oxford, was on the civil war in Sri Lanka. One conclusion she reached was that civil wars end either when the stronger side crushes the weaker side or when an outsider intervenes to force a truce. She knew that if Iraq went the first way, there would be a bloodbath; she also suspected that the United States might serve as the outsider strong enough to force a truce.

This background made her more favorably disposed toward Petraeus's views than many of her colleagues, and Petraeus launched a campaign to align her more closely still. He'd invited her, as one of the few senior civilian officials, to the COIN Field Manual Workshop at Leavenworth a couple of months earlier. In their phone conversations since, she'd expressed interest in the manual's progress.

The common perception in the White House, and in much of the Pentagon and State Department, too, was that Iraq would stabilize once Prime Minister Maliki and the various political parties cobbled together a coalition government. Violence was soaring at the moment because Sunnis felt excluded from power, and as their militias struck out at Shiites, the Shiite militias were striking back. Once a deal was reached, so this argument went, things would calm down. The upshot was that there was no need—certainly it would be premature—to change American military strategy. Better, smarter, to ride out this interregnum.

O'Sullivan had been in Iraq enough times to know that the war was going badly, more so than her political bosses were willing to admit. Still, she tended to agree that the root problem was the Iraqi government and that once it gained its footing, improvements in security would follow.

Petraeus was intent on persuading her that this analysis had things backward. The Iraqi government couldn't be effective—couldn't do the things governments do, wouldn't be seen as a legitimate authority—until the population felt secure. So security had to come first, and the Iraqi army couldn't yet provide that security by itself. Only the US military had the strength to do that, but its commanders were pursuing the wrong strategy. A new strategy was the precondition to everything else.

A few officials in Washington had reached this same conclusion, but only a few. One of them was the State Department's counselor, a former NSC official and Harvard professor named Philip Zelikow.

When Condoleezza Rice became secretary of state at the start of 2005,

Zelikow was one of her first appointments. They'd been friends since the late eighties, when they worked together in President George H. W. Bush's White House. Afterward, they coauthored a book on the reunification of Germany. More recently, when Rice was George W. Bush's national security adviser, she recruited Zelikow to come help write a new national-security strategy after the September 11 terrorist attacks.

In February, just a couple of weeks into her new cabinet job, she sent Zelikow on the first of several fact-finding trips to Iraq. He traveled lightly, taking only a staffer or two and a couple of security guards. General Casey, who'd just recently assumed command, gave him leeway to go wherever, and talk with whomever, he wanted. Zelikow came back from that trip dismayed and wrote a fifteen-page memo to Rice, concluding that—despite two years of occupation, billions of dollars in aid, and the recent free elections, which had so enthralled Bush and his top aides—Iraq "remains a failed state shadowed by constant violence."

Zelikow saw some signs of hope in what Major General Pete Chiarelli was doing with the 1st Cavalry Division in Baghdad—his emphasis on the civil and economic sides of the conflict, his views on the importance of ensuring adequate water, electricity, and sanitation services—and he recommended that Rice do what she could to fund those sorts of programs.

In subsequent trips that spring and summer, Zelikow saw a few other officers, mostly brigade commanders, following Chiarelli's lead—whether out of conscious emulation or at their own initiative, he didn't know. He spent time with Kalev Sepp, who'd embarked on the COIN Survey with Bill Hix and was seeing a similarly mixed picture.

Finally, he talked with Colonel H. R. McMaster about his accomplishments in Tal Afar. The two didn't meet face-to-face. McMaster was cautious about going outside the chain of command. When his unit first arrived in Iraq, he'd gotten into trouble complaining about a shortage of resources; he didn't want to take any chances, or give some hostile general an excuse to impose disciplinary action, just as he and his troops were making progress. But he and Zelikow did talk on the phone at great length about COIN strategy: its specific elements, history, and rationale.

When he came back from that trip in September, Zelikow wrote Rice a twenty-three-page memo. The war, he said, could go either way, but there needed to be an overall plan, a cohesive strategy from the top, and as yet there wasn't one. To avoid failure, the administration needed to come up with something in the next year.

In October he returned to Iraq, this time accompanying Rice herself as one of several staff members. She was scheduled to testify at a hearing later that month before the Senate Foreign Relations Committee, and Zelikow spent some of his time on the flight back to Washington drafting her opening statement. Rice was growing frustrated at the lack of an overarching Iraq policy. The interagency NSC meetings on the subject were useless. The White House, at Bush's direction, deferred to the commanders on the ground; Rumsfeld insisted on excluding every department but the Pentagon from any aspect of military policy. Zelikow's memos had stressed the importance of economic development and political governance to the outcome of the war; those issues fell under the State Department's purview, so Rice decided to make a policy statement of her own. Zelikow was trying to come up with a pithy phrase to encapsulate what would be her official view.

He'd been reading several books on counterinsurgency and Vietnam. One of them, Lewis Sorley's *A Better War*, delved at some length into the abortive efforts by Robert Komer and General Creighton Abrams to move away from General William Westmoreland's search-and-destroy strategy to one that stressed protecting the population. A memo cited by Sorley referred to this alternative as "clear and hold": clear an area of insurgents, then stay in the area long enough to keep it secure, to hold it, until local troops or police could manage on their own.

One of the officials traveling with Rice on the trip was General Ray Odierno, the former commander of the 4th Infantry Division in Iraq, who was now the assistant to the chairman of the Joint Chiefs of Staff and, in that capacity, the military's liaison to the secretary of state. In the year and a half since he left Iraq, even in the four months since his uncomfortable after-dinner speech at Eliot Cohen's workshop in Basin Harbor, Odierno had reflected on what went wrong, why his tactics in Tikrit—which he now realized had been too aggressive—didn't quell the insurgency, why his efforts at handing out money and cleaning up schools fell short. His daily work inside the State Department, which he'd been at for nearly a year now, deepened his understanding of the political side of conflict. Rice had sent him along with Zelikow, to be his military adviser, on the trip where he talked with Sepp about the COIN Survey and with McMaster about Tal Afar. These insights were as new to Odierno as they had been to his civilian boss.

Zelikow showed Odierno the draft of Rice's testimony that he'd been working on and asked what he thought of Sorley's phrase.

Odierno thought for a few seconds and came up with a slight revision: "Clear, hold, *and build.*" That is, after clearing and holding an area, *build* up the government so that it can provide basic services.

Zelikow liked it and inserted the phrase into his copy.

Rice appeared before the Senate committee on October 19. Early in her testimony, Rice stated: "Our political-military strategy has to be to clear, hold, and build: to clear areas from insurgent control, to hold them securely, and to build durable Iraqi institutions."

A few days later, McMaster would read a transcript of Rice's statement and notice that several passages seemed to have been taken, almost word for word, from what he'd told Zelikow in their phone conversation. He felt gratified but also a bit nervous that the line of influence might be traced.

Petraeus watched the testimony live on television from Fort Leavenworth, where he'd just arrived. (His job as commander of the Combined Arms Center would begin the next day.) He was stunned. This wasn't the strategy that he'd seen in place in Iraq. He wished that it had been, but he wondered if Rice's remarks reflected official policy and, if they did, where the administration was going to get the resources to make it so. The Army and the Marines would need more money and a lot more troops on the ground to do a real clear-hold-build operation. At the moment, Petraeus didn't see that happening.

Donald Rumsfeld watched her testimony, too, and he threw a fit. First, she was speaking publicly about military strategy—way out of her lane. Second, to the extent that he understood what she meant (and he wasn't sure he did, he hated catchphrases), he strongly disagreed with it. It seemed to imply, as Petraeus also inferred, a policy of sending more troops to Iraq for a longer time, when Rumsfeld was trying to do the opposite. He phoned Generals Casey and Abizaid to see if they'd known anything about this. Neither had, and both of them were also annoyed at Rice's intrusion on their turf. He asked General Peter Pace, the chairman of the Joint Chiefs, what he knew about it. Pace shrugged (although Zelikow had sent

Pace an advance copy of the testimony and hadn't received any objections in response).

Rumsfeld batted out a terse memo to Bush's national security adviser, Stephen Hadley, with copies to Rice, Pace, and a couple of his own staff members. Under the subject line "Talk of a New DoD Strategy," he wrote:

> I have read that both the White House and the State Department have announced that the Department of Defense has a new strategy of "clear, hold and build" or something to that effect. I don't know what it is, General Abizaid and General Casey don't know what it is, and we all would prefer it not be used.
>
> Please ask someone [to] figure out where it is coming from, who is doing it, why they are doing it, and ask them to stop.

Rumsfeld was being disingenuous; he knew who was "doing it," but he had to tread softly. He detested Rice, regarded her as a lightweight—he and Dick Cheney had run bureaucratic rings around her in Bush's first term, when she was the national security adviser—but he knew that the president liked her, admired her, relied on her for advice. He held back nothing in opposing the phrase as a matter of policy and institutional propriety, but he knew it would only hurt his case if he made it seem personal.

He also knew that Bush would do almost anything to avoid disharmony in his cabinet. The president had raised no fuss when Jerry Bremer promulgated the orders disbanding the Iraqi army and barring Baathists from public office, even though they contravened decisions that the National Security Council had approved unanimously, with Bush present and concurring. In the early stages of the occupation, when she was still in the White House, Rice had complained to Bush personally on a couple of occasions that Rumsfeld wasn't doing his part to carry out some decision or another that the NSC had assigned to the Pentagon, usually involving Iraqi reconstruction projects. Rather than confront Rumsfeld directly, Bush had told Rice that she should get together with Don and Andy Card, the White House chief of staff, and work out the problem. Of course, no such meeting ever took place. The decision-making machinery was broken when it came to national-security matters; anyone could throw a monkey wrench in the works, and Rumsfeld was a champion at wrench-throwing.

Still, it seemed for a moment that Zelikow and Odierno's phrase, and Rice's assertiveness, might stick. On October 25, six days after her testimony, Bush gave a lunchtime speech to an organization of servicemen's wives. At one point, he stated that the US-led coalition in Iraq was "moving forward with a comprehensive plan," then added, "As Secretary Rice explained last week, our strategy is to clear, hold, and build. We're working to clear areas from terrorist control, to hold those areas securely, and to build lasting, democratic Iraqi institutions."

Just over two weeks later, he was about to quote the line again in a Veterans Day speech at an Army depot in Pennsylvania, when—a half hour before the event began—Rumsfeld phoned Hadley. He'd just read the text that the White House had sent around to the various agencies, and he was furious, screaming at Hadley to delete that line about "clear, hold, and build."

The line stayed in the speech. But the president didn't follow through. It wasn't translated into an order or a strategy, it wasn't passed down, and therefore wasn't taken seriously in the chain of command or on the battlefield.

Hadley wasn't inclined to push the issue, either. In one of several tense conversations they'd had, Rumsfeld asked him rhetorically why there needed to be a secretary of defense if the White House was going to delve into military policy, and Hadley—who saw his role as facilitating the national-security bureaucracy, not overhauling it—took the point. Besides, the top military leaders, from the Joint Chiefs to the combatant commanders on down, were insisting that the war in Iraq was on the right track; that any talk of changing strategy or expanding troop levels was premature; and who was Hadley or Zelikow or Rice to contest their judgment on such matters?

Still, he and his staff had their doubts.

In April 2006, Hadley's Iraq specialist, Meghan O'Sullivan (whose own experience in Iraq gave her additional cachet, as did her formal job title of special assistant to the president), flew to Baghdad to talk with Maliki. If the failure to reach a political settlement was causing the spike in sectarian violence, what could be done to promote a settlement? Soon after arriving, she realized that her premise was mistaken. Every meeting she'd scheduled was postponed or interrupted by yet another report of an explosion or a massacre or a security alert, which, in turn, triggered a crisis. The picture was suddenly clear: people couldn't be expected to make big political decisions while they were being shelled. Security was the precondition to a political settlement, not the other way around. The Iraqi army wasn't in shape to provide security on its own, and the American Army wasn't doing the sorts of things it needed to do.

By early May, then, when O'Sullivan flew down to Fort Benning with Petraeus, she was receptive to his case for a new military strategy—specifically, the counterinsurgency strategy spelled out in his forthcoming field manual—and for more troops to carry it out.

At the time, she was worried about Iraq; a few weeks later, she was apoplectic. She and other aides, in the White House and the State Department, were hearing the reports of dead bodies piled up in the streets of Baghdad each morning, all shot in the head, hands tied behind their backs. Ordinary Iraqis, whom she'd befriended while stationed there, were phoning or emailing her in a panic. They'd heard that the American battalion in their neighborhood was about to leave; could she do something, please, to stop them? Casey and Abizaid were still claiming that the Americans' presence was the problem; she'd thought so, too, and the claim probably used to be true, but it didn't seem so any longer.

O'Sullivan was among the handful of aides who saw Bush every day. She was also talking on the phone almost every day with Petraeus. When Petraeus visited Washington, they would often have a meal together, usually at an out-of-the-way restaurant (Morton's steakhouse in the Virginia suburbs was a favorite), to minimize the chance of being spotted by a colleague. Petraeus, an active-duty three-star general, was going way outside the chain of command by giving policy advice to a White House aide. O'Sullivan used him as a frequent sounding board and a reality-check, asking questions, getting technical advice, discussing recent developments.

There was another back channel between the White House and Leavenworth. The previous fall, O'Sullivan had been looking for a military assistant, an Army officer who could provide this sort of expert support on a more routine, less surreptitious basis. Petraeus recommended a one-star general named Kevin Bergner, the deputy commander of US forces in northwestern Iraq, including Mosul. A former public-affairs officer at West Point, Bergner had, over the past year, restored order to Mosul—which had deteriorated into an insurgency stronghold after Petraeus's 101st Airborne was replaced by a brigade less than half the size—mainly by reviving Petraeus's COIN techniques. O'Sullivan had visited Bergner during one of her trips to Iraq and was impressed. When she put in a request for Bergner to be transferred to the White House, usually a pro forma matter, the Army higher-ups at first offered a couple of other one-star generals. O'Sullivan insisted on Bergner. Finally, they approved the move. He began work as the NSC's senior director for Iraq at the end of the year.

All through 2006, Petraeus, very much behind the scenes, stayed in touch regularly with both O'Sullivan and Bergner, insinuating his ideas into the daily discourse at the highest level of government.

In May, Brett McGurk, one of O'Sullivan's NSC colleagues, who'd worked in Iraq as a lawyer before joining the administration in its second term, made yet another trip to Baghdad to prod Maliki into making progress on forming a cohesive government. He'd been dealing with many of the same people as O'Sullivan; he knew about Zelikow's clear-hold-build memo; he'd befriended John Nagl and had talked with him several times about counterinsurgency and the impending field manual. And he'd also struck up several conversations with uniformed officers in the Pentagon and in Central Command who insisted that all was well with the war. McGurk spent nearly the entire month in Iraq, every night writing four-page memos to President Bush directly, reporting that the place was coming apart at the seams.

At a May 26 NSC meeting, Casey, who took part via videoconference, got into a spat with Rice over whether the State Department or the military should be doing more to salvage the situation in Iraq. Bush ended the meeting by saying, "On that happy note, we will adjourn."

Rumsfeld sent Casey a memo afterward. "My apologies to you for the comments that were made in the NSC meeting this morning," he began. At the bottom of the note, he wrote in his own hand, "You were right on the mark!"

Bush scheduled a two-day meeting at Camp David for Monday and Tuesday, June 12 and 13, to be attended by his war cabinet and—for the first time in such a setting—a small group of outside critics who to varying degrees supported the war but had problems with how it was being fought.

The critics, selected by his NSC staff, included Frederick Kagan, a defense analyst at the American Enterprise Institute, the leading neocon think tank, who'd once taught in the History Department at West Point; Michael Vickers, a former CIA official who, in the 1980s, had helped organize the mujahedeen rebels in their war against the Soviet occupiers in Afghanistan; Robert Kaplan, a widely traveled war journalist; and—the one whom the White House staffers figured would be most outspoken—Eliot Cohen, who even agreed not to wear his customary bow tie for the occasion.

Cohen argued, as diplomatically as he could, that the president might want to think about replacing his generals. He recounted the main point of his most recent book, *Supreme Command*: that presidents throughout American history have overruled their generals and were often correct to do so. Bush had once been photographed carrying the book, a fact that many saw as significant, though Cohen doubted that he'd read it; certainly, when the two were introduced, he detected no sign that the president recognized his name.

Kagan didn't argue for more troops, although he suspected more were needed, focusing instead on the need to come up with a coherent strategy that spelled out clearly what the troops—however many there were—should *do*. Kaplan made the case specifically for adopting a counterinsurgency strategy. Vickers, true to his background, called for cutting back on conventional forces and stepping up the role of Special Operations forces, as had been done during his time in Afghanistan.

The session went on for a few hours, but it had a detached quality; some of the critics—who were there for only the first day, flown out by helicopter in the morning and flown back to Washington midafternoon—had the feeling that nothing they said was sinking in. The sense was confirmed the next day, when they heard the news that Bush was in Iraq. He'd left from Camp David, at around the same time they had; the trip had been kept secret; only a few of his cabinet officers had known about it in advance.

All four outsiders had been led to believe that they were part of an extensive, possibly pivotal conversation about the war: its status, its strategy, and whether it needed more or fewer troops. Certainly that had been the hope of the White House aides who assembled the guest list. But now it seemed that the whole event—both days of the summit, with and without the outside critics—was primarily a cover, allowing Bush to slip away to Iraq without tipping off the White House press corps. They'd had a spirited discussion, but apparently that's all it was—for the moment.

Bush wasn't yet ready to take Eliot Cohen's advice; he'd always, by instinct, deferred to the commanders in the field. Still, he'd read the memos from O'Sullivan and McGurk; and as Air Force One touched down in Baghdad the evening of June 13, he was beginning to wonder about his top general in Iraq.

During the Camp David meeting (after the outside critics had departed, since they lacked the security clearances to hear it), Casey, appearing via video teleconference, briefed his latest campaign plan: the one that called for accelerating the withdrawal of US troops, at first from the cities, then from the country altogether, to the point where Iraqi forces would take the lead in all military operations by the end of the year.

A few days earlier, Maliki had finally formed a government. The week before, US Special Operations forces had hunted down and killed Abu Musab al-Zarqawi, the leader of al Qaeda in Iraq. Casey (and several others) took these events as turning points, an opportunity to accelerate the transition to full Iraqi control. He recommended to the officials at Camp David that they reverse an earlier decision to replace two brigades—seven thousand American soldiers—that were scheduled to leave Iraq in August, and he suggested that they announce this reversal in public. Doing so, he said, would demonstrate that we were leaving and thus reduce the stigma of "occupation," boost the legitimacy of Maliki's new government, and "send a signal" that the coalition was making progress in the war.

Now, face-to-face in Iraq, Bush asked his general if he had everything he needed—enough troops and other resources—to win the war. Casey repeated that, in order to win, he had to *withdraw* troops, so the Iraqis would engage more intensely in the fight, which after all was *their* fight, not ours.

This argument had maddened several officials and White House aides when they heard him make it at Camp David or when they read it in his campaign plans. Casey was frustrated at his failure to make them see that the conflict had changed, that it was no longer an insurgency but a complex sectarian power struggle. The officials and aides, some of them, anyway, were mystified by this argument. *Of course* it was a complex sectarian power struggle; it always had been, and given that the Iraqi government was a party in that struggle, they didn't see how the conflict could be stabilized by handing it more authority more quickly. Charts drawn up by Casey's own staff showed that sectarian attacks in Baghdad alone had soared to thirty or forty a day, with civilian casualties ranging from fifty to two hundred a day. It might have been one thing to say the war was hopeless, it was time to pull out; it was another thing, a sheer puzzle, to say that, under the circumstances, pulling out was the true path to victory.

Bush was a bit mystified, too. And Casey sensed that his message wasn't getting through.

Casey thought that events in the coming weeks would vindicate his position. On July 9, nearly a month after Bush's visit, he launched Operation Together Forward, a new attempt to stem the violence in Baghdad. A curfew was declared from nine at night until six in the morning, and seventy thousand Iraqi security forces were moved into the capital both to enforce the measure and to keep order in the streets during daylight. It didn't work. Bombs kept exploding.

On August 7, Casey put in motion Operation Together Forward II, a more aggressive but also more focused effort to impose order on Baghdad's seven most violent neighborhoods. At first he made this an American-led effort, moving the 3,500 soldiers of the 172nd Stryker Brigade from Mosul to the Iraqi capital.

When O'Sullivan heard about the plan, she called Petraeus to ask if a single extra US brigade would be enough to pacify the area. Petraeus, who maintained access to the daily Iraqi battle reports at his desk in Fort Leavenworth, told her it wouldn't and rattled off the reasons why.

Petraeus was proved right. The brigade "cleared" the neighborhoods of insurgents. It might have done more still, had it been given the chance. Enough officers by now had been through the COIN Academy and read Kilcullen's "Twenty-eight Articles" essay; some had followed the discussions in *Military Review* and the online soldiers' chat sites. But Casey's idea was to let the Iraqi security forces "hold" the areas by themselves while the Americans returned to Mosul before that city started collapsing, too. Six Iraqi battalions were supposed to redeploy to Baghdad from other areas of the country as part of the operation. But only two of them showed up, and they weren't up to the task. The result, predictably, was disaster. The insurgents moved back in, and the violence intensified. By the fall, the number of sectarian attacks in Baghdad was up by more than 40 percent.

Even Bush realized that Casey's plan wasn't working, that it might be time for a new strategy, maybe a new commander, too. The question was what, and who, they should be.

14.

"We Are Pulling in Different Directions"

In the summer of 2006, political pressure grew to do *something* about Iraq. Most of it came from Congress, where Democrats had always been skeptical of the war's rationale and Republicans were fearful of huge losses in the upcoming midterm elections as a result of the war's dimming prospects. And so the leaders of Congress did what they often do when disaster looms and it's risky to take a firm stance: they appointed a blue-ribbon panel of prominent Americans to study the matter.

In this case, they named ten eminences to serve on what they called the Iraq Study Group, which came to be known as the Baker-Hamilton Commission, after its chairmen, James Baker and Lee Hamilton. Baker had served as White House chief of staff and secretary of state when Bush's father was president; Hamilton, a former Democratic congressman, had cochaired a similar panel to investigate the intelligence failure that brought on the attacks of September 11.

Baker was particularly close to the Bush family: he'd been not only George H. W. Bush's campaign manager but also the chief organizer of the effort to block a recount of suspicious ballots in Florida in the 2000 presidential election; his success in this effort put Bush's son over the top in his race against Vice President Al Gore and thus into the White House. It was widely assumed that Baker's mandate now was to find some delicate way out of Iraq and, yet again, rescue George W. Bush from disaster.

All spring and into the summer, the panel, along with twenty experts hired as staff, held hearings or otherwise met with more than 170 senior administration officials, military officers, legislators, private specialists, war correspondents, and—during a five-day trip to Iraq that began on August 30—Iraqi officials.

It was on the plane ride to Baghdad that one of the panelists, William Perry, came up with a novel idea. Perry wasn't the only member of the group with experience in defense issues: Baker had negotiated Russian-American arms-reduction treaties; Robert Gates had been a career CIA analyst who'd risen, during Bush Senior's presidency, to the post of the Agency's director and was, before then, deputy national security adviser in the White House; Leon Panetta had inspected the Defense Department's accounts as Clinton's budget director; Lawrence Eagleburger had been a longtime State Department official; Charles Robb, a former senator and governor from Virginia, had been a marine who commanded a rifle company in Vietnam. But Perry was the only member who'd worked for several years at high levels inside the Pentagon, most recently as President Bill Clinton's secretary of defense. In part for that reason, he was emerging as the panel's de facto leader on substantive matters of defense policy.

Through the first few months of their work, the panelists were basically divided between those who wanted to stay the course and those who wanted to pull out of Iraq more quickly. Perry was initially in the latter camp, but on the way to Iraq, he started to mull over a third option.

Noting the front-page news reports on the spiraling violence and the slaughter of civilians in the streets of Baghdad, Perry wondered aloud to his colleagues whether it might be a good idea to send in a lot more American troops, purely as a short-term measure—say, for a single yearlong tour of duty. He had no desire to prolong the war; he still saw the panel's mandate as devising a way to cut it short. But he felt that the United States had an obligation to bring the violence under control if that was possible. A brief but massive spurt—a surge—of troops could make that happen, probably not across all Iraq (he figured, correctly, that the Army and Marines didn't have enough additional troops to control such a vast swath of territory) but perhaps in Baghdad, where most of the violence was taking place, and one other city. After a semblance of order was restored, he argued, then the pullout could begin.

Perry's colleagues thought the idea made sense, was certainly worth considering. Bob Gates and Chuck Robb were particularly intrigued.

On August 31, for its first session in Iraq, the group met with General Casey at Camp Victory, his headquarters in Baghdad's fortified Green Zone. Casey went through a shortened version of the briefing on his campaign plan. During the question-and-answer period, Perry laid out his idea for a short-term troop surge and asked the general for his response. Casey said that he didn't need more troops; there was nothing he could do with them, and, besides, they would only raise America's profile as occupiers, thus fueling the resistance.

Perry suspected that Casey might be reciting the Pentagon's party line—he knew of Rumsfeld's fierce position on the issue—so, after the briefing, he pulled the general aside for a private chat, off the record, just the two of them.

"George," Perry said, "if I were the secretary of defense and I came to you and said, 'I'm going to give you thirty thousand more troops for a limited time,' could you use them?"

Casey stood firm. He really couldn't, he assured the former secretary, and reemphasized his point that more troops might do more harm than good.

For all his experience, Perry wasn't going to presume that he knew more or had a better grasp of Iraq's security issues than the top commander on the ground. So he withdrew his proposal for a surge. The other panelists dropped it, too, except for Chuck Robb, who continued to support the idea.

The report, published with great fanfare the following December, turned out to be a mishmash, as blue-panel reports often are. Its critique of the present course was clear, and devastating. The situation in Iraq was "grave and deteriorating," with 40 percent of Iraqi citizens living in "highly insecure" provinces. Iraq's military lacked leadership, trained personnel, and equipment. Meanwhile, of the one thousand US officials in the Baghdad embassy, just thirty-three of them spoke Arabic, only six of them fluently. American policy all around was "not working."

But the report presented contradictory proposals for how to fix the problem. The authors called for a "diplomatic offensive" to push or lure Iraq's neighbors into imposing stabilizing measures—but they also concluded that nearly all of these neighbors had a vested interest in keeping Iraq unstable. The report hedged even on the core issue at hand: whether America should send more troops or withdraw the ones who were there more quickly. The key passage read: "By the first quarter of 2008 . . . all combat brigades not necessary for force protection could be out of Iraq. At that time, US combat forces in Iraq could be deployed only in units embedded with Iraqi forces." It didn't take a keen reader to notice the pertinent verb: "could." The troops *could* be out of Iraq by a particular date, but the commission skirted the question of whether they *should*.

Still, Robb insisted that the report at least mention the idea of a surge. So, four-fifths into the text (on page fifty of its sixty-two pages), after a line noting that more troops "could conceivably worsen those aspects of the security problem that are fed by the view that the US presence is intended to be a long-term 'occupation'" (a précis of Casey's argument), Perry added the following sentence:

"We could, however, support a short-term redeployment or surge of American combat forces to stabilize Baghdad, or to speed up the training and equipping mission, if the US commander in Iraq determines that such steps would be effective."

Bush dismissed the report, and not just because of its vague equivocations. The thrust of the report was a plea to prepare for withdrawal and to step up diplomacy—and Bush had no interest in either course.

However, that single sentence of conditional support for a surge would resonate in the weeks ahead and serve to legitimize (*"Even the Baker-Hamilton report says . . ."*) what Bush wound up approving.

The commission had one other effect on American military policy, more accidental but no less dramatic.

On September 3, the next-to-last day of their stay in Iraq, the panelists heard a briefing by Lieutenant General Pete Chiarelli. It was a sweeping lecture about the nature of this kind of warfare and the specific challenges of the war in Iraq: why it couldn't be won by military means alone; the correlation between areas with high violence and areas with a lack of jobs and basic services, and thus the need to undermine the insurgents' appeal by providing the people with sewage, water, electricity, and trash removal (the SWET formula). Finally, Chiarelli emphasized the big lesson that he'd learned only in the previous few months: that Maliki's government itself was fueling much of the violence and that no strategy, new or old, would have much effect until the American commanders used their strength and leverage to make him change its ways.

He said nothing about his own attempts to pressure Maliki, or about Casey's orders to leave the prime minister alone. Chiarelli valued loyalty and hierarchy, and he wasn't going to use this occasion, however tempting, to tout his own wisdom or to raise doubts about the top commander's. When Perry posed the question he'd asked Casey—whether another thirty thousand troops would have any use—Chiarelli again stood with his boss, but with a qualifier: his point (though he didn't state it quite so bluntly) was that, *as long as* Maliki kept actively preventing efforts to put down the Shiite militias, *as long as* he kept thwarting America's mission in this war, there was no point in sending still more soldiers here to fight, kill, and die.

Chiarelli's feelings on this point—his anger and bitterness at Iraq's political leaders for failing to do their part in what, ultimately, was a fight for their country—found full analytical expression in a briefing worked up around the same time by his political adviser, Celeste Ward.

Ward, thirty-five and blond, was another civilian woman, rising through the male-dominated military world, whose gender, youth, and looks deceived most officers at first sizing. As an undergraduate at Stanford University in the late 1980s and early 1990s, she'd studied aeronautical engineering and won an internship at NASA. After taking a course called Technology and National Security, she switched interests from rocket science to nuclear arms control, earned a master's degree at Harvard's John F. Kennedy School of Government, then interned in the Pentagon's nuclear policy shop before getting hired as a cost analyst, examining strategic weapons programs, at the Congressional Budget Office. After the 9/11 attacks, Ward turned to more urgent aspects of national security and, as the occupation of Iraq got under way, nabbed a job with the Coalition Provisional Authority, helping to set up a new Iraqi defense ministry. Within a few weeks, she contracted a kidney infection and had to be flown home for surgery. After recovering, she did another brief stint in the Pentagon, where a colleague recommended her to Philip Zelikow, who had just been named the State Department's counselor and needed a special assistant. Throughout 2005, Ward accompanied Zelikow on all his trips to Iraq. At the end of the year, she learned that Chiarelli was about to rotate into Baghdad as the new corps commander. She'd never met him but wanted to be in the action, so she sought him out and sat for an interview in the lobby of the Ritz-Carlton hotel in Pentagon City, after which he asked her to be his political adviser.

They both headed to Baghdad at the start of 2006 with a sense of optimism. The Iraqi parliamentary elections had taken place in December, just as Chiarelli and Ward were preparing for deployment, and the hope—

shared by most of those in command and high office—was that a competent, legitimate Iraqi government would set the stage for stability.

By late summer, Ward was at least as dispirited as Chiarelli and, if anything, more cynical about the war's prospects. What Chiarelli recognized, at least initially, as a serious problem that had to be confronted, Ward saw as a fundamental rift that called into question the rationale for continuing the fight.

She came to this realization while reading a long-out-of-print RAND Corporation monograph on the Vietnam War called *Bureaucracy Does Its Thing,* written in 1972 by Robert Komer, the ex-CIA officer and Johnson-era Pentagon official—known as "Blowtorch Bob"—who'd run the CORDS program, the most intensive but still brief and halfhearted effort to fight the Viet Cong through counterinsurgency techniques. Komer's paper criticized US policy on the same grounds that David Petraeus, Andrew Krepinevich, and John Nagl would later cover in their PhD dissertations: that the Army was trying to fight an insurgency war with conventional methods and was institutionally incapable of doing otherwise. But Komer offered two other reasons for what he saw as an impending American defeat: first, the South Vietnamese government and military were simply "inadequate to the task"; second, the United States hadn't used its power—its half million troops and tens of billions of dollars in aid—as "leverage" to make the local leaders institute reforms and deal more effectively with the threat they faced. This may have been "the most important single reason why the US achieved so little for so long in Vietnam," Komer wrote. "We became their prisoners, rather than they ours."

Komer's insight about Saigon circa 1970 resonated with Ward's own thinking about Baghdad in 2006. To win an insurgency war, the United States and the Iraqi officials it was protecting had to *want* the same basic things. If they didn't, and if the United States lacked the ability or will to make those officials change, the war was probably hopeless from the outset.

This became the core theme of Ward's briefing, titled "Analysis of Iraqi and Coalition End States": that the US-led coalition and Iraq's major political factions—very much including the Maliki government—had "considerably different," often incompatible, visions of what Iraq should look like after the war was over.

In one of her PowerPoint charts, Ward listed the various "lines of operation" found in most briefings about counterinsurgency or American strategy in Iraq—security, governance, economic development, and so forth—and then noted that the American and Iraqi views diverged drastically on every line. The coalition envisioned, in the words of its own official policy statement on the matter, an "Iraq at peace with its neighbors and an ally in the War on Terror," a "representative government that respects the human rights of all Iraqis," and a security force sufficiently strong "to maintain domestic order and to deny Iraq as a safe haven for terrorism." By contrast, the Iraqi government, judging from its own behavior, was an instrument of sectarian warfare; its security forces were dominated by Shia militias, which persistently restrained US forces from going after known Shia terrorists; and its economic ministries systematically withheld services from Sunni citizens while lavishing Western aid on programs that benefitted only Shiites.

"The result," Ward wrote on one slide, "is a real and growing tension between the Coalition and its nominal 'partner'—we are pulling in different directions."

Nor were the ambitions of Iraq's rival factions for power any closer to the coalition's vision of a new Iraq. The Kurds were explicitly demanding autonomy. The Sunni Arabs, excluded from power, were hell-bent on fragmenting the country so that they could control at least a chunk of it—even to the point of allying with foreign jihadists, if just to protect themselves from, and retaliate against, Shia terror.

Ward concluded that American and coalition leaders either had to use their strength as leverage to get Maliki to change his ways—or come up with far less ambitious goals, more compatible with the Iraqis' own visions of end-states. One such option might be to split Iraq into three ethnically distinct regions (Kurds in the north, Shiites in the south, Sunnis in the west), with a much-weakened central government in Baghdad. But this idea wasn't practical. First, Maliki would resist any step that weakened his authority. Second, the Bush administration had already dismissed a proposal by Democratic senator Joseph Biden to turn Iraq into a federal state with three semiautonomous regions. And third—the only fact pertinent to Chiarelli's domain—Casey was adamantly opposed to putting any pressure on Maliki.

In short, to invoke a word from the unmentionable Vietnam era, Iraq was looking more and more like a *quagmire.*

Chiarelli thought Ward's briefing was brilliant. It crisply summed up the deteriorating trends that they'd both observed in recent months, and it framed those trends in a coherent strategic picture. The whole idea of counterinsurgency—the whole rationale for this phase of the war—was to help make the Iraqi government more effective. But if the Iraqi government's aims were different from—even hostile to—America's aims, what was the point of going on? The more we strengthened Maliki's government, the more we might be damaging America's own interests.

Speaking to the Baker-Hamilton commissioners, Chiarelli didn't spell out the dilemma so bleakly. But as far as he did take his analysis—the promises of the SWET strategy and the need to leverage American power into making Maliki change course—he stated his case with drive and passion. He'd been over this argument more times than he could count; he didn't need notes or visual aids. He believed as deeply as ever in his conclusions, despite, or in some ways because of, the frustrations he'd experienced on the job. And Chiarelli, the popular West Point lecturer of yore, was *on* that day; he could feel this audience leaning in to his every word.

As unimpressed as the panelists had been with Casey's rote PowerPoint slide show three days earlier, they were deeply impressed with his deputy's spirited panoramic analysis. Some of them approached him afterward with warm thanks and additional questions. Bill Perry and Bob Gates were particularly lavish in their praise. They'd both heard briefings from many generals in their day, but this one was extraordinary. They hadn't met Chiarelli before, had never heard of him; but they left the room agreeing that he might well wind up as chairman of the Joint Chiefs of Staff someday.

That prediction wouldn't come true. Nor would Chiarelli's own, somewhat less lofty ambitions to succeed Casey as commander of US forces when his term ran out at the end of the year. Iraq was seen as a failure, properly so, and by dint of his position and his principled refusal to break with his boss, Chiarelli would be saddled with a share of the blame.

Few in the room could have imagined that a mere two months later, Gates would be asked by President Bush to replace Donald Rumsfeld as secretary of defense. Knowing that his main task was to "fix" Iraq, Gates would need to hire as his military assistant a general with deep knowledge of the war. And so, thinking back on that final day in the Green Zone, he would call in Pete Chiarelli for an interview and, afterward, offer him the job.

It would be through Chiarelli that the whole panoply of ideas associated with COIN and the West Point Sosh mafia flowed into the Pentagon at a pivotal moment and at the highest level.

General David Petraeus with his troops in Helmand Province, Afghanistan.

2

As a young paratrooper in the late 1970s, Petraeus read *Counterinsurgency Warfare* by the retired French officer **David Galula**, who argued that this sort of war required not just killing the enemy but reforming the government and building up the economy.

3

Colonel George "Abe" Lincoln started a Social Science Department at West Point just after World War II, realizing that the Army needed officers educated in politics and economics, not just war. This style of thinking would warm its adherents to Galula's ideas. Lincoln also created a network of "Sosh" graduates, nicknamed "the Lincoln Brigade," which persisted in Army circles for decades.

4

Petraeus served as **General John Galvin**'s aide-de-camp in the early '80s, then as his assistant in Central America a few years later, his first exposure to insurgency wars.

5

Lieutenant Colonel John Nagl, one of Petraeus's West Point protégés, wrote a book comparing the British army's victory in Malaya with America's defeat in Vietnam, then, as a high-level assistant in the Pentagon, lobbied his superiors to adopt a COIN strategy in Iraq.

6

David Kilcullen, an Australian officer-scholar on loan to the Pentagon, and later an assistant to Petraeus in Iraq, was pushing for a similar shift. He and Nagl formed a tight friendship and an alliance for the cause—though Kilcullen later grew disillusioned.

7

Eliot Cohen, a professor and Pentagon consultant, gathered thirty counterinsurgency specialists to discuss a better way to fight in Iraq. This marked the beginning of an insiders' community that pressed for a change in war policy—and in the Army's culture.

8

Kalev Sepp, an ex–West Point professor, wrote an article for *Military Review* on COIN "best practices," which widely influenced the inner circle of the strategy's advocates.

9

Sepp and **Colonel Bill Hix** *(right)*, a West Point Sosh "mafia" grad, briefly convinced the US commander in Iraq, **General George Casey** *(left)*, to adopt COIN, but later Casey changed his mind and pushed for a speedy troop withdrawal.

10

Casey's deputy, **General Pete Chiarelli**, a former Sosh professor, pushed for COIN but was overridden by Casey. **Celeste Ward**, Chiarelli's political adviser, wrote a paper concluding that the war was hopeless as long as the US and Iraqi governments' interests diverged.

11

Petraeus, back from a triumphant campaign in Mosul, Iraq, held a conference to vet a new Army field manual on COIN. His cosponsor, **Sarah Sewall**, director of Harvard University's Center for Human Rights Policy, helped legitimize the COIN concept among Iraq war critics.

12

Conrad Crane (*right*), a classmate of Petraeus's at West Point, led the COIN conference and helped write the manual, along with Nagl, Kilcullen, Sepp, Cohen, and others.

13

Shortly before Petraeus returned to Iraq, **Frederick Kagan**, a former West Point history professor now at the neocon American Enterprise Institute, wrote a paper arguing for a troop "surge" and a shift to a COIN strategy in Iraq.

14

Kagan received behind-the-scenes assistance from his former office mate at West Point, **Colonel H. R. McMaster,** who'd led a successful COIN campaign in Tal Afar, Iraq. McMaster's promotion to general, after being twice blocked by traditional officers, was seen as a sign of change within the Army.

15

General Jack Keane, a pioneer in the Army's COIN training centers, circulated Kagan's "surge" study among senior officials and urged President Bush personally to replace George Casey with Petraeus.

16

Keane also slipped the briefing to **General Ray Odierno**, a former door-bashing commander who'd been converted to COIN. **Emma Sky** (*far left*), a British Arabist, was a crucial adviser to Odierno, helping him understand Iraqi militants' motives.

17

While at Leavenworth, Petraeus cultivated a back channel to **Meghan O'Sullivan**, Bush's special assistant on Iraq.

Colonel Sean MacFarland, a former Sosh cadet who'd succeeded McMaster at Tal Afar, crafted a COIN campaign in western Iraq's Anbar Province, along with the charismatic **Sheikh Abdul Sattar**, convincing Sunni militants to ally with US forces against jihadists.

18

19

General Stanley McChrystal, a Sosh graduate, tried to apply the COIN formula in Afghanistan with the encouragement of **Defense Secretary Robert Gates** (who switched from skeptic to supporter), but the formula didn't fit.

20

Petraeus replaced McChrystal after a press scandal, assuring President Obama that he could make decisive progress within a year, but Afghanistan stumped him too. He ended his tenure exhausted, his COIN strategy discarded, and his career ambition to become Joint Chiefs chairman out of reach. Obama named him CIA director, a job he came to cherish, until a personal scandal—shocking but, in a sense, not so surprising—forced him to resign.

15.

The Field Manual

Back at Fort Leavenworth, David Petraeus was running into obstacles while pushing his COIN manual through the Army bureaucracy.

The document had sparked dozens of comments and criticisms from the standard set of reviewers in the Army's myriad agencies, institutes, and commands. Most were routine, dealing with matters of style and definitions of terms. Looking over the few substantive objections, Petraeus accommodated some, changing or deleting a sentence or two, and rebutted or simply ignored the others, as he was entitled to do; routine comments were not binding.

But the officers at the Army Intelligence Center, in Fort Huachuca, Arizona, filed a more ominous protest. "After a thorough review of the draft," the center's deputy commandant wrote in a memo on June 14, "we must nonconcur due to the number of critical and major issues."

Petraeus couldn't finesse this one. For a branch of the Army to "nonconcur" with the draft of a field manual was tantamount to a veto: its publication would be canceled; its acceptance in the annals of official doctrine would be denied. Petraeus's whole project, the fruition of his decades-long dream, would be derailed.

The Intelligence Center's problem with the manual—with the whole concept of counterinsurgency—boiled down to turf. Intelligence lay at the heart of a COIN campaign: the troops live among the people, keep them secure, and build their trust—as a result of which the people supply the troops with intelligence, which is then exploited to kill or capture insurgents, which makes the people still more secure, and so the cycle continues. The manual's chapter on "Intelligence in Counterinsurgency," the longest of its eight chapters, stated: "All Soldiers and Marines are intelligence collectors . . . Operations will be conducted for the purpose of gathering intelligence . . . Soldiers and Marines must coordinate intelligence collection and analysis with foreign militaries, foreign intelligence services, and many different US intelligence organizations."

This was what drove the officers at the Army Intelligence Center around the bend. In their eyes, and according to their own doctrine, regular soldiers had no business collecting intelligence, especially "human intelligence," or HUMINT, intelligence gathered from direct contact with ordinary people on foreign soil. "Due to legal considerations," the center's memo insisted, "only counterintelligence personnel operate a HUMINT network and develop HUMINT sources." And the notion that soldiers and marines should "coordinate intelligence collection and analysis," or had the talent or training to do so, struck them as plainly outrageous.

The manual's chapter also stressed the need for troops to understand the cultural roots of an insurgency, such as tribes, clans, or ethnic groups. The section on cultural awareness had been written by Montgomery "Mitzy" McFate, an anthropologist who'd become fascinated with military issues during her college years at Yale University and the University of California at Berkeley, partly, she would say, as a "way of rebelling against my hippie parents" (she was raised in California, in the late sixties and early seventies, on a converted barge with no plumbing) and partly as an intellectual realization—sparked by a course she took on the language of terrorist groups—that a society's style of warfare revealed at least as much about its culture as did, say, its sexual practices or table manners. McFate had written one of the first articles for the revivified *Military Review,* outlining how to find the makers of Iraqi roadside bombs by analyzing their social networks. As a result of that article, she was hired by the Army to help create "human terrain teams," which would track down Iraqi insurgents more broadly through these same methods.

In its memo objecting to the COIN field manual, the Army Intelligence Center stated that "doctrinally there is no such thing" as cultural or social network analysis.

For the next several weeks, memos flew back and forth between the analysts at Leavenworth and Huachuca. Petraeus and his team offered compromises in the language. For instance, the line "All Soldiers and Marines are intelligence collectors" was changed to describe them as "potential intelligence collectors." The sentence that envisioned regular troops coordinating intelligence was changed to stress that "commanders and staffs" would do the coordinating.

Still, the Intelligence Center's commanders were not appeased.

They had another problem besides turf: they didn't like Petraeus. Specifically, they didn't like the way he'd put together this field manual, how he'd staffed the project with his own people, circumventing normal procedures. The initial four-page memo from Fort Huachuca jabbed at the point in its final paragraph. "Our comments do not reflect on the first-rate job that CADD routinely does," it stated, referring to the Combined Arms Doctrine Directorate, the division at Fort Leavenworth that usually, and very quietly, wrote field manuals. "We realize [this] manual was drafted outside CADD's direct control. Because of this, USAIC [United States Army Intelligence Center] recommends the COIN FM be staffed again so the combined arms doctrine is captured correctly."

Fortunately for Petraeus, General Peter Schoomaker, the Army chief of staff, was in his corner for this fight. Schoomaker was in a hurry to get this manual out there; starting all over was, to say the least, not an option. In mid-August, Schoomaker was out at Leavenworth on one of his periodic trips. Conrad Crane happened to be there, tweaking the revisions. Schoomaker told him and Petraeus that he wanted all disputes settled as soon as possible; dealing with these objections had pushed back the schedule too far already. There *was* an insurgency war going on; it would be nice for the Army to have an official book on how to fight it.

At the same time, Schoomaker didn't want to step into the fray directly. He made it clear that Petraeus would have to resolve the conflict. Petraeus didn't want to antagonize the commanders at Huachuca any more than necessary; he still needed their concurrence for the manual to go forward. Still, he did have a mandate from the chief.

So while Crane sat in his office, Petraeus phoned Major General Barbara Fast, the commandant at Huachuca, and did what three-star generals sometimes do to two-star generals after exhausting all other options: he pulled rank. In a calmly chilling tone, Petraeus told Fast to get on board. This manual *had* to come out right away; the chapter on intelligence was key; the principles in that chapter were central to the whole concept of counterinsurgency; he was willing to set up a meeting to resolve the remaining differences, but they were going to be decided in *his* favor, one way or the other, that's just the way it was, and she needed to come to grips with this fact *now*.

After the call, Petraeus told Crane to arrange a meeting. It took place on Tuesday, September 13, in an office at the Institute for Defense Analyses, a largely Pentagon-funded think tank in Alexandria, Virginia, where Montgomery McFate was working at the time. Attending were Crane, McFate, two officials from the Army Intelligence Center, a colonel from the Joint Staff's intelligence branch, and the chapter's principal author, Kyle Teamey, John Nagl's former intel officer in Iraq who'd been recruited to help him write the outline of a COIN field manual at the Front Page restaurant in Dupont Circle ten months earlier.

By the end of the day, the dispute was settled. The Intelligence Center dropped its protest. Crane and Teamey made a few minor tweaks to the manual's text. But their main points remained intact.

One month later, Petraeus ran into another obstacle: Ralph Peters. A retired Army lieutenant colonel, Peters was the author of several potboiler novels, most of them about a tenacious Army officer who saves the day through acts of bravery that those around him are too corrupt or craven to muster. He was also an on-air commentator for Fox News and a columnist for the *New York Post*. In June an interim draft of the COIN field manual had been leaked to the press and was subsequently reprinted in its entirety on several websites. Petraeus was a bit annoyed—he hadn't yet given the document his final edit—but he had circulated the draft for review to every Army command (it was this draft that upset the Army Intelligence Center), so he shouldn't have been surprised that one of its hundreds (or, who knows, maybe thousands) of recipients passed it on to a reporter.

The draft sparked dozens of articles, editorials, columns, and blogs, some favorable, some not. But none was more vicious than Peters's column in the October 18 edition of the *New York Post,* titled "Politically Correct War."

Peters lambasted the field manual's authors as "dishonest and cowardly" officers of an overly academic bent who "seek to evade war's brute reality" and who "believe that being nice is more important than victory." He particularly took after the section on COIN's "paradoxes" ("Sometimes doing nothing is the best reaction," "The best weapons do not shoot," "The more force used, the less effective it is," and so forth), calling them "just nutty" and "a mush of pop-zen mantras," adding, "Unfortunately, our enemies won't sign up for a replay of the Summer of Love in San Francisco." Nor, he wrote, can we afford to "treat hardcore terrorists like Halloween pranksters on midterm break from prep school."

In a less seething tone, he complained that the manual "ignores religious belief as a motivation" for insurgents. In this sense, he argued, the communists in Malaya, whom the manual cited as a pertinent historical model, were very different from the jihadists in Iraq. "It would be a terrific manual," he wrote, "if we returned to Vietnam circa 1963, but its recommendations are profoundly misguided when it comes to fighting terrorists intoxicated with religious visions and the smell of blood."

The column set off alarm bells all over the COIN community. Peters wasn't a typical right-wing columnist. He had friends and connections high up in the military. His last assignment in the Army, just eight years earlier, had been as an aide to the deputy chief of staff for intelligence in the Pentagon. He still did consulting work for the Army and the Marines. It could reasonably be inferred that his column reflected the views of some of those contacts, senior officers who could disrupt the process of turning the field manual's doctrine into actual policy.

Short of that, the column might arouse opposition on Capitol Hill, where Peters had several fans among the hawks on the armed services committees. Not that they had the power to tamper with doctrine, but they could stir discord, which might crack the veneer of consensus that Petraeus had worked so hard to lay and polish.

Petraeus's initial response to Peters's column was bewilderment. When an old friend emailed to ask what he thought of it, Petraeus called it "a bit inexplicable." After all, he went on, "the word 'kill' is mentioned an average of once per page," and "there is a description up front of the religious extremists." Most of the manual's authors weren't merely PhDs; they'd also "served one or more years in Iraq or Afghanistan—where they did plenty of killing/capturing, in addition to trying to win the occasional heart and mind." What was Peters proposing that they do to counter the insurgents? Did he "think we can kill 'em all"? Petraeus knew that wasn't possible.

Still, Petraeus also knew that Peters was touching on a legitimate point, which the manual, in its current form, didn't address. Bing West had made the same point at the COIN conference at Leavenworth back in February. West, too, was flamboyant in his tone—less so than Peters, but enough to let many of the participants wave him off. Even then, Petraeus had conceded that the COIN paradoxes probably overstated matters. Now, the more he read through them, the more he thought they certainly did. Sometimes the best weapons *did* shoot, even in a COIN war, and the manual needed to say so more clearly.

Conrad Crane, who had written the paradoxes, was incensed by Peters's column and sent Petraeus an email urging him "to avoid overreacting to his diatribe," adding, "We must stick to our guns (or other weapons of COIN)."

Petraeus tried to tamper Crane's war fever, replying, "If you can get past the cheap shots/rhetoric, there is some merit to Ralph's critique."

Over the next week, Petraeus rewrote chapter 1, which contained most of the excesses that bothered Peters. "Not making drastic changes, rest assured," Petraeus wrote to Crane on November 3, "but am adding a bit of nuance here and there and also explicit recognition that, yes, it is necessary to kill bad guys! And that, yes, some hearts/minds can't be won."

Crane conceded the need for the revisions, allowing that the first chapter "is the only one some people will read . . . We talk plenty about targeting and killing later in the manual, but most people won't read that far back."

Petraeus replied, "You are exactly right about Chapter 1, Con, and that is, in truth, the issue with most folks. You're dead-on that many will not read beyond it. And Ralph is in that category, by his own admission . . . Anyway, thanks for not nuk'ing me for fooling with your baby! Hope to make it even prettier!"

In his rewrite, Petraeus added qualifiers to almost all the paradoxes. "The more force used, the less effective it is" became "Sometimes, the more force is used, the less effective it is." "The best weapons for COIN do not shoot" became "Some of the best weapons for counterinsurgents do not shoot." "Most of the important decisions are not made by generals" became "Many important decisions are not made by generals." (Even in the original draft, Crane was prudent enough to note that only "sometimes" is "doing nothing" the "best reaction.")

There was one more issue that Peters had raised, and Petraeus saw it as still more disturbing: whether or not insurgents fueled by religious extremism were fundamentally different from those whose motives were economic or ideological—that is, whether the lessons from past COIN campaigns, such as in Malaya or the Philippines, were relevant to the war in Iraq. Whatever the answer, the manual had to confront the question.

Petraeus had one of his aides pose the question to Montgomery McFate. She responded by writing six new paragraphs analyzing religious extremism as another form of ideology that motivated insurgents and lured a community to their cause—the difference being that these particular "true believers" embraced a "culture of martyrdom" and were willing "to use whatever means necessary to achieve their unlimited goals." As a result, "friendly actions intended to create good will among the populace are unlikely to affect religious extremists." In these circumstances, she wrote, it would take a far more focused effort to separate mere zealots from terrorists—reconcilable Muslims from irreconcilable jihadists—and, in the end, there might be more of the latter to kill.

Petraeus edited McFate's remarks and inserted them into key spots in chapter 1. He also wrote some new sentences of his own to amplify the point. In one of the manual's first paragraphs, which dealt with the need "to eliminate as many causes of the insurgency as feasible," Petraeus added, "This can include eliminating those extremists whose beliefs prevent them from ever reconciling with the government."

A few pages later, in a paragraph citing the different types of insurgents and how to co-opt them, he inserted, "True extremists are unlikely to be reconciled to any other outcome than the one they seek; therefore, they must be killed or captured."

Caveats of this sort had appeared in the leaked draft of the manual, but most of them were buried in later chapters. Petraeus saw that they needed to be placed up front, to make sure that officers—many of whom, as he said to Crane, "will not read beyond" the first chapter—didn't get the wrong idea about this kind of war. It *was* very different from traditional war. It demanded a new way of thinking. It required learning about subjects that had little or nothing to do with traditional warfare. It was about protecting the local people, undermining the insurgency's appeal, and forcing or persuading as many insurgents as possible to reconcile with the government. But some of these insurgents—maybe a lot of them—were irreconcilable; sometimes you still had to kill bad guys.

• • •

There was one more bit of business before Petraeus could turn the page on the Peters kerfuffle: a face-to-face meeting with Peters himself.

Not long after the *Post* column appeared, Petraeus had an assistant invite Peters to Leavenworth to discuss over lunch the issues he'd raised. This was one of Petraeus's specialties, bringing critics and foes into the tent, swaying them over to his side; this was another piece of information operations, a basic tool in counterinsurgencies—and insurgencies. The meeting was scheduled for Tuesday, November 21.

As it happened, Petraeus was called away that day. To take his place, he called John Nagl, who was now commanding a battalion at Fort Riley, Kansas, a two-and-a-half-hour drive away. Colonel Peter Mansoor, a former brigade commander in Iraq who'd been hired by Petraeus a few months earlier to run Leavenworth's new COIN Center, also attended as a sort of moderator. Brigadier General Mark O'Neill, the deputy commandant of the Command and General Staff College, formally hosted the affair but said little.

By this time, Petraeus had all but finished editing the field manual. Had he been at the lunch, he might have shown Peters his revisions, and Peters might have been mollified. But Nagl, who had little free time in his current job, didn't know much about these revisions. Mansoor was familiar with them—he'd been actively involved in the scrubbings—but, as the text wasn't final, he was reluctant to bring them up.

And so the lunch did not go well.

The atmosphere was icy from the start, and mutually so. Nagl viewed Peters as a bloodthirsty yahoo; Peters viewed Nagl as an overeducated priss. Peters recited his main points: that the purpose of a military is to kill the nation's enemies; that history shows this is particularly so when dealing with an insurgency fueled by religious extremism; and that the field manual's failure to mention religion as the driving force of Iraq's insurgency can be the result only of political correctness.

Nagl argued back on every charge, his main point being that in a war of insurgency, the hard thing isn't killing enemies, it's *finding* them, and for that you need to win over the people, not just shoot everybody in sight.

Starting to answer one of Peters's points, Nagl said, "Speaking as a social scientist—"

Peters interrupted: "You're not a social scientist. You're a soldier."

Nagl, a bit puzzled, replied, "Well, I'm a social scientist *and* a soldier."

"No!" Peters thundered. "You can't be both. Which is it?"

As the discussion dragged on, Nagl's aggravation deepened. Peters had never fought in battle; he'd spent most of his Army career as an intelligence analyst—which was fine—but Nagl *had* fought, day after day for a year in Iraq, and *had* killed a fair number of insurgents. Yet Peters kept lecturing *him* on the need to *kill the enemy.*

Finally, as if to prove his street cred, Nagl told him about one extremely tense day in Anbar Province, when he and his men killed a particularly nasty insurgent, tied the corpse to the front of a tank, drove it around town for everyone to see, then phoned the dead man's mother to come pick up the body.

Peters asked, "Why isn't *that* in the field manual?"

Nagl sighed. Peters flared.

The meal ended as coldly as it had started. Neither party had expected to be convinced by the other. In that sense, no one was disappointed.

The rest of that week, Petraeus made only a few additional changes to the manual. The biggest one involved resolving a dispute over how to describe the proper level of force to be used in a COIN campaign. Should the adjective be "measured," "minimal," "precise," or "discriminate"? Petraeus chose a different phrase altogether, headlining the section "Use the Appropriate Level of Force." His solution finessed the issue, but the alternative suggestions lacked clear meaning, and, besides, the manual's purpose was to lay out guiding principles; a major point in the book was that the commanders on the ground, down to lieutenants and in some cases corporals, had to use their judgment and take some initiative.

The field manual—formally titled *FM 3-24, Counterinsurgency*—was published on December 15, 2006, to much acclaim, some controversy, and a surprising level of curiosity. One-and-a-half-million people downloaded the online edition in its first month up on Fort Leavenworth's website.

Even Ralph Peters, who noticed Petraeus's changes, wrote a *New York Post* column on December 20, titled "Getting Counterinsurgency Right," hailing the manual as "the most-improved government publication of the decade" and "a genuinely useful tool" for American officers in Iraq. But six months later, he would change his mind again and revert to his original criticisms, even writing an article in the *American Interest* that slammed all officers with doctorate degrees as "theory-poisoned and indecisive" Hamlets who have learned only how to lose. (In the same issue, Petraeus—following the traditions set by the founder of West Point's Sosh department, Colonel Lincoln, and by his own mentor, General Galvin—wrote a rebuttal, extolling graduate school as a vital adjunct to a modern officer's education.)

But in his uncharacteristically positive *Post* column, Peters raised one serious question about insurgencies, a question that the manual had failed to ask, much less answer. It was, in effect, the same question that was haunting Pete Chiarelli and Celeste Ward, concerning not just Iraq's insurgents but also its leaders: *"What if they just don't want what we want?"*

Four changes would have to take place before the COIN field manual could have much effect on the war or on the American military broadly: a new commander in Iraq, a new secretary of defense, a decision by the president to send in more troops, and one clear instance where the manual's principles spawned great success on the battlefield.

In the month that the manual was published, the groundwork was laid for all four.

16.

The Surge

In mid-September David Petraeus received a phone call from General Peter Pace, chairman of the Joint Chiefs of Staff. A consensus was forming among senior officers in the Pentagon that a spurt of new thinking might help turn the war around. Pace was putting together a group of creative colonels to advise the generals on their options, and he wanted Petraeus's input on which colonels should be called.

Petraeus needed only a few seconds to respond. Here was a rare chance, still a few months before the COIN manual's publication, to install followers of the cause into the Pentagon's inner sanctum. He doubted that Pace would take anyone off the battlefield for this project, but there were two colonels—both acolytes of sorts to Petraeus and, in his eyes, brilliant—who now had some time on their hands.

One was Pete Mansoor, a West Point graduate with a concentration in history, the top-ranking cadet in the class of 1982. The other choice—an obvious one—was H. R. McMaster, the 3rd Armored Cavalry commander who had made counterinsurgency work in Tal Afar.

Mansoor could head off to Washington right away with Petraeus's blessings. But McMaster had just moved with his family to London to take a yearlong Army fellowship at the International Institute for Strategic Studies, doing research and writing on the future of US military policy in the Persian Gulf and South Asia. It was only his second day on the job when he got the call from one of General Pace's aides, asking him to come work at once on a top-secret project for the chairman.

McMaster wasn't sure what to do; the aide who called him couldn't discuss any details about the project on the phone. So McMaster called General John Abizaid, the head of US Central Command, who'd arranged for him to get the London fellowship. Abizaid had heard a little about the project. He told McMaster that it concerned the war in Iraq but that he should feel no obligation to take it; he could stay in London and do his long-term research if he preferred.

Two days later, McMaster left for Washington.

When he checked in at the Pentagon, he was taken to "the Tank," the Joint Chiefs' conference room on the building's second floor, where he found himself joined by fifteen other colonels from all the services. They were told that their work, even the very existence of the group (which came to be called the "council of colonels"), must be kept secret. Their mission was to give the chiefs unvarnished advice about the war in Iraq. They were to examine all scenarios and options—political, strategic, tactical, operational—and would be allowed access to everything they wanted, from the daily intelligence briefings to the most highly classified data on weapons systems. Once a week, sometimes twice, they would meet with the chiefs, not just to brief them on the work but to *discuss* it, without regard to the formalities of rank, as if they were peers.

McMaster had never heard of a setup like this, couldn't have conceived of such a thing. But he was heartened by the arrangement. Not only did it promise to be interesting, it might signal that the top generals finally recognized the urgency of their problems.

Petraeus had the same reaction when he first learned about the project. It seemed so unlike the JCS. Who prodded them into opening their vaults and opening themselves to self-criticism? He did have one suspicion. He called a retired four-star general, a longtime friend and mentor named Jack Keane.

"Jack," Petraeus asked, "was this council of colonels your idea?"

Keane laughed and admitted that it was.

The seeds of the council had been planted just a month and a half earlier, on the night of August 3, when Jack Keane settled into the easy chair in his McLean, Virginia, living room and watched C-Span's rebroadcast of the day's congressional hearings. Rumsfeld, Pace, and Abizaid were testifying on Iraq before the Senate Armed Services Committee, and they were claiming that all was well, that their present strategy of drawing down US forces and turning over security tasks to the Iraqis was yielding good results.

At one point in the hearing, Senator Hillary Clinton accused Rumsfeld of papering over a "failed policy" with "happy talk and rosy scenarios."

Rumsfeld, with his customary condescension, exclaimed, "My goodness!" He then acknowledged that there were problems and setbacks, but, he went on, "I don't know that there's any guidebook that tells you how to do it. There's no rule book, there's no history for this."

Keane sat up, appalled. First, he'd been to Iraq, and he'd spoken at great length with other officers, trusted friends, who were stationed there. He knew that things were not going well; that, in fact, a disaster was in the works. Second, what was Rumsfeld talking about? There *was* history; there *were* guidebooks that told you how to do this. Keane had read the books, by Galula, Kitson, Nagl, and others. He'd studied—he'd *lived*—the history.

Forty years earlier, Keane had fought as a paratrooper in Vietnam. When his tour ended in 1968, he was sent to Fort Benning, Georgia, to take an advance course for captains. One of his electives was a class on counterinsurgency, in which he read books and monographs on Algiers, Malaya, the Philippines, and the CORDS experiment in Vietnam. This was all new to him, but it rang true. He'd sensed that his commanders in Vietnam were fighting the wrong war. Now he understood the full context: that they'd been fighting against guerrillas with conventional tactics. The impression was deepened in 1975–76, when he was stationed at the Command and General Staff College and took a course on the lessons of Vietnam. The war had recently ended; all his classmates had fought in it, most of them as platoon or company commanders. The Army generals were abandoning those lessons, resuming their focus on the prospective big war in Europe and pretending that Vietnam never happened. But Keane paid attention to those lessons and tried to apply them to his soldiering, signing up for light infantry units and serving in the *moot*-wah wars in Somalia, Haiti, Bosnia, and Kosovo.

In 1987 Keane helped set up the JRTC, the Joint Readiness Training Center, in Fort Chaffee, Arkansas. (It would soon move to Fort Polk, Louisiana.) This was the "light" version of the National Training Center in California. Instead of armor officers fighting simulated tank battles on an open range in the desert, the JRTC pitted airborne infantry soldiers, Rangers, and Special Forces against guerrillas and insurgents in a mock village—to simulate the kind of battle where enemy fighters and innocent civilians mixed, almost indistinguishable from one another, and the goal was to kill or capture the former while protecting the latter.

Two decades later, after the insurgency in Iraq took off in undeniably full force, the National Training Center would follow suit, overhauling its test range, erecting mock villages, and hiring Iraqi exiles to play the parts of local citizens and terrorists. But in its beginnings, the JRTC was a novel, even controversial, enterprise. Generals came through Keane's center with their aides, often out of curiosity, to take a look and sit in on the after-action reviews.

General Gordon Sullivan, the Army chief of staff, attended one of the early reviews, in 1991. A training exercise had just taken place, and a captain with the 82nd Airborne Division was brought into a small conference room to discuss how he'd done. In the scenario, the captain and his men were to enter a village and find the gunman who'd killed one of their soldiers. The captain had decided to accomplish this mission by storming the village before daylight, guns cocked, pounding down doors, dragging the local men out of their houses, locking them in handcuffs, and interrogating them harshly, all while their families watched in horror. Of course, he came up with nothing.

The after-action review's chairman was a British officer who'd fought in Northern Ireland. Trying to prod the captain into discovering for himself where he'd gone wrong, he asked if there might have been some alternative approach to finding the killer. The captain shrugged and said, "No, I don't think so."

At this point, the man who'd played the town's mayor asked if he could say something. He gently told the captain that a better way might have been to come to the village quietly the night before and to consult with him. He would have advised the captain to wait until later in the morning, after the kids had gone to school. He then would have personally asked the townspeople to leave their homes, just for a few minutes, so that the captain's men could search for weapons. But to come in so brusquely, to let children witness such horrifying treatment of their parents—this sort of thing alienates the townspeople, makes them sympathize with, maybe join, the insurgents.

The captain was flustered. "Lookit!" he said, pounding a nearby table. "My job is not to deal with this *people thing*! My job is to *kill the enemy*!"

General Sullivan, who'd risen through the ranks as an armor officer but was beginning to sense that the end of the Cold War might spawn a different kind of warfare, watched this exchange with rapt attention. He leaned over to Keane with a smile and whispered, "Jack, this is real powerful stuff!"

Twelve years later, Keane was stunned to see the same scenario played out for real in Iraq. He was the Army's vice chief of staff when the invasion got under way in March 2003. Rumsfeld had asked him to replace General Eric Shinseki, who was about to retire as chief of staff in June. But Keane turned down the offer: his wife had recently been diagnosed with Parkinson's disease; he wouldn't have time to care for her if he took such a demanding job. (He would retire from the Army in October.) Meanwhile, in the two months between Shinseki's departure and the confirmation of his eventual successor, General Pete Schoomaker, Keane stepped up as acting chief. One of the first things he did, in late June, was to go see, six weeks into the occupation, what was happening in Iraq.

His first stop was Mosul, where he was greeted by David Petraeus, commander of the 101st Airborne Division. The two men had known each other for more than a decade. Back in 1991, when Petraeus led a battalion of the 101st at Fort Campbell, Keane was the division's assistant commander. The day when Petraeus was accidentally shot during a live-fire training exercise, Keane was the one who rushed him to the hospital, keeping up a calm chatter on the way, arguably saving his life. Ever since, Keane had remained a close friend and, perhaps second only to General Galvin, a mentor.

Petraeus gave Keane the works: the PowerPoint briefing, followed by a tour of the market, city hall, the university, the police station, then drop-ins on the brigade commanders, some of them working with the people, others going after the enemy. Keane was impressed. This was what counterinsurgency was all about. Mosul gave him hope.

His next stop was Tikrit, where Ray Odierno was commanding the 4th Infantry Division, and the news here was depressing. They had met only a couple of years earlier in the Pentagon, when Keane was vice chief of staff and Odierno was a one-star general in charge of planning the Army's force structure. In the summer of 2001, when Rumsfeld announced that he was chopping off two of the Army's ten divisions, Keane had Odierno work up a briefing overnight, explaining how force requirements were calculated and why eight divisions weren't enough. Odierno delivered the briefing the next day to Rumsfeld's deputy, Paul Wolfowitz. After Odierno finished and left the room, Wolfowitz turned to Keane and asked, "Who was *that* guy?" It was the best briefing he'd ever heard from an Army general, though, granted, the competition wasn't fierce. Wolfowitz urged Rumsfeld not to cut two divisions. Rumsfeld acceded.

But toting troops on paper was different from commanding them in the field, and, watching these troops in action, Keane concluded sadly that Odierno didn't measure up. If Petraeus in Mosul was the textbook case of how to do counterinsurgency right, Odierno was the sidebar on how to do it wrong. His PowerPoint briefing boasted how many offensive operations he'd conducted each week, how many suspected bad guys he'd killed or captured. The operations themselves, which Keane briefly observed, were no different, focusing almost exclusively on raiding, arresting, and killing—which, though clearly necessary, had little bearing on the outcome of this kind of war.

Keane thought back on the simulation at the Joint Readiness Training Center a dozen years earlier, when the captain had dragged men out of their houses and explained afterward that he had no patience for "this *people thing*," that his job was to "kill the enemy." Keane decided to pose the same Socratic questions that the British officer had that day at the after-action review. He asked Odierno to bring in one of his brigade commanders.

After the commander, a colonel, entered Odierno's office and saluted, Keane asked him what he'd been doing.

Cordoning off a village, sir, the colonel replied.

Why? Keane asked.

The enemy is in there, sir, he answered.

How do you know that? Keane asked.

Intelligence, sir.

Do you know where the insurgents are in the village?

No, sir.

How do you find them?

We go door to door, sir.

Do you knock?

No, sir. We go *through* the door.

What's on the other side?

Families, sir.

What do you do?

We take all the males outside and handcuff them, sir.

How young are these males?

As young as teenagers, sir.

What's the scene like, emotionally?

The colonel paused. Sir, it's terrible.

After the colonel left, Keane turned to Odierno. "What's going on here, Ray?" he asked. "We're breeding an insurgency here. We've got to see the people as part of the solution."

Later on, during the same trip, Keane met with Lieutenant General Ricardo Sanchez, the commander of all US forces. He'd rarely seen a general officer so in over his head. Keane spent the Fourth of July weekend with Jerry Bremer, the head of the Coalition Provisional Authority, and realized that *nobody,* civilian or military, was in charge at the top.

A week later, back in the Pentagon, Keane briefed the other chiefs on his trip. His first point was that the American troops were facing "a low-level insurgency."

Richard Myers, the Air Force general who was chairman of the Joint Chiefs of Staff, warned Keane that they all had to be careful about using that word: "insurgency."

Keane didn't know what to make of this. If we don't define the war accurately, he said, we're never going to be able to fight it effectively. We haven't been around this kind of thing for a long time. Keane admitted that his own service, the Army, was ill prepared for these wars, lacking any doctrine or training. Only one of the generals over there had any idea how to deal with the challenge (and, though he didn't say so, Keane knew that the exception—Petraeus—was hardly a favorite among the top brass).

Myers replied, "I'm just saying, the people on the third deck"—meaning Rumsfeld and his top aides, whose offices were on the Pentagon's third floor—"don't want to hear it."

End of conversation.

Keane was flustered. On his way to Iraq, he'd assumed that the war was pretty much over; that, at worst, it might be something like Bosnia on steroids. Now he realized that this fight might drag on for years, because the officers at the top lacked a strategy and seemed unaware that they needed one. He'd spent the bulk of his career preparing for this kind of war; now, just as the Army found itself fighting one, and in desperate need of leadership, he was about to leave the scene.

Like most retiring modern generals, Keane joined a few corporate boards and nabbed a lucrative job as a strategic planning executive on K Street, Washington's lobbyists row. But he ached to be a player in the war. Over the next three years, he kept in touch with former colleagues and subordinates who were in the fight; he made several trips to the war theater as a consultant of one sort or another; he saw the situation worsening and felt his frustrations mounting.

Finally on that night in August 2006, while watching the abysmal Senate hearings, he hit a boiling point. *Somebody* needed to fix American strategy. Clearly, the secretary of defense, the chairman of the Joint Chiefs of Staff, and the top commanders in the field weren't doing it, weren't even acknowledging the strategy was broken. There was no getting around it, in Jack Keane's mind: this was a job for Jack Keane.

The next day, Keane called Rumsfeld's office to ask for a meeting. It was an unusual thing for a retired general to do, but the two had gotten along when Keane was on active duty; Rumsfeld had asked him to be chief of staff, after all. The meeting took place on Tuesday, September 19, in the secretary's office. General Pace sat in, though he didn't speak, just took notes.

Keane came straight to the point: "We are edging toward strategic failure." The number of attacks was soaring, civilian casualties were skyrocketing, the Iraqi government couldn't keep the country from unraveling, and our own forces didn't have the right strategy.

Rumsfeld asked what was wrong with the strategy.

"It is not designed to defeat the insurgency," Keane replied. The only way to fight this war was through classic counterinsurgency strategy: protect the people, isolate them from the insurgents. He advised Rumsfeld to read the after-action report on Colonel H. R. McMaster's operations in Tal Afar and David Galula's book *Counterinsurgency Warfare: Theory and Practice.* Rumsfeld hated condescension when he was on the receiving end but had no leverage to fire back at a *retired* general. He shifted uncomfortably in his chair throughout the conversation.

Afterward, Pace asked Keane to come see him separately. When he did, two days later, Keane opened up the double barrels. It was widely known throughout the Pentagon that Pace, following Rumsfeld's lead, had taken his eye off Iraq, leaving the war to Casey and Abizaid while spending his own time on politically safer subjects. Keane now told him that he had to dive in, immerse himself in the issues, learn what was happening directly, and fire the commanders at fault.

Pace seemed unnerved. A few hours later, he postponed a scheduled trip to South America and started calling around to a few select generals, including Petraeus, asking for names of suitable advisers. The council of colonels held its first meeting in the Tank just six days later, on Wednesday, September 27.

When McMaster was asked to join the project, he was told it would last "weeks, not months," but it went on for three months. Workdays in the Tank began before dawn and ended after sundown, with several weekend afternoons consumed as well. McMaster felt weird on those Saturdays or Sundays, driving into a nearly empty Pentagon parking lot. There was a war going on—two wars, if you counted Afghanistan—and this was the Department of *Defense*. Why was almost nobody else working long hours?

The colonels covered a vast array of issues, not just the nitty-gritty of warfare (how many troops, and what sorts of tactics and strategies, were needed to clear and hold key cities) but also the political and strategic questions: the sectarian breakdown of Iraqi political parties, the alliance structure of the government, the preconditions of stability, the nature of US interests in the country and the region, what military objectives needed to be achieved to meet those interests. They had access to the Joint Staff's entire trove of classified files and software; they did computations, ran simulations, read reams of reports, and called in outside experts, including Eliot Cohen, who sat on the Defense Policy Board, and David Kilcullen, who was now working at the State Department. And they prepared lots of PowerPoint briefings.

At their first session with the chiefs, McMaster, Mansoor, and a Marine colonel named Tom Greenwood—who all agreed with one another on most matters—tested the limits of the top generals' tolerance for frankness. The first slide of their briefing read: "*We are losing because we are not winning. And we are running out of time.*"

This equation was straight out of Galula (the insurgent has only to sow disorder anywhere, while the counterinsurgent must maintain order everywhere), but it came as a shock to the chiefs. They seemed not to have considered this concept: that stalemate for the United States meant victory for the insurgents.

As the study progressed, almost all the colonels reached the same conclusions: that Iraq was devolving into civil war; that the Iraqi government was a faction in this war; and that, therefore, merely turning over authority to the government—as Generals Casey and Abizaid were planning to do—wouldn't break, and might escalate, the cycle of sectarian violence.

On what to do about the looming disaster, though, the colonels could form no consensus. McMaster emerged as the hardliner, adamant in arguing that the United States should mobilize as much military power as possible in order to fight and "win" the war. Mansoor was less confident about victory; he admitted that he'd never been an enthusiast of the war and didn't really know whether a good outcome was possible under any circumstances. Still, he did support a brief troop surge, to bring down the violence and restore a semblance of order, followed by a long-term counterinsurgency strategy pursued by a much smaller level of American troops. He saw this as the most that could be managed politically. Greenwood sided with Mansoor.

However, the other Army and Marine colonels, most of whom worked on the Joint Staff, were worried more about the war's effect on the military as an institution: the draining of resources, the dwindling number of recruits, and the diminishing rates of reenlistments. The Air Force and Navy colonels, who had less of a stake in the war to begin with, saw it as not only a sinkhole but also a lost cause worth no further sacrifice, and they urged getting out as quickly as possible.

The chiefs were torn. They were by nature inclined to accept the judgment of the commanders in the field. And while they were shocked by the colonels' critique of the war strategy, they also took solace at the same critics' failure to agree on a remedy. Some of the colonels urged doing more, others doing less—making it easy for the chiefs to convince themselves that a prudent compromise would be to do nothing, to stay the course.

But in the weeks ahead, McMaster's work on the council would have a profound impact, much more than even he could have imagined.

• • •

Roughly midway into McMaster's work with the council of colonels, a defense analyst named Frederick Kagan embarked on his own study to promote a surge of American troops in Iraq and the adoption of a counterinsurgency strategy.

Kagan and McMaster had known each other for almost ten years. In the mid-1990s they were both instructors—initially, they shared an office—in the History Department at West Point. Kagan was now thirty-six, eight years younger than McMaster, and he had never served in the armed forces. (West Point hired him after Congress passed a law requiring the academy to place a few civilians on its faculty.) But he came from a family of military historians. His father, Donald Kagan, a classics professor at Yale, was the author of a seminal four-volume history of the Peloponnesian War. His older brother, Robert, a prominent defense adviser in Republican circles, had written a bestselling book, *Of Paradise and Power,* about the growing rift between the United States and Western Europe regarding national-security matters. In the late 1990s, all three Kagans signed various petitions of the Project for the New American Century, the neoconservative group urging regime change by force in Iraq.

Fred Kagan had left West Point just a year earlier, in 2005, and was now ensconced at the American Enterprise Institute, Washington's most prominent neocon think tank, its roster including some of the Iraq War's most fervid supporters. Kagan was keen not only on the war but on counterinsurgency doctrine. For a few of his ten years at West Point, he taught the Revolutionary Warfare course. Now it would be through Kagan that AEI emerged as the nexus joining the neocon movement and COIN.

It was a logical convergence: the COIN revivalists saw the doctrine as a tool for fighting the small wars that were looming on the horizon; the neocons were eager to fight those wars as a way of asserting American power.

Kagan had been one of the outside critics invited to President Bush's war-strategy meeting at Camp David in June. Around the same time, he'd been one of the two dozen expert analysts invited to speak at a plenary session of the Iraq Study Group chaired by James Baker and Lee Hamilton. He'd come away from that session deeply worried. Congress had authorized the creation of the Baker-Hamilton Commission explicitly to find a way *out* of Iraq. Its ten members represented the cream of the Washington establishment. Their report was due in December, and it was likely to add a tone of gravitas to the growing calls for bringing the troops home.

To counter those calls, Kagan decided to form his own Iraq study group—which he called the Iraq Planning Group—with the idea of analyzing the war the same way that an Army commander's staff would: as a detailed problem of military strategy, tactics, and operations.

In early December, Kagan got in touch with his old West Point office mate H. R. McMaster and invited him to his apartment for dinner. McMaster couldn't talk directly about his work in the council of colonels, which Kagan vaguely knew about, but there was no prohibition against discussing his *thoughts* about the *issues* that the council happened to be covering; much of his thinking, after all, stemmed from his earlier work at Central Command, in Tal Afar—even back at West Point. So they talked, in a general way, about the conclusions he was reaching: that the Iraqis had neither the capacity nor the will to quell the violence on their own; that nothing could improve until the Iraqi population felt secure; that the way to make this happen was to adopt a counterinsurgency strategy, which involved, among other things, stationing American troops among the people instead of "commuting" them from large, heavily protected bases on the outskirts of the cities; and, finally, that such a shift would require more troops, not fewer. Kagan, from his own training and experience, was inclined to agree.

At one point during dinner, Kagan asked McMaster if he knew any recently retired Army officers who might be suitable for the project, trained staffers who had real experience in analyzing how many troops were needed to deal with a specific threat, how quickly the troops could be deployed, what they needed for support, that sort of thing.

McMaster knew exactly the right guy for the job: Colonel Joel Armstrong. He'd been McMaster's deputy commander at Tal Afar and had done much of the fine-tuned analysis that made the campaign a success. And he'd retired from the Army just a few months earlier.

The next day, Kagan sent Armstrong an email describing the project, noting that he saw Tal Afar as the model of what American forces should be doing all across Iraq and asking him to phone if he was interested in further discussion. Armstrong called back at once. Kagan offered him a contract. He took it.

Before hanging up, Kagan asked if he knew anyone else with similar skills. The job had to be professional, but it also had to be done quickly; an extra hand might be necessary. Armstrong thought at once of Dan Dwyer, a major who'd been McMaster's chief of planning in Tal Afar and, before that, an analyst in Baghdad. Dwyer was the one who had done the number-crunching, and he'd retired from the Army just a few days earlier. Kagan called Dwyer and hired him, too.

The work began right away. The Baker-Hamilton Commission was set to release its report on December 6. Kagan couldn't beat that deadline, but he hoped he could put out his alternative study very soon after. He scheduled a four-day conference to present and discuss the work, beginning on Friday, December 8—less than a week away. (Before then, Kagan, Armstrong, and Dwyer would have one more dinner with McMaster, at an Italian restaurant near Dupont Circle, to discuss how the study was going.)

Even before hiring his two new aides, Kagan and some of the staff at AEI had already gone through the vast array of open-source material—news stories, official reports, studies by private groups that assembled data on war casualties—to pinpoint the Iraqi neighborhoods with the most intense violence. They circled those areas on a large-scale map, focusing particularly on Baghdad and Anbar Province, the areas deemed most critical to the stability of Iraq overall. They then clicked on overhead images of those areas on the Google Earth website. Armstrong and Dwyer examined the images closely and calculated how many troops would be needed to secure—to clear and hold—each area.

After computing the requirements for all of these neighborhoods, running some simulations, and double-checking by altering a few assumptions and seeing if the answers came out roughly the same, they added up the numbers. It turned out that the areas could be secured with an additional five Army brigade combat teams and two Marine combat regiments (each regiment roughly equivalent in size to a brigade).

The next step was to figure out how quickly these seven extra units—about twenty-four thousand extra troops—could be mobilized to Iraq from wherever they currently were. This was Dwyer's specialty. He was one of the few people, in or out of the Army, who understood the workings of "the batting order": the sequence of which combat units were scheduled to move into Iraq, which were moving out, and which were on home leave or in training. There was a hitch: the Army's "force-generation model"—the mathematical formula that let planners plug in the numbers and find out the answers—was classified. Dwyer searched the internet, hoping to find an approximation of the real thing in the open literature. To his astonishment, he found the Army's actual, secret model on Wikipedia.

He downloaded the model, plugged in the numbers, and it turned out that five Army brigades and two Marine regiments were also the number of combat units that the military *could* put in Iraq; five plus two were all that the Army and Marines had left in reserve.

It was an unlikely coincidence that the number of troops required matched the number of troops available. When Petraeus learned of the results, he assumed that Kagan had rigged the model to make the two numbers identical, a common practice in military analysis. Kagan was a bit astonished, too; he had Armstrong and Dwyer redo the calculations, to make sure they were right. They were.

Kagan's team then laid out all the data and conclusions, replete with charts, tables, and bullet points, in fifty-five PowerPoint slides. The briefing made clear that the surge was a gamble. It would take the better part of a year to get all the extra troops in place. To sustain the surge, the standard twelve-month tour of duty would have to be extended to fifteen months for *all* American troops in Iraq, not just the newly deployed ones. Finally, because these troops would be living among the people, out in the open constantly, American combat casualties would rise, perhaps dramatically, at least for the first several months. But in the end, the group concluded, the surge, along with the shift in strategy, could make the crucial difference.

To help roll out the study and enhance its credibility, Kagan asked two retired generals to speak at the upcoming AEI conference and to lend their names to the group's roster.

One of them was David Barno, a member of the West Point Sosh network, class of 1976, and a former US commander in Afghanistan who, back in 2003–05, had put in motion a short-lived counterinsurgency strategy against the Taliban.

The other retired general was Jack Keane. Kagan hadn't known about Keane's personal campaign to change the military strategy in Iraq; the two had met only a couple of months earlier, after Keane called him to praise an article Kagan had written.

Kagan, Armstrong, and Dwyer delivered the full briefing to the two generals on the morning of Friday, December 8, just before the conference began. Both generals found it compelling. Keane saw it as precisely the sort of hard-core, detailed analysis that he needed to make his case to higher circles.

And the timing was serendipitous. Just the day before, Stephen Hadley, President Bush's national security adviser, had invited Keane to a meeting in the Oval Office. The president was coming around to the view that changes were needed in the war strategy, and some staffers on the National Security Council had put together a list of outside experts to discuss the options with him. The meeting was scheduled for the following Monday, December 11. As a further coincidence, Vice President Cheney had asked to see Keane later the same day; the two had known each other since the days when Cheney was secretary of defense for Bush's father. Keane asked Kagan if he could take a copy of the briefing slides with him and share them with the president and vice president. Kagan, of course, had no problem with that.

The White House meeting began around three thirty Monday afternoon. It had been put together by the same NSC staffers who'd organized the Camp David meeting with Bush, the war cabinet, and a few outside critics the previous June. The earlier meeting had had no effect; Bush used it as mere pretext to fly to Iraq without public notice. But the staffers had reason to believe this meeting would be different. Several crucial events had occurred since the summer: the midterm elections in November had turned over control of the House and the Senate to the Democrats; Bush's popularity was at an all-time low, mainly because of the war; he'd fired Rumsfeld right after the elections and seemed ready to make more changes still.

In the room were Bush, Cheney, Hadley, and several aides, including Karl Rove, Bush's top campaign adviser, who had started to take a more active role in policy matters. The outsiders this time around, besides Keane, were retired generals Barry McCaffrey and Wayne Downing, and two civilians: Stephen Biddle, a former professor at the Army War College, now with the Council on Foreign Relations, who had written an article calling for a new strategy; and—the one repeat from the Camp David session—Eliot Cohen.

Cohen had regretted not taking a firmer stance back in June, so this time he steeled himself and advised the president to fire some of his generals. He knew that Bush was disinclined to challenge the judgment of commanders, so Cohen rattled off a list of presidents and prime ministers in history—most notably Winston Churchill and Abraham Lincoln—who had done just that, with fruitful results.

When Bush asked who should replace General Casey as the commander in Iraq, Cohen had a ready answer: David Petraeus.

Some of the NSC advisers had mentioned Petraeus as a strong candidate for the job, especially Meghan O'Sullivan, Bush's top aide on Iraq, with whom Petraeus was still in regular contact. The president now went around the room, asking the other outsiders if they agreed with Cohen. They all nodded. Petraeus, they said, was the right man.

Keane launched into a very abbreviated version of his case for a counterinsurgency strategy and more troops. Cohen and Biddle, the civilians, agreed with him. McCaffrey and Downing, the other retired generals, did not, arguing that a surge probably wouldn't work and couldn't be sustained, in any event.

After the meeting, Keane followed Cheney down the hall into his office. He went through the fifty-five slides from Kagan's briefing. Cheney said he'd show them to the president.

One week later, on December 18, Robert Gates was sworn in as secretary of defense. The next day, he flew to Iraq. Among the aides flying with him was Eric Edelman, the undersecretary of defense for policy. For the previous year and a half, Edelman had been handing out copies of John Nagl's *Learning to Eat Soup with a Knife* to every Iraq policy hand he knew. He'd also been instrumental in pushing DoD Directive 3000.05—the policy statement that declared stability operations were "a core US military mission," to be given "priority comparable to combat operations"—through the Pentagon's top echelons.

From his White House contacts, Edelman knew that Jack Keane had given Cheney the slides from Fred Kagan's briefing and that Cheney had, in turn, shared at least their conclusions with Bush. Edelman knew Kagan. He'd been friends with his father. And as a Soviet-affairs specialist in the Pentagon during George H. W. Bush's presidency, he'd hired young Fred as an intern. Knowing that he was going to be on the plane with Gates, Edelman called Kagan and asked for a set of the same slides. Kagan sent them over. En route to Iraq, Edelman brought them over to the new secretary of defense and said, "The president has seen these. You should, too."

What none of these people knew—not Gates, Edelman, Casey, Abizaid, nor, for that matter, Kagan—was that Keane had also shared the slides with Ray Odierno.

It had been announced in the spring that Odierno would be returning to Iraq at the end of the year to replace Pete Chiarelli as deputy commander of US forces.

Odierno had come a long way in the two-and-a-half years since his first tour, when he was commander of the 4th Infantry Division and Keane criticized him (as others would later do) for running operations that inflamed the insurgency. He left Iraq in the summer of 2004, knowing that he'd made mistakes and determined to learn as much as he could about Iraq and counterinsurgency before going back. He spent the next year and a half as the JCS chairman's liaison to the State Department and accompanied Condi Rice, Phil Zelikow, and Eliot Cohen on their trips to the war theater, gaining a broader perspective than he'd managed either as a division commander or, years earlier, as a rising artillery officer. In May 2006 he was named commanding general of Army III Corps in Fort Hood, Texas, and spent the next seven months—before the multidivision corps was scheduled to rotate into Iraq—organizing seminars, conferring with experts (including Cohen and David Kilcullen), reading lots of books (including the draft of David Petraeus's COIN field manual), and taking the COIN-heavy Battle Command Training Program that Petraeus had created at Fort Leavenworth.

A crucial moment in this reeducation took place late that fall, when an old friend, General J. D. Thurman, came to Fort Hood for a visit. Thurman was on break from a tour in Iraq, where he was serving as Odierno's successor, commanding the 4th Infantry Division. Over cigars and brandy, they talked about the war's frustrations. By this time, many officers were at least somewhat versed in counterinsurgency theory, but they were ill equipped to apply it in practice. Thurman's troops had tried to "protect the population," and they'd swatted away the insurgents from an area with little problem. But then they'd turn over the piece of land to the Iraqi army, and within a month, the insurgents would return and resume full control.

Suddenly, in Odierno's mind, everything clicked into place. He remembered the memo he'd helped Zelikow write on the plane back to Washington from Baghdad in the fall of 2005, the memo that introduced the phrase "clear, hold, and build." Thurman was now telling him, essentially, that his troops could *clear* an area of insurgents but that the Iraqi soldiers couldn't *hold* it. Until this moment, Odierno had found much of the COIN reading material a bit abstract. Now it struck him as stunningly tangible. The problem in Iraq seemed obvious: the American commanders were turning over operations to the Iraqis too quickly. The solution seemed equally clear: we had to stay in place longer; we had to clear *and* hold.

Keane sent Odierno the data from the Kagan-Armstrong-Dwyer study at just the right moment. How to manage and sustain a clear-and-hold strategy (the *build* part, as in clear-hold-build, seemed at this point a long way off) would be the key task and biggest challenge of Odierno's new job. And from his own background in quantitative analysis, he knew that the only way to meet this challenge was somehow to get more troops.

Odierno did not know that Keane was sharing the same data with the White House or that Edelman had passed on the same information to the new defense secretary. So when Gates met with Odierno in Baghdad and asked if he could use some more troops, he quickly affirmed that he could. He didn't realize—nobody in the room realized—that his answer and the secretary's question had stemmed from the same analysis, the same source. Neither of them knew that Keane had been pushing the top officials on both sides of the water toward the same conclusion.

Casey was also in the room. He was still the commander and would remain so for another seven weeks. (His replacement hadn't yet been announced, but rumors were flying that it would be Petraeus.) Odierno had privately told some officials that he needed an additional five Army brigades and two Marine regiments—reflecting the data Keane had passed along. But Casey, while ceding somewhat to the new political realities, had told his new deputy before the meeting with Gates that he would agree to no more than two extra brigades—one in Baghdad and a Marine equivalent in Anbar Province. So Odierno, who'd been on the job for barely a week and was respectful of hierarchy (while knowing that the scene was about to change very soon), parroted his commander's reply.

Soon after this session, Gates met with Prime Minister Maliki to sell him on the idea of accepting two extra American brigades. After three hours of suasion, Maliki finally signed on.

On the plane ride home, Edelman and some of the other staffers, mainly from the NSC, wondered if they'd sold themselves short. Were two extra brigades just enough to fail? Should they have gone for the full seven, for everything they could muster? Gates said he wasn't opposed to the idea but that he would have a hard time convincing Maliki.

Meanwhile, back at Fort Leavenworth, Petraeus was following the whole chess game through his elaborate network of contacts in the national-security bureaucracy. He'd kept track of every move: the council of colonels, McMaster's influence on Kagan, Keane's pushing the Kagan study through the White House and to Odierno.

Now that Rumsfeld was gone, Casey on his way out, and Bush on the verge of pushing for a surge and a shift in strategy, some of the holdouts among the top brass were gearing up a case that the two extra brigades allowed by Casey were all that the Army *could* send; there weren't any more available. The campaign was beginning to take its toll. In a recent interagency meeting, Secretary of State Condoleezza Rice had opposed a surge because her counselor, Philip Zelikow, who might have favored the idea in principle, had been told by one of his Pentagon contacts that a surge was simply infeasible. Though Zelikow possessed enormous self-confidence, he would not have presumed to challenge an Army general on such an esoteric calculation.

Petraeus rallied his own resources at Leavenworth and elsewhere to identify the five brigades that could be mobilized over a six-month period to Iraq. Keane, who by this time was delving into the issue and its politics with the imprimatur of the president and vice president, finally prodded General Pace, the JCS chairman, to concede that the task was not physically impossible.

Bush scheduled a meeting of all his national-security advisers for December 28 at his ranch in Crawford, Texas, where he was spending the holidays. The question at this point, everyone realized, wasn't whether to send more troops but how many.

Petraeus heard from Meghan O'Sullivan, his main source in the White House, that Casey was holding firm on no more than two extra brigades, with the further condition that only one of those brigades should deploy directly to Iraq; the other one should stay in Kuwait as a backup, to be moved on to Baghdad or Anbar Province only if needed. Although he didn't say so, Petraeus had heard the same report from his contacts in the operations directorate of the Pentagon's Joint Staff.

O'Sullivan asked Petraeus what he thought of the idea. He replied that it would be a disaster. First, he said, two brigades weren't enough. Second, rolling them in one at a time would make the situation worse; every time he asked for an extra brigade, it would look like an admission of failure. Petraeus knew that he topped the extremely short list of candidates to replace Casey as commander. But, he told O'Sullivan, if the president approved Casey's idea—if, in fact, he decided on any sort of surge smaller than five brigades—he would turn down the offer, because he simply couldn't succeed with such skimpy resources.

He knew that O'Sullivan would pass this message on to Hadley, who would in turn convey it to Bush. It was an audacious ploy, a bit of a gamble. Would he really say no if the president asked him personally to take the job? Three-star generals weren't supposed to reject a request from their commander in chief. Certainly they didn't do so and retain hopes of earning a fourth star. Still, Petraeus wanted to clarify, dramatize, the stakes. And he was telling her the truth: he didn't think he could do his job under Casey's conditions.

Meanwhile, Keane was hearing from his contacts that Pace would be briefing Casey's proposal at Crawford as the Joint Chiefs' official position. He called John Hannah, Vice President Cheney's national security adviser, to give him a heads-up on what was going on and to make the same case against Casey's position that Petraeus had laid out to O'Sullivan. He threw Hannah one additional line of argument in case Pace went ahead with the briefing. He should tell Cheney to ask Pace whether those extra two brigades would constitute "a decisive force" for victory. The key word was "decisive": Pace would have no choice but to answer, "No."

Keane also circulated word that Odierno, with whom he was talking on the phone once or twice a week, would much prefer a larger surge force and that he and his staff were developing a campaign plan to exploit the full five-plus-two brigades. If the deputy commander wanted a full surge, if the top candidate for new commander was threatening to turn down the job if he didn't get the full surge, and if even the nation's top general had to admit that something less than a full surge wouldn't be a "decisive force," Keane figured the game might be won.

On January 4, 2007, administration officials told reporters that President Bush would award David Petraeus a fourth star and name him as the new commander of US and coalition forces in Iraq. Six days later, in a nationally televised prime-time speech, Bush declared that the situation in Iraq was "unacceptable" and that "we need to change our strategy." To facilitate the change, he had decided to send "more than twenty thousand additional American troops" to the battlefield—five Army brigades to Baghdad and another four thousand marines to Anbar Province (a bit less than Kagan's two Marine regiments but deemed enough).

"In earlier operations," Bush said, "Iraqi and American forces cleared many neighborhoods of terrorists and insurgents, but when our forces moved on to other targets, the killers returned. This time we will have the force levels we need to *hold* the areas that have been *cleared*."

COIN was now the official policy.

17.
Awakenings

While the maneuverings over COIN and the surge played out on the home front, something was happening at the epicenter of violence in Iraq.

Seventy miles west of Baghdad, in Ramadi, the capital of Anbar Province, a city of nearly a half million people where all pretenses of order had long since been abandoned—where Sunni insurgents ran free and al Qaeda gunmen enjoyed unchecked control—suddenly, a mere six thousand American troops were turning the war around through the classic methods of counterinsurgency.

The reversal came to be called the Anbar Awakening, but it rose and rallied so abruptly and rapidly in the fall of 2006 that the most alert observers, back in the States and even elsewhere in Iraq, barely detected the rumbles.

And the Awakening's chief strategist, Colonel Sean MacFarland, a brigade commander with the 1st Armored Division, was equally oblivious to the political struggles going on back in Washington.

Yet the two breakthroughs—the rise of COIN doctrine in American policy circles and the success of COIN practice on Iraq's most dangerous landscape—arose from the same set of ideas, networks, and influences: the classic books, the West Point nexus, the lessons learned or relearned from the small wars of history, David Petraeus's experiment in Mosul three years earlier, and the mediation of all these factors through Colonel H. R. McMaster.

McMaster's role in this shift was indirect but pivotal: when his 3rd Armored Cavalry Regiment pulled out of Tal Afar the previous January, it was Sean MacFarland's brigade that moved in as the replacement.

During the transition, McMaster gave MacFarland a complete tour of the area, introduced him to the players, briefed him on every aspect of the clear-hold-build campaign that had pacified what was once an insurgent stronghold: the outreach to tribal leaders, the isolation of extremist Islamists from merely devout Muslims, the swift construction of American outposts in the heart of the city, and the generous outlay of cash to buy off fence-sitters and hire workers for reconstruction projects.

MacFarland grasped the concept quickly. Ten years earlier, he'd been one of the first squadron leaders to separate the warring sectarian militias in Bosnia as part of the effort to enforce the Dayton peace accords—a task that had forced him to figure out who was in charge, arrange power-sharing schemes with local factions, and help reconstitute a local government.

He'd also long been an avid reader of military history, first as a cadet at West Point (class of 1981, three years ahead of McMaster), then as one of the elite junior officers at Leavenworth's School of Advanced Military Studies, where he pored over T. E. Lawrence's insurgent memoir and every chronicle of the war in Vietnam—books that well disposed him to John Nagl's *Learning to Eat Soup with a Knife* when it was published a few years later.

In short, COIN was not at all a new concept to MacFarland.

During his command at Tal Afar, he built on the foundations that McMaster had laid, getting a feel for what this kind of warfare involved: the balancing act of offense, defense, and stability operations. In late May, when his brigade was transferred to Ramadi, he set out to apply the same approach.

Initially, it was unclear whether these principles would be relevant. When McMaster came to Tal Afar, there was at least a functioning city government; not so when MacFarland arrived in Ramadi. Tal Afar's population was a mix of Sunnis, Shiites, Turkomen, and Kurds, so McMaster could play them off one another; Ramadi consisted almost entirely of Sunnis, many of them well-armed Baathists still angry at Saddam's ouster and their own loss of power. Tal Afar was small and surrounded by desert, so McMaster could keep out foreign jihadists by building a wall around the town; Ramadi was much larger, it was surrounded by suburbs, and jihadists were already dug in and allied with the more militant tribal elders.

MacFarland's brigade was part of a multiservice force that included three other Army battalions (which, together, were roughly the size of another brigade) as well as a Marine regiment and a few teams of Navy SEALs. Still, they didn't add up to much. To amass a force with any potency, he would have to recruit local police and soldiers to join the Americans' side in a very hostile environment. In Tal Afar, MacFarland had benefited from a thick binder that McMaster left behind, listing the tribes, the key players, and all of his contacts. In Ramadi, he had nothing; he and the other units would have to start from scratch, one neighborhood at a time.

As a first step, the "clear" phase of clear-hold-build, MacFarland launched an offensive against some of the heaviest al Qaeda strongholds. Once he secured those areas, he set up combat outposts, like those McMaster had set up in Tal Afar: small bases inside the neighborhood, where he and his troops would live, patrol, and protect the population from any returning jihadists. From there, he established contact with tribal leaders and swayed them to help screen and recruit a police force, whose members he armed and trained. MacFarland also started reconstruction projects right away, in some cases while the fighting was still raging, again using the tribal sheikhs as the legitimizing funnel to direct the spending. (In COIN, as Petraeus had said in Mosul, cash was a form of ammunition.)

In establishing these contacts, MacFarland was fortunate to have on his staff an outgoing former Special Forces soldier, Captain Travis Patriquin, who was conversant in Arabic. Patriquin served as interpreter, negotiated the payment schemes, set up the meetings with sheikhs, got to know their families, and earned their trust.

One thing Patriquin learned quickly was that the townspeople, even some of the most militant Baathists, were turning against al Qaeda; the jihadists, it seemed, had overstepped their welcome, robbing businesses, stealing away the daughters of prominent families, and assassinating the parents who refused to comply. A year earlier, some sheikhs and Sunni nationalists had formed a resistance group called the al Anbar People's Council; but, outnumbered and racked by internal disputes, they were crushed, many of the group's leaders brutally murdered. The survivors were primed to try again, but only if the Americans promised to stay for the fight till the finish.

MacFarland gave the guarantee, though he had no authority to do so. He was freelancing a fair bit of this whole campaign, as Petraeus had in Mosul and McMaster had in Tal Afar. General Casey paid a visit once to see how things were going and was clearly skeptical. Casey's larger campaign plan leaned toward pulling out, and here was MacFarland burrowing in. Casey also worried about the idea of a neighborhood watch program on its own terms. It was one thing to encourage reconciliation with Sunni tribes; but MacFarland was arming militiamen who had been killing American troops just a few months earlier and—who knows?—might resume killing them, this time with American-supplied weapons, a few months hence.

Casey's doubts were fueled by an August 16 report by Colonel Peter Devlin, the US military's intelligence chief for the province, declaring that the American forces were "no longer capable of militarily defeating the insurgency in al Anbar." The previous few months, he wrote, had seen "the near complete collapse of social order." Al Qaeda had emerged as "the dominant organization of influence" and was viewed by many local Sunnis as "their only hope for protection" against fears of "ethnic cleansing" by the Shia-dominated central government—fears that had some basis, as General Chiarelli was witnessing in the bloody streets of Baghdad around this time. Devlin concluded that "there is nothing" the US-led coalition could do to change this dynamic.

Yet this dynamic started to change less than a week later, on August 21, when al Qaeda fighters attacked a new police station with overwhelming force, and the police fought back. Hours later, the jihadists upped the stakes by murdering Abu Ali-Jassim, a particularly beloved sheikh who had encouraged his tribesmen to join the resistance, and then—in a blatant violation of Muslim law—dumping his body in a field to rot rather than bringing it home for a proper burial. The jihadists had gone too far, and several sheikhs, who until then had been reluctant to ally with "infidel occupiers," flipped to the Americans' side.

A new figure emerged in the backlash, Sheikh Abdul Sattar Abu Risha. Sattar was a shady character who had earned much of his wealth through smuggling. But one of MacFarland's battalion commanders, a jovial, cigar-chomping lieutenant colonel named Tony Deane, happened to run across Sattar, struck up a conversation, and came back to the base, telling MacFarland that this was a great guy—he loves America, loves George Bush, and wants to meet the commander. MacFarland went to meet him. It turned out that the jihadists had killed Sattar's father and two of his brothers; he wanted to sign up for the resistance.

In the aftermath of the August 21 attacks, Sattar became MacFarland's main agent in the Ramadi Street, the charismatic figure who persuaded other sheikhs not only to rise up against al Qaeda but to do so in open alliance with the Americans. On September 9 he organized a tribal council attended by MacFarland, his staff, and over fifty sheikhs. Sattar called it the Awakening Council. They approved a resolution to expel al Qaeda from all of Anbar Province, form a local government, and reestablish the rule of law.

With the legitimacy of these local leaders, the police force swelled from roughly one hundred officers to over four thousand. The number of neighborhood combat outposts, which were now manned jointly by American and Iraqi soldiers, expanded from four to twenty-four. By November, nearly every tribe, not just in Ramadi but also on the city's northern and western outskirts, declared support for the Awakening.

The American troops in Ramadi were technically under the purview of a Marine expeditionary force, whose commander, Major General Richard Zilmer, had given MacFarland remarkably free rein in his unconventional approaches. At the end of the year, Zilmer was replaced by another marine, Brigadier General John Allen, who, after getting briefed by MacFarland, endorsed the idea explicitly, built on the Awakening Council's momentum, and extended the operations, first to Ramadi's eastern outskirts, where the jihadists retained control, then ultimately across Anbar Province. Allen stepped up the pressure, calling in tank assaults and air strikes to clear al Qaeda's remaining strongholds. Then, emulating MacFarland, he set up neighborhood outposts to hold the areas, build up local government, and fund reconstruction projects—which, like MacFarland's, were administered through the sheikhs.

The fighting continued for several months. In early December, a roadside bomb killed Captain Patriquin; more than a dozen sheikhs attended his memorial service. Sheikh Sattar would be assassinated the following September. But by the end of 2006, the tide had clearly turned: violence was cut in half; the incidence of insurgent attacks, which had numbered fifty a day when Colonel Devlin wrote his gloomy intel report, plummeted to a couple of dozen and, by the following spring, to nearly zero. The city was crawling back to somewhat civilized life.

When General Ray Odierno took his predeployment tour of Iraq in early December, he paid a visit to Ramadi. He'd seen the city briefly three years earlier, when he commanded the 4th Infantry Division; now he could hardly believe the change. This was clearly the new model of what COIN could accomplish in Iraq.

David Petraeus traveled to Ramadi soon after assuming his post as top commander in early February 2007. He asked MacFarland if he'd read the COIN field manual. MacFarland replied that he hadn't. "That's all right, you don't have to," Petraeus said. "You've been *doing* it."

Odierno took over from Pete Chiarelli as deputy commander on December 14, 2006. But George Casey still held the reins, and his latest campaign plan, issued on December 5, bore no sign of retreat from his previous plan, no acknowledgment of the new developments either in Anbar or back in Washington. In fact, his plan, called the "Transition Bridging Strategy," ordered a "speed up" in the handoff to the Iraqis. Specifically, American troops were to "move outside all major cities" over the next three months and, after that, do little more than guard the borders and provide Iraqi troops with logistical support.

Odierno was in a bit of a bind. Casey was his boss, but only for another two months, and he knew from various contacts, especially Jack Keane, that his new boss was likely to be Petraeus. Not only was Petraeus certain to take a different direction; his very appointment would indicate that the president of the United States had decided to change course as well. So Odierno and his staff would have to write their own campaign plan, something that Petraeus could adopt, modify, and build upon the moment he arrived. The two couldn't communicate directly during this time, lest they be accused of subverting the chain of command. But they kept in touch indirectly—Odierno informing Petraeus of the plan's progress and Petraeus sending Odierno his feedback—through Jack Keane in his well-honed role as middleman.

Drawing up some sort of plan would not have been out of place for Odierno. His formal title, corps commander, meant that he was not only deputy to the force commander (Casey) but also in charge of day-to-day military operations. The force commander's campaign plan outlined the basic strategy and guidance; one of the corps commander's jobs was to turn that guidance into a detailed plan of action. The difference, in this case, was that Odierno, anticipating Petraeus's arrival, was also quietly outlining a new strategy.

The first thing Odierno did was to list the campaign's goals, the various obstacles to those goals, and some ways to surmount—to defeat, preempt, or co-opt—those obstacles. This was basic stuff, the sort of three-column outline that junior officers learned to do in strategy courses at the Command and General Staff College. Casey's strategy relied on a similar method. But Casey's premise was that the occupation had run its course; that there was little the American military could do, or should do, to improve Iraq's security; that, in fact, the mere presence of foreign troops was making things worse.

Odierno started with a different premise: that there was still one more chance to get the war right.

At the top of a yellow legal pad, Odierno jotted down the main problem: a "failing state." Below that heading, he wrote that a "large gap" was separating the Iraqi government from its people and that "malign actors" were exploiting this gap. The task was to figure out how US and coalition forces could step in and help fill the gap. He titled the memo "Closing the Gap."

In the first column, he listed the "needs and desires" of "the Iraqi individual" that the Iraqi government was not fulfilling. Among them: "physical security," "essential services," "justice under the rule of law," and fair "political representation." He broke down "security"—which, as he'd been learning, was the precondition for everything else—into three parts: "Protect the population, priority to Baghdad"; "Engagement [with the tribes] leading to local cease-fires and popular rejection of extremists"; and "Develop capable, credible ISF [Iraqi security forces]."

In the second column, he listed the groups that were "exploiting the gap": Shia extremists, Sunni rejectionists, organized crime, al Qaeda, and external forces such as Iran and Syria.

In the third column, he listed several ways that American troops could fill the gap. The main thing was to rebuild the failing state. This would mean helping the government protect the population, reform its ministries to make them less corrupt, provide basic services (including sewage, clean water, and electricity—the elements of Pete Chiarelli's aborted SWET plan), and reconcile with sectarian foes (as MacFarland was doing in Anbar), so that people would see their government not as "Shia-based" but as a ruling body "advancing the interests of all Iraqis."

Odierno's memo was a complete repudiation of Casey's latest campaign plan. It resembled, in certain respects, the plan that Casey had briefly put in place in the summer and fall of 2005, under the tutelage of Bill Hix and

Kalev Sepp, who'd also encouraged him to create the COIN Academy. In short, Odierno was spearheading a campaign to restore a counterinsurgency strategy.

To help him translate these principles into a military plan, he brought with him to Baghdad a staff well suited to the task. He'd been assembling much of this staff through the fall while he was still in Fort Hood, before the surge briefings—and before it was clear that Petraeus would soon be replacing Casey. As a result, back then the two could still talk directly with each other, and they often did. And among the topics they discussed was the staff's composition.

For his chief of staff, Odierno picked Brigadier General Joe Anderson, who as a colonel had been Petraeus's 2nd brigade commander in Mosul, the one who had most actively helped him make contact with the city's tribal chiefs, merchants, and prospective political leaders.

Also at Petraeus's suggestion, Odierno picked as his executive officer Colonel Mike Meese, the chairman of West Point's Social Science Department, who'd served Petraeus in that role in Bosnia and Mosul. (After Petraeus came to Baghdad, Meese moved his office to work for him once again.)

And there was Odierno's own wild card, a short, slight, thirty-eight-year-old British development worker and self-described pacifist named Emma Sky.

Odierno had met Sky in 2003, when she was a civilian adviser in Kirkuk, the city in northern Iraq with the thickest mix of Sunni Arabs, Kurds, Turkomen, and a few Shiites. Sky had volunteered for the assignment from her post at the British Foreign Office. She'd opposed the war but spoke Arabic, had experience mediating conflicts between Israelis and Palestinians (she spoke Hebrew as well), and thought she could help keep Kirkuk from going up in flames.

When Sky started out, she was formally working for Jerry Bremer's Coalition Provisional Authority, but she was attached to the US Army's 173rd Airborne Brigade, which itself had links to the 4th Infantry Division, so Odierno would see her when he visited Kirkuk. Her presence puzzled him at first, but the more he watched her in action, the more she impressed him. She seemed in control of everything in her domain: reaching out to all the sectarian groups; coordinating the brigade's civil-affairs soldiers with AID officials and nonprofit volunteers, and, all the while speaking to any and all military officers, of whatever rank, with brutal frankness, telling them they didn't know what they were talking about (usually they didn't), asking why they were doing things that made no sense (most of them had no explanation), and spelling out local political realities with a stark clarity that jarred them into changing course. Some officers resented her, but Odierno liked her style.

When he knew that he'd be heading back to Iraq as corps commander in the fall of 2006, he sent Sky an email asking her to come be his political adviser. Sky was reluctant. She'd gone back to Jerusalem to work on Middle East peace talks, which were going nowhere, but she'd had it with the war in Iraq; she was impatient with the narrowness of American military culture and saw the whole enterprise as hopeless.

In a return email, she inveighed against the war that he'd asked her to rejoin, calling it the most colossal strategic failure in American history.

Odierno wrote back with a question: What should we do about it?

She liked that, liked the fact that he didn't deny her indictment or get defensive about it, as many officers she'd met would have done. She'd always thought that Odierno asked good questions; that for all his flaws as commander of the 4th Infantry Division, he seemed genuinely curious about how to do things better and about what she was doing at her job. She accepted the offer.

When Sky first returned, she was appalled that so little had changed. During one briefing, she noticed several slides referring to the enemy as "AIF."

"What does AIF mean?" she asked.

"Anti-Iraq Forces, ma'am," the briefer answered.

She chewed him out. These people *are Iraqis,* she told him. How can they be *anti-Iraq*? They're Jaysh al Rashideen, Jaysh Muhammad, Jaysh Rijal al-Tariq al-Naqshabandi, she said, listing the names of just some of the groups. If you don't understand that, she went on, you don't know who they are, what they want, or why they're resorting to violence. And if you don't know that, you can't come up with ways of getting them to stop.

Odierno took the point to heart. The second slide of his campaign-plan briefing, right after the slide on closing the gap, read:

The term AIF is not adequate to describe:

1. Shia vs. Sunni Sectarian Violence.
2. AQ and AQI [al Qaeda and al Qaeda in Iraq].
3. Sunni Insurgency.
4. Kurdish Expansionism.
5. Shia on Shia Violence.
6. External Influences (Iranian, Syrian, and Turkish).

He was acknowledging that there were multiple threats, each distinct, some of which could be co-opted or played off one another, some of which couldn't. You had to know which were which before you could figure out what to do with each.

Sky knew little and cared less about counterinsurgency theory. But her knowledge of local political cultures, and her broader background in development, placed her on the same track as the COIN strategists, made her look at the war in a similar way—as a contest for the people's loyalty, a contest that, therefore, had to be fought in a way that honored their interests, offered them livelihoods, and ensured their security.

In the first few weeks of 2007, Sky used her facility with the language and familiarity with the culture to open doors all over Baghdad and to build some degree of trust, not just with Maliki's ministries but also with the Shiite militias. And because they trusted her, they trusted Odierno.

Over the coming months, wherever Odierno went, whether to explain the mission to American troops, to meet with Iraqi officials, or to explore deals with militants, he brought Sky along. The pair made an odd sight, the general towering over his aide by more than a foot. Odierno was once asked by a fellow general officer what he got from her. He replied, "She helps me with the *why*."

The month before Odierno came back to Iraq, the seventeen thousand soldiers of the 1st Cavalry Division returned as well, for their second tour of duty, as the main US force in Baghdad. Since securing Baghdad was Odierno's top priority, his staff worked in tandem with the 1st Cav's staff, especially with its planning chief, a lieutenant colonel named Doug Ollivant.

Ollivant came out of the West Point Social Science Department, having taught there from 1999 to 2002, overlapping with John Nagl, Ike Wilson, and the others who thought and talked about the future of the Army in the age of the "*moot*-wah wars" in Bosnia, Somalia, and other third-world hot spots. Afterward, he studied at the School of Advanced Military Studies, in Leavenworth, during which time he missed the invasion of Iraq, but he was deployed during the first troop-rotation as operations chief for one of the battalions in the 5th Cavalry Regiment.

In the early fall of 2004, as the resistance was intensifying, Ollivant's battalion was rounding up insurgents at an impressive clip, owing to a trick that he'd figured out along with the unit's assistant intelligence officer, a University of Chicago graduate named Eric Chewning, who had quit his Wall Street job to enlist in an Army officers' program after some of his friends were killed in the September 11 attacks. On his own initiative, Chewning was making pals with Shia and Sunni militiamen, some of whom had joined the armed wing of the Supreme Council for the Islamic Revolution in Iraq. As such, they were bad guys in the eyes of the US-led coalition, but there were varying degrees of bad: some were shooting at American soldiers, some weren't for the moment. In any case, between one group and another, Chewning's sources knew who the shooters were and where they were hiding. So Chewning would put together the intel, and Ollivant would form the raiding party. At their peak, they were running three-day targeting cycles: making an arrest, getting new intel, making another arrest—all in a three-day period. After a while, Chewning's cell phone contained the numbers for dozens of friendly bad guys from a wide array of sects and militias, and those of several ordinary Iraqis as well. When gunfire sounded, he could make a few calls and learn right away who was shooting.

Neither he nor Ollivant knew much about counterinsurgency. Chewning was essentially doing the same thing that he'd learned as a mergers and acquisitions broker at Merrill Lynch—he was networking. The difference was that in Baghdad, the local power brokers in his network were Shia militiamen.

Ollivant's tour ended in February 2005. Back in the States, he talked with some of his Army friends about what he'd been doing. He was eager to put the experience in perspective, to see if it held any lessons for the future. John Nagl told him that he should get hold of Galula's *Counterinsurgency Warfare*. Ollivant found a copy and read it with astonishment. He and Chewning had been following several of Galula's principles, especially the idea that intelligence was the springboard for operations and that acquiring intelligence required living among the people in order to earn their trust. They'd been doing COIN without knowing it.

That fall, Ollivant learned that David Petraeus, the new commanding general of the Combined Arms Center at Fort Leavenworth, was posting a writing contest: whichever officer wrote the best essay on countering insurgencies would win $1,000 and get the piece published in *Military Review*.

Ollivant and Chewning had already started jotting down a list of what they'd done, what worked, what didn't, and how it all fit into Galula's theories of counterinsurgency, which, they now believed, should guide the Army's strategy in Iraq more broadly. When Ollivant heard about the contest, the pair sharpened their prose, threw in a lot more references to "counterinsurgency," and submitted it under the title "Producing Victory: Rethinking Conventional Forces in COIN Operations."

Their essay won.

The contest's judges included Ollivant's old colleague from West Point John Nagl, as well as Conrad Crane, Kalev Sepp, and Jan Horvath—who, at the time, were putting together the first full draft of the COIN field manual. Petraeus, who'd handpicked the judges, liked the essay, too. The contest was but one piece of Petraeus's War of Information campaign to spread COIN throughout the officer corps, and the Ollivant-Chewning piece most closely matched the message that he was promoting. It was telling that the runner-up prize of $500 went to a major named Paul Stanton, who had written an essay about Petraeus's stability operations in Mosul; though the official announcement of the contest's winners didn't say so, Stanton had participated in those operations as one of Petraeus's company commanders.

A half year later, in early January 2007, just a few days after being named the next commander of US forces in Iraq, Petraeus learned that Ollivant was working as the planning chief of the 1st Cavalry Division, known in Army circles as First Team. He sent Ollivant an email: "Doug, if this reaches you, pls let me know if you still believe in the thesis in your article, 'Producing Victory.' If so, can you execute it with First Team? Thx."

Ollivant wrote back, assuring Petraeus that he still did believe in what he'd written and that he was executing it at that moment.

Through their varying backgrounds and experiences, Ollivant's team and Odierno's staff were coming to similar conclusions about how to secure Baghdad. Ever since Odierno's return, members of the two staffs had been getting together two or three times a week. On Christmas Eve, Odierno met in a conference room with the 1st Cav's commander, Major General Joseph Fil, and their respective staffs, to lay down the guidance for a common campaign plan.

They all agreed on the basic challenge: how to break the cycle of sectarian violence, especially in Baghdad, while helping to bolster the legitimacy of the Iraqi government. Odierno laid out the main points of his "Closing the Gap" memo, which his staff had by now refined to a single PowerPoint slide: protect the population, live where the people live, build trust, use that trust to gather intelligence on extremists, and go after them relentlessly while also reaching out to reconcilable elements.

For Odierno, these ideas stemmed from everything he'd learned in the previous three years—from his time in the State Department with Eliot Cohen and Phil Zelikow, his command training sessions with David Petraeus, his reading of the COIN field manual (and every other book on the subject he could lay his hands on), the brainstorming with fellow officers, and, most recently, his trip to Ramadi, where for the first time he actually *saw* how this sort of operation worked. For Ollivant, the ideas resonated with his earlier time in country and the lessons he and Eric Chewning had drawn in their contest-winning essay.

The biggest decision that came out of both headquarters, Odierno's and the 1st Cav's, was to move the troops out of the superbases on the outskirts of town and install them in "joint security stations," which would rapidly be built—eventually, seventy-seven of them—in Baghdad's neighborhoods. As with McMaster's combat outposts in Tal Afar and MacFarland's in Ramadi, the troops would eat, sleep, and patrol in and around these stations twenty-four hours a day, seven days a week, to keep the insurgents from coming back after they'd been pushed out. This was the clear-hold-build strategy put in motion, only now Odierno called it "clear-control-retain"—in part to play down "build" (which seemed overly ambitious, given the depths of the crisis) and in part to emphasize "retain" (the idea being that he would not hand over an area to Iraqi troops until they were ready to control it by themselves).

Odierno and the 1st Cav did differ on one aspect of the new campaign plan. Ollivant assumed, in drawing up his part of it, that all five surge brigades would be deployed in Baghdad; that was what President Bush had said when he announced the surge on January 10.

In the meantime, though, new intelligence had come to light that pushed Odierno and his staff in a different direction. During a recent sweep of a jihadist hideout, American Special Ops forces had come across a hand-drawn map that appeared to illustrate al Qaeda's plan for an assault on Baghdad. There were markings near various cities and villages encircling the capital—the Baghdad Belts, they came to be called—as well as lines drawn along roadways from the belts into Baghdad, like the spokes on a wheel, suggesting that those would be the assault routes.

The map only added credence to a massive analysis of insurgent activity along the belts that had already been produced by a team of three Army majors on Odierno's intelligence staff: Nichoel Brooks, Ketti Davison, and Monica Miller—all three, strikingly, women in their late thirties, who were known collectively to the officers around them (for the most part, good-naturedly) as "General O's Girls," "Odierno's Chicks," and (the nickname the women themselves liked best) "the Coven."

None of the three were West Pointers; they were, in fact, all autodidacts. Brooks, tall and athletic, had gone to the University of Nevada on a basketball scholarship before earning a master's degree in information systems at the University of Texas and joining the Army through an officer candidates' school program with a specialty in tactical intelligence. She'd first deployed to Iraq at the end of 2003 and acquired deep expertise in Shia militias, tribes, and families, tracking their movements, alliances, gains, losses, and shifts. When Odierno returned to Baghdad, she was well into her tenure as chief of the command's analytic center, fusing and analyzing data from more than three hundred intel officers, about fifty of them embedded with US combat brigades.

Miller had taken ROTC to fulfill her phys ed requirement at Texas A&I University, liked it, won her officer's commission, fell into the intelligence ranks, impressed her commanders, and wound up in Iraq, immersing herself in the data about Saddam's former entourage and Sunni militias, in tandem with Brooks's work on the Shia.

Davison was the one who took the thousands of scattered data points and put them all together in a series of interactive graphs, charts, and tables. As a junior officer at Fort Leavenworth's School of Advanced Military Studies, she'd taken a course on systems design and written her thesis on applying its principles to intelligence analysis. Her work in Iraq put the thesis into practice.

With Brooks's and Miller's analysis plugged into Davison's models, the team could brief Odierno on the daily shifts in Iraqi sectarian politics: who was doing what where, to what effect, and with what consequences for American strategy, tactics, and policy.

To the Coven, the al Qaeda map was nothing new. They'd pieced together a much more detailed map, from their own analyses, which pinpointed the bomb-making sites of the various militias as well as the supply routes that they followed into Baghdad. The Sunnis' sites were to the north, along a trail that began in Fallujah. The Shiites' were to the south, centered in the cities of Karbala' and Najaf. The road to Baghdad from al Kut was a favored route for criminal smugglers. The most violent areas along the Baghdad Belts—in Baqubah to the northeast and Yusifiyah to the southwest—were "friction points," where the various support zones and supply routes overlapped and the various factions fought one another for dominance.

This discovery wasn't merely interesting: it uncovered a major flaw in the impending plan for President Bush's troop surge. Putting all five of the extra Army brigades in Baghdad wouldn't solve the problem, because the bombs were being built—and the militias inside Baghdad were being supplied—by extremist leaders in the belts outside the capital. At least some of the extra brigades had to attack the belts and interdict the supply routes.

The Coven's intelligence analysis provided daily updates on precisely where the bomb sites were along the belts—and precisely who was controlling the routes. In the end, Odierno decided to split the five brigades between Baghdad and the belts. (The two Marine battalions were sent, as had always been the plan, to shore up Anbar Province, which was already well into the hold-and-build phase of clear-hold-build.) And he used the Coven's analysis to pinpoint exactly where to send the brigades along the belts.

On February 10, 2007, General David Petraeus assumed command of US and coalition forces in Iraq. The same day, Odierno briefed him on the campaign plan. Petraeus approved it—no surprise, since its overarching ideas had come from Petraeus, directly or indirectly, and the operational details that hadn't, including the innovative intelligence on the belts, struck him as sensible.

Odierno would remain in charge of day-to-day military operations. Petraeus would fit those operations into a broader strategic and political framework, a Joint Campaign Plan, which he coordinated with the US ambassador, Ryan Crocker, to ensure that every aspect of politico-military policy—strategy, tactics, intelligence gathering, and all the pieces of nation-building too—flowed in alignment with the overall plan. There had long been a brigade here, a battalion there, whose commanders understood what counterinsurgency was about and who tried to apply its principles to the narrow areas they covered. Petraeus would now give them "top cover," legitimizing what they'd been doing and actively making sure that other colonels and captains who hadn't been doing COIN—whether because they didn't get it, resisted it, or had just been following contrary orders—now joined the program.

Finally, Petraeus would be the point man for visiting legislators, journalists, and other opinion-makers—a role that he'd always performed shrewdly. This was classic information operations, which he saw as an integral part of war, especially counterinsurgency war. The "center of gravity" in such a war was the people—not just the people in the country where the war was being fought but also the people on the home front, whose children and spouses were fighting the war, whose tax dollars were funding it, and who needed some hope, some reason, for remaining patient a while longer.

The war was unpopular back home, and with good reason; the chances of a turnaround seemed dim. Yet Petraeus was widely seen as a different kind of general. He was still basking in the plaudits for his campaign in Mosul;

his COIN field manual was touted as the work of a creative strategist; if he could replicate what he'd done in Mosul, if he could turn the field manual's ideas into reality, maybe the war wasn't such a losing proposition; maybe *he* could turn it around. That was why Bush ordered the surge and chose Petraeus to install a new strategy: this was the last chance for redemption; Petraeus was typecast as the redeemer.

Petraeus brought along his full entourage, the officers he'd been grooming and encouraging, whose views he'd sought out and found compatible or promising, for several years. There was Mike Meese, the West Point Sosh chairman, serving as his special assistant; H. R. McMaster, called in just as the council of colonels was breaking up (he never would resume that fellowship in London); Pete Mansoor, also from the colonels' council and, before then, Petraeus's handpicked director of Leavenworth's COIN Center; Joel Rayburn, McMaster's political adviser at Tal Afar, who, for the past year, had been an internal dissident on General Abizaid's staff, grinding out memo after unread memo (though some outsiders, including Petraeus, had been reading them) on why Casey's transition strategy wouldn't work. And there was Dave Kilcullen, the Australian COIN soldier-scholar who'd drafted the irregular-warfare section of the Pentagon's Quadrennial Defense Review, written the "Twenty-eight Articles" essay that so many junior officers had read on how to perform COIN in their daily patrols, and spoken at so many of the culture-changing COIN conferences since. (John Nagl was not among the chosen; he had recently been named commander of a battalion in Fort Riley, Kansas, that was being reorganized into a dedicated cadre of Army officers who would train other countries' security forces, a mission that Petraeus saw as too important—possibly for the Iraq War, certainly for future insurgency wars—to interrupt.)

As part of his information operations campaign, Petraeus asked McMaster to bring together twenty experts—fellow officers, embassy officials, and prominent academics—to form what he called the Joint Strategic Assessment Team. The stated rationale of the team was to help the commander decide on a new strategy. In fact, though, Petraeus already had a new strategy; the team's real purpose was to rally buy-in for the strategy from critics and institutions whose support Petraeus knew would be politically useful. In this sense, the JSAT was similar to the workshop that Petraeus had put together at Leavenworth a year earlier to vet the COIN field manual. The conference hadn't been entirely a ruse; some of its participants did raise provocative questions, point out problems, and make useful suggestions. The same was true of the JSAT, especially since Petraeus hadn't yet completely thought through the Joint Campaign Plan's political section. But in both cases, it was Petraeus and his inner circle who did most of the work; the others were selected to widen the circle of support, to impart a sense of ownership to the diplomats who would have to carry out the political part of the plan and to the academics who might write articles about the new strategy in major magazines and newspapers back home.

The JSAT's members met in one of Saddam's former palaces, now an annex of the American embassy, with marble floors and thirty-foot-high ceilings. They met every day, sometimes twelve to fifteen hours a day, for three weeks, usually splitting off into plenary groups to hammer out the details of specific issues.

One issue that the JSAT fiercely debated was how far to extend what Sean MacFarland had done in Anbar. Turning and reconciling with former insurgents was a big part of counterinsurgency; Petraeus had written much about the subject in the field manual; Odierno had called for it, at least selectively, in his campaign plan. But were there limits? Should the United States try to co-opt *all* the Sunni insurgents into an alliance of convenience against jihadists? Or were some of them so militant, had they killed so many American soldiers, that the very idea of allying with them went beyond the pale?

Dave Kilcullen was on the side of pushing deals as far as they could go. This was a sectarian civil war, he would say. Intervening powers in a civil war have two choices: they can pick one side and annihilate the other, something that the United States wouldn't and shouldn't do; or they can broker a deal and set up a power-sharing arrangement.

Stephen Biddle, one of the few civilians in the group, agreed. Biddle had been among the handful of critics, along with Jack Keane and Eliot Cohen, to discuss the war with President Bush in the Oval Office the previous December. Biddle was more pessimistic about the course of the war than most of the JSAT members, which was why he favored making deals, even ugly deals. To his mind, the whole campaign should be built around devising incentives for bad guys to stop fighting and start talking.

But several of the military officers in the room resisted the idea, and

H. R. McMaster was the most vehement. McMaster was all for reconciling with reconcilables; he'd shown MacFarland how to do it in Tal Afar. But some of the guys that Kilcullen and Biddle wanted to work with were brutal gangsters, monsters. He'd seen what they'd done, not just to Americans but to innocent Iraqis, to women and children. It didn't take much for McMaster to get emotional; he started screaming, at its peak with an intimidating tone, which spurred others to scream just as loud.

Biddle, a soft-spoken academic, was alarmed by the ferocity of the argument. At one point, he looked around and realized, with a slight shiver, that he was the only one in the room who wasn't carrying a gun.

Out of this discussion, though, came a consensus of support for one of the decisive turns in the war: the Sons of Iraq. This was the moniker that Petraeus gave to Sunni Arabs, many of them armed militiamen, who agreed to stop shooting at coalition soldiers and to start cooperating with them instead—patrolling neighborhoods, unearthing hidden caches of weapons, and joining in the fight against al Qaeda, sometimes even against other Sunni militiamen who had chosen not to change sides. In exchange for flipping, they would earn a regular salary; and unlike MacFarland's Anbar Awakening, which paid co-opted Sunnis out of the Iraqi government's budget, Petraeus paid the Sons of Iraq from the American military's cash fund.

Petraeus had tapped a similar fund to great effect in Mosul. But there, the money had been spent on small local projects: sweeping streets, cleaning sewers, building schools. Buying off insurgents who had been killing American soldiers was different, and Petraeus knew it.

Looking for legal cover, he asked the command's lawyers if he could use the funds to pay the Sons of Iraq under the rubric of "site security." The lawyers squirmed but concluded that it would probably be all right. So he did it. And because the funds could be disbursed at the commander's discretion, Petraeus felt no obligation to tell the president, the Congress, or anyone else in Washington exactly how he was spending the money. So he didn't.

But before many Sunnis could be persuaded to give up the resistance and join forces with foreign infidels, some groundwork had to be laid. Not least, Petraeus had to crush the main Shiite militias; they were the ones whose death squads were killing Sunnis, compelling many survivors to support or join Sunni militias and even to turn to al Qaeda for protection against ethnic cleansing.

This was the "cycle of sectarian violence" that Petraeus and Odierno were determined to break: a "spectacular attack" by al Qaeda or another jihadist group, followed by retaliation from Shia militants, followed by counter-retaliation from Sunnis, then counter-counterretaliation from Shiites, and on and on the killing spiraled.

When Pete Chiarelli had been corps commander, he understood this cycle as well. To help break the cycle, he planned targeted raids on Shia militias, especially soldiers in Muqtada al-Sadr's Mahdi Army in Sadr City. But Prime Minister Maliki would always warn Casey to stay away from Sadr, and Casey would order Chiarelli to comply. Toward the end of his tenure, Chiarelli opposed the surge, figuring that there was no point in sending more troops if the Iraqi government blocked them from doing what they needed to do.

Petraeus got around this obstacle by simply ignoring it. He sent his troops into Sadr City without telling Maliki in advance. It was here that the Joint Strategic Assessment Team served its most useful purpose. In their briefings to the JSAT, H. R. McMaster and Joel Rayburn emphasized what they'd learned from their tenures in Tal Afar and Central Command headquarters: that the Iraqi government was a party to the civil war; that many of their police were, in effect, Shia death squads, whose killing sprees against Sunnis were ratcheting up the sectarian violence.

Rayburn had read the "end-states" briefing that Celeste Ward had written for Chiarelli, with its conclusion that the coalition and the Iraqi government possessed divergent interests and pursued divergent goals. Ward and Chiarelli had inferred from this that the war was all but hopeless; by contrast, Rayburn inferred that the United States should use its leverage to get Maliki to change course.

The embassy officials on the JSAT agreed. When Maliki called Ambassador Crocker to complain about Petraeus's insolence, he received no sympathy. It was made clear that the days of blank checks were over; that, as long as Maliki and his ministries were pushing sectarian violence, the United States would push back.

Petraeus and his aides stepped up the pressure on all the parties. When they discovered that a national police brigade in southern Baghdad was murdering Sunnis, they told the interior ministry that the coalition was withdrawing all support for that brigade until it stopped the killing. Suddenly it had no fuel, spare parts, money, or equipment; nor were its men allowed into any area controlled by American troops. The brigade backed off within days. Some (though far from all) of the other police squads, watching the standoff play out, followed suit.

Maliki tried to regain the upper hand, giving Crocker a list of fourteen demands. Most of them called on him to resume policies that Casey had pursued but that Petraeus had ended. Among them: withdraw all US troops from Iraqi cities, release all Shia detainees, and accelerate the transfer of authority to the government. Maliki had been pushing for these moves all along, so that he could intensify the attacks on Sunnis without American interference.

Petraeus called for a meeting with Maliki's national security adviser, Mowaffak al-Rubaie, and told him that none of the demands would be met. If the prime minister wanted to phone President Bush and complain, Petraeus himself would take the next plane back to Washington, go directly to the Oval Office, and explain the situation.

At other times, Petraeus would cozy up to Maliki, play good cop to his own bad cop, pump the prime minister with pep talks about his destiny as a great national leader, and brief him—share sensitive intelligence with him—on the many ways in which Sadr was an unreliable ally, serving interests, including Iranian interests, that were hostile to Iraq's long-term security.

Maliki backed off, at least for the moment.

Petraeus's biggest gamble was his literal application of Galula's dictum to live among the people. Very soon after taking command, he ordered joint security stations to be constructed all over Baghdad—seventy-seven of them, in all—starting in Ghazaliya, the once-prosperous neighborhood that Meghan O'Sullivan, his White House contact, had personally witnessed plunging into chaos.

Some of these stations were modifications of outposts that Casey had built, although back then, the troops had used them as day stations and would return to their large bases on the city's outskirts at dusk. Most of the new ones had to be constructed from scratch, in one night; otherwise they would come under fire the next morning. Crews would roll in after sundown with a flatbed and crane, sometimes two cranes. By sunrise, the station would be fully erected, manned, and guarded, as if it had been there for months.

Petraeus also ordered the construction of concrete walls, winding all through Baghdad, as a brusque way of separating Sunni from Shia neighborhoods, thus keeping the peace between them, at least for a while.

The idea was that the constant presence of American troops would reduce the violence and that this, in turn, might make the local people feel sufficiently secure to help the troops find insurgents in their midst; this would reduce violence further, and on the cycle would spiral, resulting eventually in support for the war effort—and ultimately for the Iraqi government.

Several officers got the concept right away. They'd understood it for some time, having taken the course at the COIN Academy and read several articles, the online forums, and the recently issued COIN field manual. Now, with top cover from Petraeus, they pushed further, taking still greater risks at making contact and striking deals on their own initiative with local citizens, fence-sitters, and, in a few cases, militants.

But some officers resisted; the whole notion rubbed against everything they'd been taught about respecting a host-government's sovereignty and the Army's traditional primary mission of self-protection. Others were eager to follow the new commander's orders but didn't know what specifically to do.

So Petraeus asked Dave Kilcullen to write another essay, similar to his "Twenty-eight Articles," which had circulated widely a year earlier. This one, Petraeus told him, should translate the principles of Odierno's campaign plan into point-by-point instructions.

Kilcullen swiftly wrote a three-page memo called "Counterinsurgency Guidance." It began with a précis of what Petraeus had said repeatedly in public: that the Iraqis will have to work out their own political solutions, but they can't be expected to do so in a climate of "chaos, violence, and fear." They needed help to change this climate, to create some breathing space—a zone of security—in which they might resolve their disputes calmly. "This," Kilcullen wrote, addressing the troops, "is where you come in . . . Your actions at the tactical level resonate throughout the communities you protect and are amplified beyond."

He listed ten things they needed to do, chief among them: "Secure the people where they sleep" (because securing them only in the daytime will make them more vulnerable to revenge by insurgents at night). Another point: "Get out and walk." Armored vehicles were necessary to get from one place to another, but once you're there, mingle among the people; the vehicles offer self-protection but "at the cost of a great deal of effectiveness"; patrolling by foot is the only way to build trust, and building trust is essential to gathering reliable intelligence.

With Kilcullen in the room, Petraeus read his memo, picked up a pen, and seemed about to sign it. Then he stopped, thought for a moment, and said, "Take this over to Emma and tell her that Ray should sign it."

It was another instance of Petraeus seeking buy-in from those he needed to carry out a policy. Kilcullen took the document to Odierno's office. Emma Sky went over it, making a few small changes. Odierno later signed it, sent it to all combat units, and also came up with the idea of having it translated into Arabic and circulated through the local media, so that the Iraqi people would have a sense of American intentions.

Petraeus and Odierno understood that the guidance was risky, that it would expose their troops to greater danger. Petraeus publicly acknowledged that, as a result of his new policy, more American soldiers would probably be killed, at least in the short run. They would be spending more time out in the open, near the enemy, in the fight. And because of the surge, there would be more of those troops taking risks. If the strategy worked, though, the payoff would be a steep reduction in military and civilian casualties over the long haul—and, further out into the future, a more secure and stable Iraq.

But this was a gamble. It was sure to work in theory; no one knew what would happen in practice.

For the first half of 2007, the violence didn't let up in the slightest. Roadside bomb explosions hovered between 400 and 500 a month; suicide bombers set off another 200 or so blasts a month. And because the troops were now out in the open almost constantly, American combat fatalities soared by 50 percent, reaching a peak of 120 in the month of May.

But *civilian* casualties were dropping: from a high of 3,700 in January to 2,500 in March and 2,000 in June. Still, the death toll was too high, for Iraqis and for Americans. Back home, the surge was widely declared a failure. Even the commanders were getting a bit nervous.

Then on June 15, all five surge brigades were finally in place. (They had been mobilized at the rate of roughly one per month.) The next day, Petraeus and Odierno launched Operation Phantom Thunder, the long-planned, multipronged assault on the Baghdad Belts. Five days after that, a joint US-Iraqi Special Operations team mounted a raid on a key Mahdi Army stronghold in Sadr City.

The effects were almost immediate. The jihadists' bomb-making operations were disrupted; their supply routes—both to Baghdad and to one another—were cut off; their veneer of invincibility was shattered. Meanwhile, the attacks on Sadr City persuaded many Sunnis that maybe the Americans weren't taking the side of Shia militants after all. In August, Muqtada al-Sadr himself declared a cease-fire and took refuge in Iran. The same month, Odierno mopped up the al Qaeda cells that had eluded the first round of attacks and began putting into motion the hold-and-build (or, as he now called it, secure-and-sustain) phase of the COIN campaign.

The next few months saw a steep decline in all measures of violence. By August, explosions of roadside bombs dropped to three hundred a month, car bombings to fewer than one hundred; by the end of the year, the figures plummeted, respectively, to under one hundred and barely twenty. Sectarian deaths fell to fewer than five hundred in August and, by the end of the year, to nearly zero. American combat casualties began to drop as well, reaching numbers—ten to twenty a month—that hadn't been seen since the start of the occupation.

As the violence subsided and the most militant insurgents lost their strength and appeal, the Sons of Iraq saw their ranks swell, which reduced the violence further. The recruitment lines were so long, the desire to sign up so feverish, that even some of the program's supporters were a bit concerned—it wasn't clear who some of these new comrades were or how enduring their allegiances might be.

Still, American soldiers and marines knew something new was in the air when they noticed Shiite and Sunni militiamen consorting openly in the streets of the capital. In the short run, this all worked to the Americans' advantage.

The long run would be up to the Iraqis.

And that was the problem.

In the euphoria over the undeniable improvements in Iraq, the emergence of near-normal everyday life, a tendency arose both in the field and back in Washington to give all credit to the American military, to the surge, or to General Petraeus and his counterinsurgency strategy.

But there were other factors having little to do with anything that the Americans had done—apart from starting the war and thus triggering the social disruptions in the first place.

First, Petraeus and the surge had come late to the civil war. Many areas of violence had already been "cleared" through ethnic cleansing and exile; hundreds of thousands of Sunnis had abandoned their homes under threat of death for points west, either in Anbar Province or across the border into Lebanon or Syria.

Second, the Sunnis would not have been so eager to split from al Qaeda, much less join the Sons of Iraq, had they not begun to realize that they were losing the civil war with the Shiites. Only then did they see an alliance with the Americans as their best hope for survival.

Similarly, Maliki consented to the American assault on Shia militias in part because he had no choice, in part because he was slowly realizing that the Mahdi Army was at least as much a threat as an ally, that Sadr had joined his political coalition in order to take it over. And so Maliki allied with the Americans for the same reason the Sunni tribesmen did: to boost the prospects of his survival.

The surge facilitated this cooperation. It conveyed to everyone concerned that the Americans weren't leaving after all. They were staying, in strengthened numbers; they had to be contended with, and perhaps they could be trusted.

True, the Anbar Awakening had preceded the surge, preceded the arrival of Petraeus, was well under way before publication of the COIN field manual, and was initiated by Sunnis, not by Americans. But it took a commander like Sean MacFarland to grasp the Awakening's potential and respond sagely to the Sunnis' initiative. That is, it took someone who'd been trained in COIN and influenced by the same events and ideas that had sired the field manual, not least Petraeus's own experiences in Mosul. More conventional commanders would have responded to the violence by killing as many Sunnis as they could—with disastrous results on all sides.

Even with MacFarland in place, the Awakening would have remained a mere local phenomenon, had it not been for the changes that followed. The surge enabled Petraeus to spread variations of the Awakening across the rest of Iraq; it gave him enough troops to clear and hold more than one area at a time.

Finally, it took a commander with Petraeus's background, instincts, and brazen assertiveness to know what to do with the surge—how to make twenty-one thousand extra combat troops (not exactly a massive escalation) the hinge of a strategic shift.

Even so, in the broader scheme, this shift, however dramatic, had only tactical consequences. The surge and the COIN campaign that went with it were—explicitly—mere means to an end. Petraeus said many times, as did Kilcullen in his Odierno-signed counterinsurgency guidance, that the point of it all was to give Iraq's factions some "breathing space" so that they could focus in peace on hammering out their differences and forming a cohesive government with widespread legitimacy.

By the summer of 2007, it was clear that the American troops were fulfilling their part of the bargain. The question was whether the Iraqi factions would take advantage of the breathing space. Would they strike an agreement on sharing oil wealth? Would the Kurds and Sunni Arabs settle their property disputes in Kirkuk? Perhaps most important for the country's future, would Maliki incorporate the Sons of Iraq into the national Iraqi army?

And if these things didn't happen, would the surge and the new strategy turn out to have only prolonged the fighting and compounded the war's tragic waste?

18.

The Insurgent in the Pentagon

Whenever David Petraeus needed something from the Pentagon—when one of his policies faced resistance from the chiefs, when critical supplies hit a clog in the bureaucracy, when he'd find it useful to have an argument made at a high-level meeting—he would often send a note or put in a call to his old friend and fellow member of the West Point Sosh network, Pete Chiarelli.

In early March 2007, just a few weeks after Petraeus assumed command of US forces in Iraq, the new secretary of defense, Robert Gates, chose Chiarelli to be his senior military assistant. Gates needed a general with an intimate understanding of the war. He'd been impressed with Chiarelli's briefing six months earlier in Baghdad, when Chiarelli was Casey's deputy and Gates was a member of the Baker-Hamilton Commission. Hearing that Chiarelli was now back in the States, he called him in for an interview and hired him.

Gates's own rise had been sudden and swift. On November 7, 2006, the Republican Party lost both houses of Congress in midterm elections, due in large part to the war's declining popularity. The next day, President Bush announced that Donald Rumsfeld had resigned as defense secretary and that Bob Gates would take his place. Four weeks later, the Senate confirmed Gates's nomination, 95–2. On December 18, he was sworn into office.

His priorities were Iraq, Iraq, and Iraq. The day after he took the oath, he made the trip to Baghdad. On the flight over, he read Fred Kagan's surge briefing, then, upon touching down, talked with Casey and Odierno about its prospects. When he got back to the Pentagon and began to settle in, the first thing that struck him was how few people in the building seemed to share his sense of urgency.

Gates was sixty-three. He'd never worked in the Pentagon, but he had spent his entire career in other top-secret compartments of the Washington bureaucracy, rising through the ranks of the CIA—from staff Kremlinologist to director—and spending two-and-a-half years in the White House as deputy national security adviser to Bush's father. Those were Cold War times, when some crisis was always riveting everyone's attention late into the night. Now there was a real war going on, yet the senior officers in the Pentagon were shuffling through their routines as if Americans in uniform weren't fighting and dying anywhere on the planet. The generals and admirals would haul their PowerPoint briefings into his office, urging him to spend more money on the Air Force's F-22 stealth fighter jet, the Army's high-tech Future Combat System, or yet another Navy nuclear-powered aircraft carrier. These pitches had their place, and so perhaps did the weapons in some big war of the future; but they were *all* the brass wanted to talk about, and they had *nothing* to do with the wars going on *now*.

The first glaring sign of these jumbled priorities came on February 18, 2007, two months into his job, when the *Washington Post* published a front-page story revealing the dreadful neglect of wounded soldiers at Walter Reed Army Medical Center, six miles north of the White House. Gates cleared his schedule, conducted his own investigation, and ordered sweeping changes, including firing the secretary of the Army, Francis Harvey.

Before long, Gates realized that the problems he faced ran much deeper than that of a few officials' negligence at a military hospital.

Even before Chiarelli took his new job, Gates had asked him what the troops in Iraq needed most. From his own experiences the previous year and from talks with Petraeus since, Chiarelli cited two huge priorities: ISR and MRAP.

ISR—intelligence, surveillance, and reconnaissance—referred mainly to the unmanned aerial vehicles, or drones, that flew over the battlefield with cameras (and sometimes missiles) attached to their bellies, streaming video images back to stateside bases where Air Force officers watched the pictures on monitors and steered the drones with remote-control joysticks, sending signals through GPS satellites. The drones, with names like Predator and Global Hawk, were the realizations of John Foster's dream, hatched thirty-five years earlier with a model airplane and a lawn-mower engine. The irony was that they'd originally been conceived and developed as weapons that could strike Soviet targets behind enemy lines—a tool of "deep-strike interdiction" in the titanic war to come between the Warsaw Pact and NATO. Now the drones were helping soldiers and marines—grunts on the ground—track down insurgents and terrorists in a kind of warfare that the Joint Chiefs, a few years earlier, had refused to call a "war."

For that reason, though, the top Air Force generals had little interest in unmanned aircraft; the centerpiece of their culture was still the agile pilot in a fast plane's cockpit. So they held up the drones' production. When Gates accelerated production, they held up delivery. Gates then ordered a step-up in the deliveries, but got word that only a few were up in the air.

Gates had his staff call the bases where the drones were stationed and discovered that they were operating at just half the rate they could have been. When he took office, barely twenty drones were flying combat air patrols at any one time, and almost all of those were allocated to the Joint Special Operations Command, the secretive commandos hunting down the most wanted jihadists. Very few drones were let loose on the insurgent foot soldiers setting off bombs in Iraqi cities or planting them along roads used by American convoys. Some test runs against these sorts of targets had demonstrated their value; the drone's camera would observe insurgents planting a bomb and then follow them back to their hideouts, where soldiers or marines were sent to kill or capture them. But, Chiarelli told Gates, in all the time he'd been corps commander in Iraq, he'd never been allowed more than a single Predator drone at any one time.

Roadside bombs were the biggest threat facing soldiers in Iraq, the cause of nearly two-thirds of American combat casualties. And, Chiarelli added, the Pentagon could be doing one more thing to bring down those numbers: there was a new kind of armored troop-carrying vehicle, the Mine-Resistant Ambush-Protected vehicle, or MRAP (pronounced "M-Rap"). It really did what its name suggested: resist mines and protect against ambushes. But the senior officers in the Army and the Marines didn't want it. The vehicles were expensive, a half million dollars each, more than three times the price of armored Humvees. But they would save lives—hundreds, potentially thousands—that the Humvees couldn't.

Gates was detecting a pattern. The Air Force didn't want drones because they might subvert its plans to build advanced manned fighter planes for the big war of the future. The Army and the Marines didn't want the MRAP because it would take money away from other armored vehicles, especially the Future Combat System, which was designed to fight this same big war of the future. What *was* this big future war? When would we be fighting it, against whom? Gates wasn't opposed to planning for a wide range of contingencies, and he had no desire to retract the reach of American global power. But he found it perverse—it took him a while to believe—that the senior officers in the Department of Defense were so uninterested in the wars going on at the moment. It was clear they wanted out of this war; this wasn't what they had in mind when they thought about war ("real men don't do *moot*-wah"); they couldn't wait until this war was over, so they could go back to preparing for the war they'd *rather* fight. Unmanned planes wouldn't play as much of a role in the big war; slow, bulky troop carriers like the MRAP might be fine for urban guerrilla wars, but sleeker ones would be better for the rolling hills of a conventional battlefield.

Chiarelli had to be a bit cautious in this dispute. Soon after he came on board as Gates's assistant, General George Casey, his old boss and frequent antagonist from Iraq days, became the Army chief of staff. President Bush had felt bad about rejecting Casey's advice and relieving him of his command, so he promoted him to chief of staff as a consolation prize. Casey was well aware that he'd lost the battle over policy; and as chief of staff, he had no formal control over the war's operations. But he had his ideas about the Army's proper priorities, and he had a big say about the Army's budget. So he kept up his resistance to the push toward COIN. He worried—and others, even those less resistant to COIN, shared this concern—that the Army was pulling back too far from the task, arguably the more vital task, of arming and training for major combat against a comparably mighty foe.

Gates took up Chiarelli's battles, often with his guidance. At first glance, the new defense secretary struck an unassuming profile. He'd grown up in Wichita, Kansas, and still spoke with a midwesterner's slight twang and steady cadence. Short, with thin white hair and a bit of a waddle in his walk, he could pass as a small-town banker. But there was a steely glint in his eyes when he confronted a challenger. He hadn't climbed the rough ropes at the CIA, survived scandals, or learned to navigate the corridors of power all across the nation's capital by being a milquetoast.

Early on in the new job, he called a meeting of senior Pentagon officials, civilian and military, to tell them he wanted 1,500 MRAPs in Iraq by the end of the year. Several in the room protested that it couldn't, and shouldn't, be done: the production lines were slow, the logistics were difficult, the vehicles weren't needed anyway—a dozen more reasons.

After a few minutes of this moaning, Gates flashed that glint and told them—still in a soft voice, there was no need to yell—that maybe they didn't understand: there *will be* 1,500 new MRAPs deployed to Iraq by the end of the year; *their* job is to figure out how to get them there.

It was clear to everyone in the room that the meeting was over.

Not long after, during a review of the upcoming supplemental bill, a midyear add-on to the defense budget that covered unanticipated war costs, Gates unilaterally tacked on an extra $16 billion to build more MRAPs as quickly as possible—an unprecedented sum to spend on a single weapons program in a single year.

He launched similar machinations to push for more drones but faced still fiercer resistance from the Air Force; it took a year for Gates to win this contest decisively. His break came in the summer of 2007, when an Air Force bomber pilot mistakenly (and against all safety regulations) flew over American territory with live nuclear weapons under the plane's wings. Gates used the occasion to fire the Air Force chief of staff, General T. Michael Moseley, and the service's civilian secretary, Michael Wynne. His official rationale was the nuclear mishap, but the real reason was their persistent insubordination on the F-22 fighter (by this time, Gates had decided to stop building more of the planes, though Moseley and Wynne kept arguing publicly for more) and their refusal to get with the drone program.

This was a stunning move. Four-star generals were almost never fired. Hardly less remarkable was Gates's choice as Moseley's replacement—General Norton Schwartz.

Ever since 1947, when the Air Force split away from the Army to become an independent service, its chiefs of staff had always risen through the ranks of its dominant branch. Until the early 1980s, every chief had been a nuclear-bomber pilot. From that point on, they'd all been fighter pilots. But Norty Schwartz had come up through the Special Operations Command, and when Gates nominated him as chief, he was head of the Air Force's Transportation Command, which managed cargo-transport planes; that is, he was in charge of airlifting supplies and troops to foreign bases or war zones, mainly for soldiers and marines. Schwartz impressed Gates because when all the other senior Air Force officers were claiming that it was impossible to fly MRAPs to Iraq in any great number, Schwartz worked out a plan on how to do it.

By promoting Schwartz, not only did Gates promote a general who was focused on the war of the moment, he also laid the groundwork for the next cultural shift of the Air Force itself. Schwartz announced that drones would play a central role in the conflicts to come and that the drones' joystick pilots would be rewarded accordingly. Within months, the drone fleet's flight hours doubled. By the end of the following year, the Air Force was training more joystick pilots than cockpit pilots, and the former's ranks included a growing share of the elite. Flying an F-15 jet might have been fun, but the nation was fighting two wars, and manned fighter planes were barely involved in either. (The F-22 wasn't involved at all.) Steering a Predator or any of the other growing number of drones, the pilots were above—they were *in*—the action nonstop, increasingly so as the drones emerged as vital tools in the fight against insurgents in Iraq and Afghanistan.

Gates saw that the entire Defense Department needed an overhaul—in the way its leaders bought weapons, managed budgets, promoted officers, and fought wars. He had just two years, the time left in Bush's second term as president: not enough time to do much besides deal with Iraq. But he could outline an agenda of change for his successor, and he decided to do this through a series of speeches.

The head speechwriter in the Office of the Secretary of Defense was a thirty-six-year-old former Army lieutenant named Thayer Scott. He'd been the number-two speechwriter when Donald Rumsfeld was secretary and initially relished working for a kick-ass reformer. But he grew weary of Rumsfeld (who turned out to be more kick-ass than reformer) and wearier still of the war in Iraq.

A Princeton graduate (he'd come into the Army through ROTC) and the son of two Foreign Service Officers, Scott had grown more reflective and started reading lots of articles about what went wrong in Iraq, including the officers' debates in *Military Review* and *Small Wars Journal.* When Rumsfeld left the Pentagon, the top speechwriter went with him, so Scott took over the slot.

Scott had little one-on-one contact with the new secretary, just a single meeting, in his first four months. But he watched Bob Gates in action, saw how directly, even bluntly, he dealt with the Walter Reed scandal and with the obstructionists on MRAP and the drones. He read about Gates's tenure as CIA director in the wake of the Cold War, when he shifted the Agency away from its obsession with Russia (which had been Gates's own specialty) to focus more on terrorism and unstable states. He also read an article in *Texas Monthly* magazine about Gates's tenure as president of Texas A&M University, his last job before coming to the Pentagon, where he'd overhauled the admissions policy (more minorities, fewer unqualified children of alumni), fired incompetent department managers, hired more faculty to bring down class rolls, even ordered a more diverse menu in the dining halls. Maybe this guy was the real agent of change.

That summer, Gates was invited to speak at the upcoming convention of the Association of the United States Army, the lobbying organization of retired Army officers. It was an annual rite for defense secretaries, a surefire forum for pandering applause-lines. Scott decided to draft a different sort of speech, one that described the changes that he knew Gates wanted to make.

Scott hadn't talked with Pete Chiarelli much, either, but he knew that Gates and the general were close, that they talked with each other at least twice a day and usually had dinner together on trips abroad. Scott had read Chiarelli's article in *Military Review* two years earlier about counterinsurgency operations in Iraq, and he obtained an advance copy of his article for the upcoming issue of *Military Review* (he knew that Gates had a copy of it, too), called "Learning from Our Modern Wars," in which Chiarelli urged the Army to shift its focus away from large-scale tank maneuvers on wide-open battlefields to smaller-scale, urban COIN campaigns.

From there, Scott read John Nagl's *Learning to Eat Soup with a Knife*. He talked with Colonel Sean MacFarland—who, at this point, was working for the Joint Staff in the Pentagon—about the Sunni Awakening that he'd led in Ramadi. He had lunch with Andrew Krepinevich, whose book about Vietnam (which Scott read) had argued that the Army lost the war because its commanders fought as if it were a conventional battle instead of a competition for the allegiance of the people. He even read David Petraeus's PhD dissertation, which made the same point and extended it to a broader argument that the Army should get over its Vietnam complex and prepare for the growing trend of low-intensity conflicts.

Finally, Scott took another look at the transcript of Gates's confirmation hearings and noticed one passage in particular, in which he'd stressed the importance of "continuing to strengthen our capacity to fight irregular wars," adding, "I think that's where the action is going—is most likely to be for the foreseeable future."

By the time he started writing, Scott had a good idea of the sort of speech Gates himself would write if he had the time.

The first half of the draft was boilerplate: some banal but crowd-pleasing jokes about the self-centeredness of Washington (Gates wrote these himself, and would repeat them in many speeches to come), followed by praise for the Army's proud traditions and brave soldiers.

He eased gently into the innovative section, the assault on conventional wisdom held not only by Gates's challengers inside the Pentagon but also by the vast majority of retired officers who would be sitting in the audience. "In the years following the Vietnam War," Scott wrote, taking his cues from the writings of Petraeus, Krepinevich, and Nagl, "the Army relegated unconventional war to the margins of training, doctrine, and budget priorities," leaving itself "unprepared to deal with the operations that followed—Somalia, Haiti, the Balkans, and, more recently, Afghanistan and Iraq—the consequences and costs of which we are still struggling with today." He noted signs of progress—the revamping of the National Training Center, the publication of the counterinsurgency field manual—but stressed, "This work and these lessons in irregular warfare need to be retained and institutionalized, and should not be allowed to wither on the bureaucratic vine."

Then came the lines that would make many in the audience flinch: "It is hard to conceive of any country challenging the United States directly on the ground—at least for some years to come. Indeed, history shows us that smaller, irregular forces—insurgents, guerrillas, terrorists—have for centuries found ways to harass and frustrate larger, regular armies and sow chaos . . . We can expect that asymmetric warfare will remain the mainstay of the contemporary battlefield for some time."

Finally, he told the tale—which was still not widely known—about the Army's "Ready First" Brigade, which pacified Ramadi one neighborhood at a time, and he memorialized in particular Captain Travis Patriquin, who gave his life while forming alliances with the town's tribal elders to defeat al Qaeda and win the peace. "It is stories and soldiers like these," the speech concluded, "that inspire us and make us proud and hopeful about the future of America's Army."

It was a bold claim to make before a hall of hidebound veterans: that their Army's future lay not with gold-plated weapons or sweeping tank maneuvers across an open battlefield—the projects and scenarios that had been driving its budgets and activities for decades—but rather with some junior officer who'd struck deals with Arab sheikhs.

Scott turned in the draft, not knowing what to expect. Gates looked it over with Chiarelli, approved it with only a few stylistic changes, and, on October 10, read it aloud to the vets and their lobbyists at the Washington Convention Center as the lunchtime keynote speaker.

The reactions were what Scott had hoped. The Army traditionalists—those who watched the speech delivered live and those who read the transcript later—were alarmed that the defense secretary might really cut into the heart of the Army they knew and loved, might change its mission and its whole concept of a soldier. The COINdinistas were stunned in a different way. They realized that they now had an ally and spokesman in the highest of places. The secretary of defense himself, it seemed, was *one of them*.

Another eyebrow-raising line in Gates's speech came toward the end, when he praised the junior and midgrade officers "who have been tested in battle like none other in decades" and who "have seen the complex, grueling face of war in the twenty-first century up close." He then said: "These men and women need to be retained, and the best and brightest advanced to the point that they can use their experience to shape the institution to which they have given so much. And this may mean reexamining assignments and promotion policies that, in many cases, are unchanged since the Cold War."

To an extent that Gates himself didn't realize, this was the most radical passage in the speech.

Scott got the idea for this passage from an article written a year earlier, in *Armed Forces Journal*, by John Nagl and another lieutenant colonel named Paul Yingling, who'd been a colleague of Nagl's on the West Point Sosh department's faculty back in the 1990s. Their article, titled "New

Rules for New Enemies," noted that the officer promotion boards were "the surest means the Army has to communicate which skills, knowledge, and abilities it prizes most highly." All executives tend to promote underlings whose styles and career paths resemble their own; that was the purpose of a promotion system—to perpetuate an organization's dominant culture. Most of the Army's generals had risen through the ranks during the Cold War as armor, infantry, or artillery officers, trained to lead men in large-scale, head-on battles against enemies of comparable strength. And so they tended to promote officers with that same experience. But today's wars, the authors argued, were more likely to be asymmetric conflicts against guerrillas, insurgents, or terrorists. Fighting these wars required more adaptive officers and thus "a more adaptive organizational culture." The best way to change the Army's organizational culture, they wrote, was "to change the pathways for professional advancement within its officer corps. The Army will become more adaptive only when being adaptive offers the surest path to promotion."

Nagl and Yingling didn't say so, but it was widely known throughout the Army that one of those adaptive officers—who, true to form, had not been promoted when he should have been—was H. R. McMaster.

McMaster was the commander of the 3rd Armored Cavalry Regiment who pushed back jihadists in Tal Afar with the clear-hold-build approach inspired by the classic COIN books and by the more recent example of Petraeus's campaign in Mosul. If the Army wanted to promote officers who "got" the new style of warfare and who knew how to defeat an adaptive foe, McMaster was their man. Yet around the time that Nagl and Yingling wrote their article, the board that picked which colonels would be promoted to one-star general each year didn't pick him.

The article didn't mention that the authors and McMaster were colleagues and friends: Yingling had been McMaster's assistant in Tal Afar; he and Nagl had taught in West Point's Sosh department at the same time McMaster was teaching in its History Department.

When the news of McMaster's nonpromotion came down the line, Nagl was outraged. One place where he often stormed off to vent his outrage was the office of Pete Geren, the undersecretary of the Army.

Back in the fall of 2004, when Nagl first came to the Pentagon and spent his spare time prowling the corridors in search of someone—anyone—with an interest in counterinsurgency, Geren was among the few who lent an ear. At the time, Geren was one of Rumsfeld's special assistants, a former four-term congressman from Texas—a "Blue Dog Democrat," meaning a Democrat hawkish on defense issues—who'd quit the House in 1997 and moved back to Texas. Rumsfeld offered him the Pentagon job in the early summer of 2001. He hadn't known Rumsfeld, though he was a longtime friend of George W. Bush's. Some House members had advised Rumsfeld that Geren would make a good liaison with both the White House and the Congress.

Geren sat down with Nagl several times, but their meetings became more frequent after February 2006, when Geren was appointed undersecretary of the Army. Geren didn't know much about the nuts and bolts of the service, and he gladly accepted Nagl's tutelage about everything from the fine points of tactics and strategy to the design flaws of a proposed new armored vehicle.

Even before McMaster was passed over, before he and Yingling wrote their article, Nagl spent several sessions with Geren, railing against the conformist coterie that ruled the Army's archaic promotion boards.

"Why haven't *I* been promoted?" Nagl moaned on a couple of occasions. "We've got idiots running this place!"

When Gates fired Francis Harvey as Army secretary over the Walter Reed scandal, he moved up Geren to take Harvey's place. Geren tried to talk Gates out of the promotion, noting that, given the wars going on, the job should go to someone with active-duty Army experience. But Gates insisted. Geren knew the ropes, and, besides, a new administration would take over in less than two years: better to maintain continuity than to bring in a new secretary, who, after the vetting and the confirmation hearings and all the rest, would just be getting up to speed by the time the job ended.

Geren was confirmed as secretary of the Army on July 16, 2007. Not long after, he received—along with the dozens of other documents that passed his desk each day—a memo from GOMO, the Army's General Officer Management Office, listing the generals who'd been nominated to sit on the upcoming promotion board.

This was usually a pro forma memo, but by statute, the civilian service secretary had to sign off on such a list. If Francis Harvey had still been Army secretary—which is to say, if Bob Gates hadn't fired Harvey over the

Walter Reed scandal (which is to say, if George W. Bush hadn't fired Donald Rumsfeld over the Iraq War's unpopularity)—the list almost certainly would have been approved without a moment's thought.

But Pete Geren, who had won his job through a series of flukes, remembered those conversations he'd had with John Nagl about the promotion system. So he took a close look at the list of generals who were going to pick tomorrow's generals and who would thus send the signals—as Nagl and Yingling put it—about which "skills, knowledge, and ability" the Army prized most highly. And he realized that these were not the right generals for such a sensitive task; they were not the Army's movers and shakers.

The board's chairman was by tradition the Army vice chief of staff, but Geren suddenly realized it didn't have to be that way. And the current vice, General Richard Cody, though a decent man, was completely wrong for this part of the job: his only combat tour had been as an aviation battalion commander in Desert Storm, and he appeared to have no understanding of the current wars. Once, during a conversation about Petraeus and counterinsurgency, Cody had told Geren, "You can't run an Army based on the flavor of the month." Clearly he was one of the generals who couldn't wait to drop this irregular warfare fad and get back to the Army's *real* business. Most of the generals on this list were of the same view.

Geren was also picking up signals that this type of general *didn't like* H. R. McMaster. And he knew by this time that the failure to promote McMaster the previous year had widely been seen as a symbol of the Army's hidebound ways, not just by the COIN enthusiasts but by junior officers who had served in Iraq or Afghanistan, learned new skills, and now wondered if they would be rewarded or punished for adapting well to the kind of war they were fighting. Geren had read these young officers' bitter comments in Army blog posts and in a few mainstream news stories. Geren had once asked Casey, who by now was chief of staff, why so many generals had a problem with McMaster. Casey replied, in a tone that suggested he was a member of the club, "If McMaster weren't such a smart-ass, he would have been promoted a long time ago."

So, looking at the list of prospective board members, Geren did what no one else in his job had ever done: he sent it back with a rejection note and said he'd pick them himself.

Geren spent the next week canvassing every smart officer he knew, including Nagl, and assembling a list of the Army's most dynamic generals. He whittled down that list to fifteen and asked them all to serve on the promotion board. They included David Petraeus; Pete Chiarelli; Stanley McChrystal, head of the Joint Special Operations Command; John Mulholland, head of Special Operations for Central Command; and Ann Dunwoody, a former parachutist in the 82nd Airborne Division who was the Army's highest-ranking woman and so might be disposed to the idea of opening doors.

There was one possible hitch. Only the secretary of defense could call back a wartime commander to serve on a domestic panel like the promotion board, which is to say Geren needed Gates's authorization to call back Petraeus. Gates thought Geren had a terrific idea; he signed the form without hesitation. Chiarelli was also an unusual choice; some might see the appointment of the defense secretary's military assistant as a political move, but Gates allowed that, too.

When word got out that Petraeus was chairing the board and that Chiarelli was one of its members, it was widely inferred—celebrated in some quarters, lamented in others—that McMaster would finally get his star. Some even dubbed it "the H. R. McMaster promotion board."

The board met from November 8 to 13 in the Hoffman Town Center, a bland office and retail complex in Alexandria, Virginia, seven miles south of the Pentagon, adjacent to the Army's Human Resources Command.

McMaster got his star, but that wasn't the board's only breakthrough.

Among the forty colonels it advanced to brigadier general were Sean MacFarland, the commander who led the Awakening in Ramadi; Steve Townsend, who cleared and held Baqubah; Michael Garrett, who commanded an infantry brigade that helped turn around the "Triangle of Death" south of Baghdad; Colleen McGuire, an officer in the military police, a branch of the Army that had almost never produced a general; as well as eight Special Forces officers and a few commanders of "light" forces—Stryker brigades and units of the 10th Mountain Division—which previous boards had systematically ignored.

Nearly all of these new generals had served multiple tours of duty in Iraq or Afghanistan. They had a depth of knowledge about asymmetric warfare that the generals at the start of those wars lacked entirely. And many of them were promoted straight from their combat commands; they weren't forced to scurry through the bureaucratic maze as a prerequisite to advancement.

This alone was a big shift. The year before, when Cody chaired the promotion board, nine of the thirty-eight new one-stars had been executive officers to a commanding general—and in most cases, not a combat commander. Only four of the forty rewarded by the Petraeus-led board were executive officers, and all of them had served commanders who were directly involved in the war.

In short, the fall 2007 promotion board marked a major cultural change in the Army. From then on, every brigadier-general board had to include at least one general who'd commanded troops in Iraq and another who'd done so in Afghanistan. (The chairman of the 2008 board would be Ray Odierno. Three years later, McMaster would be awarded his second star, although the revolution was still a halting one; the year before, he was once again passed over.)

Nagl and Yingling had written in their article, "The Army will become more adaptive only when being adaptive offers the surest path to promotion." Gates expressed the same idea in his speech to the retired Army officers. With the Petraeus-led board, which was created under Nagl's influence and with Gates's assent, the Army became "a more adaptive organizational culture"—or, as Nagl had put it in his book a few years earlier, "a learning organization."

But in the months and years ahead, what would this organization learn, and where would that lead it?

19.

"It Is Folly"

David Kilcullen had cause to be pleased with himself at the end of 2007. The Iraq War had taken a turn for the better, and the COIN doctrine he'd long pushed had played a substantial role in that turn. The secretary of defense was force-feeding its lessons to the Army, which as a result was changing its ways, in some cases dramatically.

In fact, though, Kilcullen's mood was apprehensive. He was concerned that too many people—officers, journalists, politicians, and policy makers—would see Iraq as a template for future wars and how to fight them, when, to his mind, it was a botch from the get-go: a terrible mistake that was steered away from disaster at the last minute, and, even then, no one should call the save a "victory." It was unclear whether the Iraqi government had really adopted the same goals as its American rescuers, whether the country's sectarian factions were capable of reconciling with one another, or whether Prime Minister Nouri al-Maliki and his top ministers were interested in reconciliation. Nor was it clear, even if all did end well, whether the crushing costs—in lives, money, and strategic position, for Iraq and the United States—had been commensurate with the gains.

Until recently, these issues wouldn't have disturbed Kilcullen. He'd built up a reputation for speaking his mind, often colorfully; but he'd also come up in the school of thought, common among soldiers, even intellectual ones, that his job wasn't to make policy but merely to carry it out in a way that minimized the pain and suffering.

His thinking on this point changed over the summer during a series of emails with a few anthropologists who had criticized some members of their profession for helping the US military in Iraq and other theaters in the global war on terror, which they saw as a cover for "indirect colonial rule." Toward the end of 2006, a group calling itself the Network of Concerned Anthropologists sent around a petition titled "Pledge of Nonparticipation in Counterinsurgency," which blasted those who engaged in such work for abetting "a brutal war of occupation which has entailed massive casualties." The executive board of the American Anthropological Association went so far as to condemn such work as "an unacceptable application of anthropological expertise."

The group's main target was Montgomery McFate, who had coauthored the intelligence chapter of David Petraeus's COIN field manual and had also helped design the Army's program of human terrain teams, which instructed brigades on the tribal cultures of the people they were both fighting and defending. But some in the group also went after Kilcullen, who had a doctorate in political anthropology and who had written articles stressing cultural understanding as a component of COIN.

McFate rattled off several spirited rebuttals, noting that such eminent anthropologists as Margaret Mead and Gregory Bateson had helped the Allied armies understand the cultures of the Pacific Islanders during World War II, and arguing that her own work in Iraq and Afghanistan had persuaded many American soldiers to use less force and kill fewer civilians.

Kilcullen went further, writing a lengthy response to an article titled "Toward Mercenary Anthropology?" in the June 2007 issue of *Anthropology Today,* a British journal that served as a forum for these charges. Afterward, he extended the dialogue in email correspondence with the magazine's editor, Gustaaf Houtman, and with Hugh Gusterson, an anthropologist at George Mason University who had helped launch the anti-COIN petition.

In one email addressed to both of them in late July, Kilcullen defended the "humanitarian effects of applying sound social science in Iraq," citing "measurable data" on the decline in civilian deaths, car bombings, and sectarian murders, as well as the proliferation of peace treaties signed among local tribal leaders—all the result, at least in part, of counterinsurgency methods. As for the war itself, he wrote, "I am not political in any way." Yes, he was working in the Bush administration, but merely as a "technical specialist." He'd opposed the war from the beginning, because it was a strategic blunder and because he figured it would take much longer and cause much greater suffering than the policy makers realized. When the administration switched to a COIN strategy at the start of 2007, and when General Petraeus asked him to come to Iraq to help implement it, he agreed, "not because I'm a Bush administration supporter," he wrote, but because "I felt a sense of obligation to put my money where my mouth was."

Houtman replied with a gracious note, beginning, "I am very impressed with your frankness and vision." In an earlier email, Gusterson had drawn comparisons between the COIN anthropologists and the German scientists in World War II. Houtman assured Kilcullen that this wasn't meant as a personal attack on him but rather as a restatement of the well-known fact "that an academic establishment can sometimes collaborate in the wrong way with their governments, with disastrous consequences." However, the editor added, not wishing to inflame his correspondence even to that degree, "the vision you sketch here bears no comparison to that at all."

Over the next few weeks and months, Kilcullen wondered whether Gusterson's comparison might have some validity. Did his role as a "technical specialist" really let him off the hook? Was joining an administration to help set right one of its own foolish decisions, and thereby make the military occupation of a foreign country go down more easily, a politically neutral act? Was he right to have excluded his judgments on the larger issue—the wisdom of the invasion itself—from his consultations?

The more he thought about it, the more Kilcullen realized that the anthropologists had a point. He didn't think that they were *right*. He was proud of the work that he and his colleagues had done; they'd helped clean up a mess left by others, and that didn't make them aligned with the culprits. To the extent they did share culpability, they had a moral obligation, having invaded the country, to keep it from crumbling into chaos.

Still, he was coming to the view that *as* a specialist and a professional, he also had an obligation to state his views on the whole picture: not just on how to improve the conduct of the war but also on whether going to war—this war or some future war—was a good idea in the first place. Questions of policy, not merely the execution of it, should very much be within his purview.

At the moment, Kilcullen was working as the special adviser on counterinsurgency for Secretary of State Condoleezza Rice, and he was spearheading a project that might offer a good platform for this new take on his responsibilities.

The project was a counterinsurgency guide for the civilian side of the US government. The project stemmed from Galula's dictum that insurgency wars were "80 percent political, 20 percent military" and from the line in Petraeus's field manual that counterinsurgents should use "*all* instruments of national power." Contrary to these basic principles, COIN in Iraq was in fact performed almost entirely by the military; even the few civilian field specialists from State and AID were attached to Army brigades, and mainly in advisory roles. There must be plenty of officials in the Departments of Justice, Agriculture, Commerce, and Transportation who knew more than any Army officer about setting up courts, growing crops, financing businesses, and building roads—the elements of the civil society that counterinsurgents were supposed to be creating. But where were they? The premise of the project was that these agencies' leaders didn't understand the COIN concept. They needed to be brought in; they needed, to use one of Petraeus's favorite phrases, to buy in.

The seeds for such a guide had been planted two years earlier, in the spring of 2006, when Petraeus, soon after his COIN conference at Fort Leavenworth, approached John Hillen, the assistant secretary of state for politico-military affairs, and asked him when State and all the other civilian agencies were going to get behind the policy.

In response, Hillen and his assistant, a Foreign Service Officer named Donna Hopkins, organized a similar sort of conference. It took place on September 28 and 29 at the International Trade Center in downtown Washington, a few blocks from the White House. Petraeus's field manual was about to be published; the interim draft had leaked to the press a few months earlier. A companion volume for the rest of the government might form the basis for a truly integrated civil-military policy. And this conference, Hillen thought, might do for the interagency COIN guide what Petraeus's Leavenworth conference, seven months earlier, had done for the Army field manual. Hillen, too, it seemed, knew something about buy-in.

The conference—called the Interagency Counterinsurgency Initiative—was a big event. More than a hundred officials attended from seventeen federal departments and agencies. Hillen's cosponsor was Jeb Nadaner, the Pentagon official who had shepherded the DoD directive declaring stability operations to have the same priority as combat operations. And there were speeches by the usual suspects, including Petraeus himself, Kilcullen, John Nagl, Conrad Crane, Eliot Cohen, Eric Edelman, Janine Davidson, and Sarah Sewall, whose Carr Center for Human Rights Policy at Harvard had cosponsored the Leavenworth conference.

But over the next year, the initiative fell apart. Kilcullen had been assigned to take the lead in drafting a report, but one chapter into it, Petraeus was promoted to commander of US forces in Iraq, and he asked Kilcullen to come along as an aide. Midlevel officials from several different agencies formed a team to write a new draft. After reading it, Conrad Crane told them that it was a mere laundry list of little use. From there, the project deteriorated further. An AID official wrote one section proposing that US law-enforcement officers train local police in a COIN campaign. Crane told him that this was a bad idea; they'd tried it in Iraq, and it failed miserably. The official replied that he couldn't delete the passage because his bosses were planning to invest a big chunk of their budget in just such a project. As the writing team progressed, the draft devolved, with officials from the disparate agencies disagreeing over clauses large and small. Nothing materialized.

The fact was, the US government wasn't set up as a colonial enterprise. The Justice Department ran some intelligence and counter-narcotics operations in dozens of unstable and dangerous countries; Agriculture administered food programs abroad; Commerce promoted exports. But these activities followed their own logic: their managers wanted nothing to do with counterinsurgency; any formal ties to the military would hinder their effectiveness.

By the time Kilcullen returned from Iraq in the fall of 2007, the project had dwindled to three core agencies: State, Defense, and AID, with some input from the CIA and the White House. The original idea had been to produce a how-to guide, similar to the Army field manual but for civilian experts assigned to counterinsurgency campaigns. This notion was moot, now that so many agencies had dropped out. So Kilcullen, who took over the writing job on his own, turned it into a guide for senior policy makers, and he decided to give them the advice he now wished he'd dispensed long ago.

This guide, he wrote up front in his draft, would focus above all on the "formulation of policy," the factors that policy makers should consider when "determining *whether* the US should become engaged in a COIN campaign overseas"—precisely the question that he'd once thought he had no business addressing. The decision to intervene, he went on, "should not be taken lightly," as "historically, COIN campaigns have almost always been more costly, more protracted, and more difficult than first anticipated."

The authors of the Army's field manual had dropped hints along these lines: brief, elbow-nudging passages noting that insurgency wars were "protracted by nature," requiring "firm political will and substantial patience" as well as "considerable expenditures of time and resources." Some of its authors had wanted to insert an explicit warning: if you're not willing to spend the time and the money, then don't start a COIN war in the first place. But an Army field manual was no place for policy advice: by nature, it assumed that the political leaders had decided to fight this kind of war; the field manual's purpose was to instruct soldiers on how to proceed.

Kilcullen had long thought—and still believed—that it was important to study insurgency wars because big powers, including the United States, tend to get involved in these kinds of wars at least once every generation, whether willingly or incrementally, and they can turn disastrous if their armies didn't know how to fight them. If you were going to engage in a COIN campaign, there were certain things you had to do. Those things were what he'd spent his entire professional life learning and setting down. But he also thought—he'd always thought—that it was usually best not to undertake COIN campaigns in the first place. They took a long time, cost a lot of money, got a lot of people killed, and often didn't work. This side of his thinking, though, he'd discussed only with his friends.

But now Kilcullen had retired from the military; he was writing a guide for the political leaders who help make the decisions on going, or not going, to war; so he flashed the warning lights brightly. The theme throughout his fifty-page guide, sometimes implicit, quite often unabashed, was basically: *don't do this!*

On its first page, echoing the themes of Robert Komer's Vietnam-era *Bureaucracy Does Its Thing* and Celeste Ward's briefing from the previous year on diverging American and Iraqi interests, Kilcullen emphasized that success in COIN often depends on whether the host government is willing to make the sorts of reforms that earn its people's loyalty. "However great its know-how and enthusiasm," he wrote, "an outside actor can never fully compensate for lack of will, incapacity, or counterproductive behavior on the part of the supported government."

This was a greater obstacle than some might think, he went on, because the fact is, a government needing outside help to stave off insurgents probably *does* lack the will or capacity to fight on its own; and, since insurgencies thrive on real grievances, it probably *is* resistant to reform. In these cases, a country that intervenes to wage a COIN campaign "will almost always need to co-opt, persuade, or occasionally pressure the local government to give up counterproductive behavior, take genuine steps to reform its actions, win the support of its people, and demonstrate effectiveness and legitimacy."

Kilcullen then hammered home the main point:

> It is folly to become engaged with counterinsurgency in a foreign country unless there is a reasonable likelihood that the affected government will introduce necessary reforms and will demonstrate adequate willpower and capacity to defeat insurgents (or at least be willing to accept advice as well as assistance). Before deciding to provide overseas COIN assistance, US officials must determine how likely it is that the local government will cooperate and how willing it is to undertake necessary reforms.

Reduced to a syllogism, his argument went like this: we shouldn't engage in counterinsurgency unless the government we're helping is effective and legitimate; a government that needs foreign help to fight an insurgency generally isn't effective or legitimate; therefore, we generally shouldn't engage in counterinsurgency.

Few of these ideas were original; similar points about favorable and unfavorable conditions for insurgents had been made by Galula and the Army field manual. But for Kilcullen, this was a departure from the scope and nature of the arguments that he'd been accustomed to making in a public, political forum.

On July 9, 2008, Kilcullen hosted an all-day workshop in a large classroom at the Foreign Service Institute in Arlington, Virginia, to vet his draft of the civilian COIN guide. It was Kilcullen's show: he made the opening remarks at 8:30 a.m., as well as the closing remarks at 4:30 p.m., and he led several of the discussions in between.

The most heated arguments took place over what he'd figured would be the eyebrow-raiser: the passage about the "folly" of counterinsurgency and the edict that American officials "must" determine if a foreign government will make reforms before they decide whether to intervene.

Conrad Crane protested that Kilcullen had gone too far. Certainly, Crane said, we should try to use our leverage to persuade the foreign government's leaders to reform. But how can we *make* them do that? And besides, if they did everything we demanded, wouldn't the local population view them as American puppets? The war in El Salvador took more than ten years to settle. Should we have decided not to intervene just because, especially at the beginning, the Salvadoran government was corrupt and oppressive?

Crane lost the argument, not just with Kilcullen but with the majority of officials and consultants in the room. As a compromise, Kilcullen did insert a sentence after his "folly" line: "Unfortunately, there will inevitably be occasions when the assessment of the insurgency situation will weigh heavily against US involvement, but specific US national interests will drive policy makers towards engagement." But, he added, even in these cases, an assessment should still be made, as it may "prompt caution over the *form* of engagement to be used, perhaps encouraging a more limited involvement from which a subsequent exit can be made with less political consequences . . . It is often the case that the less intrusive and more indirect the approach selected, the more likely it is to succeed."

Kilcullen was reciting the argument made by some of the Special Forces veterans at Petraeus's COIN conference nearly two-and-a-half years earlier: that a small footprint is often best, in that it gives us more leverage and focuses attention on the fact that the fight is ultimately the host government's, not ours.

Dealing with the Iraqi insurgency required a lot of troops, Kilcullen wrote on, but that war wasn't a typical case of COIN. America had sent troops in the first place "to bring about regime change," not to help prop up a government. When the social and political order collapsed—a nearly inevitable result of the regime change itself and of the subsequent (and still mystifying) decision to disband the Iraqi army—America had an obligation to repair the damage it wreaked. But, he noted, Iraq should not be regarded as a case to emulate when thinking about counterinsurgency.

Crane wasn't the only one in the room who had problems with Kilcullen's language. Several others thought that "folly" was too snarky a word for this sort of document and that it seemed presumptuous to tell senior officials they "must" weigh certain factors before deciding on a policy.

But Kilcullen noticed that these critics weren't quarreling with him on substance; they only thought he should express the points more cautiously. He fired back. As the professionals who executed this fuckup, he said, we have to lay down a marker; we have an obligation to say what we think. If our bosses think we've gone too far, they'll notch it down. But let's not censor ourselves preemptively.

By a vote, the room agreed with Kilcullen.

Over the next few weeks, he tightened the prose, circulated revisions for final comments, and sent the finished product to the officials who would sign it.

He was feeling good about having expressed his views so clearly, and completely, for once. He gave advance copies of the guide to a few journalists he knew. When one of them, Spencer Ackerman, called to ask some questions, Kilcullen opened up.

If future policy makers follow the guide's lessons, he said, maybe they'll avoid another war like Iraq. He then added, "The biggest fucking stupid idea was to invade Iraq in the first place."

Ackerman's story, written for the *Washington Independent*, quoted Kilcullen's line in full. *The Huffington Post*, a much more widely read site, picked up the story, running it under the headline "Rice Adviser: Iraq Invasion Was 'F*cking Stupid.'"

Within hours, Kilcullen got a phone call from Eliot Cohen. "What the fuck, Dave?" Cohen exclaimed. Condi had seen the piece and was very displeased.

Kilcullen posted a response on the *Small Wars Journal* site, stating that Ackerman "did not seek to clear that quote with me, and I would not have approved it if he had." Tellingly, Kilcullen did not retract, or deny uttering, the remark; nor did he claim, as many do under similar circumstances, that he'd been speaking off the record. In fact, he restated his point, though more politely. "If [Ackerman] had sought a formal comment," Kilcullen wrote, "I would have told him what I have said publicly before: in my view, the decision to invade Iraq in 2003 was an extremely serious strategic error."

Cohen and Rice were hardly mollified. An "extremely serious strategic error" was only a notch or two below "fucking stupid" when it came to remarks that a special adviser to the secretary of state shouldn't say in public about the defining decision of a presidency.

Ten days later, on August 8, a brief war broke out between Russia and the Republic of Georgia, a crisis atmosphere enveloped the administration, and the F-bomb affair vanished in the fog. The next time Rice saw Kilcullen at a meeting, she looked at him as if she should be angry but couldn't remember why.

Meanwhile, the civilian COIN guide moved forward. Robert Gates at the Pentagon and Henrietta Fore, the administrator of AID, gave it their signatures. But Condi Rice didn't, not right away. Cohen told Kilcullen that she had definitely received it and had probably read it. But by the end of the year, it still sat on her desk. Was she still ticked off at Kilcullen? Did she realize, reading it in the context of the Ackerman interview, that the guide was a harsh critique of her own time in office?

Rice finally signed the guide on January 13, 2009. Kilcullen's prose was left unchanged. But the document was dead on arrival. Barack Obama would be sworn in as president in a week's time. New teams tend to ignore what the old team leaves behind, especially something dropped on the doormat so late in the day.

In this case, though, the warnings might best have been noted.

20.

COIN Versus CT

On January 20, 2009, Barack Obama moved into the White House with a path already laid for an exit from Iraq. Two months earlier, the Bush administration and Nouri al-Maliki's government had signed a Status of Forces Agreement, which required all American troops "to withdraw from all Iraqi territory, waters, and airspace no later than the 31st of December of 2011." The details of the transition still needed to be worked out, but the American side of the war was practically over.

Now, though, the other, forgotten war, in Afghanistan, was spiraling out of control.

During his presidential campaign, candidate Obama had repeatedly called for sending more troops to Afghanistan, which he called the center of global terrorism. As far back as October 2002, when he was still an Illinois state senator, Obama, in a speech against the then-impending invasion of Iraq, had said, "I don't oppose all wars. What I am opposed to is a dumb war . . . a rash war, a war based not on reason but on passion, not on principle but on politics." Iraq was the dumb war. But there was a smarter war that Obama favored waging. "You want a fight, President Bush?" he said in that same speech. "Let's finish the fight with bin Laden and al Qaeda."

When he gave that speech, serious fighting hadn't yet resumed in Afghanistan. But by the time Obama was running for president, the Taliban had come out of hiding and were attacking American and NATO troops in the eastern and southern parts of the country, and so he spoke out explicitly for sending in more troops. Many thought he was playing politics: Iraq was Bush's war, and therefore bad; Afghanistan was the war that Bush had neglected, and therefore good. There may have been some truth to this, but another, substantive factor was at play: the fact that one of Obama's foreign-policy advisers was Bruce Riedel.

Riedel was a recently retired career CIA analyst with a specialty in South

Asia and a deep knowledge of terrorist groups in Afghanistan and Pakistan. Still a consultant, and plugged into a network of associates, Riedel knew that the Taliban fighters were on the rise in Afghanistan, that they had ties to al Qaeda, and that a restoration of their rule in Kabul could destabilize neighboring Pakistan, which possessed a nuclear arsenal and an intelligence service rife with Islamist extremists. Riedel joined the Obama campaign because of his speech against the war in Iraq, which he opposed for the same reason as Dave Kilcullen and other strategically minded analysts: because it distracted resources and attention from the real center stage, Afghanistan and Pakistan. Obama heeded Riedel's briefings on the dangers in that part of the world; his call for sending more troops there was based on more than electoral calculations.

Soon after he won the November 2008 election, Obama asked Admiral Mike Mullen, the chairman of the Joint Chiefs of Staff, to come talk with him at his transition headquarters in Chicago. Mullen told him the same thing about Afghanistan that Riedel had, with the additional admission that the Bush administration had devoted too few resources to the region (they'd all been diverted to Iraq) and had devised no strategy for it whatever.

In early January, Obama sent his vice president–elect, Joe Biden, to Afghanistan on a fact-finding mission. Biden had long been a senior member of the Senate Foreign Relations Committee; this was far from his first trip. When he returned, he told Obama, with his usual theatricality, "I bring back one big headline for you: if you ask ten of our people over there what we're trying to accomplish, you get ten different answers."

So, one week after his inauguration, Obama phoned Riedel and asked him to chair a White House review of America's policy in Afghanistan and Pakistan. He would need the report in sixty days, in time for a NATO summit in early April. Riedel had told Obama that he wanted no administration job, but he agreed to do this.

Riedel's report painted a gloomy, though not quite dire, picture. His bottom line: "We are losing the war in Afghanistan, but it is not yet lost." He rejected Bush's notion of creating a Western-style democracy in Kabul and recommended instead a set of challenging though feasible strategic goals: to "degrade, dismantle, and destroy al Qaeda"; to train the Afghan military, so that it could secure the country after Western troops leave; and to stabilize Afghanistan, build up its government, and thus leave no pockets of anarchy for al Qaeda to exploit.

The best way to accomplish these goals, his report concluded, was to pursue, at least in the southern part of the country, a "fully resourced counterinsurgency strategy."

Riedel had no background in counterinsurgency. He was influenced on this point by one of the key members of the interagency group that worked on the report—General David Petraeus.

Petraeus had wrapped up his tour as commander in Iraq the previous September on a note of triumph. George Bush promoted his deputy, General Ray Odierno, to take over the job of commander, and he put Petraeus in charge of US Central Command, which supervised all American military operations in the Persian Gulf and Southwest Asia, including Iraq and Afghanistan. But the command's headquarters were at MacDill Air Force Base in Tampa, Florida, giving Petraeus closer access to the powers in Washington.

The Riedel group had started meeting in February 2009, just weeks after Obama took office. As with most policy-review groups of this sort, it included second- and third-tiered officials from all the agencies with any stake in the policy: CIA, AID, Justice, Agriculture, and several others. But the three main players, besides Riedel, were Richard Holbrooke, the State Department's envoy to Afghanistan and Pakistan; Michèle Flournoy, the undersecretary of defense for policy; and Petraeus, representing the military.

Flournoy backed Petraeus on a counterinsurgency approach with some authority. The two had known each other from the COIN field manual workshop at Fort Leavenworth three years earlier and from the Clinton administration's policy reviews of Haiti back in the mid-1990s. In 2007 Flournoy had cofounded a Washington think tank called the Center for a New American Security. Its purpose was to build bridges between Republicans and Democrats on defense policy, but the two wars going on happened to be insurgency wars, so it evolved into a locus of thinking and writing on counterinsurgency; some called it "COIN Central." (Fittingly, when John Nagl retired from the Army in 2008, he joined the center as a senior fellow; when Flournoy left to join the Obama administration, Nagl replaced her as the center's president.) Flournoy thus approached the Riedel group's tasks as an analyst well versed in COIN doctrine and, though not as fervent as some, an advocate.

On March 12, Obama's top national-security advisers met to discuss the Riedel report and touched off an argument that wouldn't be settled completely for another three years.

Joe Biden instigated the dispute. Biden could go off on tangents at self-indulgent length; many saw him as a blowhard. But Obama had privately asked his vice president to raise questions in these sorts of meetings, to challenge every assumption, to highlight a policy option's unstated implications. Obama was a famously fast learner, but military issues were new to him. And he was preoccupied, to the exclusion of nearly everything else, with the economy, which was plunging in steeper free fall than anyone had calculated just a few months earlier.

So Biden asked hard questions and, in this case, not merely as a devil's advocate. He'd first been elected to the Senate when he wasn't quite thirty, in 1972, during the final throes of the Vietnam War, and so he was suspicious of counterinsurgency, suspicious of any sort of military escalation based on a theory. If the strategic goal was to defeat al Qaeda, whose leaders were based mainly in Pakistan, he asked, why should we deploy a lot of troops to do nation-building in Afghanistan? Why not just send drones and small teams of Special Ops forces to go directly after al Qaeda fighters along the border?

Admiral Mullen, the Joint Chiefs chairman, explained patiently that chasing insurgents wouldn't solve the problem and, worse still, would allow them the initiative. The best way to defeat insurgents, he said, reciting the standard COIN argument, was to protect the population, earn its trust and loyalty, and thus dry up its support for the insurgents.

Biden said he understood all that, acknowledged that Mullen's case had logic. But, he argued, this course wasn't *politically* sustainable; it would require a lot of troops, a lot of money, a lot of time, and the American people wouldn't put up with it.

At this point, Hillary Clinton, Obama's erstwhile rival in the Democratic primaries and now his secretary of state, spoke up. She thought that the mission *was* sustainable, that the American people *would* put up with it, if we succeeded at meeting our objectives.

Mullen seemed to win the day on substance. Biden, besides being the sole outright dissenter in the room, had objected mainly on grounds of domestic politics; and one could argue that Clinton—who'd crushed Biden in the Democratic primaries and had spent eight years in the White House as a very policy-driven First Lady—possessed a firmer grasp of domestic politics than he did.

Obama endorsed the Riedel report, but with caveats. He didn't take his vice president's side, but he shared his apprehensions. So, importantly, did his secretary of defense, Robert Gates.

When Gates agreed to replace Donald Rumsfeld in the final two years of the Bush administration, he had no intention of staying any longer. He'd taken the job in part as a favor to the Bush family, in part out of a patrician sense of obligation to the nation in a time of crisis. And he found the experience wearying. He hated Washington and longed to get back to his two houses in the Pacific Northwest: one lakeside, the other overlooking the ocean. A friend had given him a digital "countdown meter" displaying how many days remained before Bush's term was over, and Gates showed it to visiting legislators, journalists, and lobbyists with mischievous glee. The sentiment was far from reciprocal. Gates was respected in all corners of the capital for his experience and well-worn gravitas. Several senators, on both sides of the aisle, hoped out loud that he would stay on, no matter who won the upcoming election. Gates discouraged all such speculation, telling one reporter, "The circumstances under which I would do that are inconceivable to me."

He later confessed that his dismissiveness had been part of a "covert action" (a serious phrase for a man who'd spent the bulk of his career in the CIA) to convince everyone that he didn't want to stay, so that no one would ask him to. But he knew all along that if the president did ask, he would feel duty-bound to comply. Besides, as much as he hated to admit it, he was growing comfortable in the job; he liked being in the thick of things and having influence with those at the zenith of national power.

Finally, when he met with Obama, he found himself, to his surprise, liking *him*. Gates was a Republican, but he saw in this Democrat a man with a similar temperament: a thinker and a reformer, but one with a pragmatic bent and an impatience for party dogma of whatever stripe. He sensed that he could work with Obama and make a difference. All those speeches

Gates had given under Bush, outlining the changes that his successor should put in place—it might be best if he were that successor. Gates agreed to stay on, for one year; he ended up staying for two and a half.

For all his agitated efforts to change the Pentagon, Gates was at heart a conservative. He killed or slashed thirty weapons systems in his first two years as Obama's defense secretary, including some of the services' dearest projects (the Air Force's F-22 stealth fighter and the Army's Future Combat Systems vehicle, among others), but he had no interest in cutting back the military's size or America's global reach.

Yet when it came to Afghanistan, Gates was leery. He'd been deputy director of the CIA when the Soviet Union crashed and burned on the country's rugged terrain, despite nearly a decade of pummeling the mujahedeen rebels with all the firepower it could muster. And he'd been the Agency's director when, partly as a result of that fiasco, the once-mighty Communist empire collapsed. Contemplating America's options, he had to consider that there was still some way to go in Iraq; he wasn't at all eager to step up yet another war in another Muslim nation.

Gates didn't say much at the White House meeting on Riedel's report; he rarely said much in large meetings, holding his fire for key moments or, better yet, for the smaller sessions, preferably face-to-face, with the decision-maker. But at Senate hearings a month and a half earlier, Gates had testified that he would be "deeply skeptical" of a request to deploy a lot more troops. It would be best, he said, to keep America's "footprint" relatively small. If the Afghan people begin to see the war as our war, not theirs, he warned, "we will go the way of other imperial occupiers."

There was one other aspect of Afghanistan that weighed on President Obama: the war's cost. His senior advisers met one last time on March 17 to approve the Riedel report. The next day, Obama flew on Air Force One to Los Angeles for a political event and to appear on Jay Leno's *Tonight Show*. His chief of staff, Rahm Emanuel, told Riedel to get on that plane; the cross-country flight would pose a perfect opportunity for a discussion about the report—and, more to the point, a discussion with no generals present.

A couple of hours into the flight, Riedel was called into the president's cabin to go over the whole report: its grim analysis of the situation in Afghanistan and Pakistan, and its twenty recommendations of what to do about it. But one remark in his briefing seemed to impress Obama particularly. Riedel told him that the annual cost of arming and supporting one American soldier in Afghanistan was $250,000 (he'd been given the number by the Pentagon, but, as he discovered later, the real cost was at least three times as much). By contrast, the cost of one Afghan soldier was $12,000. You could pay twenty Afghan soldiers for the same price as a single American soldier.

Riedel could practically see a lightbulb switch on above the president's head. This would be the logical exit strategy: to turn the fight over to the Afghans. And the calculation—this ratio of the two soldiers' costs—would be a sobering constraint, especially given America's financial crunch, on any pressure to send tens of thousands of more US troops into battle.

In the end, buffeted by the crosswinds of the military's advice, Biden's dissent, Gates's qualms, and Riedel's recital of the costs, Obama took a middle course.

At a press conference on Friday, March 27, one week before the NATO summit in Strasbourg, Obama announced what he called a "comprehensive strategy" for Pakistan and Afghanistan; but, in fact, it was not a strategy at all. His declared *goal* for the war—taken straight from Riedel's report, and a sober scaling-back from Bush's dreams of erecting a Western-style democracy with the full panoply of human rights—was simply "to disrupt, dismantle, and defeat al Qaeda in Pakistan and Afghanistan, and to prevent their return to either country in the future." How to do this—whether to pursue the COIN approach, which had been endorsed by nearly everyone in his cabinet, or Joe Biden's more limited counterterrorism approach, which some dubbed CT—the president didn't exactly say. Or, rather, he straddled both.

Even before the Riedel report was finished, Obama had approved an urgent request from the Joint Chiefs for twenty-one thousand more troops to be sent right away to Afghanistan, on top of the thirty-seven thousand already there. Presidential elections in Afghanistan were scheduled for August. One reason the Taliban insurgents were gaining strength was that Hamid Karzai—who had been installed in his office by Western powers—wasn't seen by many of his own people as quite legitimate. The elections could change that, but first there had to *be* elections, and they had to be seen as fair. The areas around polling places had to be secure so that people would feel safe going to vote. More troops were needed for that security, and only the United States could provide them. To get them there in time for the election, they had to be mobilized now. Obama had hoped to wait for Riedel's report before making any decisions on troops, but the request had logic; Riedel thought so, too.

Now, at his March 27 press conference, Obama declared that these extra troops "will take the fight to the Taliban in the south and the east and . . . go after insurgents along the border" between Afghanistan and Pakistan—with one exception, this urged on him by Bob Gates: one brigade of the 82nd Airborne Division, four thousand troops in all, would beef up the training of the Afghan army.

Had he stopped there, the new policy would have amounted to an acceptance of Biden's CT strategy and a desire, perhaps prompted by Riedel's economic argument, to jump-start the transition to the Afghans.

However, Obama went on to say, "To succeed, we and our friends and allies must . . . promote a more capable and accountable Afghan government." This goal, he said, will require "a dramatic increase in our civilian effort," including the deployment of "agricultural specialists and educators, engineers and lawyers," all of whom must, of course, be protected by soldiers as they go about their work. He also said that the United States and its NATO allies must compel Karzai's government to reduce the "corruption that causes Afghans to lose faith in their own leaders."

This part of the speech sounded like an endorsement of COIN. In fact, at a press briefing afterward, Michèle Flournoy called the new policy "very much a counterinsurgency approach," although she added that military operations against "high-value targets"—meaning al Qaeda and Taliban leaders—would also remain "a central part of this mission."

The problem was that twenty-one thousand extra troops wouldn't be enough to carry out both CT and COIN strategies. Besides, these troops would have little to do with either mission; they were being sent to boost security before the election. One thing the Riedel report did not deal with, at all, was how many troops would be needed to do whatever it was that the president decided to do: this sort of calculation lay outside Riedel's lane and beyond his competency; he left it to the military.

Obama put off all these questions until after the Afghan elections—a deferral that stemmed from his indecision on the basic question but also made sense. If, as he'd been told, a key issue in COIN was whether the host government was seen by its people as legitimate, it would be wise to wait for the results of the election—to see whether or not they legitimized Karzai or whichever candidate won—before upping the stakes any further.

The president went off to Strasbourg, his first official trip to Europe, to declare the new policy and to rally allied support. Then he went home to deal with his own country's gravest economic crisis since the Great Depression.

Meanwhile, Bob Gates continued to deal with all the relevant players, including the US commander in Afghanistan, General Dave McKiernan. For some time, McKiernan had a request on the table for an additional ten thousand troops beyond the twenty-one thousand that Obama had approved. But the more Gates talked with him, the more he realized that McKiernan had little idea of what he would do with them. He was devoting all of his effort to battling al Qaeda and Taliban militants along the eastern border with Pakistan, while doing almost nothing in the southern cities, where the Taliban were strengthening their hold, especially in Kandahar. McKiernan also acknowledged that he'd been devoting all his intelligence assets to pinning down the locations of the Taliban fighters, and none at all to analyzing the Afghan people: their tribal allegiances, sectarian splits, or any of the other sociocultural tags that would have been vital inputs in a counterinsurgency campaign. Petraeus, who also spoke often with Gates, was particularly annoyed at this neglect, which amounted to a violation of his own directive as CentCom commander to shift more to a COIN strategy.

McKiernan wasn't entirely to blame; he barely had enough resources to fight along the border. But he was seen as old-school Army, an armor officer who hadn't made the conversion to the new way of thinking that some other tank men, such as Pete Chiarelli, H. R. McMaster, and John Nagl, had made.

On May 11, after consulting with Mullen, Petraeus, Clinton, and the president, Gates announced that he was relieving McKiernan of duty one year before his term in Afghanistan was due to expire—effectively ending his Army career. It was the first time that an American wartime commander had been fired since Harry Truman dismissed General Douglas

MacArthur during the Korean War a half century earlier. (It was the second time Gates had fired any sort of general, but the earlier dismissal, handed to T. Michael Moseley, the Air Force chief of staff, had been on grounds of malfeasance.) At a press conference, Gates said that McKiernan hadn't done anything wrong specifically; it was just that the war needed "fresh thinking."

By "fresh thinking," Gates meant a working knowledge of COIN. He announced at the same news conference that McKiernan's replacement would be General Stanley McChrystal, whose main qualification, Gates said, was his "unique skill set in counterinsurgency."

Several officers who'd worked with McChrystal were puzzled by his appointment. As far as they knew, he had *no* skill set in counterinsurgency, much less a unique one, at least not as the COINdinistas defined the term. He was an exceptionally creative officer, but his creativity seemed to reside in the art and science of finding and killing bad guys—and, at least in Iraq and Afghanistan, he hadn't done this by winning hearts or minds.

McChrystal came from a military family: his father was a two-star general who'd fought in Korea and Vietnam; all four of his brothers enlisted in the Army; even his sister wound up marrying an Army officer. But Stan was the only son who'd gone to West Point, graduating in the class of 1976. Afterward, he entered the force as a parachutist in the 82nd Airborne, then rose through the ranks in Ranger and Special Forces units, climaxing in the fall of 2003, when he took control of the Joint Special Operations Command. JSOC was the most clandestine branch of the American military, the black-ops ninjas—Delta Force, Navy SEALs, Night Stalker pilots, and various specialized Task Forces identified only by their numbers (TF 11, TF 6-26, TF 121, among others)—that swooped down on terrorists in the dead of night. After the September 11 attacks, JSOC expanded enormously. In September 2003, Donald Rumsfeld signed an executive order authorizing the command to take any action against al Qaeda without prior approval of the president or secretary of defense and without notifying the intelligence committees of Congress.

McChrystal became commanding general of JSOC the same month that Rumsfeld's order took effect. Still, for all his command's power, he found its reach limited. Each branch was cut off from one another, not to mention from the rest of the military and the national intelligence agencies. McChrystal saw that al Qaeda was a network, each cell's powers multiplied by its ties with other cells. It would take a network to fight a network, so McChrystal built one of his own.

Before taking command at JSOC, he had worked in the Pentagon as the Joint Staff's vice director of operations. He saw how different elements of the national-security bureaucracy did or did not connect. Applying those lessons, he now reached out to the CIA, the National Security Agency, the National Geospatial-Intelligence Agency, regional specialists from the State Department, and the top officers of Central Command: making deals and exchanging services, while at the same time remaining sensitive to each fiefdom's turf. As a result, when JSOC was searching for a terrorist, tracking an insurgent, or planning and executing a raid, everyone involved had continuous access to a vast range of real-time intelligence—drone imagery, satellite signals, cell phone intercepts, and much more—as well as the support of conventional Army forces. By fusing all this intelligence, McChrystal's men in Iraq were able to perform dozens of raids a night; it was his team that found Saddam Hussein's hideout and that killed Abu Musab al-Zarqawi, the leader of al Qaeda in Iraq.

McChrystal was driven, even obsessed. It was well known that he ran seven miles a day, ate just one meal, and slept only four hours a night. After his men killed Zarqawi, he insisted on personally inspecting and identifying the corpse.

JSOC's nature—elite, hard-core violent, and unaccountable—sometimes sowed a toxic atmosphere. Several raids targeted the wrong house, killing innocent people. A top-secret detention center known as Camp Nama, run by JSOC's thousand-man Task Force 6-26 at Baghdad airport, came to resemble a torture chamber, so brutal that the US Army stepped in and disciplined thirty-four of its members. McChrystal wasn't involved personally in its operations; the first time he toured the center and saw what was happening, he muttered, "This is how we lose." After the disciplining, he set new rules for interrogation. Still, he had at least tolerated the climate that produced such practices. Members of the Task Force had posted placards all over the center reading, "No Blood, No Foul." In other words: feel free to do anything to a prisoner, as long as the pain and bruises you inflict don't make him bleed.

And yet McChrystal knew more about counterinsurgency than his career path suggested. As a cadet at West Point, his favorite course had been the History Department's offering on Revolutionary Warfare—the academy's sole concession, at the time, to the study of COIN—which included readings from Galula, Mao, *The Centurions,* and the assorted classics that David Petraeus and others had also read in their formative years.

When he was named commander of US and NATO forces in Afghanistan, he knew it was time to reactivate that aspect of his education. Up till then, though, McChrystal's experience in this side of insurgency warfare had been, literally, academic, derived strictly from reading books. He hadn't maneuvered to find the right balance, hadn't navigated the shoals between killing and co-opting, that Petraeus and others had done in sustained operations—and, even then, with uneven success—in Iraq. The consequences would soon show.

McChrystal won Senate confirmation as commander on June 10. The first thing he did was to emulate his old friend and fellow West Point alumnus Dave Petraeus: he recruited a group of experts to come to Afghanistan for a month and write an assessment of the situation. Petraeus had put together these groups to get political buy-in for what he'd already decided to do. McChrystal had the same idea in mind, but he also really wanted the outsiders' advice and reality-check.

The questions he asked the "assessment team" to answer came in a directive from Petraeus himself, in his role as head of Central Command: Can ISAF—the International Security Assistance Force, the formal name of NATO's coalition in Afghanistan—achieve its mission? If so, how should it go about the task?

In choosing his team, McChrystal again followed Petraeus's example by picking a dozen specialists, many of them PhDs from leading Washington think tanks. Among them were Fred Kagan, the former West Point history professor at the American Enterprise Institute, who'd made the crucial case for a surge in Iraq; his wife, Kimberly Kagan, who'd since formed her own think tank to tout and document the surge; and Stephen Biddle of the Council on Foreign Relations, who'd served on a similar team when Petraeus took command in Iraq.

McChrystal asked John Nagl to participate, too, but he had just taken over as president of the Center for a New American Security. Most of its top analysts—not just Michèle Flournoy, whom he'd replaced—had gone off to join the Obama administration; so he was too busy raising money and recruiting new staff, both unfamiliar tasks. Instead, he offered up one of his new hires, Andrew Exum, an intense, scholarly former Special Ops officer who'd not only earned a master's degree at the American University of Beirut and a PhD in war studies at the University of London but had also commanded Ranger platoons in Iraq and Afghanistan.

The team visited American and NATO troops all over Afghanistan and spoke with high-ranking Afghan officials in Kabul. By the time of its interim briefing to McChrystal on July 4, barely a week after the members' arrival, the picture was clear. The country was falling apart, the government was corrupt and incompetent, the Taliban were gaining strength and popular favor, ISAF had no coherent strategy, and its troops were "commuting to the war"—just as most American troops had done in Iraq before Petraeus—patrolling the streets by day, usually in armored vehicles, almost never getting out to walk among the people, and returning to their large, gated bases at night. If nothing was changed, defeat was inevitable.

There was unanimity on this grim finding, but not on what to do about it. A few of the team's members, including Jeremy Shapiro of the Brookings Institution, came away from the tour deeply skeptical that the mission was feasible under any circumstances. To varying degrees, the others saw the prospects as dim but not hopeless and thought that the stakes were high enough to justify giving the mission a shot—as long as there was a surge in troops and a shift to a counterinsurgency strategy, the same formula that seemed to have turned things around in Iraq (though none of the experts had any illusions that the two countries were otherwise similar).

Eventually the dissenters were brought around, on the condition that the report made clear that success was by no means certain even if its recommendations were followed. Nobody had a problem with that. Even Fred Kagan, the most enthusiastic team member, put the chances of success—with an adequate surge and a shift to COIN—at less than fifty-fifty.

McChrystal was briefed on the study periodically. During the drafting stage (and the document went through a few drafts), he sat with the team and went over every line, rewriting many.

The final sixty-six-page report began with an attention-grabber: "The overall situation is deteriorating . . . Success is achievable, but it will not be attained simply by trying harder or 'doubling down' on the previous strategy." There was an "urgent need for a significant change to our strategy and the way that we think and operate." This "new strategy," it went on, must be "an integrated civilian-military counterinsurgency campaign."

In language familiar to anyone who had studied COIN, the report outlined the implications: "This is a different kind of fight . . . Our strategy cannot be focused on seizing terrain or destroying insurgent forces; our objective must be the population." To gain the people's support, the troops must maintain "a persistent presence" in the neighborhoods (the report called this approach "shape / clear / hold / build," a slight rephrasing of the by-now-standard phrase "clear, hold, and build") and cultivate a "better understanding" of their needs.

Victory was defined as "a condition where the insurgency no longer threatens the viability of the state." This suggested a two-pronged approach: fighting the *insurgency* directly, when that was necessary; and, at least as important, bolstering the Afghan *state,* making it a viable, legitimate entity that fulfilled the needs of its people and thus preempted or co-opted the insurgents' appeal.

McChrystal and his team realized that bolstering the state was a bigger task than battling the Taliban. Their insight about the nature of Karzai's government was reminiscent of the realization that dawned on American commanders in Iraq rather late in the day about the nature of Nouri al-Maliki's regime. "Progress is hindered," they wrote, by "a crisis of confidence in the government," owing to "the weakness of state institutions, malign actions of power brokers, widespread corruption and abuse of power by various officials." All of these failings "have given Afghans little reason to support their government" and have created "fertile ground for the insurgency." To win the people's support, ISAF "must protect the people from both of these threats": the insurgents and their own government.

Yet the essence of COIN was to provide for the people's needs "by, with, and through" the local government. Therefore, ISAF would need to shore up the legitimacy of Karzai's regime: strengthen its institutions, clean up its corruption, help it deliver basic services. And none of this could be accomplished simply by killing insurgents.

The report stressed that another obstacle, besides the Afghan government's malfeasances, was ISAF itself, in two ways. First, ISAF was "a conventional force . . . poorly configured for COIN, inexperienced in local languages and culture." Second, it was "under-resourced." A new COIN strategy would require more money, more civilian experts, and more troops.

How many more troops, the report's authors didn't say, and deliberately so. Fred and Kim Kagan argued during the team's deliberations that it should recommend a precise number of additional brigades, as Fred had done two-and-a-half years earlier in his AEI report on the Iraq surge. But Steve Biddle argued that the team had neither the access to data nor the analytical tools to make this sort of judgment. Fred did, in fact, know intelligence officers at ISAF headquarters who could have supplied him with the data and the tools, just as H. R. McMaster's former staff aides from Tal Afar had done on his AEI study. But Biddle figured that he and the other members might be called upon to defend this report in articles, media appearances, or congressional hearings. (He well knew that this was one of the functions of these teams: the commander gets buy-in from outside experts, who in turn make statements or write articles that get buy-in from the public.) And he had no desire to defend a number without knowing how it was reached or whether some other number might be better.

Biddle's view won out. McChrystal would make his recommendation on troop levels separately, after an analysis by his headquarters' staff.

On August 30 McChrystal signed the team's report, formally titled "Commander's Initial Assessment," and sent it to Secretary of Defense Robert Gates, who, in turn, passed along copies to the Joint Chiefs and the White House.

A few days before Gates received McChrystal's assessment, he took a brief vacation, during which he caught up on some outside reading. Friends and colleagues were always sending him articles that they thought he should read, on top of the mounds of official memos and reports that filled his working days. Away from the mounds, he flipped through some of these articles, especially those on Afghanistan, a topic with which he was still wrestling. One in particular caught his attention, a piece in the American Enterprise Institute's magazine, the *Weekly Standard,* titled "We're Not the Soviets in Afghanistan," written by Frederick Kagan.

Gates knew the Kagan name. He remembered the slides from Fred's briefing that called for a surge in Iraq. He knew of the book comparing American and European foreign policy by Fred's brother, Robert. And Gates had long regarded their father, Donald, as one of the great military historians of all time. Once, after learning that Kimberly Kagan would be briefing him on developments in Baghdad, Gates turned to an aide and asked, "How many of these fucking Kagans *are* there?"

But the *Weekly Standard* article's subject matter was what drew Gates's interest. He had been leery of expanding the mission in Afghanistan precisely because he'd seen close-up how badly the same course had turned out for the Russians. Yet Kagan was arguing that history didn't have to repeat itself: when the Soviet army entered Afghanistan, it had virtually no prior experience at counterinsurgency—in fact, no experience at any sort of combat since World War II. Its tanks and artillery rolled in with brute force; its arsenals contained no precision weapons; its troops, many of them drunk and half-literate, killed civilians with no compunction, destroyed their villages, defoliated their crops. An American campaign, particularly a counterinsurgency campaign, would be very different; the results needn't be the same.

Gates had forgotten the details of the Russians' brutality in the war, the crassness of their strategy and tactics. Maybe, he thought, we *could* do things differently.

Then, a few days later, McChrystal's assessment arrived, laying out a path of *how* to do things differently, advocating a COIN strategy, which Gates himself had been pushing the Army to adopt as mainstream policy. His views on Afghanistan began to shift; he opened up to the idea of escalation.

It was a crucial shift. Over the next few months, in the president's meetings with his national-security team, Joe Biden remained the only outright opponent of McChrystal's push for a surge and a switch to COIN. By this time, Gates and Obama had grown close. Obama respected his views, trusted his judgment; Gates was one of just three cabinet officers—the others were Hillary Clinton and Treasury Secretary Tim Geithner—who met with the president at the White House one-on-one every week.

At NSC meetings on a variety of topics, Gates would frequently emerge as a center of gravity. He didn't speak much, but when he did, he shifted people's opinions or at least altered the boundaries of what differences in opinion they'd tolerate, and coaxed them into a consensus with others whose positions they'd previously opposed. He'd honed this craft during his time as deputy national security adviser in George H. W. Bush's White House. Right before a meeting of the various departments' deputy secretaries, who routinely set an administration's foreign policy agenda, Gates would sit down with his boss, retired general Brent Scowcroft, Bush's national security adviser, and work out what position they wanted the group to adopt. Gates would then guide the meeting in such a way that all the deputies came to precisely that view and walked away thinking that it had been their idea.

Several aides who observed the national-security meetings on Afghanistan through the fall of 2009 later reflected that if Gates had remained skeptical of escalation, if he *and* Biden had opposed McChrystal's recommendations, President Obama might well have settled on a different policy, involving fewer troops and a less ambitious strategy.

On September 13, two weeks after McChrystal submitted his assessment, President Obama brought together his top national-security advisers—the same officers, officials, and aides who had met in March after the Riedel report came in—to discuss what to do about Afghanistan.

Obama was ambivalent about the war. He had been persuaded that the stakes were high; that if the Kabul government fell, the Taliban would easily take over, with al Qaeda not far behind, and Afghanistan would devolve once again into a haven for terrorists. He'd decided that he would not pull out altogether.

Yet as a student of history, he knew well the pitfalls of escalation and overconfidence. That summer, he'd invited a group of presidential historians to the White House for an off-the-record dinner. They included Robert Caro, Robert Dallek, Doris Kearns Goodwin, and Michael Beschloss, all of whom had written books about Lyndon Johnson. The conversation turned inevitably to the Vietnam War, which had taken down that earlier progressive president, and some of the historians told reporters afterward that Obama seemed mindful of the potential parallels.

The specter of Vietnam haunted conversations throughout the White House and the Pentagon that summer. Skeptics of escalation in Afghanistan brandished copies of a new book called *Lessons in Disaster* by Gordon Goldstein, about how some of Johnson's smartest advisers, including

McGeorge Bundy (for whom Goldstein had later worked as a research assistant), led the nation into a tragic quagmire. Advocates of sending in more troops were seen carrying around Lewis Sorley's *A Better War,* the revisionist tome, published a decade earlier, which contended that the Vietnam War could have been won if only the commanders had stuck to a COIN strategy from start to finish.

The September 13 meeting was, in many ways, a reprise of the debates—COIN, CT, or something in between—from the previous March. Eleven days later, McChrystal submitted his follow-on report, stating how many troops he needed to carry out his assessment's strategy. Obama and his advisers met again six days after that, on September 30, to discuss those numbers. McChrystal had listed a range of options: ten thousand more troops if the president wanted merely to accelerate the training of the Afghan army; forty thousand for a counterinsurgency strategy with some risk, sending the troops first to fight in the south, then to push their way to the east; eighty-five thousand for a "more robust counterinsurgency" strategy across both regions simultaneously.

It seemed to some a standard ploy: lay out three options—one too small, one too big, and one in the middle, which, by process of elimination, looks just right. And as his "professional military judgment," McChrystal recommended forty thousand—the number in the middle. But, in fact, he'd played it straight. His staff had calculated that the highest number, eighty-five thousand, while preferable in theory, was neither practical nor worth the extra effort: by the time the military built all the additional bases, airstrips, and other logistical networks to support so many troops, the course of the war would already be decided. McChrystal's forty thousand was not a political compromise; it was his genuine preference.

Still, the reaction inside the White House was sticker shock. Obama had approved the military's request for twenty-one thousand extra troops just six months earlier; they'd barely started to arrive in country, and now—already—the generals were hitting him up for twice as many more. If the situation didn't improve, would they ask for another forty thousand the next year and one hundred thousand the year after that? This had all the earmarks of the endless escalation he most feared.

Clearly, he was going to send *some* increment of more troops, and however small or large it was, the Afghanistan War would from that moment on be "Obama's war." He'd called it the war of necessity on the campaign trail, as distinct from Bush's war of choice in Iraq. He'd authorized his secretary of defense to fire the commander he inherited, General McKiernan, on the grounds that he lacked a winning strategy. This new recommendation of forty thousand more troops and a COIN strategy came from the commander that Obama had hired as McKiernan's replacement. There was pressure to take his commander's advice. But he didn't want to get boxed in. He had lots of questions, and he wanted more options.

The group would meet eight more times over the next two months. Obama's Republican critics, especially former vice president Dick Cheney, accused him of "dithering." In fact, Obama was asking the chiefs pointed questions, and the answers they'd bring to the next meeting only raised more questions. When one official raised the possibility of working less with Karzai's central government and more with local officials across Afghanistan, Obama asked for a rundown of which provincial and district governors had the tightest and loosest connections with Karzai or seemed to be the most and least likely to cooperate with US interests. No one around the table knew the answers, so back they went to their offices at the Pentagon or the CIA and ordered an intelligence analysis.

And the chiefs never did satisfy Obama's request for more options; they never answered his question of what could be done, say, with thirty thousand more troops or with twenty thousand. (The vice chairman of the JCS, Marine General James "Hoss" Cartwright, drew up such an option, figuring that his job was to comply with the president's lawful orders. He got an earful from the chiefs; Mullen never sent his paper up the chain to the White House. Cartwright pulled an end run and took his paper to Biden's office; the vice president at least put it on the agenda, but the chiefs discussed it only to dismiss it.)

Some of the aides sitting behind the officials around the table found the whole process a bit dumbfounding. Petraeus, the most persuasive advocate for McChrystal's numbers, barely mentioned Afghanistan as a distinct country; his main interest seemed to be defending his own COIN philosophy as a principle of warfare. Mullen and Gates backed their commanders. In some past administrations, the secretary of state might have risen in opposition, but Obama's team players were remarkably unified in their views;

Hillary Clinton herself was more hawkish than some had anticipated, so she went along as well.

Two events outside the Situation Room intensified the political tensions and pressures within.

First, on September 21, a few days before McChrystal submitted his recommendation on troop levels, the *Washington Post* printed a front-page story by Bob Woodward summarizing the main points of McChrystal's sixty-six-page assessment, and the *Post*'s website reproduced a leaked copy of the entire document. There was no evidence that the leak had come from McChrystal or his staff, but it compounded the feeling among White House political advisers that the generals were trying to box in the president.

The second event amounted to pressure from the opposition. On November 9, the ambassador to Afghanistan, Karl Eikenberry, a retired three-star general who had been commander of US forces in Afghanistan for eighteen months between 2005 and 2007, sent a secret cable to Secretary of State Hillary Clinton titled "COIN Strategy: Civilian Concerns."

It was a lengthy critique of McChrystal's entire presentation: his assessment of the security situation, his request for more troops, and his call for a shift to a counterinsurgency strategy. Eikenberry stated the reasons for his objections in a simple, shocking sentence: "President Karzai," he wrote, "is not an adequate strategic partner."

He elaborated that COIN

> assumes an Afghan political leadership that is both able to take responsibility and to exert sovereignty in the furtherance of our goal—a secure, peaceful, minimally self-sufficient Afghanistan hardened against transnational terrorist groups. Yet Karzai continues to shun responsibility for any sovereign burden . . . He and much of his circle do not want the US to leave and are only too happy to see us invest further . . . It strains credulity to expect Karzai to change fundamentally this late in his life and in our relationship.

Eikenberry also criticized McChrystal's analysis for assuming that once US forces clear and hold an area, the Afghan government will quickly step in and provide basic services. "In reality," he argued, "the process of restoring Afghan government is likely to be slow and uneven, no matter how many US and other foreign civilian experts are involved."

Finally, there was the matter of the safe havens across the porous border with Pakistan. "More troops won't end the insurgency," the ambassador wrote, "as long as Pakistan sanctuaries remain."

He acknowledged that McChrystal's analysis was "logical and compelling within his narrow mandate to define the need for a military counterinsurgency campaign within Afghanistan." However, he went on, it failed to take into account several "real-world variables": not only Pakistan's sanctuaries and Karzai's weak leadership but also America's own "national will to bear the human and fiscal costs over many years." Any one of these variables, he observed, could potentially "block us from achieving our strategic goals, regardless of the number of additional troops we may send."

Eikenberry urged instead that the president conduct a "comprehensive, interdisciplinary analysis of all our strategic options," going well beyond an up-or-down verdict on COIN—in essence, that Obama start his review all over. "For now," Eikenberry summed up, "I cannot support DoD's recommendation for an immediate Presidential decision to deploy another 40,000 troops here."

In one sense, Eikenberry's cable wasn't surprising. He had been making some of the same points, though less forcefully, in some of the national-security meetings, which he attended via video teleconference. Nor were most of his points particularly novel: McChrystal's own assessment had spelled them out as serious problems; Petraeus and Mullen had testified in congressional hearings that cleaning up Karzai's corruption and shutting down Pakistan's sanctuaries were just as important as battling the Taliban. At a Senate hearing in mid-September, Mullen had acknowledged that the main problem in Afghanistan was "clearly the lack of legitimacy in the government."

Senator Lindsey Graham, Republican of South Carolina, asked, "We could send a million troops, and that will not restore legitimacy in the government?"

Mullen replied, "That is correct."

But Petraeus, Mullen, and McChrystal saw these matters as obstacles to overcome, not as reasons to call off the campaign. All three were furious when they heard about Eikenberry's cable, and more so when it leaked to the press a few days later. It wasn't just that they disagreed with his conclusions. They felt ambushed by his abruptness; he hadn't consulted with any of his former brothers in arms or alerted them that he was writing such a document. How was the United States supposed to run an "integrated civilian-military counterinsurgency campaign," as McChrystal's memo recommended—or, for that matter, any kind of coherent campaign, COIN or otherwise—when the top diplomat in the country was rejecting the game plan and, more than that, hadn't bothered to discuss his qualms with the top officers?

Another reason for the officers' ire may have been that the ambassador's main points were so clearly accurate. The Afghan president's behavior was increasingly erratic and self-destructive; Eikenberry's description of him ("not an adequate strategic partner") barely began to capture the concerns about his shortcomings. There were reports that Karzai was on medication for bipolar disorder, that his brother was a major drug runner, that he and his entourage were siphoning money abroad through corrupt state banks.

Finally, the presidential election, which had been expected to bolster Karzai's legitimacy, in fact diminished it further. So many ballot boxes had been so blatantly stuffed that nobody believed the official outcome. Western inspectors calculated that fully one-third of the ballots were fraudulent. Subtracting those from Karzai's tally gave him a plurality but one that fell just under 50 percent of the vote—the bar he needed to cross to avoid a second-round runoff against the second-place candidate, former foreign minister Abdullah Abdullah. To make matters worse, Karzai condemned the inspectors as imperialist trespassers, declared himself the winner, and refused to hold a runoff. Obama dispatched John Kerry, the Democratic chairman of the Senate Foreign Relations Committee, who had traveled extensively in that part of the world, to calm Karzai down. It took five days of soothing talk—and, as Kerry later put it, "three *hundred* cups of tea"—before Karzai agreed to accept the monitors' report and to abide by his own country's election laws.

In the end, Abdullah dropped out before the runoff took place. Karzai retained the presidency by default, lending some hope for his redemption.

Yet the harsh dilemmas remained. On the one hand, the case for COIN in Afghanistan seemed far from plausible. On the other hand, the case for

Biden's position—to do little more than keep sending drones and Special Ops commandos to kill insurgents along the AfPak border—was still less compelling; that's what McChrystal's predecessor, Dave McKiernan, had been doing, with little to show for it.

There was another dilemma. On the one hand, Karzai was now the duly reelected president of Afghanistan and thus the only national leader with whom Obama could deal. On the other hand, Obama would have to pressure Karzai into reforming his government if COIN had a chance of succeeding; he needed to make Karzai realize that America's patience wasn't endless.

Back in March, when he announced his first escalation of the war, Obama had said, "We will not *blindly* stay the course" and "We will not, and cannot, produce a blank check." Eight months later, after nine meetings of intense deliberations on the subject, he was still insistent on those points.

On Sunday, November 29, around five in the afternoon, Obama held his final meeting on the new strategy. This one was in the Oval Office and involved a smaller group than usual, restricted mainly to his top defense advisers: Gates, Mullen, the service chiefs, and Petraeus, along with Biden, national security adviser Jim Jones, and the president's senior adviser on Afghanistan, Doug Lute.

In a little over forty-eight hours, Obama would deliver a much-anticipated address at West Point, spelling out his decision on troop levels and a new strategy. He called the Sunday afternoon meeting to inform his advisers of what he'd decided and to give them each a copy of his orders, which he'd written himself.

In the order, he wrote that the "core goal" of the war would be the same as the one he'd announced back in March: "disrupting, dismantling, and eventually defeating al Qaeda and preventing al Qaeda's return to safe haven in Afghanistan and Pakistan." However, he now emphasized that his approach for doing this was "*not* fully resourced counterinsurgency or nation-building."

Rather, the strategy would be to *deny* the Taliban access to key population centers, but merely to *disrupt* the Taliban outside those areas and, overall, not to defeat but rather to *degrade* their forces to levels that the Afghan army and police could eventually handle by themselves after an enlarged and reinvigorated training program.

In short, Obama was calling for a mix: COIN in the large cities, CT elsewhere.

To this end, Obama had decided to deploy a "surge"—he called it by that name—of thirty thousand additional American troops, plus three thousand "enablers" (headquarters staff, extra logistical support, and so forth), while also pushing the NATO allies to send seven thousand more of their troops. That would add up to the forty thousand that McChrystal had recommended.

Finally, Obama would *begin* to withdraw these surge troops in July 2011, just eighteen months hence, assuming that the Taliban would be degraded and the Afghans would get better at securing and governing their own country.

This last part was the shocker; none of the officers in the room had seen it coming. Obama was coupling the surge and the drawdown for two reasons. First, he wanted to convey a sense of urgency to Karzai; the Americans weren't going to be around forever, so he had to make reforms now. Second, Obama regarded this whole business—the escalation and the partial adoption of COIN—as an experiment, a useful experiment, probably unavoidable, and, in any case, less risky than not trying. But if it didn't achieve results after what he saw as a reasonable length of time, he wasn't going to extend it.

Obama spoke directly to his top defense advisers: Gates, Mullen, and Petraeus. With these additional forces, he asked them, will you be able to clear, hold, and transfer to the point where—within eighteen months—the Afghan security forces can take the lead in the fight? He emphasized that this was a pivotal moment. If they said they could do this, and it turned out they couldn't, he wasn't going to double down. There wasn't going to be another round of escalation. This was all they were going to get.

So he asked them, one at a time, if they could perform this mission with these resources: Bob? Mike? Dave?

Each of them replied, one after the other, "Yes, sir."

Doug Lute, the three-star general who had been brought over from the Pentagon to serve as Bush's "war czar" and who stayed on to work for Obama, was taking notes. He was startled that all three agreed to the terms. Lute had been a West Point cadet, class of 1975, and, a decade later, had taught international relations in the Sosh department for three years, overlapping with Petraeus's tenures as a cadet and as an instructor. He had read the COIN literature, including Petraeus's field manual, and he knew that no serious scholar or practitioner in the field would promise that a campaign of this sort, especially in Afghanistan, could succeed so rapidly. Counterinsurgency wars were by nature protracted wars; they usually took years, sometimes decades, to resolve.

Petraeus was asked afterward by a number of colleagues why he didn't speak up and tell the president that the timetable wasn't plausible. Petraeus replied that it wasn't that kind of meeting; he got the clear sense that the advisers were there to take orders, not discuss options; that what Obama put on the table was a take-it-or-leave-it deal, and that if you wanted to stay on the team, you would take it. He also calculated, in his own head, that if *enough* progress had been made by the eighteen-month deadline, even if not quite as much progress as the president was now demanding, a case could be made to stay on a bit longer.

Everyone in the room was making a gamble. Obama was making at least four: that Karzai would reform his government and thus remake himself; that the Afghan army would shape up to a competent force; that Pakistan would alter its calculus of national-security interests and go after the Taliban on the border more forcefully; and that the NATO coalition would hold together.

Petraeus and the other top officers were making just one gamble: that, in the end, Obama would soften his position.

None of the bets would pay out.

21.

"Storm Clouds"

It was by this point forgotten—few knew it at the time—that, six years earlier, the United States had pursued a classic counterinsurgency strategy in Afghanistan. It was headed up by a three-star general named David Barno, who in October 2003 became commander of US forces in the country, just the second officer to hold the position since the invasion that had toppled the Taliban two years earlier.

Not that Barno had many US forces to command. President George W. Bush and his defense secretary, Donald Rumsfeld, had long ago declared victory in Afghanistan and shifted focus—and resources—to the new war in Iraq.

When Barno arrived, he found himself in charge of just two brigades, a smattering of Special Ops forces, and a handful of close aides, augmented by a small staff of reservists in their forties or fifties. During one lunch hour in the mess hall early on in his tenure, he sat down next to one of these reservists, an overweight, middle-aged master sergeant, and asked how he happened to be there.

The sergeant replied cheerfully that he'd recently had triple-bypass heart surgery, which was a good thing, since the Army wouldn't have let him come if he'd had a quadruple bypass.

Barno quickly grasped that Afghanistan was not regarded as a high-priority mission.

On his predeployment tour of the country a month earlier, he'd been shocked by how scattershot the effort was. There was no unity of effort: the military did its thing, the embassy did its thing, and their two paths neither crossed nor ran parallel. The military's headquarters were at Bagram Air Force Base, more than an hour's drive from the embassy in Kabul; the diplomats and the officers rarely met or spoke. Similarly, the Army had troops in the field; AID had provincial reconstruction teams in a handful of villages, some nearby, but they, too, never coordinated their efforts. The entire enterprise reeked of complacency. The war was considered over. Yet the Taliban were still putting up a fight in the eastern provinces along the Pakistani border and, to a lesser but worrisome degree, in the south.

To Barno's mind, the setting was ripe for a counterinsurgency strategy.

Barno had been a cadet at West Point, class of 1976, with a heavy concentration in the Social Science Department. An avid reader of military history since his teens, he particularly liked the academy's course on the history of Revolutionary Warfare. After graduating, he chose to make a career in the Army's light infantry branch. Over the next three decades, he was never stationed in Europe, never assigned to an armored unit; rather, he deployed as a Ranger to the era's "*moot*-wah wars" in Panama and Grenada.

The Army had no doctrine on counterinsurgency when his command in Afghanistan began, so Barno brought with him the textbook that he'd used in the Revolutionary Warfare class as a second-year cadet and reread it thoroughly. He also dipped into his discretionary fund to order several copies of every book about COIN that he could find on the BooksAMillion.com website—including the Marine Corps's *Small Wars Manual,* T. E. Lawrence's *Seven Pillars of Wisdom,* Lewis Sorley's *A Better War,* and John Nagl's *Learning to Eat Soup with a Knife* (in the expensive hardcover edition, since the paperback wasn't out yet)—and distributed them to all his officers, from brigade commander on down to platoon leader.

From these readings, Barno devised a strategy that he called, with a nod to Lawrence, the "Five Pillars." The central pillar was to secure the population; the others were to defeat the terrorists, help with reconstruction and good governance, seek support from regional powers and international organizations, and order the troops to live alongside the people in their neighborhoods.

In short, it was classic clear-hold-build—a drastic departure from the search-and-destroy tactics that had been pursued previously. Before Barno arrived, American troops would mount their raids, then head back to their base in the outskirts, to no effect; the Taliban would simply melt away during the attacks, then return to the village at night, after the American big guns were gone.

Barno's plan also called for unified social, political, economic, and military operations. The US ambassador, Zalmay Khalilzad, arrived in Afghanistan just a few weeks after Barno. Khalilzad had been born in Afghanistan to a Muslim family (his father was Sunni, his mother Shiite); he understood the culture, knew some of the tribal elders and warlords, and knew how to cultivate their interests. Barno moved his military headquarters into the Kabul embassy and set up his office just twenty feet from Khalilzad's. The two struck up a close relationship, consulting and coordinating with each other on every aspect of policy. They also hooked up the four civilian provincial reconstruction teams with military battalions in their areas, partly to give them security but more to get them working jointly toward the same objectives.

The two also brought in specialists: successful corporate executives—some retired, some not—who'd been recruited by Martin Hoffman, a former secretary of the Army, to volunteer for what he called the Afghanistan Reconstruction Group. Led by Louis Hughes, vice president of General Motors, the group included Mitchell Shivers, a managing director at Merrill Lynch, who was assigned to work with the Afghan finance minister, and David Grizzle, a senior vice president at Continental Airlines, who worked with the transportation minister, among others.

By the time Barno rotated out of command in May 2005, support for the Taliban seemed to be waning and support for the provisional government booming. He thought he'd dealt a fatal blow to the insurgency.

Soon after returning to the Pentagon, he briefed Lieutenant General James Lovelace, the Army's chief of operations. Lovelace said afterward that he'd had no idea what Barno had been doing in Afghanistan. Nor did any of the other senior officers; nor did they care to learn. No one else in the Pentagon, civilian or military, asked Barno for any further briefings. Nor was he rewarded for his creativity: his next posting was assistant chief of staff for installations management, a clerical job supervising the supply depots for the Army's bases around the world. He retired from the Army one year later and, after a four-year teaching stint at the National Defense University, went to work as a senior fellow at John Nagl's think tank.

When Barno rotated out of Afghanistan as commander, so did Zal Khalilzad as ambassador (he was transferred to Iraq), and so did the troops from the 25th Infantry Division who had carried out Barno's plan. Barno's successor would have had a hard time staying the course if he'd wanted to. It was a moot point, though, because he didn't want to.

The new commander was Lieutenant General Karl Eikenberry, who four years later would return to Afghanistan as Obama's ambassador and, among other things, write the secret cable that criticized the proposals for a troop surge and a counterinsurgency strategy.

Eikenberry had also been a West Point cadet, class of 1973. His career as an officer started out much like Barno's, in the light infantry, but he then took a broader path, serving not only in airborne and Ranger units but also in mechanized infantry. He then moved into the policy world, earning a master's degree from Harvard in East Asian studies, studying Chinese language and history in Hong Kong and Nanjing, and serving as a military attaché at the US embassy in Beijing, before a tenure at the Army's Office of Plans, Policy, and Programs in the Pentagon.

In short, Eikenberry knew about COIN as a cadet and junior officer, but he never made it the focus of his interests or ambitions.

His first tour in Afghanistan, from 2002 to 2003, was as the US security coordinator, helping the Afghan army set up its first corps. When he returned as US commander two years later, his natural inclination was to resume where he'd left off. He knocked down four of Barno's Five Pillars, retaining only the strictly military operations: going after insurgents and training the Afghan army. He disbanded the joint civilian-military teams in the field and sent the corporate volunteers home. He also moved his headquarters out of the embassy and cut off all coordination with its diplomatic corps. The new ambassador, Ron Neumann, didn't mind; he and Eikenberry didn't get along, and, in any case, he was under orders from Secretary of State Condoleezza Rice to turn his shop into a "normal embassy"—a reflection of the Bush administration's deliberate neglect of Afghanistan as it switched gears to Iraq.

By the time Eikenberry's tenure ended at the start of 2007, Afghanistan was coming apart. The summer before, NATO's International Security Assistance Force had taken command of the war, except in the area along the eastern border with Pakistan—the scene of the most intense fighting, where American troops retained independent control. This was fine with the European allies, who didn't want to fight much anyway. The ISAF commander, British general David Richards, saw his job as principally a peacekeeping operation. But as the European troops moved down south, the Taliban—who, it turned out, had never gone away—came out to fight. Suddenly, each of the allied powers—whose leaders hadn't known they were getting into a *war*—declared a list of "caveats," conditions under which its troops could and could not be deployed: one country would defend territory but not go on the offensive; another would keep the peace in the north but not in the south; still another would fly helicopters but not put troops on the ground. All in all, the NATO allies issued eighty-three caveats, strangling the top commanders' flexibility.

The American military was hardly a model of cohesiveness, either. Eliot Cohen traveled to Afghanistan in April—he'd been hired as Condoleezza Rice's counselor at the State Department the month before—and was appalled by how fractured the effort was. Some American officers were leading the autonomous combat units in the east; others were reporting to ISAF at Kabul headquarters; then there were the Army Special Forces, covert JSOC teams, and CIA agents scattered all about. And each of these entities was fighting its own war; there was no unified command, even on a strictly military level, much less a socioeconomic one. (General Richards had started to revive some of Barno's joint civil-military development programs, but the new ISAF commander, a traditional US Army general named Dan McNeil, dismantled them once more.) Cohen told his colleagues that the campaign reeked of "military malpractice."

Cohen worked closely with Lieutenant General Doug Lute. In November 2008, two months before the end of Bush's second term, Lute delivered a briefing to Bush, spelling out all the problems that he and Cohen had uncovered: the Taliban's widening offensives, Karzai's corruption, the Afghan army's weakness, and, not least, ISAF's own internal chaos.

This was the state of the Afghan War when Barack Obama moved into the White House. Lute stayed at his job through the transition and after. His briefing to Bush served as the starting point for Bruce Riedel's report to Obama. General Dave McKiernan, the commander in Afghanistan whom Gates had appointed in 2008 to replace McNeil, started to unify at least the military side of the campaign. But the basic situation didn't change much during his tenure, which lasted less than a year.

And so, this was also the state of the Afghan War when Stanley McChrystal took over as commander.

• • •

One of the first things McChrystal did upon arriving in Kabul was reach out to Hamid Karzai. McChrystal knew that tensions between the Afghan president and Washington were high-strung and that, more often than not, the problems stemmed from Karzai: his regime's corruption, his lack of discipline, and possibly his state of mind. But McChrystal also knew that COIN involved working "by, with, and through" the host nation's government, and in this case, that meant working by, with, and through Karzai.

So McChrystal endeavored to make Karzai his pal and his peer, treating him with the utmost respect. Each time they met, he would assure Karzai that he regarded Afghanistan as a sovereign state and that, therefore, ISAF and its armed forces were all under the command of the country's duly elected president. Karzai would beam at the kowtowing.

When McChrystal asked Karzai what troubled him most about the ISAF troops' actions, his reply was instant: they were killing too many Afghan civilians. Dropping bombs on residential areas, smashing down doors of people's homes in the dead of night, shooting at cars that veered too close to armored convoys—these raids and attacks were damaging, disrespectful, even criminal, and often based on mistaken intelligence.

McChrystal sympathized, and not just for show. Everywhere he went, from the ministries in Kabul to the markets in the villages, he heard the same complaints about the night raids and the bombing runs, even from people who had never personally witnessed raids or bombings. McChrystal knew that this was serious, potentially catastrophic. In conventional warfare, killing innocent civilians fell under the rubric of collateral damage: regrettable but unavoidable by-products of firing or dropping weapons in a populated area. But counterinsurgency warfare was all about *protecting* the people. Killing civilians in the course of chasing bad guys would breed local outrage, distrust, alienation, and blood revenge from the victims' relatives; it would spur many people to ally with, even join, the insurgency. As Petraeus's field manual had put it, "An operation that kills five insurgents is counterproductive if collateral damage leads to the recruitment of fifty more insurgents."

It wasn't just the killing that did damage to the war cause; it was the conventional mind-set that dominated the behavior of too many of his men in everything they did. Even when they drove him someplace in an armored convoy, they would barrel down the middle of the road, forcing cars on both sides into the ditch. Looking out the slotted window, McChrystal saw the expressions on the civilians' faces: the horror and humiliation from suffering yet another indignity at the hands of foreign occupiers. Yet his men thought they were doing the right thing: they'd been taught that *self*-protection was the primary mission—and protecting the commanding general, a higher mission still. He needed to shift the mind-set, to convince his troops that winning the war meant winning the support of the Afghan people; if the people weren't convinced that ISAF was there to support them, the war would be lost for sure.

On July 2, well before his assessment team had finished its work, two days before he would hear the team's first interim briefing, McChrystal issued a document called the "Tactical Directive," addressed to all American and ISAF military units in Afghanistan.

The main struggle in this war, he wrote, was "for the support and will of the population." Winning and maintaining that support "must be our overriding operational imperative—and the ultimate objective of every action we take." This kind of war, he stressed, as many other commanders had stressed in similar documents through the years, "is different from conventional combat . . . We must avoid the trap of winning tactical victories—but suffering strategic defeats—by causing civilian casualties or excessive damage and thus alienating the people." He allowed, "We must fight the insurgents and . . . defeat the enemy," but then reemphasized that "we will not win based on the number of Taliban we kill." Victory will instead depend on "our ability to separate insurgents from the center of gravity—the people."

He continued, in a passage that he knew would arouse the ire of some of his men, "I recognize that the carefully controlled and disciplined employment of force entails risk to our troops." They should take steps to mitigate those risks; certainly they should take whatever action they felt necessary for self-defense. "But," he wrote, "excessive use of force resulting in an alienated population will produce far greater risks. We must understand this reality at every level in our force."

Then came the hammer: "I expect leaders at all levels to scrutinize and limit the use of force," especially air strikes, "against residential compounds and other locations likely to produce civilian casualties." Following this directive, he acknowledged, "requires a cultural shift within our forces—and complete understanding at every level—down to the most junior soldiers."

Eight weeks later, on August 26, as the final draft of his assessment team's report was being completed—and a full three months before President Obama decided whether even to pursue a COIN strategy—McChrystal sent all of his troops another document, called "ISAF Commander's Counterinsurgency Guidance."

It was an elaboration of his "Tactical Directive" but written in still starker language. Directly below the heading, almost as if it were a subtitle, he wrote, in italics, *"Protecting the people is the mission. The conflict will be won by persuading the population, not by destroying the enemy. ISAF will succeed when [the Afghan government] . . . earns the support of the people."*

Key phrases were certain to jump out at most American soldiers and marines:

> We will not win simply by killing insurgents . . . This means that we must change the way that we think, act, and operate . . . Every action we take must reflect this change: how we interact with people, how we drive or fly, how we patrol, how we use force . . . This is their country, and we are their guests . . . Large-scale operations to kill or capture militants carry a significant risk of causing civilian casualties and collateral damage. If civilians die in a firefight, it does not matter who shot them—we still failed to protect them from harm . . . Think of counterinsurgency as an argument to earn the support of the people . . . Earn the support of the people and the war is won, regardless of how many militants are killed or captured. We must undermine the insurgent argument while offering a more compelling alternative . . . There is clearly a role for precise operations that keep the insurgents off balance, take the fight to their sanctuaries, and prevent them from affecting the population. These operations are important, but, in and of themselves, are not necessarily decisive.

McChrystal meant to be laying down basic principles; the document was his *guidance*. "Keeping the right balance over time is critical," he wrote, "and there is no mathematical formula for it." But then he supplied just such a formula: "Strive to focus 95% of our energy on the 95% of the population that deserves and needs our support. Doing so will isolate the insurgents. Take action against the 5%—the insurgents—as necessary or when the right opportunities present themselves. Do not let them distract you from your primary tasks."

Even some COIN enthusiasts thought McChrystal was going too far. It was a provocative enough departure from conventional wisdom when Mao and Galula had described insurgency wars as 80 percent political, 20 percent military. Now McChrystal was splitting it at 95 and 5. And he was expressing this equation well before enough American troops had arrived to carry out a counterinsurgency strategy—well before the president had decided to send enough troops or to adopt such a strategy.

When David Petraeus edited the COIN field manual, he'd toned down some of his writing team's more exuberant passages, for instance changing "The best weapons don't shoot" to "*Sometimes* the best weapons don't shoot" and inserting several paragraphs throughout the text, making it clear that sometimes a soldier had to go kill bad guys. Petraeus's final draft didn't define "sometimes." Several officers had raised the question at his COIN conference in Fort Leavenworth and afterward: where to draw that line and how soldiers were supposed to recognize the line when they saw it. In the scheme of the "three-block war" (combat on one block, peacekeeping on the next block, and handing out humanitarian aid on the next), how would they know which block they were occupying? Petraeus had tried to capture the fine line in the *tone* of his prose (he often told officers that setting the right tone was one of a commander's most vital tasks), but the ambiguity remained. Probably it could never be resolved fully; it was something a soldier felt in his bones after months or years of experience; in any case, it was a shortcoming in the manual that some still criticized.

There was nothing nuanced at all, though, about the tone of McChrystal's "Counterinsurgency Guidance": it sounded a stern order for strict restraint; it sent a signal that soldiers could get into serious trouble if they killed a single civilian, whatever the circumstances; it thus had the effect of encouraging not merely restraint but passivity, a dangerous trait in any war.

McChrystal's impulse was well founded. Before he took command, civilian casualties were soaring, and one reason was that nobody had issued an order to minimize them. His directives marked an attempt, if overwrought, to do that.

• • •

Around this time, Sarah Sewall, the director of Harvard's Carr Center for Human Rights Policy, wrote David Petraeus a note offering to conduct an on-site study of CIVCAS incidents, the military term for civilian casualties.

The two had stayed in touch ever since they cosponsored the COIN field manual conference at Fort Leavenworth three-and-a-half years earlier. Petraeus liked the idea and passed it on to McChrystal. As head of Central Command, which had authority over US military operations in Iraq and Afghanistan, Petraeus could have ordered the study himself. But he knew the art and value of getting buy-in from the crucial players, and McChrystal was the commander on the ground. The study would get a better hearing, and Sewall's very presence would be better tolerated, if the project appeared to be McChrystal's idea. So Petraeus forwarded her proposal with as much aloofness as he could muster.

McChrystal recognized what Petraeus was doing, but he liked the idea, too, so he commissioned Sewall to do the study. He was deeply concerned that his officers weren't following his "Tactical Directive" or his "Counterinsurgency Guidance"; he wanted her study to include an assessment of how closely they were following the orders and some suggestions on how to push through his message more clearly.

Sewall began work in November, though not in earnest until the following February. As she and her team—nearly forty analysts, civilian and military—were flown and driven all over Afghanistan, talking with American and ISAF planners, staff officers, and troops in the field, she realized that McChrystal's directives, far from being ignored, were instilling fear up and down the ranks. Many of the troops understood the reasoning behind the rules of engagement, but many others didn't; it had never been explained to them. They would call in air strikes when they *knew* that insurgents were in a building; their superior officers, also drenched in fear, would deny the request, and everyone involved would walk away from the scene, feeling not just hamstrung but demoralized and vulnerable.

Whenever Sewall dropped in on ISAF headquarters in the course of her work, she could practically smell the toxic sweat beads. McChrystal's staff formed a tight clique. They were all Rangers, as McChrystal had been, and they all tried to act just like the boss: a groupthink seemed to have taken hold, a shared conviction that they were right about everything and that everyone else was wrong, naïve, or stupid. Sewall understood why McChrystal had tightened the troops' rules of engagement, and she lauded him for doing so; that was how a commander made his troops understand and internalize his intent. But usually commanders adjusted these rules now and then to accommodate new realities or incorporate lessons learned. The insularity of McChrystal's staff suppressed the normal tendency to reassess the situation or modify a decision. (Petraeus had a loyal entourage of aides as well, but he'd gathered them from various branches of the Army and even included civilians; his management style welcomed new ideas, to a point.)

Sewall wrote up her findings in a 147-page report. On Tuesday, April 13, 2010, she and a few members of her team briefed McChrystal on their main findings. In one part of the briefing, she told the general that, contrary to his concerns, most of the troops *did* understand his guidance and how it fit into a counterinsurgency strategy.

McChrystal reacted with skepticism. How could that be true? Too many civilians were still getting killed. Just the week before, an American unit had sprayed a busload of innocent people with gunfire. *Those* troops didn't "get it."

Sewall decided to put it all out there. She told him about the frustrations and complaints she'd heard, the times when an attack or air strike seemed warranted but permission was denied. This was nothing new to McChrystal. He regarded himself as a soldier above all; he frequently visited the troops in the field, even went out with them on patrols; he'd heard the same stories and would respond by trying to explain his guidance more clearly.

She then went one step further. Sarah Sewall, the Ivy League human-rights scholar and the only woman in the room, looked unblinkingly at Stan McChrystal, the peerless professional killer, and said, "General, counterinsurgency is a combination of offense, defense, and stability operations. Don't forget the offense."

McChrystal growled, "Don't tell me how to run my war."

Meanwhile, the war—McChrystal's war—wasn't going well.

The clearest and most disturbing sign was the battle for Marja, a district of roughly eighty thousand people in southern Afghanistan's Helmand Province, where the Taliban had seized the reins of power two years earlier.

McChrystal saw the battle as a key test of his counterinsurgency plan, and publicly said as much. He'd been preparing for the battle since September, not long after his arrival as commander. Dubbed Operation Moshtarak (the Dari word for "together" or "joint"), it got under way in the predawn hours of Saturday, February 13, 2010, as an advance force of American, British, French, and Afghan troops, most of them marines and Special Forces, poured into the province and occupied key sites, confiscated weapons caches, and began to push out the insurgents. At its full flush, the operation pulled together fifteen thousand ISAF and Afghan troops, the largest American-led offensive since the invasion that toppled the Taliban more than eight years earlier.

In McChrystal's plan, the assault marked the opening volley of a broader campaign: the "clear" phase in a full-fledged attempt at COIN's clear-hold-build. He told Dexter Filkins, the *New York Times*'s war correspondent, "We've got a government in a box, ready to roll in."

He went on to describe an enormous apparatus—more than a thousand police, a new governor, and vast teams of administrators, all Afghans—standing by, all set to swoop into Marja the moment the shooting was over and the insurgents were cleared. As the tens of thousands of America's surge troops began to arrive in country, the process would start up again in another town, then another, all along the Helmand River, out to the edge of the border with Pakistan. At that point, he predicted, a critical mass of Taliban leaders would abandon their hopes for victory and seek a political settlement, which would soon spark the end of the war.

Filkins's article about his interview with McChrystal was published on February 12, the day before the offensive was to begin.

Heidi Meyer was among the many political officials who read the *Times* that day in a state of shock. She'd been working on Afghanistan's problems for nearly four years: first as a civilian aide inside the US military command, then on the Pentagon's Afghan policy desk, and now, for the past year, as the US embassy's team leader for stabilization, the official in charge of helping to stand up institutions of governance in Kabul and out in the districts and provinces. And she knew for sure that there was no such thing as "government in a box," especially in Afghanistan, which lacked the barest prerequisites for government of any sort.

A few months earlier, Meyer had heard McChrystal's staff brief the general on the idea of dropping in schools, businesses, a hospital, a governor's office—replete with adequate supplies and trained personnel—as soon as the fighting was over. The briefer talked casually about doing this in forty-eight "focus districts," eventually in eighty "key terrain districts," of which Marja would be merely the first. She told the staffers afterward that the idea was preposterous. This wasn't the way governance developed, anywhere, and certainly not in Afghanistan, which had no capacity to deliver services so quickly. Its people, including most of its officials, were illiterate; they lacked the skills or technology to draw up a budget or to administer a payroll. This dream, she said, would take a decade or more to realize. Other officials from the AID office told them much the same.

McChrystal knew about the skeptics, but he asked what they would do instead and heard no answer. "Clear" had to be followed by "hold" and "build"; this was the plan on how to do that. His staff officers dismissed the pessimism out of hand. They were Rangers, flush with a can-do confidence, emboldened by their recent tours in Iraq. If the civilian bureaucrats couldn't get the job done, they'd do it themselves.

And now here they were, actually setting out to do it.

Two days before the offensive began, McChrystal felt confident enough to dispatch the Afghan interior minister, Hanif Atmar, to meet with more than three hundred of the area's tribal elders, brief them about the impending offensive, and assure them that the fighting wouldn't last long, that police would be brought in to keep the Taliban out after the military pushed them out, and that the government would follow up with roads, medical clinics, and other vital projects.

McChrystal's staff figured that Marja would be conquered in a matter of days, at most a few weeks. By the time Sarah Sewall briefed the general on her civilian-casualties report in mid-April, the operation had gone on for two months; the troops had captured a lot of territory, but they hadn't yet secured it, not to the point where they could safely transfer control to the Afghan police. Even by the end of the year, Taliban fighters still lingered, sniping from rooftops, setting off bombs, beheading collaborators, and knocking on doors at night to warn of the same fate for those who consorted with the infidel occupiers.

The ISAF troops could clear but not hold, and the "build" phase of the plan lay in the incalculably distant future. As Meyer and other civilian specialists had warned, there *was* no government in the box, no pool of administrators standing by. Some of Karzai's ministers had nodded their heads when American officers asked if such things were in the works; they'd learned to tell a man with power and money what he wanted to hear. The Independent Directorate of Local Governance, the Afghan agency that funneled much of this money, had recruited a fair number of Afghans to come take the new jobs, but most of the men vanished once the battle dragged on for much longer than expected, once it was clear that Marja was still too dangerous to police and govern.

In the late fall of 2009, as McChrystal was preparing for his battle in the south, Colonel Randy George, brigade commander of the US Army's Task Force Mountain Warrior, and a career diplomat named Dante Paradiso were engaged in a different kind of counterinsurgency, dealing not with Karzai's government—which they viewed as fatally corrupt—but with the tribal elders of Nangarhar Province along the craggy border with Pakistan.

On January 21, 2010, their campaign culminated in what should have been rewarded as a triumph. They brought together 160 of the most influential elders of the Shinwari tribe—one of the area's largest, encompassing about a half million people—to sign a pact denouncing the Taliban, threatening to punish anyone in their tribe who supported the Taliban, pledging to stop growing poppies, and declaring their allegiance to the central government in Kabul, despite grave misgivings over Karzai and his cronies.

In exchange, the elders asked the Americans for more development assistance, the removal of some particularly corrupt local officials, and the right to have a say in which Afghan security forces would be stationed in their province.

George pledged $1 million from his commander's discretionary fund for development, but emphasized that while the elders could suggest local projects, he, not they, would handle and distribute the money. As for the other demands, he and Paradiso would do their best to persuade their higher-ups but could make no guarantees. That was good enough for the elders; the deal was struck.

It was a remarkable pact. There had been nothing like it, in scope or substance, in the eight years since the Taliban had been overthrown.

And yet the pact was sabotaged by the Afghan president and by the American ambassador.

• • •

Randy George had some background in counterinsurgency and the art of dealing with tribal cultures. He'd served three tours of duty in Iraq. The first was as part of the invasion force, but the second was more intriguing: a brigade commander in Kirkuk, where he wound up spending most of his time arbitrating property disputes between local Kurds and Sunni Arabs.

He was in frequent contact with Dave Petraeus, who'd been following his career since the early 1990s, when Petraeus commanded a battalion in the 101st Airborne Division and George was his top lieutenant. George also read the classic counterinsurgency books, including John Nagl's (the two had been classmates at West Point in the mid-to-late 1980s), and he absorbed their principles. But George also realized that Iraq was very different from Malaya and that the modern American military had much less sway over a sovereign country in the media age than the British army had possessed over one of its colonies in the aftermath of World War II. He gained deeper wisdom about how to apply COIN's basic principles from reading histories of the Kurds and the Sunnis and from observing the role that history and culture were playing in the tenuous borderline between war and peace that he himself was treading every day.

In Kirkuk, he also met and worked with Emma Sky, the British Arabist who was trying to help American officers understand why the insurgents were fighting. General Ray Odierno had met them both when he was commander of the 4th Infantry Division. When Odierno was promoted to corps commander in the early days of the surge and hired Sky as his political adviser, she suggested that he bring George into his circle, too. Odierno put George to work on a road map for Iraq's future: what if the surge didn't work, what if it did, what might happen next in either case, and how would various outcomes affect US interests?

George came away from Iraq with a knack for solving gritty human disputes, and for spinning grand strategic scenarios, in a very foreign land.

He came to Afghanistan about the same time McChrystal did, as commander of an infantry brigade—6,500 American soldiers—spread out across four provinces in the country's desolate eastern region. Some of his men had been sent to occupy fortified bastions on remote cliffs, positions inherited from the reign of earlier commanders, whose battle plan had been to shoot the Taliban as they crossed over the border from Pakistan. It was a strategy of static defensiveness and, in the end, futility, as the Taliban would simply cross a few mountain paths away.

Early on in his deployment, George wrote a twenty-one-page strategy paper that called for shifting the focus away from "attacking the enemy in remote areas" to "protecting and developing the major population centers" in order to "separate the enemy from the local population" and "connect local populations to a responsive Afghan government." He also called for a thorough anticorruption campaign. The Taliban were winning the fight for popular support, he observed, by setting up their own courts, which, for all their faults, did at least mete out swift justice while barring bribes—a stark contrast with the official courts, which were both inefficient and corrupt. For the United States and ISAF to tolerate this corruption, he wrote, would only validate the Taliban's claims to moral authority.

George briefed his plan to McChrystal, who approved it.

Around this time, firefights between the Shinwari tribesmen and the Taliban were intensifying. A Shinwari elder named Malik Niaz appealed to Colonel George for help. Not long after, another elder, Malik Usman, whose brother had been killed by the Taliban earlier in the year, approached George as well.

George and Paradiso learned that Niaz and Usman were rivals (the Shinwari tribe was rife with ancient feuds and factions), and they saw this coincidence as an opportunity to reunite the two elders in a common cause. With the two Americans' guidance, they drew up a ten-point pledge to band together against the Taliban. George and Paradiso encouraged them to reach out to other elders and get them to sign the pledge, too. Over the next few months, the elders expanded the roster from two to four to sixteen and beyond, culminating in the signing ceremony of January 21, 2010.

The two Americans saw this meeting as a very big deal, maybe the start of an Afghan parallel to the Anbar Awakening, which had sparked the turning point in Iraq three years earlier and which had stemmed from much the same impulse—tribal elders turning to a foreign army, despite their prior antipathy, because they felt more threatened by Islamist militants.

One week after the signing, a story about the Shinwari pact appeared on the front page of the *New York Times*. Secretary of State Hillary Clinton happened to be in London at a conference of international donors to Afghanistan. She read the story and publicly hailed the pact as a reflection of America's new strategy.

"This is classic counterinsurgency," she proclaimed in an interview with CNN. "As General McChrystal said, you're never going to kill or capture everybody calling himself a Taliban. But you can change the political environment, so that those who continue to call themselves Taliban become more and more isolated, and that's what we're seeking."

Clinton had good reason to believe her comments were in line with broad US policy. In his memo on the new war strategy two months earlier, President Obama had written that "we must focus on what is realistic . . . working with Karzai when we can, working around him when we must"— the latter, in order to improve governance and reduce corruption at the local level. The Shinwari pact seemed a textbook case of working around Karzai when we must.

For precisely that reason, Karzai loathed the pact. It had been conceived, written, and endorsed without his involvement, outside the realm of his control.

Karzai had always opposed plans to build up a base of independent local power because they had the effect—and, he suspected (sometimes rightly), the intent—of stripping away the central government's powers, which is to say his own power and that of his cronies, whom he'd installed as provincial or district governors, jobs that they treated as cash cows, collecting bribes, extorting farmers, and pocketing revenue. Any plan that empowered people outside this network—for instance, Shinwari tribal elders in Nangarhar Province—threatened to undermine Karzai's true constituents and thus the foundations of his power. In this sense, it didn't matter that the Shinwari had pledged to oppose the Taliban or even to support Karzai's government; the problem was that they were assuming the right to make such a pledge of their own volition.

Karzai complained about the pact to Ambassador Eikenberry and General McChrystal. Dante Paradiso—who was the embassy's chief representative in the four eastern provinces, heading a team of forty civilian diplomats and aid workers attached to Colonel George's brigade—expected Eikenberry to stand up for their work. After all, his now-famous critique of McChrystal's proposal to send more troops and switch to a classic COIN strategy had stemmed from a judgment that Karzai was not a suitable strategic partner. Surely, then, making a deal with influential tribal leaders—real local powers—to band against the Taliban, and even pledge fealty to the central government, would be seen as a step in the right direction.

Instead, Eikenberry stood up for Karzai. The ambassador was also in London when Secretary Clinton touted the Shinwari pact on CNN. The thing he didn't like was that the pact was news to him. Paradiso had sent the embassy a cable outlining the deal, emphasizing that he and George had not promised to give the elders money outright or to provide them with weapons. Somehow, though, the ambassador never saw the cable. Eikenberry was obsessed with control; he demanded to be—and, just as important, to be seen as—the dominant actor in his realm. He had no patience with minions who tried to make policy or tamper with the delicate machinery of diplomacy on their own, and that's what he thought Paradiso was doing.

After Eikenberry made his displeasure known, his senior staff followed through. One embassy official complained to a *Washington Post* reporter that the pact had "really stirred things up." It was like telling the Shinwari, "Congratulations, you get a pony." Now, the official said, "other tribes are saying, 'Why don't *I* get a pony?'"

This made no sense to Paradiso. The same thing could be said about any development project. (Why don't *I* get a dam? Why don't I get *my* sewers cleaned up?) And what would be so bad about giving other tribes a "pony" if they, too, signed a pact against the Taliban? The whole point of the commander's discretionary fund was to improve battlefield conditions: to pay communities to support the coalition's cause and to oppose the enemy's. That's what Petraeus and MacFarland had done in Mosul and Anbar Province. Meanwhile, Eikenberry's embassy staff was handing out hundreds of millions of dollars for power plants and construction projects without any trade-offs, guarantees, or accountability.

McChrystal privately supported the pact; he had no problems with what George was doing. But he was in the final stages of preparing the battle for Marja, which he saw as essential to his own broader strategy, and Karzai hadn't yet granted him permission to move on the city. He needed to coax and massage Karzai to approve it; this was no time to oppose him on a peripheral point.

So Eikenberry won the day. He not only disavowed the Shinwari pact, he issued an edict barring all embassy officials from engaging with any tribes in any setting where a "pact" might be discussed—this, in a country of tribes.

The decision drove a deeper wedge between the embassy and the military. Officers could still reach out to tribes, and often did; the civilians were supposed to lead the way in reforming Afghan governance, but they couldn't, since governance required dealing with tribes, which they were now barred from doing.

Meanwhile, George and Paradiso were forced to cut off the flow of money to the Shinwari and to retract their part of the deal. Two weeks after the pact's signing, a violent land dispute had erupted between two factions within the tribe. Some embassy officials pointed to the fight, with some gloating, as proof that the deal was doomed from the outset. Maybe it was; probably it wouldn't have lasted long or spread far. Still, it was something, which was more than what most districts or provinces had going for them. Even while the Shinwari factions were squabbling, they reaffirmed their commitment to the pact. But after the money stopped flowing and the consultations ended, the elders grew more distrustful toward George and Paradiso as well as toward one another. They saw the cave-in to Karzai as proof that the Americans were complicit with the corruption. The pact collapsed.

It was no wonder that when Sarah Sewall briefed McChrystal on her civilian-casualties report in mid-April 2010, she found the general grumpier than usual.

A few days later, McChrystal and his staff made their ill-fated trip to a NATO conference in Europe, where they were joined by a *Rolling Stone* reporter named Michael Hastings, who taped some of them making crude and demeaning remarks about Obama, Biden, a few other American officials, and the French foreign minister. It was the toxic atmosphere that Sewall had observed, puffed up to self-destructive levels.

President Obama obtained an advance copy of the article. He read the first few paragraphs and put it down in disgust. He called a staff meeting that night. By the next morning, he knew he had no choice: McChrystal had to go.

He called the general to the White House for a one-on-one meeting on

June 23. McChrystal had tendered his resignation the day before. At the meeting, Obama accepted it. That afternoon, he announced the move at a press conference, saying that the behavior depicted in the article, for which McChrystal had taken full responsibility, "erodes the trust that is necessary for our team to work together to achieve our objectives in Afghanistan." He also emphasized, "This is a change in personnel, but it is not a change in policy."

The president then introduced the general he'd chosen as McChrystal's replacement—David Petraeus.

Choosing Petraeus was an exceptionally shrewd move, preempting the otherwise inevitable complaint that Obama was crippling the war effort by removing a perfectly fine commander and replacing him with someone who, competent though he may be, would take months to get up to speed.

Petraeus, of course, was no newbie. He was immersed in the fight, having been CentCom commander for nearly two years. More than that, he was David Petraeus, the best-known, most admired American general in a generation, the author of the COIN field manual, the miracle worker of Iraq. Maybe he could work miracles in Afghanistan, too.

Petraeus took command in Kabul on the Fourth of July, 2010. As his helicopter landed on the grounds of ISAF headquarters, a small group of civilian analysts mingled with the official welcoming party.

The analysts didn't quite know what they were doing there. McChrystal had invited them on an "opinion leaders" tour of the war, one of several such tours that he'd organized for prominent experts and analysts. Upon their arrival, they'd learned of McChrystal's dismissal. No one could tell them whether or not the tour was still on.

Still, they weren't fazed by their odd status. They were by now familiar figures in these settings: Fred and Kimberly Kagan, Steve Biddle, the neocon historian-columnist Max Boot, and Sarah Chayes, a former National Public Radio war reporter who'd moved to Kandahar eight years earlier, learned to speak Pashto, set up some small development projects to wean local farmers away from growing poppies, moved on to join the staff at ISAF headquarters, and was now about to become the Afghan-policy adviser to Admiral Mike Mullen, the chairman of the Joint Chiefs of Staff.

They were all familiar figures to Petraeus, too. He knew most of them from his own opinion leaders' tours or assessment teams back in Iraq. He was surprised to see them in Kabul, but he also saw an opportunity.

After his opening remarks and other ceremonial obligations, Petraeus approached them and asked if they'd be willing to stay on for a monthlong project. He knew that one of the biggest obstacles in the war was the Afghan government itself. He could design the most brilliant counterinsurgency campaign, but it would be for naught if Karzai, his ministers, and key district governors failed to follow through with sustained security and basic services—which would require thoroughgoing reforms.

He wanted the analysts to draft a detailed plan on how to get these reforms going. He also asked them to keep mum on what they were doing. McChrystal's assessment team had set off enough of a commotion with its famous sixty-six-page memo, and the Obama administration had long since carved its policy in stone. Petraeus didn't want anyone in Washington to get the idea that he was reopening long-settled debates.

Though he could not have known it, Petraeus *was* reopening one of the unsettled debates that had haunted some members of McChrystal's assessment team, including a few who were now on Petraeus's secret new advisory group.

Sarah Chayes had raised the issue during that earlier assessment, not as a team member but as one of McChrystal's staffers who'd been asked to give the team a briefing. Chayes had concluded that the problem with the Afghan government wasn't that it lacked competence or resources, but, rather, that it was corrupt and predatory. Simply training officials wouldn't improve matters; it might only make them more effective predators.

Chayes's briefing had carried weight among several analysts on the team. Most of them had only visited Afghanistan now and then for a few days or weeks at a time; she'd actually been living there, outside the embassy's gates, for years. They also saw evidence of her argument as they toured the country and talked with local officials and ordinary citizens.

In their report for McChrystal, they'd warned that corruption was pervasive and that the war might be lost without serious reforms. But they had neither the mandate nor the time to delve into the problem. Now Petraeus was asking them to put the issue front and center and to devise a plan for action.

The new team finished its report in early August and briefed it to

Petraeus. Afghanistan's governing apparatus, the analysts concluded, was basically a network of malign actors. Pushing for reform at the top of the network, within Karzai's central government, wouldn't work. Better, they suggested, to undermine the network by shutting off its levers of patronage at the bottom and to make this effort part of every brigade commander's mission. A senior officer should be named to coordinate the campaign, roaming across the country to make sure that the commanders were enforcing the edict. The team recommended that this job be given to H. R. McMaster, who had just arrived in Kabul to serve on Petraeus's staff.

Petraeus was impressed with their analysis but found most of their proposals impractical. First, he couldn't simply bypass Karzai. One of Petraeus's strategic goals was to help stabilize Afghanistan; overhauling all the districts' local governing boards and spreading power to a new array of warlords was hardly a recipe for stability.

Second, the plan would undermine another one of his strategic goals: protecting the Afghan population. The local officials who were taking bribes and extorting businesses (with or without Karzai's complicity) were also helping with local security and, in some parts of the country, guarding convoys of ISAF supply trucks as they drove through dangerous areas. If the cash spigot was shut off, they'd let the Taliban attack the supply trucks and maybe join in, attacking not only the trucks but the troops and their local collaborators.

The team's briefing acknowledged the risk, outlining precisely that scenario as a potential side effect of the plan. But Petraeus saw it as an inevitable and dangerous consequence of their proposal, not a potential side effect. And even if it did work, even if it was possible to devolve power to the local districts, it would take way too much time. Petraeus was under pressure to show fast results in improving security; the plan's effects would be slow and murky at best.

Steve Biddle, who had also worked on McChrystal's assessment team and a similar team that Petraeus had appointed in Iraq, was disturbed by the broader implications of Chayes's analysis. Two years earlier, Biddle had written an article, pointing out a logical hole in Petraeus's field manual. The manual envisioned America's role in a COIN campaign as helping the host government fulfill its own best interests by becoming a more legitimate defender of its peaceful citizens' well-being. But what if the host government had a different view of its best interests? What if it was more interested in catering not to the population as a whole but to a particular sectarian group that was hostile to rival groups? Helping that sort of government perform more effectively might make things worse.

When Biddle wrote the piece, he was thinking of Maliki's Shiite-dominated government in Iraq; but after hearing Chayes's briefing, he realized his critique had far greater relevance in Afghanistan. If Chayes was right, if the Afghan government was beholden to a criminal network of patronage, then its leaders would never warm to the notion of reform. The implications were these: either a COIN campaign in this country was futile because America's "strategic partner" wasn't really a partner (as Eikenberry had argued in his cables the previous November) or Petraeus would have to persuade, manipulate, and coerce Hamid Karzai into altering his own concept of Afghanistan's national interests.

This was essentially the conclusion that General Pete Chiarelli and his political adviser, Celeste Ward, had reached about the diverging American and Iraqi interests back in the fall of 2006. And it was the conclusion that Dave Kilcullen had reached more generally in 2008, when he wrote in the interagency guide on COIN that it would be "folly" to engage in counter-insurgency abroad "unless there is a reasonable likelihood that the affected government will introduce necessary reforms."

Petraeus knew all about this. He'd done quite a lot of persuading and coercing with Maliki in Iraq, and he figured that he'd need to do the same with Karzai. He'd achieved some success with Karzai already. For months, McChrystal had tried to set up Afghan self-defense units in local districts, but Karzai had always blocked him, fearing (not unreasonably) that they would empower warlords and weaken the national army's authority—*his* authority. Through a mix of cajoling, arguing, arm twisting, and soothing (and finally agreeing to place the units, ultimately, under the interior ministry's authority), Petraeus won Karzai's endorsement for the local units just ten days after taking command.

The team members did inspire Petraeus to issue a document called "Counterinsurgency Contracting Guidance," outlining new rules for buying goods and services from Afghan companies without fueling corruption or financing insurgents.

But Petraeus recognized that these were first steps, fraught with risk and reversible at any moment.

He also well understood the same broader, more worrisome implication that Biddle had detected: the possibility that, despite his best efforts, COIN simply might not work in a country where the government's leaders didn't want to reform—in effect, didn't want COIN to work.

In the PowerPoint briefing that he delivered to countless congressional delegations at his Kabul headquarters, Petraeus titled one of the slides "Storm Clouds," which listed all the aspects of Afghanistan that bode ill for the war's prospects. Topping the list was the Afghan government's incapacity; cited not far below was the government's network of criminal patronage.

David Galula's classic book *Counterinsurgency Warfare,* which Petraeus was still consulting, contained a chapter titled "The Prerequisites for a Successful Insurgency." According to Galula, these prerequisites included a weak government, a neighboring country that offers safe havens, and a predominantly rural, illiterate population—precisely the traits marking Karzai's Afghanistan. Even the country's geography, it seemed, favored insurgents. As Galula put it, "the ideal situation for the insurgent would be a large land-locked country, shaped like a blunt-tipped star, with jungle-covered mountains along the borders and scattered swamps in the plains, in a temperate zone with a large and dispersed rural population and a primitive economy."

In other words, an insurgent's ideal situation was the topography and demography of Afghanistan.

Petraeus saw all this as a daunting stack of obstacles, but surmounting obstacles was his specialty; it was what he *did.* He'd placed first at Ranger school; he'd survived a bullet wound, a collapsed parachute, and, just a year before taking command of ISAF, a bout of early-stage prostate cancer. More pertinent still, he'd defied the odds in Iraq, with the surge and the spread of the Anbar Awakening. Taming Afghanistan might be his hardest challenge, but "hard" was not the same as "impossible." Others had failed, but most of them hadn't seen the war correctly. Petraeus liked to say that once you got "the inputs right"—the right strategy, personnel, tactical guidance, and metrics of success—you were more likely to get the right outcome. The commanders before him didn't get the inputs right. McChrystal came close, but he went too far on some points, not far enough on others, and, finally, he ran out of time.

Petraeus was confident about inputs; his biggest doubts concerned time. He had a year—six months had already passed in the president's eighteen-month deadline—to show results. That wasn't nearly enough time for classical COIN techniques alone, which usually took, as his field manual noted, a decade or longer to play out. (Yes, this war had been going on for almost a decade by the time Petraeus took command, but it hadn't been waged as a COIN campaign. As several Army officers liked to say, "We haven't been fighting in Afghanistan for eight years; we've been fighting there for one year, eight years in a row.") Petraeus would have to throw everything he could muster into the war all at once—more COIN, more killing bad guys, more training Afghan soldiers—and hope that all the pieces fell into place, and quickly.

One thing he did early on, both to facilitate this all-out effort and to correct what he saw as overreach, was to revise McChrystal's signature documents: his "Tactical Directive" and his "Counterinsurgency Guidance."

Petraeus's revisions, both issued on August 1, four weeks into his command, recited many of the same basic principles: to "secure and serve the population," to "live among the people," to "help Afghans build accountable governance," and to "reduce the loss of innocent civilian life to an absolute minimum," in order to avoid alienating the Afghan people, who are "the center of gravity in this struggle."

But gone were McChrystal's rigid formulas that had frustrated so many troops in the year since his rules of engagement had gone into effect. Where McChrystal had stressed the need to avoid violence except under limited circumstances (seeing COIN as 95 percent political, only 5 percent military), Petraeus wrote explicitly, "Protecting the Afghan people does require killing, capturing, or turning the insurgents. Indeed . . . we must pursue the Taliban tenaciously." In his revised "Counterinsurgency Guidance," he stated the point more aggressively: "Pursue the enemy relentlessly. Together with our Afghan partners, get our teeth into the insurgents and don't let go." It was within this context that he summed up his directive: to "fight with great discipline and tactical patience" and "use only the firepower needed to win a fight."

The new orders were still ambiguous; they still harked back to the unanswered questions at Petraeus's COIN conference in Fort Leavenworth four years earlier: at what stage *is* force justified in a counterinsurgency campaign, and how do the troops know when they've crossed that line? Still, Petraeus's guidance set a new tone, one meant to let the troops breathe easier, insisting that they act with an awareness of COIN principles but not to the point where they feared the prospect of court-martial if they accidentally killed a civilian in the course of staving off bad guys.

From that moment, Petraeus stepped up the kill-and-capture side of the operation. In his first three months as commander, US warplanes and drones dropped 1,600 weapons on targets in Afghanistan—nearly half the number that had been dropped in the entire previous year. He also let loose the JSOC Special Ops forces all over the country, to a greater extent than even McChrystal, who'd practically invented JSOC.

The new twist in strategy seemed to have some tactical effect, killing or capturing three hundred midlevel Taliban leaders (including a number of shadow provincial governors and district commanders), as well as killing more than eight hundred rank-and-file insurgents and capturing another two thousand. And the attacks were fairly precise; civilian casualties, caused by air strikes and raids, were down.

Petraeus had long been saying in speeches and congressional testimony that you can't simply kill your way to victory in these kinds of wars; they usually end with a negotiated settlement, not a surrender ceremony. But he also thought that you did have to kill a lot of insurgents to get them to the bargaining table. He and Karzai had said they would reconcile with any insurgents who pledged to lay down arms and uphold the Afghan constitution. Insurgents weren't likely to do those things if they thought they were winning the fight.

Hy Rothstein, a retired Special Forces colonel who was now teaching at the Naval Postgraduate School in Monterey, took a fact-finding trip to Afghanistan a few months after Petraeus had taken command. The two had been classmates at West Point and had stayed in touch since. Eight years earlier, in late 2002, Rothstein had written a secret report for the Pentagon, concluding that the US military in Afghanistan had failed to translate tactical success into strategic victory; yes, the Taliban had been ousted from power, but al Qaeda still thrived, and, meanwhile, militant warlords were taking over many villages. The problem, as Rothstein saw it, was that the Americans were putting too much emphasis on bombing, when they should be putting boots on the ground and engaging in "unconventional warfare"—another term for "counterinsurgency," when that word was still banned from use. (The Pentagon, still run by Donald Rumsfeld, returned the report to Rothstein and asked that he tone it down; he refused.)

Rothstein had made a few trips to Afghanistan since then and had come away shaking his head on each occasion. This time, he was impressed with what Petraeus was doing; finally, a strategy, a coherent plan, was in place.

But Rothstein was concerned about a larger question: Where was this going? Petraeus was achieving some impressive *effects* (Taliban killed, terrain cleared, local police recruited), but the measure of real, sustained success was *outcomes*. When the West eventually pulled the plug on this place, *outcomes* would determine whether it survived on its own.

He came away with the impression that Petraeus was hoping to rack up enough effects, for a long enough time, that at some point they'd spill over into outcomes. Maybe so, but Rothstein saw no sign of a tipping point just yet.

Even Petraeus knew that Afghanistan was a long shot. Then again, Iraq had been a long shot, too. He understood, intellectually, that the two wars and the two countries were very different; in his PowerPoint briefings, he'd often include a slide that read, "Afghanistan Is Not Iraq." But Iraq was what he knew best; he'd spent three tours there, all in command slots, spanning a total of nearly four years. Afghanistan, by his own admission, he barely knew at all; so it was natural for him to view its problems through an Iraqi prism. But some of his aides and officers found the tendency disturbing. His instinctive reaction to *every* new challenge was to seek a parallel from his years in Iraq. *We solved that this way in Mosul . . . We did this when that happened in Anbar . . . I said this when Maliki threatened to do that . . .*

Once, he drew a comparison between Kabul and Baghdad in a conversation *with Karzai*. Matt Sherman, one of Petraeus's advisers who had spent considerable time in Iraq and Afghanistan, told him bluntly as they walked away from the meeting, "Don't talk about Iraq so much," adding, "It might be a great mental exercise for you to try not thinking about Iraq at all."

Petraeus nodded and said, "I'm working on it."

Afghanistan, on its own terms, was a stumper: the levers weren't working; the effects weren't producing outcomes. A major obstacle was Karzai himself, and Petraeus couldn't figure out a way to play him: he was clearly shrewder than Maliki had been; his hold on power relied on more networks that Petraeus couldn't disrupt.

In October, Karzai threatened to kick all foreign-owned private security guards out of the country. In a rare show of unity, Petraeus and Eikenberry went to see him together and urged him to reverse his decision; otherwise, they said, every economic-development project would shut down, as the aid workers and business executives couldn't stay without reliable protection. Karzai insisted that the Afghan police could do the job; the two Americans expressed their doubts.

Karzai threw a fit. He told them, "I have three main enemies"—the Taliban, the United States, and the international community—and "if I had to choose today, I'd choose the Taliban!"

At the last minute, Karzai backed down. But a few weeks later, in an interview with the *Washington Post,* he went on the rampage again, demanding that the Americans cut back on their military operations and end the Special Ops forces' nighttime raids altogether.

When he'd first assumed command, Petraeus told himself that if he ever thought the mission simply could not be accomplished, he would tell the president, and that would probably mean he'd have to resign. If Karzai really did forbid the nighttime raids, he knew he'd have to push that button.

Petraeus didn't want to take that step, so he played what leverage he had. He phoned Ashraf Ghani, one of Karzai's top national-security advisers, and said, "Your president has put me in an *untenable* position. Please take note of that word. I chose it carefully."

Ghani rushed to ISAF headquarters to assure Petraeus face-to-face that Karzai wasn't serious. A few days later, the Afghan president backed off again, for a while.

It wasn't the first or last time that Karzai made trouble or howled in protest or denounced the Americans or threatened to go join the insurgency. Eikenberry was right: Karzai was not a suitable strategic partner. But the problem wasn't Karzai personally. He had multiple constituencies: the Americans and NATO, for their money and security; his patronage network, for extending his power across the country; certain elements of the Taliban, with whom he'd have to make a deal at some point; and ordinary Afghans, for their complicity, if not quite warm support. The Americans and NATO, he could toy with; he'd learned that they were invested in this mission at least as much as he was, and so they weren't going away. (Petraeus's "untenable" threat to do just that was an exception, and all the more potent as a result.) His other constituents Karzai needed to placate more consistently, and they didn't like nighttime raids; they didn't like foreign soldiers, period. Whatever Karzai's mental state, he wasn't behaving much differently from the way that any Afghan president would have behaved in his situation.

Petraeus's frustrations, in short, stemmed not so much from Karzai as from the nature of Afghanistan itself: its primitive economy (which impeded the rise of an educated, entrepreneurial class); its vastly scattered, rural population (which a weak central government could rule only through a corrupt patronage network); and its long border with a state whose leaders were assisting the insurgency (which limited the success of any fight confined to Afghan territory).

A glance at a map, a few villages, or some key passages from Galula would have revealed that Afghanistan and COIN made an unlikely match.

Petraeus had glimpsed a bit of this himself five years earlier in the fall of 2005. He was about to complete his stint as commander of the mission to train the Iraqi army, when Donald Rumsfeld called and asked him to stop off in Afghanistan on his way home to assess the security situation. The Joint Chiefs of Staff were beginning to call the global war on terror the "long war," a seamless campaign that could stretch on for decades. Noting Afghanistan's widespread illiteracy, its lack of infrastructure and investment, the poor shape of its armed forces, and the signs of a rising insurgency, Petraeus told Rumsfeld, "Of all the long wars, this one is going to be the longest."

Now here he was, engulfed in its tidal waves himself.

At Petraeus's urging, and with President Obama's authorization (as well as, more often than not, the Pakistani military's compliance), the CIA stepped up its drone strikes against insurgent leaders basking in sanctuaries across the border. But despite an impressive hit rate (and relatively few civilian casualties), US intelligence reported that the campaign was doing little to alter the militants' behavior; they were still able to retreat to safe havens at will. It was another case of effects without outcomes.

To combat corruption, Petraeus set up a special command and put his favorite one-star general, H. R. McMaster, in charge. McMaster linked up with the intelligence community and special FBI agents. He and his team interviewed hundreds of Afghan officials and citizens, mapped out the networks of criminal patronage from the most powerful ministries to the most remote district governors, and drew up a list of nine objectives and fifty-four tasks they had to accomplish. He compiled evidence of massive malfeasance by some of Karzai's top officials and cronies. They included the chairman of Kabul Bank, who'd spent over $150 million of state deposits on personal villas in Dubai; the Afghan surgeon general, who'd stolen tens of millions of dollars' worth of drugs from the main military hospital; and officers in the Afghan air force, who were moving narcotics around the country on behalf of drug lords.

His efforts resulted in the firing of a few dozen police chiefs and local government officials, but not much more. No higher-ups were prosecuted; a few were taken into custody briefly, until Karzai set them free.

Petraeus was rotated out of Kabul on July 18, 2011, just as Obama's troop cuts were about to get under way. He hadn't made as much progress as he'd pledged toward accomplishing the mission. Probably no one could have.

He was also exhausted: dark circles under his eyes, his back slightly bent when he walked, his concentration a bit less steely than usual. This was, to say the least, normal for a twice-injured fifty-eight-year-old cancer survivor wrapping up his sixth consecutive command in a span of nine years, the last three of those commands and the last four of those years deployed abroad in combat. But Petraeus would heatedly deny that he was at all tired, challenging anyone who commented on his signs of fatigue to a five-mile foot race at dawn.

A few nights before his farewell ceremony, Petraeus sat in his office with a small group of aides and visitors, watching videos of his days back in Mosul as commander of the 101st Airborne Division, then more videos, archival films of the 101st of yore, the Screaming Eagles from World War II. It was an evening of unwinding, an immersion in nostalgia and glory.

They watched no videos from his year in Afghanistan.

22.

"A New American Way of War"

David Petraeus had once hoped, even expected, that after Afghanistan would come the promotion of his careerlong dream: to chairman of the Joint Chiefs of Staff. But the post went instead to his West Point classmate Martin Dempsey.

With the pending budget cuts and the doctrinal retreats, Petraeus half convinced himself that it was just as well he didn't get the job. As he told one friend, "I'm better at buildups than drawdowns."

He'd learned back in December 2010 that the promotion wouldn't be coming. Bob Gates, the secretary of defense and an ally in the quest, delivered the news during a trip that month to Afghanistan. Petraeus was crushed but not too surprised. He knew about what he called, with a rueful smirk, the "Petraeus problem." A number of President Obama's White House aides didn't trust Petraeus; they thought that he'd tried to box in the president during the deliberations on Afghan war policy; Rahm Emanuel, Obama's chief of staff, openly worried that the most famous general of his generation might possess a white-knight complex, an urge of destiny to run for president. Petraeus disabused him of this notion.

But even those who dismissed Emanuel's fears were leery of giving too much power to a general of such prominence, ambition, and agility. The JCS chairman was a position of potentially enormous power; he would have control of the Joint Staff, a multiservice body of nine directorates, manned by several hundred of the military's smartest officers. The last chairman who'd molded the Joint Staff into a bureaucratic weapon—who'd figured out how to use its collective talents and inside knowledge to win arguments and pursue his agenda—was General Colin Powell, during the presidencies of George H. W. Bush and, briefly, Bill Clinton. It was no accident that almost every chairman since had been fairly unassertive by inclination. Doug Lute, who'd known Petraeus since their days at West

Point and who was now Obama's adviser on Afghanistan, told some of his colleagues, "Dave Petraeus will never be chairman as long as anyone still remembers how Powell ran circles around the interagency process."

At the same time, any president, especially a Democrat, would want to keep a general like Petraeus on the inside. He might not run for high office, but he could go write policy papers for a think tank like the American Enterprise Institute, where he had many friends. A paper by retired general Petraeus, criticizing the administration's policy on Afghanistan or the defense budget, would be treated as front-page news. Obama would be asked about "the Petraeus study" at his next press conference. Out of uniform and cast to the winds, Petraeus could set the national-security agenda.

After Gates gave Petraeus the news, they discussed other job possibilities. Petraeus raised one idea: director of the Central Intelligence Agency. He had the right experience, as a consumer of intelligence and as a prodder and a collector, not just in Iraq and Afghanistan—where he'd worked with JSOC, Special Forces, and the entire range of the intelligence community—but also during his time running counterterrorism operations in Bosnia. Gates, who'd been a CIA director himself, thought that Petraeus would be terrific at the job. It would keep him on the front lines of the war on terror (the Agency operated the drone strikes in Pakistan, Yemen, Somalia—every place except Afghanistan, where the military controlled them), and it would fit well with his analytical talents.

Petraeus started lobbying informally for the job—with, crucially, Gates's strong endorsement. He was eager to demonstrate that he could be a solid team player. Three months after his conversation with Gates, he had a chance. He returned to Washington for congressional hearings on Afghanistan and, during his testimony, defended every aspect of the administration's policy, including Obama's decision to set a date when American troops would start to come home, a decision that most COIN scholars—and, privately, many of Petraeus's fellow senior officers—had sharply criticized.

Toward the end of that trip, he met with the president to discuss his recommendations on Afghanistan—and, on the side, his own future. Obama offered Petraeus the CIA job on condition that he first resign from the military, to avoid conflicting loyalties. Petraeus accepted the deal.

A mere six weeks later, he once again took the long flight from Kabul to Washington, so he could stand in the East Room of the White House while Obama announced the grand shuffle in his national-security team: Gates was retiring; Panetta was shifting from the CIA to replace Gates at the Pentagon; and Petraeus was leaving Afghanistan, several weeks ahead of schedule, to replace Panetta at CIA.

On June 30, the Senate confirmed Petraeus's nomination, 94–0. He returned to Afghanistan for his last two weeks as commander in a state of rush and ambivalence: on the one hand, eager to turn a new page in his life (Gates had advised him to get out of the car at headquarters in Langley all alone, to cut loose the entourage that he'd cultivated over the past twenty years as an officer); on the other hand, frustrated that his final command post was ending on a less than triumphant note.

He retired from the Army on August 31, with a full-colors ceremony on the parade field at Fort Myer, not far from the Pentagon. He was sworn in as CIA director six days later.

In the weeks between his return and his retirement, Petraeus attended a spate of welcome-home parties, with many of his fellow COINdinistas in attendance.

At one party, John Nagl rose to make a toast, hailing the guest of honor as a model soldier-scholar deserving mention alongside Ulysses S. Grant and Dwight D. Eisenhower as American generals who had commanded successfully in two theaters of war—and perhaps someday, Nagl added with a wink and a smile directed at his former mentor, he would follow those generals' footsteps in another way as well.

Petraeus stared straight ahead with a deadpan expression, avoiding the slightest visible response to both of Nagl's improbable references: the prospect of a Petraeus presidency and the notion that he'd been successful in Afghanistan as well as Iraq.

Afterward, as the crowd around Petraeus dwindled to just a few friends, Dave Kilcullen approached. "Do you really believe what John said about *two* successful commands?" he asked.

"No," Petraeus said, shaking his head slowly. "There's still a long way to go."

On June 22, 2011, a few weeks before the end of David Petraeus's tenure as commander in Afghanistan, President Obama delivered a fifteen-minute address on national prime-time television, announcing that he would withdraw ten thousand troops from Afghanistan by Christmas and another twenty-three thousand by the end of the following summer.

This amounted to pulling out the entire "surge" force: all thirty-three thousand of the extra troops that he'd decided to send in December 2009 after the series of ten meetings with his national-security advisers. These troops were scheduled to rotate out by then anyway, but Obama was now saying that they would not be replaced by a new rotation of troops. The sixty-eight thousand troops that remained after their departure would be it—and *their* ranks would be reduced steadily until 2014, the year when the NATO ministers had decided, with Karzai's consent, to end their occupation altogether.

In short, Obama was announcing the end of the surge—and, with it, the end of its underlying strategy.

His top defense advisers were stunned. They'd known that *some* troops would be coming out: when Obama announced the escalation eighteen months earlier, he also announced that he would *begin* to pull them out in July 2011. But the advisers had urged him not to withdraw more than a few thousand, at least for the moment.

They'd apparently forgotten, or had never taken seriously, Obama's words at the last of those ten meetings, the Sunday afternoon session in the Oval Office two days before his West Point address, when he asked these advisers whether the thirty thousand extra troops he'd decided to send would improve things to the point where the Afghan army could lead the fight within eighteen months. He warned them that this would be the final escalation; they shouldn't count on him to double down or extend their stay if they couldn't do the job in that time span.

He'd viewed the generals' COIN strategy as a gamble—a worthwhile gamble, but a gamble nonetheless—and he wasn't going to bet more lives or treasure than he'd already put on the table. At that Sunday meeting, the defense secretary, the JCS chairman, and the commander on the ground—Gates, Mullen, and Petraeus—had assured him one by one that, yes, they could accomplish the mission with the resources and time that he was giving them.

Now those eighteen months had passed, and the gamble hadn't paid off. By all accounts, only a handful of Afghan army units were capable of taking the lead. So, as he'd warned, Obama was scaling back the war substantially.

He didn't put it that way in his TV address. To the contrary, he all but declared victory. The United States and NATO, he proclaimed, "are meeting our goals" of defeating al Qaeda, reversing the Taliban's momentum, and training Afghanistan's security forces. So it was time to begin turning the mission over to the Afghans.

By that measure of success, he was right. Two months earlier, on his orders, a team of SEALs had killed Osama bin Laden—the mastermind of the 9/11 attacks, the figure who'd provoked the American invasion from the outset, the wanted-dead-or-alive target that George W. Bush had been chasing for years but had never been able to find.

Yet if Obama's war aims had been merely to kill bin Laden, push back the Taliban a bit, and step up the training of the Afghan army, he wouldn't have needed to send so many extra troops to begin with. He'd decided to send thirty-three thousand more troops because that number (augmented by seven thousand more from NATO allies) was the minimum needed to carry out the counterinsurgency strategy that Petraeus and McChrystal were urging him to adopt.

Pulling them all out, and thus returning to the level of troops in place before the surge, meant pulling the plug on COIN.

Obama wasn't getting out entirely. The Special Ops commandos who were mounting raids on Taliban hideouts, the drones and other aircraft that were dropping smart bombs on high-value targets both in Afghanistan and across the border in Pakistan—those forces, he emphasized, would stay in place, would not be reduced at all.

But they were the tools of a counterterrorism strategy: the "CT" approach that Joe Biden had favored in the White House debates toward the end of 2009. They had once been elements of a counterinsurgency strategy: tools that would clear an area of insurgents, after which conventional troops would hold the area and then build support for the local government by helping to provide basic services. But with cuts as deep as those Obama was now announcing, "hold" and "build" could not be sustained—not by American troops, anyway, not for long. Pretty much all they could do was go after insurgents and train the Afghan army to go after insurgents once the NATO troops were all gone.

Those forty thousand extra troops that Obama had deployed for the more ambitious strategy—the troop levels and the strategy that his top generals had requested—weren't able to hold or build much in any case, not even after a year and a half of a COIN-driven surge. The failure had stemmed not so much from the troops or their commanders as from the nature of Afghanistan and its regime. That being the case, there was no reason to believe that another year and a half and thirty thousand troops would make much difference. Nor, probably, would another ten years and one hundred thousand troops.

Back in March 2009, just two months into his presidency, while announcing his first escalation in Afghanistan—the twenty-one thousand extra troops sent to provide security for the country's elections—Obama had said that he would not "*blindly* stay the course" or "provide a blank check" for the mission.

He was now making good on that promise.

On September 30, General Martin Dempsey was sworn in as chairman of the Joint Chiefs of Staff. Three weeks earlier, General Ray Odierno had taken the oath as the new chief of staff of the Army.

Had the war in Afghanistan gone better, their promotions might have been seen as a solidification of COIN culture in the highest echelons of the Pentagon.

But the ground was shifting rapidly under their feet.

Within days of his ascension, Dempsey got word from the White House—as did Secretary of Defense Leon Panetta—that the president wanted a formal review of American military policy. Specifically, he wanted to put an end to interventions—large-scale, protracted "stability operations"—like those in Iraq and Afghanistan. Their costs were unsustainable in a time of fiscal pressures; their benefits were uncertain in any event.

For the next two months, the Pentagon's leaders—first just the chiefs, then an expanded group that included the senior civilian officials—met roughly once a week to discuss a wide range of military issues: a possible shift of forces from Europe to the Pacific, another shift from manned aircraft to drones, the proper mix of active-duty soldiers and reservists, of conventional troops and Special Ops commandos.

And they talked about the future of stability operations, the issue of greatest concern to those who had taken part in the COIN revolution of the previous decade and had seen their own views on the nature of warfare evolve and harden. Among the officials in the room who felt the pangs most intensely were Ray Odierno, the COIN convert who was now the Army's top general; Michèle Flournoy, the former president of the Center for a New American Security, who was now in her final months (by her choice) as undersecretary of defense for policy; and Robert Schmidle, the Marine three-star general who organized the first Irregular Warfare Conference at Quantico back in the fall of 2004.

Schmidle, who was now deputy director of the new US Cyber Command, had been recruited by Dempsey to run his transition team in the weeks before taking over as Joint Chiefs chairman. Now that a strategic review was in the works, he asked Schmidle to stay on a few more weeks to run it again alongside Flournoy's deputy, Kathleen Hicks. Schmidle and Hicks had worked together once before, on the team of analysts—including, most prominently, David Kilcullen—who wrote the chapters on irregular warfare for the Pentagon's 2005 Quadrennial Defense Review.

The officials involved in these new discussions understood the president's—and the American public's—reluctance to get embroiled in another Iraq. But they were also keen to preserve what the chiefs were now calling the "lessons learned from ten years of war." Among these lessons: that conflicts of the future were likely to be a mix of offense, defense, and stability operations; that, in such wars, awareness of the local culture would be as important as an assessment of the enemy's order of battle; and that, therefore, it was essential to retain officers who were skilled in this sort of warfare—and to educate and train the coming generation of officers in its principles and techniques.

Schmidle knew that, historically, few American presidents had plunged into long insurgency wars on purpose; usually they'd backed into them, or they'd sent troops to a foreign land for a completely different reason, then got sucked into the "stability" mission as the country fell apart. Vietnam was a case of the former; Iraq, the latter. The pattern tended to repeat itself, one way or another, every generation—at intervals just long enough for the people in power during one war to forget the lessons of the previous war.

The commanders of these past ten years of war—Petraeus, Odierno, Chiarelli, McMaster, and the others—had to excavate the few useful lessons from Vietnam, because the senior Army officers of the earlier generation had deliberately buried the records. And now the new top officers were determined that the next time a president got them involved in a war of this sort, a ledger of lessons, a guide to action—their ledger, their guide—would still be in active circulation.

In one slide of their PowerPoint briefings, Schmidle and Hicks assembled a list of irregular wars, low-intensity conflicts, and counterinsurgency campaigns that the American military had waged over the years. They focused particularly on the "*moot*-wah" wars of the nineties—among them Somalia, Haiti, Panama, Grenada, Bosnia, Kosovo—the same wars that Petraeus, Nagl, Crane, and others had cited to justify a revival of COIN doctrine. They argued that even another war in Korea—one of the few scenarios that would involve large-scale maneuvers of tanks and artillery—might require stability operations if North Korea's regime crumbled and the country tumbled into chaos.

By December, the top Pentagon officials were ready to make their case to the White House. Several meetings, in one building or the other, took place over the next few weeks.

Obama himself attended and took an active part in three of these meetings: two in the Oval Office, one in the Pentagon. He quickly grasped the generals' argument: that no one could predict what sorts of wars we might wind up fighting and that skills in stability operations should be retained in case this particular kind of war arose again for whatever reason. But that left open the question of priorities. How far did the military and the country need to go to make *preparations* for that kind of war? How many troops and how much money should be pegged to stability operations instead of other types of operations?

By the start of 2012, a consensus had formed around an answer.

On January 5, Obama traveled across the Potomac, stood at the podium in the newsroom of the Pentagon, and—with Secretary Panetta and the entire Joint Chiefs of Staff standing behind him—outlined the main tenets of the new "strategic guidance" for the Defense Department.

No president had ever before held a press conference at the Pentagon; Obama's appearance to trumpet this policy signaled clearly that it was far from routine.

The eight-page document, titled "Sustaining US Global Leadership: Priorities for 21st Century Defense," focused mainly on the shift of security concerns and resources from Europe to the Pacific and the role that the American military's technological edge could play in countering the rise of China's power.

But one section also dealt with stability operations. Obama summed it up in his opening remarks: "As we look beyond the wars in Iraq and Afghanistan—and the end of long-term nation-building with large military footprints—we'll be able to ensure our security with smaller conventional ground forces."

For the Army, the key phrase here was "smaller conventional ground forces." For the COINdinistas, it was "the end of long-term nation-building with large military footprints."

The document noted that "for the foreseeable future," the United States would "take an active approach" in countering threats posed by al Qaeda and other jihadist terrorist groups around the world. But, it went on, this approach would "emphasize nonmilitary means," and, to the extent that arms were necessary, it would focus more on assisting other nations' security forces so that they could stave off homegrown threats on their own.

Occasionally, the guidance acknowledged, American forces would need to get involved in "directly striking the most dangerous groups and individuals." But even then, it added, in italics: *"Whenever possible, we will develop innovative, low-cost, small-footprint approaches to achieve our security objectives."*

In the key passage, it stated that the American military would remain "ready to conduct limited counterinsurgency and other stability operations if required" and, therefore, would "retain and continue to refine the lessons learned, expertise, and specialized capabilities that have been developed over the past ten years . . . in Iraq and Afghanistan."

"However," it proclaimed, again in italics, *"US forces will no longer be sized to conduct large-scale, prolonged stability operations."*

Back in late 2005, David Kilcullen, Bob Schmidle, and the other authors of the Pentagon's Quadrennial Defense Review had called for boosting the Army's size and resources, so that it *could* "conduct a large-scale, potentially long-duration irregular warfare campaign." Now, six years later, Obama was reversing course. With his strategic guidance, he wasn't merely saying "Never again" to another war like Iraq or Afghanistan, at least as long as he was commander in chief; he was telling the generals that when they calculated how many troops were needed for various contingencies, they were not to assume that one of those contingencies might be a long war involving lots of troops engaged in anything like a COIN campaign.

The strategic guidance nullified another key COIN document from late 2005: Defense Department Directive 3000.05, which declared that stability operations were "a core US military mission" to be "given priority comparable to combat operations."

That was clearly no longer the case. Planning and preparing for those sorts of wars would be a part of the armed forces' repertory but not a centerpiece—not a scenario to shape or justify its size or its budget. It was no longer a "core mission" of the American military.

Exactly how to go about retaining and refining the lessons learned from ten years of war, Obama left to the chiefs. Odierno and Dempsey spent a lot of their time filling in the blank spaces.

One space they filled was to transform the Army's Maneuver Center of Excellence, a school for armor and infantry officers at Fort Benning, Georgia, into a training ground for "full-spectrum operations," combining tank maneuvers with counterinsurgency and humanitarian assistance, devising scenarios and exercises in which junior officers would have to switch back and forth from one mode of warfare to another, teaching them how to make judgments and decisions in a complex environment.

As the center's new director, Odierno appointed H. R. McMaster, now a two-star general, who'd been the peerless tank-killer in Desert Storm and the COIN commander par excellence in Tal Afar, Iraq.

Odierno also drew up new rules for the Army's promotion boards, a long list of skills and experiences that colonels must amass before advancing to the rank of brigadier general. Scoring well at commanding a combat battalion would no longer be sufficient; they'd also need experience at posts that had required cultural awareness and complex decision-making. And to make sure that the guidelines were followed, Odierno would personally pick the generals who served on the boards—generals that he knew were in synch with his approach.

But the larger picture was still hazy. There had never really been an official, thorough study on the military implications of a post–Cold War world. Now the Army was facing a post–Iraq War world as well. What were its roles and missions in this world? If it wasn't going to fight the Red Army in Europe, or wage large-scale, prolonged stability operations, what *should* it be sized, structured, trained, and equipped to do? What priority should be given to options for *short-term* or *small-scale* stability ops? And what should those ops involve specifically: Would regular Army soldiers be trained and organized to fight in small wars or merely to "advise and assist" allied armies, embedding small teams of trainers and enablers in their midst? Special Operations forces had focused on these missions in the past; to what extent would, or could, the regular Army now join along?

During the initial meetings where the chiefs discussed these ideas, Dempsey wondered out loud whether they were all teetering toward uncharted territory: some nexus of Special Ops forces, drones, networked intelligence, and cybertechnology that added up to "a new American way of war."

It was reminiscent, though he might not have known it, of the moment just before Operation Desert Storm, more than twenty years earlier, when Andy Marshall, the Pentagon's director of net assessment, wondered if the US Air Force, with its emerging smart bombs and high-tech sensors, might be on the edge of a "revolution in military affairs"—a concept and phrase that Donald Rumsfeld drew on when planning his light, swift shock-and-awe invasion of Iraq.

In some respects, the Obama-Panetta strategic guidance—with its vision of future forces that were "smaller and leaner . . . agile, flexible, ready, and technologically advanced"—bore a striking resemblance to the Marshall-Rumsfeld language of "military transformation."

There were, of course, differences. Obama saw force as a means of stabilizing the international order, and in his surprisingly numerous decisions to use force, he stressed the legitimizing role of fighting alongside allies in coalitions; Rumsfeld, by contrast, saw force as a tool for toppling rogue regimes that were impeding American primacy, and he celebrated the new wonder weapons as gateways to unilateralism.

But both tugged on technology as an alluring anesthetic that numbed the senses to the pain of warfare: the grit, grime, and mayhem of its consequences on the ground. In this sense, neither vision was so different from the *old* "American way of war," with precision bombing now serving as a substitute for annihilating firepower. The modern variant was more humane, less grotesquely destructive, but each had the effect, in its own way and time, of rendering war easier, more *comfortable*.

In the article that he ghostwrote for General John Galvin in the mid-1980s, David Petraeus, then an ambitious young major, noted the military's tendency "to invent for ourselves a comfortable vision of war, a theater with battlefields we know, conflict that fits our understanding of strategy and tactics . . . that fits our plans, our assumptions, our hopes, and our preconceived ideas." Galvin and Petraeus had urged the military's leadership to prepare for what they called the "uncomfortable wars" ahead: wars of subversion, terrorism, and guerrillas that conformed to no assumptions, confounded all preset plans, and required a whole new way of looking at warfare. Petraeus spent much of the next twenty years preparing to tear down the old edifice and construct a new one that he saw as better suited for the age.

But these uncomfortable wars turned unacceptable once the stakes seemed minor, the duration seemed endless, or the chance of "winning" (however the word was defined) seemed dim. Comfortable wars—small, cheap, and, for all practical purposes, invisible to those not directly fighting them—were back in fashion.

Two or three times a year, Conrad Crane goes back to West Point to attend a conference or give a lecture, and when he does, he always makes a point of strolling through the cemetery. It's laid out on flat, grassy land overlooking the Hudson, an old country churchyard, modest and intimate. Crane regards it as the most hallowed plot of ground on the planet, "the soul of West Point," a sanctuary of its values: honor, sacrifice, service, and, too often, tragedy.

Six thousand former cadets are buried there, dating back to the American Revolution. The carvings on the older headstones are rich with the lore of history. But Crane usually heads straight to the back rows—Section 36, as the area is known—where the fallen from the Iraq and Afghanistan Wars are laid to rest.

Fifty-nine West Point alumni were killed in Iraq, and nineteen of their bodies lie here. They include nine lieutenants, eight captains, a major, and a colonel. All but four were younger than thirty years of age; one was over forty. They left behind a total of seventeen children (none older than twelve years of age), eleven widows, and four fiancées.

At least three of them were once students of Crane's, a fact that pains him when he stands over their gravestones. He is intensely aware that some of them died while following the instructions he'd helped write in the counterinsurgency field manual. He hopes—he has to *believe*—that the manual, and the new strategy it brought forth, saved more soldiers' lives than it cost and that the outcome of the wars, still unclear, will at some point prove worthy of their sacrifice.

But he knows he will never be sure.

David Petraeus and his fellow plotters succeeded in fomenting great change. By the time he hung up his uniform, not quite five years after signing his counterinsurgency manual, the American Army had evolved into a different institution. It was more flexible, more adaptive; it was, in John Nagl's phrase, a "learning organization."

In the aftermath of wars, especially unpopular ones, armies tend to revert to traditional practices. But this was less likely to happen after the wars in Iraq and Afghanistan. There would be no going back to a frame of mind that defined "war" strictly as a titanic clash between uniformed foes of comparable strength—and not just because the prospective foe in that clash, the Soviet Union, had in the meantime imploded. Another factor at play was that an entire generation of American officers had risen through the ranks fighting what were once called small wars, waged among the people in villages and cities, wars in which lieutenants often took as much initiative as commanders, and soldiers of all rank were as attentive to the local culture as to the enemy's order of battle.

It was extremely unlikely that official Army doctrine would ever again refer to these sorts of battles as "low-intensity conflicts," much less as "military operations other than war." The colonels and generals of the post-Petraeus era had spent what seemed like a lifetime fighting in these sorts of battles; they were not low intensity, and they certainly felt like wars.

Petraeus, Nagl, and the others fulfilled their main ambition of wresting away the Army from Cold War habits and adapting it to the new era: an era of what John F. Kennedy had called, a half century earlier, "another type of warfare, new in its intensity, ancient in its origins—war by guerrillas, subversives, insurgents, assassins." These were the sorts of threats and modes of warfare that the world was once again facing. And to the extent that the regular US Army, not just the Special Forces, had learned how to fight them, it was the result of the plot that the West Point Sosh mafia had sired.

But knowing how to fight these wars didn't necessarily mean winning them. There's an old military adage: "The enemy has a vote." You can go into battle with a brilliant plan, but if the enemy adapts and shifts gears, the plan is rendered worthless after the first shots are fired. In counterinsurgency wars, it's not just the enemy that has a vote; the ally does, too. If you send troops overseas to bolster a regime whose leaders lack legitimacy or the will to reform, the most brilliant strategy—and strategist—will have little chance of prevailing.

Robert "Blowtorch" Komer realized this, too late, in Vietnam. Peter Chiarelli and Celeste Ward experienced their own Komer moment in Iraq, as did Steve Biddle in Afghanistan and Dave Kilcullen while reassessing the entire COIN enterprise.

Petraeus knew all this, too. He'd read Komer and the other historians and chroniclers; he'd absorbed every nuance and checklist of caveats in the classic theoretical tracts. Yet, in part from overconfidence, in part from inertia, he came to view the doctrine as a set of universal principles: "the *laws* of counterrevolutionary warfare," as Galula had put it.

As a commander, Petraeus had stressed the importance of getting "the big ideas" right, but the ideas in COIN theory weren't as big as he seemed to believe. Counterinsurgency is a technique, not a grand strategy. Field manuals are guides for officers preparing to fight in a specific setting; and in that sense, a COIN field manual isn't so different from a field manual on mountain warfare, amphibious operations, or armored maneuver combat. If the setting is appropriate, and the conditions seem ripe for success, a good field manual is essential. But if a mountain is too steep to climb, if a beach is too turbulent to storm, or if a field is too cluttered for tanks to maneuver across, the manual won't be worth much—and it's a commander's responsibility to say so.

In assessing the prospects of a COIN campaign, if the insurgents are out of reach, or if the government being challenged is too corrupt to reform, or if the war is likely to take longer and cost more than a president or a nation is willing to commit, in these cases, too, it's the commander's responsibility to say so. David Petraeus knew that all these things were true of the war in Afghanistan, but he stopped short of saying so; he thought he could overcome the odds, as he had so many times before.

Petraeus's COIN field manual caused such a stir when it was published at the end of 2006 because the Army brass had deliberately avoided writing such a guide—had avoided even thinking about the subject—for two decades, and now here they were, in Iraq, caught in a war that had begun as a blitzkrieg invasion but had quickly devolved into an insurgency revolt.

Ideally in a war, civilian authorities set the strategic goals, and military commanders devise the plans and tactics to achieve those objectives. But the Bush administration had no strategy in Iraq beyond toppling Saddam; and in Afghanistan, it had no strategy beyond ousting the Taliban. Petraeus's manual seemed to offer a way out, a recipe for action, a set of plausible criteria for a victory of sorts.

The manual's authors, including Petraeus, wove this perception into being. They set out explicitly to write something much more than the usual field manual; they meant it to serve as a manifesto—and, in its official acceptance, the spearhead—of a revolution within the Army as an institution and a culture.

This was asking too much of mere doctrine. COIN—the field manual and the long history of ideas it embodied—was like a set of instructions on how to drill an oil well: it didn't guarantee that there was oil in the ground or that drilling for oil was the wisest energy policy.

It was a useful guide for conflicts where the insurgents could be contained within a clear-cut area and where the intervening power and the foreign government had interests that aligned. The COIN approach helped produce stunning results in *parts* of Iraq and Afghanistan: Mosul, Tal Afar, Anbar Province (whose Awakening then spread to many other Sunni districts), and, briefly, the Shinwari pact in Nangarhar Province.

The distinctive thing about all those areas was that the Americans and the *local* powers—the mayor, provincial council, or tribal elders—shared common interests or, at least, common enemies.

But the *central governments*, which COIN was ultimately supposed to strengthen, were another matter. A much larger, more pertinent "big idea"—which neither Petraeus nor any other outsider could ultimately control—was the identity and interests of the foreign country's ruling elite. If that identity and those interests obstructed the regime's willingness or ability to govern its people with legitimacy, and if the intervening power had little leverage to alter this fact, then—as Dave Kilcullen concluded in the end—it was "folly" to embark on a counterinsurgency campaign in the first place.

In that respect, the modern age itself has reduced much of the whole COIN concept to folly. The most often-cited models of successful counterinsurgencies—Malaya, Kenya, the Philippines, Algeria, and Northern Ireland—were colonial wars. There was no divergence of interests between the country sending the troops and the local authorities welcoming them, because they were one and the same or at least fragments of the same empire. When Field Marshal Sir Gerald Templer commanded the British colonial army in Malaya, he didn't have to persuade the local government to do what he wanted; for all practical purposes, he *was* the local government.

The successful COIN campaigns of lore were also wars of stunning brutality: in Malaya, four hundred thousand civilians forcibly relocated and thousands of insurgents starved to death; in the Philippines, sixteen thousand guerrillas killed in battle, and two hundred thousand civilians killed by disease and starvation spreading through the relocation centers (formally called "concentration camps"); in Algeria, the routine use of torture in the "pacification" campaigns.

This was the dark side of counterinsurgency, but it had also been seen by its practitioners as an essential side. And it was far too dark an alleyway for a democracy to roam in the global-media age—too savage, and prone to drag on far too long.

Even John Nagl allowed as much. He would often tell friends that, judging from the lessons of Malaya, the ideal counterinsurgency campaign was one fought "on a peninsula against a visibly obvious ethnic minority before CNN is invented." Eating soup with a knife, as he'd quoted Lawrence cautioning, was "messy and slow" indeed.

Modern-day America does not like messy and slow, especially slow. David Petraeus had written in his PhD dissertation, nearly a quarter century before retiring from the Army, "Vietnam was an extremely painful reminder that when it comes to intervention, time and patience are not American virtues in abundant supply."

Were he to update his thesis, he might note that Iraq and Afghanistan are reminders as well.

Yet Nagl did not step back from his standing as COIN's most ardent public enthusiast, nor did Petraeus repudiate the doctrine he'd done more than anyone to revive. As they saw it, and still do see it, American armed forces might once again find themselves in an insurgency war. It had happened at least once each generation, and rarely by design. Such wars, like any wars, went better if the Army sent to fight it knew how: if its commanders knew that firepower alone wouldn't do the trick and might make things worse; and if the soldiers had some understanding not only of battlefield tactics but also of the local culture of the people they were protecting.

Petraeus, Nagl, and their compatriots reshaped the American Army so that a core group of officers knew how to do those things—and a body of doctrine existed so they could train their successors to do them, too.

But in the aftermath of the Iraq War and as American involvement in Afghanistan was winding down, it seemed unlikely that any president would soon get involved in this sort of war again, not on a scale as large or long-lasting as those wars had proved to be. COIN may have made for a "smarter" or "better" war than the bash-down-doors, shoot-first alternative, but that didn't make it a *smart* war or a *good* war. The COIN strategists made the American military more adept at fighting this kind of war, but they didn't—they couldn't—succeed at making this kind of war acceptable, either to the American public or to the people in the lands where it was fought. They didn't, they couldn't, instill the broader message that these kinds of wars—protracted, large-scale battles in the "long war" on global terror—were now permanent fixtures on the landscape and that the COIN way was the right way, the only way, to fight them.

In the end, they didn't, they couldn't, change—at least in the way they intended to change—the American way of war.

Postscript

On November 9, 2012, the mystique that had shrouded David Petraeus for nearly a decade suddenly shattered. That afternoon, he resigned as director of the CIA, admitting to an extramarital affair—a firing offense in the military officers' code and, though Petraeus had retired from the Army, he still felt bound by the code: at least after he'd been caught.

The news stunned his longtime associates. He'd seemed a figure of such rectitude, had spoken with contempt of other officers who'd committed infidelities. Yet in at least one sense, the lapse flowed naturally from the course of his career.

His mistress, it turned out, was Paula Broadwell, the author of *All In: The Education of General David Petraeus,* a fawning biography published earlier in the year. More to the point, she was an aspiring denizen of the cabal that he'd created. They'd met in 2006, when she was in graduate school at Harvard and he came to give a talk about COIN. She approached him afterward, expressed interest in the subject. Soon she began a PhD dissertation on his leadership style and, when he took command in Afghanistan, asked if she could come observe him in action. He agreed.

She was twenty years his junior, and beautiful, but her initial appeal lay more in her CV than in her glamour. She'd been a West Point cadet, she'd trained as a parachutist, she was an obsessive runner, *and* she was an Ivy League grad student. In short, she seemed just the sort of officer-intellectual that Petraeus had long been keen to mentor—a promising candidate for the West Point mafia, the Lincoln Brigade.

But, unlike other protégés, Broadwell didn't merely admire Petraeus, she adored him—and Petraeus let her, to a degree that discomfited some of his aides. In Kabul, he gave her extraordinarily close access; they ran five-mile jogs at dawn together, traveled together, shared endless hours for weeks at a time. Petraeus had invented his own rules before, though strictly for military reasons. Now, after so many years of deployments, on a turf more primal, the allure proved overwhelming, the famous discipline broke down.

In the end, the decade of war punctured many myths that were long overdue for rethinking. It revealed COIN as a tool, not a cure-all—and David Petraeus as a man, not an icon.

Notes

Most of the material in this book is based on interviews with more than one hundred players. Their names are listed after these notes, though the interviews themselves were conducted on a confidential basis. I have not footnoted information that comes strictly from interviews, though in almost every case I have confirmed the facts from at least two sources. When something is based in part on published sources and in part on interviews, I cite the source, then add "and interviews."

Chapter 1: "What We Need Is an Officer with Three Heads"

1 *Lieutenant Nagl was a platoon leader:* 1st Lieutenant John Nagl, "A Tale of Two Battles: Victorious in Iraq, An Experienced Armor Task Force Gets Waxed at the NTC," *Armor,* May–June 1992; and interviews.

3 *if you can lick the cat:* The phrase is widely attributed to General Curtis LeMay, commander of the US Strategic Air Command in the 1950s.

3 *published as a book:* John Nagl, *Learning to Eat Soup with a Knife: Counterinsurgency Lessons from Malaya and Vietnam* (Westport, CT: Praeger, 2002; reprinted in paperback by University of Chicago Press, 2005).

3 *"An Insurgent Within the COIN Revolution":* Dr. Conrad Crane, PowerPoint presentation, New York City, May 2006 (provided to author). Crane, as we shall later see, was General David Petraeus's chief collaborator on the COIN field manual, which was being written at the time.

3 *"COINdinistas":* A defense reporter and former Marine named Carl Prine has claimed (and regretted) credit for inventing the term; he also came up with "COINtras" as a name for the group's critics, though that never caught on. See www.lineofdeparture.com/2011/04/25/dazed-and-coinfused.

4 *West Point was where . . . General George Washington:* "A History of West Point," www.usma.edu/history.asp.

5 *"Two Hundred Years of Tradition":* Nobody seems to know who first came up with this one, though in some recitations, "unhindered" is rendered as "unmarred" or "unimpeded."

5 *George Arthur Lincoln:* For biographical information, see Lincoln's personal history sheet on his application to West Point, in George A. Lincoln Collection, Biographical Cover, US Military Academy Archive, West Point, NY; Obituary, "George Arthur Lincoln, Class of 1929," *Assembly* (published by Association of Graduates, US Military Academy), March 1976, 121; Charles F. Brower Jr., "Sophisticated Strategist: Gen. George A. Lincoln and the Defeat of Japan," *Diplomatic History,* Summer 1991; Captain Martha S. H. VanDriel, "The Lincoln Brigade: One Story of the Faculty of the USMA Department of Social Science," n.d., on file at the Social Science Dept., US Military Academy (although VanDriel mistakenly reports that Lincoln was a two-star general before

taking his demotion, when he was a one-star, and that he asked Marshall for the demotion when in fact he asked Eisenhower).

6 *thirteen Rhodes Scholars:* Letter, George A. Lincoln to Herman Beukema, April 23, 1947, George A. Lincoln Collection, Box 3.

6 *"very broad-gauged individuals":* Letter, Lincoln to Beukema, March 16, 1946, ibid.

6 *"a little late":* Letter, Lincoln to Beukema, August 27, 1946, ibid.

6 *"I am beginning to think":* Letter, Lincoln to Beukema, May 20, 1945, ibid.

6 *the two officers struck up a correspondence:* Besides the ones cited here, see also Letters, Lincoln to Beukema, December 16, 1945; February 12, July 20, July 22, 1946, ibid.

6 *"baptizing":* Letter, Lincoln to Beukema, November 20, 1945, ibid.

7 *made it clear:* Letter, Beukema to Lincoln, December 19, 1945, ibid.

7 *In August 1945, soon after:* "Summary of Plan for Returning to Four-Year Course," August 18, 1945, George A. Lincoln Collection, Box 100, "Report of Post-War Curriculum Committee" folder.

7 *In June 1946, Congress passed a bill:* Letter, Beukema to Lincoln, June 26, 1946, George A. Lincoln Collection, Box 3.

7 *In July, Lincoln told Beukema:* Letters, Lincoln to Beukema, July 14, 19, and 22, 1946, ibid.

7 *Lincoln started his new job:* Letter, Lincoln to Beukema, March 10, 1947, ibid.

7 *West Point's curriculum:* See "Summary of Plan for Returning to Four-Year Course," op. cit.

7 *Lincoln wrote one:* George A. Lincoln and Norman J. Padelford, *International Politics: Foundations of International Relations* (NY: Macmillan, 1954).

8 *"I am certain that we must make":* Letter, Lincoln to Beukema, May 17, 1947, George A. Lincoln Collection, Box 3.

8 *"a couple of left-wing pinko":* General Norman Schwarzkopf, Lecture at West Point, May 15, 1991; and interviews. (Schwarzkopf's lecture was videotaped; a DVD copy of the video was provided to author.)

9 *"Pick good people":* Quoted in obituary, "George Arthur Lincoln," *Assembly,* op. cit.

Chapter 2: "Another Type of Warfare"

12 *"Every cadet an athlete":* Quoted in "A Brief History of West Point," www.usma.edu/history.asp.

13 *Petraeus, who was ranked forty-third:* David Cloud and Greg Jaffe, *The Fourth Star* (New York: Crown, 2009), 18; and interviews.

14 *Shortly after graduating:* Ibid., 21; and interviews.

15 *Marcel "Bruno" Bigeard:* See obituary, *London Telegraph,* July 22, 2011; and interviews.

15 *Bernard Fall's volumes about Vietnam: Hell in a Very Small Place: The Siege of Dien Bien Phu* (New York: Lippincott, 1966); *Street Without Joy: The French Debacle in Vietnam* (New York: Schocken Books, 1961).

15 The Centurions: It was published in a bestselling English translation in 1961, and turned into a popular movie, *Lost Command,* in 1966. But it is presently out of print and, perhaps because it's known to be General Petraeus's favorite novel, selling for several hundred dollars on the secondhand market.

16 *"When we make war":* Jean Larteguy, *The Centurions* (New York: E. P. Dutton, 1961), 181–82.
17 *"the 'how-to' book in the field":* Fall, *Street Without Joy,* 400.
17 *He had just retired from the French army:* Ann Marlowe, *David Galula: His Life and Intellectual Context* (Carlisle, PA: Strategic Studies Institute, US Army War College, 2010), esp. 21ff.
18 *"Revolutionary war . . . special rules":* David Galula, *Counterinsurgency Warfare: Theory and Practice* (Westport, CT: Praeger, 1964), xii. (Page numbers refer to the 2006 paperback edition published in Praeger Security International's series "The Classics of the Counterinsurgency Era," with a foreword by John A. Nagl.)
18 *"In a fight between a fly":* Ibid., xii–xiii.
18 *the "insurgent" and the "counterinsurgent":* Ibid., xiv.
18 *"to define the* laws*":* Ibid., xiii (italics added).
18 *"is fluid because he has neither":* Ibid., 7.
19 *fish swimming in water:* Ibid., 33–34.
19 *In his days as a military attaché:* Marlowe, op. cit., 25–32.
19 *"step-by-step" process:* Galula, op. cit., 55–56.
19 *a matter not of adding:* Ibid., 61.
19 *"20 percent military":* Ibid., 63.
20 *"[C]onventional operations by themselves":* Ibid., 51–52.
20 *"be prepared to become a propagandist":* Ibid., 62.
20 *"a mimeograph machine":* Ibid., 66.
20 *"primarily a war of infantry":* Ibid., 21, 65.
20 *Meanwhile, at the end of 1978:* Cloud and Jaffe, op. cit., 35–42; and interviews.
22 *Jack Galvin was an unusual Army general:* James Kitfield, *Prodigal Soldiers* (New York: Simon & Schuster, 1995), 68, passim; and interviews.
22 *Over the years, . . . he would write . . . books:* Galvin, *The Minute Men: The First Fight—Myths and Realities of the American Revolution* (Portland, OR: Hawthorne Books, 1967); *Three Men of Boston* (John R. Crowell, 1976); *Air Assault: The Development of Air Mobile Warfare* (Portland, OR: Hawthorne Books, 1969).
25 *"Holy cow!" Petraeus thought to himself:* Interviews for this book were conducted mainly on "background," but I should clarify that whenever I have someone saying or thinking something, and there's no endnote given, the source is almost always the person saying it; on a very few occasions (not this one), it's someone who heard him say it or to whom he recited his thoughts.
26 *By the time the war ended:* Cynthia J. Arnson, *Crossroads: Congress, the President, and Central America, 1976–1993* (University Park, PA: Pennsylvania State University Press, 2d ed., 1993); Todd Greentree, *Crossroads of Intervention: Insurgency and Counterinsurgency Lessons from Central America* (Annapolis, MD: Naval Institute Press, 2008); John D. Waghelstein, "Military-to-Military Contacts: Personal Observations—The El Salvador Case," *Low Intensity Conflict and Law Enforcement,* Summer 2003.
26 *Kennedy set up a secret panel:* See Douglas S. Blaufarb, *The Counterinsurgency Era: US Doctrine and Performance* (New York: Free Press, 1977), 64ff.
27 *"another type of warfare":* Quoted in John A. Nagl, *Learning to Eat Soup with a Knife,* 125.

27 *CORDS was led by . . . Robert Komer:* See especially Neil Sheehan, *A Bright Shining Lie* (New York: Random House, 1988), 652–57.

27 *The whole branch was seen as a career dead-ender:* Colonel John D. Waghelstein, *El Salvador: Observations and Experiences in Counterinsurgency* (Carlisle, PA: US Army War College, 1985), introduction; and interviews.

28 *Brigadier General Fred Woerner:* The so-called Woerner Report was declassified only in 1993 and, even then, with many deletions and after a long legal battle, waged by Kate Doyle and the National Security Archive. www.gwu.edu/~nsarchiv/nsa/DOCUMENT/930325.htm.

28 *Woerner drafted a National Campaign Plan:* As far as I can tell, the plan is still classified; it's unclear whether there ever was a document beyond the briefing delivered to the Salvadoran government. However, it is summarized in detail in Waghelstein, op. cit., v–vi, 48–62, and Appendix G. I also received some information from interviews.

29 *John Waghelstein, a Special Forces colonel:* Waghelstein, "What's Wrong in Iraq: Or Ruminations of a Pachyderm," *Military Review,* January–February 2006.

29 *"Simply killing guerrillas":* Waghelstein, *El Salvador,* 62.

29 *Woerner's National Campaign Plan, at this point:* Ibid., 64–66.

29 *"LIC is a growth industry":* Clifford Krauss and Tim Carrington, "Latin Lesson: US Effort to Win 'Hearts and Minds' Gains in El Salvador," *Wall Street Journal,* September 8, 1986.

29 *in fact, he and several of the Special Forces officers:* Waghelstein, op. cit., 40; and interviews.

30 *We in the military:* General John R. Galvin, "Uncomfortable Wars: Toward a New Paradigm," *Parameters,* Winter 1986.

32 *"General Galvin's words were relevant then":* Lieutenant General David H. Petraeus, "Learning Counterinsurgency: Observations from Soldiering in Iraq," *Military Review,* January–February 1986.

32 *The "reluctance to get involved":* David Howell Petraeus, *The American Military and the Lessons of Vietnam: A Study of Military Influence and the Use of Force in the Post-Vietnam Era.* PhD dissertation, Princeton University, 1987, 287.

32 *"come to grips":* Ibid., 309. See also 281–82.

32 *"Lessons of history":* Ibid., 292, 297.

32 *"We should be careful":* Ibid., 299.

33 *"will depend . . . on forthcoming":* Ibid., 279.

33 *"crippling naivete":* Quoted in ibid., 282–83n. The fate of Krepinevich's book, and his meeting with Petraeus, come from interviews.

Chapter 3: "Eating Soup with a Knife"

37 *"decimated by a light-infantry company":* 1st Lieutenant John Nagl, "A Tale of Two Battles: Victorious in Iraq, An Experienced Armor Task Force Gets Waxed at the NTC," *Armor,* May–June 1992; and interviews.

38 *While pursuing this odd new interest:* He was especially drawn to Alexander George, "Case Studies and Theory Development: The Method of Structured, Focused Comparison," in Paul Gordon Lauren, ed., *Diplomacy* (New York: Macmillan, 1979); and interviews.

39 *"best explained by the differing":* John A. Nagl, *Learning to Eat Soup with a Knife,* xxii. (The book was first published in hardcover by Praeger, in 2002, with the title and subtitle switched, at Praeger's insistence. The page numbers cited, here and elsewhere, are from the University of Chicago paperback edition.)
40 *"You know, some brigadiers":* Ibid., 74–75.
40 *"an understanding of the nature":* Ibid., 41.
40 *"I have been impressed":* Ibid., 97.
41 *"the eradication of threats":* Ibid., 43.
41 *"the strategy of annihilation":* Quoted in ibid., from Russell Weigley, *The American Way of War: A History of United States Military Policy and Strategy* (Bloomington: Indiana University Press, 1973), xxii.
41 *"were quickly lost to the belief":* Nagl, ibid., 46.
41 *"another type of warfare":* Quoted in ibid., 126.
41 *"strategic hamlets":* Ibid., 164–66.
41 *General Creighton Abrams:* Ibid., 168–72, 175. This same point is made by Andrew Krepinevich, *The Army and Vietnam,* which Nagl cites.
41 *General William Westmoreland:* Ibid., 200.
41 *In the spring of 1965, in response:* Ibid., 130–31.
41 *"I guess I should have studied":* Quoted in ibid., 142.
41 *After the war, he was put in charge:* Ibid., 206. The Army field manual that DePuy led was the 1976 edition of *FM 100-5: Operations.* It sparked enormous controversy, not so much from "small wars" advocates, of whom there were few (and fewer still who had interest in publicizing their views on this score), but more from those who thought DePuy's views of strategy were too static, defense-minded, and unrealistically mathematical.
42 *"Like most Americans who served in Vietnam":* Quoted in Nagl, ibid., 203.
42 *"may well have been an aberration":* Ibid., 222–23.
43 *The title he emblazoned:* Nagl titled his DPhil dissertation *Learning to Eat Soup with a Knife: British and American Army Counterinsurgency Learning During the Malayan Emergency and the Vietnam War.* In its first book form, published by Praeger in October 2002, during (coincidentally) the lead-up to the invasion of Iraq, the title and (a pared-down version of) the subtitle were reversed, at the editor's insistence and over Nagl's opposition, as *Counterinsurgency Lessons from Malaya and Vietnam: Learning to Eat Soup with a Knife.* At a retail price of $81.95, it lured few buyers; as discussed later, it gained cult status mainly through word-of-mouth and Nagl's PowerPoint summaries. The University of Chicago paperback edition, published in September 2005, as (again coincidentally) the US occupation of Iraq was about to spin out of control, for a more commercially appealing $17, sold (relatively speaking) in droves.

Chapter 4: Revolutions

45 *A new Army field manual stated:* Janine Davidson, *Lifting the Fog of Peace: How Americans Learned to Fight Modern War* (Ann Arbor: University of Michigan Press, 2010), 114; and interviews.
45 *"Real men don't do* moot-*wah":* Quoted in ibid., 143.
46 *The revolution in military affairs began:* Much of this section is based on parts

of chapter 1 of my book, *Daydream Believers: How a Few Grand Ideas Wrecked American Power* (Hoboken: John Wiley & Sons, 2008). In addition to the documents noted below, the material here also comes from interviews conducted, during research for *Daydream,* with Richard Armitage, David Deptula, Richard Garwin, Andrew Krepinevich, Andrew Marshall, Donald Rice, James Wade, Huba Wass de Czege, and Barry Watts.

46 *John Foster, a nuclear physicist:* Richard H. Van Atta, et al., *Transformation and Transition: DARPA's Role in Fostering an Emerging Revolution in Military Affairs, Vol. 1—Overall Assessment,* IDA Paper P-3698 (Alexandria, VA: Institute for Defense Analyses, 2003), 40.

47 *"identify and characterize":* DARPA and Defense Nuclear Agency, *Summary Report of the Long Range Research and Development Planning Program,* DNA–75–03055, February 7, 1975 (declassified December 31, 1983). The primary author of the study was Albert Wohlstetter, a prominent nuclear strategist who, through the 1950s, had been a colleague, and initially a mentor, of Andrew Marshall at the RAND Corporation. For more about Wohlstetter and Marshall in those days, see my book *The Wizards of Armageddon* (New York: Simon & Schuster, 1983), esp. chs. 6 and 7.

48 *In the summer of 1986:* Commission on Integrated Long-Term Strategy, *Discriminate Deterrence,* January 1988. Wohlstetter and another former RAND analyst, Fred Iklé, were the main authors of this report as well.

49 *The final version was finished:* Department of the Air Force, *The Air Force and U.S. National Security: Global Reach—Global Power, A White Paper,* June 1990. See also Major Barbara J. Faulkenberry, *Global Reach—Global Power: Air Force Strategic Vision, Past and Future* (Maxwell Air Force Base: Air University Press, 1996), 46.

49 *A few had been dropped toward the end of the Vietnam War:* Barry Watts, *Six Decades of Guided Munitions and Battle Networks* (Washington, DC: Center for Strategic and Budget Assessments, 2007), 185ff.; Kenney Werrell, "Did USAF Technology Fail in Vietnam?" *Airpower Journal,* Spring 1998.

50 *Deptula had drawn up a chart:* Michael R. Gordon and Bernard E. Trainor, *The Generals' War* (New York: Little Brown, 1995), ch. 4; and interviews.

50 *The actual upshot turned:* Thomas Keaney and Eliot Cohen, *Revolution in Warfare? Air Power in the Persian Gulf* (Annapolis: Naval Institute Press, 1995), esp. 191. This was a declassified version of the executive summary of the Air Force's official study of airpower in the Gulf War. The conclusions were so discomfiting that the report was thrown out (it has long gone missing), and the book version was published by the *Naval* Institute Press.

50 *Now he was assessing:* Krepinevich was one of the few COIN advocates who also celebrated RMA and transformation. In 1992, Krepinevich presented a summary of his work for Marshall at the Naval Postgraduate School. Harvard professor Samuel Huntington, who knew Krepinevich's work on Vietnam, asked him, "Andy, if we'd had all these great weapons in Vietnam, would we have still lost?" Krepinevich laughed but thought it over; it was a serious question. He reasoned that Vietnam and a NATO–Warsaw Pact war were two different wars, requiring different strategies. Blitzkrieg worked for the Germans in Poland and France; it wouldn't have worked in an invasion of England.

50 *"Quality is becoming far more important":* The paper was declassified a decade later and published, with a foreword by Marshall, as Andrew F. Krepinevich Jr., *The Military-Technical Revolution: A Preliminary Assessment* (Washington, DC: Center for Strategy and Budgetary Assessments, 2002). CSBA is Krepinevich's think tank.

51 *"We are on the cusp":* National Defense Panel, *Transforming Defense,* December 1987, iii.

51 *"revolution in the technology of war":* Governor George W. Bush, "A Period of Consequences," speech, the Citadel, September 23, 1999.

52 *"to stun, and then rapidly defeat":* Harlan Ullman and James Wade, *Shock and Awe: Achieving Rapid Dominance* (Philadelphia: Pavilion Press, 1998).

52 *Soon after the war began, Franks:* Michael R. Gordon and Bernard E. Trainor, *Cobra II: The Inside Story of the Invasion and Occupation of Iraq* (New York: Pantheon, 2006), 35.

53 *"the ongoing revolution":* Department of Defense, *The Quadrennial Defense Review Report,* September 30, 2001, esp. 6, 23, 27, 44.

54 *Then, on October 15:* The story has been told many times. E.g., Max Boot, *War Made New: Technology, Warfare, and the Course of History, 1500 to Today* (New York: Gotham, 2006), 369–73; Fred Kaplan, "High-Tech US Arsenal Proves Its Worth," *Boston Globe,* December 9, 2001.

55 *Rumsfeld was overstating the case:* Stephen Biddle, "Afghanistan and the Future of Warfare," *Foreign Affairs,* March/April 2003; Sean Naylor, *Not a Good Day to Die: The Untold Story of Operation Anaconda* (New York: Berkley Books, 2005), esp. 56–57.

57 AirLand Battle: US Army, *FM 100-5 (Revised),* 1981; see also Huba Wass de Czege, "How to Change an Army," *Military Review,* November 1984; "Advanced Studies," *Soldier,* July 1986.

58 *In the early 1990s:* Richard M. Swain, *Lucky War: Third Army in Desert Storm* (Fort Leavenworth: US Army Command & General Staff College Press, 1994), ch. 3.

60 *"tend to devote more attention":* Wass de Czege published a slightly condensed version of this memo as "Wargaming Insights," *Army,* March 2003. (The original memo, which he gave me, is called "'02 Wargaming Insights.")

Chapter 5: The Insurgent at War

62 *He would later joke that getting shot:* Cloud and Jaffe, op. cit., 97; cf. also 94–97, 115. The stories of the injuries are told in most accounts of Petraeus's life. Rick Atkinson, *In the Company of Soldiers* (New York: Henry Holt & Co., 2005), 37–38, 72; and interviews.

64 *After one of these sessions:* Cloud and Jaffe, 98; and interviews.

65 *a presence of al Qaeda fighters:* Robert M. Cassidy, *Counterinsurgency and the Global War on Terror* (Westport, CT: Praeger Security International, 2006); Douglas Frantz, "US-Based Charity Is Under Scrutiny," *New York Times,* June 14, 2002; "Islamic Charity Still Faces Charges," *New York Times,* May 14, 2002; and interviews.

72 *Petraeus arrived the next day:* The account of Petraeus and the 101st Airborne Division in Mosul is based mainly on interviews but also on Kirsten Lundberg, *The*

Accidental Statesman: General Petraeus and the City of Mosul, Iraq (Kennedy School of Government Case Program, C15-06-1834.0, Harvard University, 2006); and Isaiah Wilson, *Thinking Beyond War: Civil-Military Relations and Why America Fails to Win the Peace* (New York: Palgrave Macmillan, 2007).

74 *CPA Order No. 1:* At this writing, nearly ten years after the fact, it is still not known who wrote Bremer's orders or where the idea behind them came from. Bremer wrote in his memoir (*My Year in Iraq* [New York: Threshold Editions, 2006]) that Doug Feith, an undersecretary of defense and member of Rumsfeld's inner circle, handed him the orders before he left for Iraq. Rumsfeld, in his memoir (*Known and Unknown* [New York: Penguin Sentinel, 2012], 514–18), puts all blame on Bremer and the State Department (even though Bremer reported to *him* at the Pentagon) and acknowledges that the issues addressed by the orders "did not receive the full interagency discussion [they] merited." But in fact, they were discussed in detail at two NSC Principals' Meetings. At one, on March 10, 2003, everyone in attendance—including President Bush—agreed that the vast majority of Baathists should be allowed to stay in the government and that the senior members (estimated to be about 5 percent of the total) would be vetted by a Truth and Reconciliation Commission, modeled on those in postapartheid South Africa and parts of post-Communist Eastern Europe. At the other meeting, on March 12, they all agreed to disband the Republican Guard but to call the regular army back to duty after a proper vetting of the senior officer corps. Bremer's orders, whoever wrote them, contravened these presidential decisions. Bush, who found out about them the way everyone else did (from the daily newspapers), let it go, saying Bremer should be given leeway. (See my account of the NSC meetings in Fred Kaplan, *Daydream Believers,* 150–52.) My *guess* is that the orders were the creation of Ahmed Chalabi, the Iraqi exile who had enormous influence in the Bush White House and Pentagon and who'd long been lobbying for an invasion. First, he was a fanatical proponent of total de-Baathification (after Saddam's ouster, Chalabi managed to get himself appointed as chairman of the official de-Baathification board). Second, he'd organized a militia of exiles, called the Free Iraqi Forces, that he wanted to supplant the Iraqi army. (The FIF melted into the Iraqi crowd upon landing and was never heard from again.) Another guess is that the orders came to Chalabi via Vice President Dick Cheney's office. First, Chalabi had several close allies there. Second, Cheney's office has remained the most tight-lipped chamber of the Bush administration; the fact that the orders' origins have remained secret, after all these years, suggests (like Sherlock Holmes's case of the dog that didn't bark) Cheney as the source.

77 *Two months before they left:* 101st Airborne Division (Assault), PowerPoint Briefing, *Transition: Outstanding Issues and Concerns* (obtained by author).

77 *Instead, they focused:* The brigade, with its Stryker light armored vehicles, was deployed to Iraq in October 2003, initially joining the 4th Infantry Division in the extremely violent Sunni Triangle districts in the central part of the country. The 4th ID commander, Major General Roy Odierno, assigned them to exclusively "kinetic" tasks: i.e., killing, raiding, and capturing. That was their introduction to the war, and that was what they continued when assigned to replace the 101st Airborne in Mosul. (Interviews.)

77 *"There was no Phase IV plan":* Isaiah (Ike) Wilson III, "Thinking Beyond War: Civil-Military Operational Planning in Northern Iraq," speech, Peace Studies Program, Cornell University, October 14, 2004. He gave a similar speech to the annual conference of the American Political Science Association in early September.

78 *Tom Ricks:* Thomas E. Ricks, "Army Historian Cites Lack of Postwar Plan: Major Calls Effort in Iraq 'Mediocre,'" *Washington Post,* December 25, 2004; and interviews.

Chapter 6: The Irregulars

79 *One of them drew a parody:* Peter Maass, "Professor Nagl's War," *New York Times Magazine,* January 11, 2004.

79 *"something of a blithe sense":* In the introduction to the paperback edition, Nagl assesses the strengths and weaknesses of his book from the vantage of having fought in a real insurgency war (Nagl, op. cit., xii).

80 *Nagl remembered a line:* Quoted in Maass, op. cit.

80 *Nagl was surprised by how much:* Nagl, op. cit., xiii.

80 *"Iraq 2003–2004":* Maass, op. cit.

81 *"protracted guerrilla war":* Gary Anderson, "Saddam's Greater Game," *Washington Post,* April 2, 2003.

83 *"represent the normal":* US Marine Corps, *Small Wars Manual* (1940) (published commercially by Skyhorse Publishing, 2009), 2–3.

84 *"three-block war":* General Charles Krulak, "The Strategic Corporal: Leadership in the Three Block War," *Marines Magazine,* January 1999.

84 *There was family lineage:* Late in 1962, JFK sent Krulak and Joseph Mendenhall, a senior Foreign Service Officer with experience in Vietnam, on a fact-finding trip to gauge the progress of the war and the stability of Diem's regime. Krulak reported that everything was great; Mendenhall, in retrospect correctly, said the opposite. After their briefings, Kennedy said, "You two *did* visit the same country, didn't you?" David Halberstam, *The Best and the Brightest* (New York: Random House, 1972), 339 (page number refers to the Hawcett paperback edition).

86 *He moved on to West Java:* This story comes from George Packer, "Knowing the Enemy," *New Yorker,* December 18, 2006. The rest of the section comes from interviews and, a bit, from David Kilcullen, *The Accidental Guerrilla: Fighting Small Wars in the Midst of a Big One* (Oxford and New York: Oxford University Press, 2009), esp. prologue and ch. 1.

86 *"The thing that drives these guys":* Quoted in Packer, op. cit.

88 *Kilcullen's briefing:* Lieutenant Colonel (Dr.) David Kilcullen, PowerPoint, "United States Counterinsurgency: An Australian View" (provided to author); and interviews.

89 *The last QDR:* US Dept. of Defense, *Quadrennial Defense Review Report,* September 30, 2001, www.dod.gov/pubs/qdr2001.pdf.

90 *While he was in Anbar:* Maass, op. cit.

Chapter 7: "Where's My Counterinsurgency Plan?"

95 *"become more like":* Quoted in Thomas Baines, "An Assessment of Joint Doctrine," Center for Defense Information, March 2001.

95 *"warrior-diplomats":* Quoted in Eli Cohen and Noel Tichy, "Operation-Leadership," *Fast Company,* August 31, 1999.

95 *In the year Schoomaker wrote:* Cited by Braddock Caesar, "Reshaping the Army Through Reconcilement [*sic*] of Conventional and Special Forces," Commandos and Special Operations Discussion Board, January 6, 2006. www.strategypage.com/militaryforums/516-867.aspx.

95 *In 1974 he'd gone to Ranger School:* Cloud and Jaffe, op. cit., 21–22.

98 *"Partnership: From Occupation":* HQ, MNF-I, Baghdad, *Multi-National Force-Iraq, Campaign Plan: Operation Iraqi Freedom, Partnership: From Occupation to Constitutional Elections,* August 5, 2004 (declassified).

104 *"Successful and Unsuccessful":* Reprinted in Kalev I. Sepp, "Best Practices in Counterinsurgency," *Military Review,* May–June 2005.

106 *"The enemy we're fighting":* Jim Dwyer, "A Gulf Commander Sees a Longer Road," *New York Times,* March 28, 2003.

107 *In Darley's first year, he published twenty-nine:* David H. Ucko, *The New Counterinsurgency Era: Transforming the US Military for Modern Wars* (Washington, DC: Georgetown University Press, 2009), 77.

107 *The footnoted essay appeared: Military Review,* May–June 2005. cgsc.contentdm.oclc.org/cdm/fullbrowser/collection/p124201coll1/id/171/rv/singleitem. The articles were Montgomery McFate, "Iraq: The Social Context of IEDs"; Lieutenant Colonel Robert Cassidy, "The British Army and Counterinsurgency: The Salience of Military Culture"; Charles Byler, "Pacifying the Moros: American Military Government in the Southern Philippines, 1899–1913"; and Lieutenant Colonel Conrad Crane, "Phase IV Operations: Where Wars Are Really Won."

Chapter 8: The Basin Harbor Gang

109 *Over the next few years, Cohen emerged:* Along with Donald Rumsfeld, Dick Cheney, Paul Wolfowitz, Eliot Abrams, and others, Cohen signed the June 3, 1997, "statement of principles" of the Project for the New American Century, the prominent neocon group that called for greater military spending, unabashed American preeminence in the post–Cold War world, and, starting in the following year, "regime change" in Iraq. (See www.newamericancentury.org/statementofprinciples.htm.) He advocated the forcible overthrow of Saddam Hussein in two early *Wall Street Journal* op-ed pieces: "World War IV: Let's Call This Conflict What It Is" (November 20, 2001) and "Iraq Can't Resist Us" (December 23, 2001).

110 *the study's executive summary:* Eliot A. Cohen and Thomas A. Keaney, *Revolution in Warfare? Air Power in the Persian Gulf* (Annapolis: Naval Institute Press, 1995); and interviews.

110 *The year before, Cohen had coauthored:* Eliot A. Cohen and John Gooch, *Military Misfortunes: The Anatomy of Failure in War* (New York: Free Press, 1990).

111 *There was another factor:* Cohen wrote an unusually impassioned, much-discussed article about his personal and political anguish, "A Hawk Questions Himself as His Son Goes to War," *Washington Post,* Outlook section, July 20, 2005. He also

talked at length about the article and what drove him to write it on C-Span's *Q&A* program on July 31, 2005, www.qanda.org/Transcript/?ProgramID=1034.

111 *Others on Cohen's list:* The full list of participants can be found at www.sais-jhu.edu/merrillcenter-original/workshops/2005/Participant_list.pdf; the backstory is from interviews.

112 *They met twice a day:* For the schedule, see www.sais-jhu.edu/sebin/y/d/Schedule2005.pdf; backstory from interviews.

112 *Some of the participants recited:* A summary of the workshop's discussion can be found at merrillcenter.sais-jhu.edu/outreach/Summary2005.pdf; and interviews.

113 *The 4th Infantry had entered the war late:* Thomas E. Ricks, *Fiasco: The American Military Adventure in Iraq* (New York: Penguin Press, 2006), esp. 232–34, 279–90; and (mostly) interviews.

115 *"We in the Army don't think":* This remark is quoted in Thomas E. Ricks, *The Gamble: General David Petraeus and the American Military Adventure in Iraq, 2006–2008* (New York: Penguin Press, 2009), 109. But the details of the speech, and the audience's response, come from my interviews with nine participants at the conference, whose accounts were consistent with one another, on most points identical. I should note that General Odierno told me that he remembers giving a talk at Basin Harbor but has no memory of what he said. When I recited other sources' accounts of his talk (without identifying their names), he said that none of it rang a bell.

Chapter 9: The Directive

117 *"especially relevant today":* General Peter J. Schoomaker, foreword to John A. Nagl, *Learning to Eat Soup with a Knife*, x.

119 *"Stability and reconstruction missions":* Defense Science Board 2004 Summer Study, *Transition to and from Hostilities*, Undersecretary of Defense for Acquisition, Technology, and Logistics, 2004, www.acq.osd.mil/dsb/reports/ADA430116.pdf.

122 *Stability operations are a core:* Department of Defense Directive No. 3000.05, "Military Support for Stability, Security, Transition, and Reconstruction (SSTR) Operations," signed by Gordon England, acting deputy secretary of defense, November 28, 2005.

123 *"long war . . . a war that is irregular":* Department of Defense, *Quadrennial Defense Review Report*, February 6, 2006, 1.

124 *"conduct a large-scale":* Ibid., 38.

124 *"a new breed of warrior":* Ibid., 42.

124 *"new direction":* Ibid., 4.

124 *"There is a tendency":* Ibid., v.

124 *"it is important to note":* Ibid., ix.

Chapter 10: The Insurgent in the Engine Room of Change

126 *Had it been up to:* Harvey had been acting secretary of the Army since the previous September, but the Senate had only recently confirmed him.

126 *"Sir . . . that is the stupidest thing":* Cloud and Jaffe, op. cit., 210; and interviews.

128 *Petraeus's outlook on his own status:* In his official end-of-tour interview as CAC commander, Petraeus said: "I have to tell you candidly, when I was told I was

going to be the CAC commander, I thought, 'What do you do out there? Harass the students in CGSC [Command and General Staff College] that day? What is this all about?'" (William G. Robertson and Kevin D. Crow, CAC History Office, "End of Tour Interview with Lt. Gen. David Petraeus, Commandant, Combined Arms Center," January 27, 2007, 42); and interviews.

130 *It was a long drive:* Ibid., 2; and interviews.

130 *Wallace told the historian:* William G. Robertson and Kevin D. Crow, "Interview with Lieutenant General William S. Wallace, Commandant, Combined Arms Center," September 8, 2005; and interviews.

132 *Early on, Petraeus visited:* Robertson and Crow, "End of Tour Interview with Lieutenant General David Petraeus," op. cit., 36–37; and interviews.

135 *"is a protracted politico-military":* US Army, *FMI-3-07.22, Counterinsurgency Operations,* October 2004.

136 *The students were brutal:* Comments provided to author.

137 *He finished the slide show:* Briefing provided to author. The subsequent article, Lieutenant General David H. Petraeus, "Learning Counterinsurgency: Observations from Soldiering in Iraq," was published in *Military Review,* January–February 2006. Petraeus credited Nagl's book with inspiring the title change during his talk at the Workshop on the Counterinsurgency Field Manual, Fort Leavenworth, February 23–24, 2006; the entire conference was videotaped; a DVD transfer was provided to author.

137 *"great strides":* Remarks by Lieutenant General David Petraeus, CSIS, "Iraq's Evolving Forces," November 7, 2005, www.comw.org/warreport/fulltext/0512petraeus.pdf.

138 *The event was a conference:* The agenda and list of participants can be found at www.hks.harvard.edu/cchrp/programareas/conferences/november2005.php.

141 *"Observation number one":* Prepared text of Petraeus's speech, provided to author. There is no transcript.

143 *"Not as well as it should . . . and that's why":* Dr. Don Wright, Combat Studies Institute, Fort Leavenworth, "Interview with John Nagl," October 20, 2010; and interviews.

144 *The five of them sat at a table:* There is a slight disagreement over whether Nagl scribbled the outline on a napkin or a notepad. Nagl, Davidson, and Simpson insist it was a napkin; Lacquement recalls it as a notepad; Teamey can't remember. So I went with a napkin. Either way, the document is now lost; Nagl says he's looked for it several times, to no avail. However, he also proposed an outline in an email to Conrad Crane (provided to author), dated November 18, 2005, just ten days later, and Nagl (to whom I sent a copy of the email to refresh his memory) says the contents are basically the same as what he'd written at the restaurant. I am quoting or paraphrasing from the email.

145 *"the ubiquitous John Nagl":* Video, COIN Field Manual Workshop, Fort Leavenworth, February 23–24, 2006 (provided to author).

145 *One of the speakers was Conrad Crane:* www.sais-jhu.edu/merrillcenter-original/Iraq_Panel2_Summary.pdf.

145 *Crane wrote a paper:* Conrad Crane, "Avoiding Vietnam: The US Army's Re-

sponse to Defeat in Southwest Asia," Strategic Studies Institute, US Army War College, September 2002.

146 *Crane led the team:* Conrad Crane and Andrew Terrill, *Reconstructing Iraq: Insights, Challenges, and Missions for Military Forces in a Post-Conflict Scenario* (Ann Arbor: University of Michigan Library, January 1, 2003; reprinted by University Press of the Pacific, October 2004).

146 *"It is an imposing task":* Email, Crane to Petraeus, November 17, 2005 (provided to author).

146 *"Super news, Conrad":* Email, Petraeus to Crane, November 17, 2005 (provided to author).

146 *"some major distractions":* Email, Crane to Petraeus, op. cit.

147 *"and sincere concern for your health":* Email and attachments, Nagl to Crane, November 18, 2005. Petraeus must have *b*cc'd Nagl the correspondence, as there is no "cc" designation in the headers.

147 *These activities could include electronic jamming:* US Army, *FM-3-13, Information Operations: Doctrine, Tactics, Techniques, and Procedures,* November 2003.

149 *even getting the Carr Center:* The center contributed $10,000.

149 *"COIN Principles, Imperatives and Paradoxes":* These were first published, around the time of the conference, as Eliot Cohen, Lieutenant Colonel (ret.) Conrad Crane, Lieutenant Colonel Jan Horvath, and Lieutenant Colonel John Nagl, "Principles, Imperatives, and Paradoxes of Counterinsurgency," *Military Review,* March–April 2006. They also appear, in significantly revised form, in US Army, *FM 3-24, Counterinsurgency Operations,* December 2006, ch. 1. They are discussed in Conrad Crane, "United States," in Thomas Rid and Thomas Keaney, *Understanding Counterinsurgency: Doctrine, Operations and Challenges* (London and New York: Routledge, 2010), 61–63; and interviews.

Chapter 11: The Workshop at Tatooine

154 *Petraeus brought the meeting to order:* The entire conference was videotaped. A DVD transfer of the full proceedings was provided to author. All quotes and paraphrases come from that disc. The background, behind-the-scenes conversations, and people's thoughts come from interviews.

158 *Back in the 1980s:* Manwaring did this study as codirector of a project at US Southern Command called the Small Wars Operations Research Directorate, or SWORD. (The acronym came first; what it stood for was contrived after the fact.) John T. Fishel and Max G. Manwaring, *Uncomfortable Wars Revisited* (Norman, OK: University of Oklahoma Press, 2006); Fishel and Manwaring, "The SWORD Model of Counterinsurgency: A Summary and Update," *Small Wars Journal,* December 20, 2008; and interviews.

158 *"should strive to avoid imposing":* US Army Field Manual, *3-24, Counterinsurgency Operations,* December 2006, III–11.

158 *"a culturally acceptable level":* Ibid., III–12.

159 *John Waghelstein, who had been the MilGroup:* see ch. 2.

160 *Even Galula, his other model:* Galula recounts the brick oven episode in David Galula, *Pacification in Algeria, 1956–1958,* RAND Corp., December 1963 (re-

printed by RAND in 2006), 118–19. He sums up the tale: "This police work was not to my liking, but it was vital and therefore I accepted it. My only concerns were (1) that it be kept within decent limits, and (2) that it not produce irreparable damage to my more constructive pacification work."

161 *His book:* Bing West, *The Village: The True Story of 17 Months in the Life of a Vietnamese Village, Where a Handful of American Volunteers and Vietnamese Militia Lived and Died Together Trying to Defend It* (New York: Harper & Row, 1972).

163 *"at every echelon":* US Army Field Manual, *FM 3-24: Counterinsurgency Operations,* "(Final Draft—Not for Implementation)," June 2006, 1-18 to 1-19; leaked to the press, printed in full by Steve Aftergood's Secrecy News at www.fas.org/irp/doddir/army/fm3-24fd.pdf.

163 *"a clear . . . appreciation":* US Army Field Manual, *FM 3-24: Counterinsurgency,* December 15, 2006, 1-23. (This is the actual published field manual.)

165 *Bill Darley, the journal's editor:* The article was in the March–April 2006 issue of *Military Review.*

165 FM 3-24: In an unusual, perhaps unprecedented step, the field manual was republished, in unedited form, by the University of Chicago Press, with separate forewords by General David Petraeus, General James Amos, and John Nagl, as well as an introduction by Sarah Sewall. US Army and Marine Corps, *Counterinsurgency Field Manual: US Army Field Manual No. 3-24, Marine Corps Warfighting Publication No. 3-33.5* (Chicago and London: University of Chicago Press, 2007).

Chapter 12: Hearts & Minds

168 *H. R. McMaster had made his mark:* H. R. McMaster, *Dereliction of Duty: Lyndon Johnson, Robert McNamara, the Joint Chiefs of Staff, and the Lies That Led to Vietnam* (New York: HarperCollins, 1997).

169 *At the time of Desert Storm:* Rick Atkinson, *Crusade: The Untold Story of the Persian Gulf War* (New York: Houghton Mifflin, 1993), 443ff; and interviews.

172 *The regiment headed to Iraq in February:* The story of McMaster at Tal Afar comes from George Packer, "The Lesson of Tal Afar," *New Yorker,* April 10, 2006; Regimental After-Action Report, "The 3rd Armored Cavalry Regiment in Operation Iraqi Freedom III" (n.d., provided to author); Contemporary Operations Study Team, On Point III, "Interview with Colonel H. R. McMaster" (Combat Studies Institute, Fort Leavenworth, KS), January 7, 2008; Major Jay B. Baker, "Tal Afar 2005: Laying the Counterinsurgency Groundwork," *Army,* June 2009; Christopher J. Lamb and Evan Munsing, *Secret Weapon: High-Value Target Teams as an Organizational Innovation* (Washington, DC: National Defense University Press, March 2011); and interviews.

174 *"key strategic tasks":* Multi-National Forces-Iraq, Security Strategy, Counterinsurgency Center of Excellence, "*Ilitzam Mushtarak*—United Commitment," November 5, 2005 (provided to author); and interviews.

175 *If you have not studied counterinsurgency:* The paper, "Twenty-eight Articles: Fundamentals of Company-Level Counterinsurgency," was published in a number

of places, including *Small Wars Journal,* April 2006, and *Military Review,* May–June 2006; backstory comes from interviews.

177 *He emailed the draft:* The like-minded friends are all listed in the author's acknowledgments; and interviews.

177 *The same week that Kilcullen:* Packer, op. cit.; Cohen, Crane, Nagl, Horvath, op. cit.; Stephen T. Hosmer and Sibylle O. Crane, *Counterinsurgency: A Symposium, April 16–20, 1962,* R-412-1, RAND Corp. (1963), republished (April 2006); David Galula, *Counterinsurgency Warfare: Theory and Practice* (Westport, CT: Praeger Security International, 2006 reissue).

179 *"This strategy is shaped":* Multi-National Force Iraq Security Strategy, "*Ilitzam Mushtarak*—United Commitment," July 1, 2006; and interviews.

182 *Which made Rayburn all the more impassioned and insistent:* Besides his many memos, which he circulated to other, more sympathetic officers once Abizaid clearly stopped reading them, Rayburn wrote an article pointedly comparing the emerging US drawdown strategy in Iraq to the British strategy in Mesopotamia in the 1920s, a similar sequence of an invasion followed by exhaustion and withdrawal, which led to the rise of the Wahhabi Muslims, whose descendants were now dominating the Iraqi insurgency. Joel Rayburn, "The Last Exit from Iraq," *Foreign Affairs,* March–April 2006; and interviews.

185 *On August 3 . . . Four months earlier, on April 4:* Cloud and Jaffe, op. cit., 148–52, 157–60; and interviews.

187 *It was published:* Major General Peter W. Chiarelli and Major Patrick P. Michaelis, "Winning the Peace: The Requirements for Full-Spectrum Operations," *Military Review,* July–Aug. 2005; backstory comes from interviews.

187 *"Anytime you fight":* Cloud and Jaffe, 225–26, 236–37; and interviews.

189 *Three months later, he joined:* "Revolt of the Generals," *Time,* April 16, 2006; Ricks, op. cit., 38.

190 *in fact, it aroused anger:* Fred Kaplan, "Challenging the Generals," *New York Times Magazine,* August 26, 2007.

Chapter 13: "Clear, Hold, and Build"

191 *More pertinent still, her dissertation:* Steve Coll, "The General's Dilemma," *New Yorker,* December 8, 2008.

193 *Afterward, they coauthored a book:* Philip D. Zelikow and Condoleezza Rice, *Germany Unified and Europe Transformed: A Study in Statecraft* (Cambridge, MA: Harvard University Press, 1995).

193 *"remains a failed state":* Bob Woodward, *State of Denial: Bush at War, Part III* (New York: Simon & Schuster, 2006), 388; and interviews.

193 *When he came back from that trip:* Ibid., 412–14; and interviews.

194 *"clear and hold":* Lewis Sorley, *A Better War: The Unexamined Victories and the Final Tragedy of America's Last Years in Vietnam* (New York: Houghton Mifflin, 1999), 7, 29. Sorley's was one of a few books, published around this time, arguing that the United States could have won the Vietnam War with a bit more patience. That view is very controversial; few find it convincing (I don't); but, more valuably, this was also one of the few books between the end of the war and John

Nagl's dissertation that described the Komer-Abrams strategy and contrasted it with Westmoreland's clearly failed approach. For a cogent critique of Sorley, see H. D. S. Greenway, "The Revisionist Approach to Vietnam," *Boston Globe*, February 19, 2008.

196 *I have read that both:* Memo, Donald Rumsfeld to Stephen J. Hadley, "Talk of a New DoD Strategy," November 7, 2005.

197 *Just over two weeks later, he was about to quote:* Woodward, op. cit., 422.

199 *"On that happy note . . . My apologies":* Memo, Donald Rumsfeld to General George Casey, "Comments in This Morning's NSC," May 26, 2006. The Rumsfeld Papers website, library.rumsfeld.com/doclib/sp/3945/2006-05-30%20to%20George%20Casey%20re%20Comments%20in%20This%20Mornings%20NSC.pdf. (The memo, as it appears in the Rumsfeld Papers, is stamped May 30, but a copy of the original, which was provided to author, is dated May 26.)

199 *Bush scheduled a two-day meeting:* Thomas E. Ricks, *The Gamble* (New York: Penguin Press, 2009), 42–45; and interviews.

201 *During the Camp David meeting:* MNF-I, *2006 Joint Campaign Action Plan: "Unity, Security, Prosperity,"* July 9, 2006; and interviews. Casey's briefings, once Secret, have now been declassified. *Joint Campaign Plan: Camp David Briefing; COIN Strategy: Camp David Briefing;* and *Strategic Assessment: Camp David Briefing,* all dated June 12, 2006. Some of the material also came from *Force Structure Assessment,* June 21, 2006.

201 *Now, face-to-face in Iraq:* Woodward, *The War Within,* 3–7; and interviews.

202 *Charts drawn up by Casey's: MNF Iraq Update,* July 19, 2006.

Chapter 14: "We Are Pulling in Different Directions"

204 *And so the leaders of Congress:* The Iraq Study Group's roster of Republicans initially consisted of James Baker, former CIA director Robert Gates, former Supreme Court Justice Sandra Day O'Connor, former senator Alan Simpson, and former New York City mayor Rudolph Giuliani. The Democrats were Lee Hamilton, former secretary of defense William Perry, former White House chief of staff Leon Panetta, business executive (and erstwhile Bill Clinton adviser) Vernon Jordan, and former senator and governor Charles Robb. Early on, Giuliani quit, ostensibly because he was about to run for president but actually because he'd decided to spend the panel's first month racking up $1.7 million in speaking fees to twenty different private groups. Gates resigned toward the end of the process, in November, after President Bush nominated him to replace Donald Rumsfeld as his secretary of defense. They were replaced by former attorney general Edwin Meese and former ambassador Lawrence Eagleburger, respectively.

204 *All spring and into the summer:* The schedule and number of experts and witnesses come from *The Iraq Study Group Report* (US Institute of Peace, December 6, 2006), Appendices.media.usip.org/reports/iraq_study_group_report.pdf.

206 *"grave and deteriorating":* Ibid., 6, 11, 13, 23, 30, 57, 60.

207 *"could conceivably worsen":* Ibid., 50.

207 *On September 3:* Cloud and Jaffe, op. cit., 238–39; and interviews.

209 *"inadequate to the task":* R. W. Komer, *Bureaucracy Does Its Thing: Constraints on U.S.-G.V.N. Performance in Vietnam.* RAND Corp., R-967-ARPA, August 1972, vi. Komer's influence here comes from interviews.

209 *"considerably different":* "Analysis of Iraqi and Coalition End States" [n.d., circa October 2006], provided to author; and interviews.

Chapter 15: The Field Manual

213 *"After a thorough review":* Jerry V. Proctor, SES, Deputy Commandant, Futures, US Army Intelligence Center, Memorandum for Commander, Combined Arms Center, "Review of FM 3-24, Counterinsurgency Operations," June 14, 2006 (provided to author).

213 *"all Soldiers and Marines are intelligence":* US Army, *FM 3-24: Counterinsurgency Operations (Final Draft—Not for Implementation),* June 2006, esp. 3-1 [hereinafter called "FM 3-24, June draft"].

214 *McFate had written one of the first:* Montgomery McFate, "The Social Context of IEDs," *Military Review,* May/June 2005.

214 *"potential intelligence collectors":* US Army, *FM 3-24: Counterinsurgency,* December 2006, 3-1.

215 *In mid-August, Schoomaker:* Email, Conrad Crane to Montgomery McFate, Kyle Teamey, "The Battle over Chapter 3," August 22, 2006. (This and all other emails noted were provided to author.) Crane notes in the email: "The CSA [chief of staff of the Army] came by to see us at Leavenworth last week, and told us to get the manual out as soon as possible. LTG [Lieutenant General] Petraeus is looking for a way to do that without completely antagonizing Huachuca."

216 *It took place on Tuesday, September 13:* Email, Conrad Crane to LTC Lance McDaniel, Colonel Douglas King, "Intelligence changes to COIN FM," September 14, 2006, refers to "our meeting in Alexandria yesterday . . . to do some reconciliation with some new doctrine . . . particularly dealing with HUMINT." The substance of the discussion comes from interviews.

216 *"dishonest and cowardly":* Ralph Peters, "Politically Correct War," *New York Post,* October 18, 2006. The column was attached to a number of emails to and from Petraeus and others at Fort Leavenworth.

217 *"a bit inexplicable":* Email, David Petraeus to Keith Nightingale, "Ralph Peters column today . . . ," October 20, 2006.

218 *"to avoid overreacting":* Email, Conrad Crane to David Petraeus, John Nagl, "NY Times, 29 Oct 06," October 29, 2006.

218 *"If you can get past the cheap shots":* Email, David Petraeus to Conrad Crane, Clinton Ancker, October 27, 2006. (This was in response to an email from Conrad Crane, saying much the same thing as the October 29 email quoted above.)

218 *"Not making drastic changes":* Email, David Petraeus to Conrad Crane, "Counterinsurgency Field Manual for the Senate," November 3, 2006, 11:32 a.m.

218 *"is the only one some people will read":* Email, Conrad Crane to David Petraeus, "Counterinsurgency Field Manual for the Senate," November 3, 2006, 11:11 a.m.

218 *"You are exactly right":* Email, David Petraeus to Conrad Crane, "Counterinsurgency Field Manual for the Senate," November 3, 2006, 1:14 p.m.

218 *"The more force used":* FM 3-24, June Draft, 1–26ff.
218 *"Sometimes, the more force is used": FM 3-24, Counterinsurgency,* 1–26ff.
219 *Petraeus had one of his aides:* Email, Barry Periatt to Montgomery McFate, "FW: Ralph Peters column today . . . ," October 24, 2006. Major Periatt had replaced Jan Horvath as chief writer of Leavenworth's doctrine office after Horvath was deployed to the COIN Academy in Iraq.
219 *"true believers":* McFate's paragraphs were incorporated in email, Clinton Ancker to David Petraeus, [no subject line], October 27, 2006.
219 *Petraeus edited McFate's remarks:* They are in *FM 3-24, Counterinsurgency,* 1–14ff.
219 *"to eliminate as many causes":* Ibid., 1, 9.
220 *"Speaking as a social scientist":* This exchange is quoted in Ralph Peters, "Learning to Lose," *American Interest,* July/August 2007. Nagl confirms it in an interview and remains baffled as to why he can't be both. Other tales about the lunch come from interviews.
221 *"measured," "minimal":* Email, Conrad Crane to David Petraeus, Steve Capps, "Measured Force," November 24, 2006.
221 *"Use the Appropriate Level of Force":* Email, David Petraeus to Steve Capps, Conrad Crane, "FM 3-24, ch. 1, showing changes," November 27, 2006.
221 *One-and-a-half-million:* US Army, *Counterinsurgency Field Manual* (Chicago: University of Chicago Press, 2007), introduction by John A. Nagl, xviii.
221 *"the most-improved":* Ralph Peters, "Getting Counterinsurgency Right," *New York Post,* December 20, 2006.
222 *"theory-poisoned and indecisive":* Peters, "Learning to Lose," op. cit.
222 *In the same issue:* David Petraeus, "Beyond the Cloister," *American Journal,* July/August 2007.

Chapter 16: The Surge

223 *In mid-September David Petraeus:* Some aspects of the "council of colonels" are reported in Bob Woodward, *The War Within,* 145–52ff., passim, and Thomas Ricks, *The Gamble,* 90, 96, 101–4; but most of the tale told here comes from interviews.
224 *The seeds of the council had been planted:* The story about Keane watching C-Span comes from Ricks, 80, 83–84; the rest, including all the material about Keane's background, comes from interviews.
225 *"I don't know that there's any guidebook":* Quoted in ibid., 84. Keane's reaction and the chronicle of his background with the JRTC and COIN doctrine come from interviews.
227 *when Petraeus was accidentally shot:* Cloud and Jaffe, op. cit., 94–96.
230 *"We are edging toward strategic failure":* Ricks, op. cit., 88–90; and interviews.
236 *But in the end, the group concluded:* The forty-seven-page study was published as F. W. Kagan, *Choosing Victory: A Plan for Success in Iraq* (Washington, DC: American Enterprise Institute, January 5, 2007). General Keane briefed the study at a press conference on December 14, 2006, www.aei.org/events/2006/12/14/choosing-victory-a-plan-for-success-in-iraq-event. The story of how it came about, and how the analysts did their work, comes from interviews.

237 *The White House meeting began around three thirty:* Ricks, op. cit., 98–101; Woodward, op. cit., 279–82; and interviews.

Chapter 17: Awakenings

244 *The reversal came to be called:* The section on the Anbar Awakening is based on Major Niel Smith and Colonel Sean MacFarland, "Anbar Awakens: The Tipping Point," *Military Review,* March–April, 2008; Smith and MacFarland, "Addendum: Anbar Awakens," *Military Review,* May–June 2008; Michael J. Totten, "Anbar Awakens, Part I: The Battle of Ramadi," *Middle East Journal,* September 10, 2007, www.michaeltotten.com/archives/001514.html; David Kilcullen, "Anatomy of a Tribal Revolt," *Small Wars Journal,* August 29, 2007; and interviews. (The Devlin report is quoted in Ricks, op. cit., 47, 331–35.)

249 *"speed up . . . move outside all major cities":* Reprinted in Ricks, op. cit., 337–41; and interviews.

250 *"Closing the Gap":* There are a few versions of this briefing. The earliest, written in December 2006 and known as "the Gap slide," was obtained by the author; a later one, from January 2007, incorporated into Odierno's campaign plan, is reproduced in Ricks, op. cit., 344. The background comes from interviews.

255 *The contest's judges included:* The names of the judges and the winners are cited in US Army Combined Arms Center, "2005–2006 Writing Contest Winners: Combined Arms Center Commanding General's Special Topic Writing Competition: Countering Insurgencies," babylonscovertwar.com/Analysis/Conventional Force_COIN.pdf; the background and the story of Ollivant and Chewning in Baghdad come from interviews.

255 *"Doug, if this reaches you":* Email, Petraeus to Ollivant, January 8, 2007 (obtained by author).

257 *"clear-control-retain":* Cited in MNC-I [Odierno] Campaign Plan, February 2007; and interviews.

258 *The Coven's intelligence analysis:* Most of this section relies on interviews, although I was also provided with some of their briefing slides on the maps and the Baghdad Belts.

265 *"chaos, violence, and fear . . . This . . . is where you":* General Raymond Odierno, MNC-I, "Counterinsurgency Guidance," June 2007 (provided to author); backstory on the memo's origins comes from interviews.

266 *For the first half of 2007, the violence:* Data come from briefings and charts assembled by MNC-I and US Central Command; the material on Phantom Thunder comes from those sources and from interviews.

Chapter 18: The Insurgent in the Pentagon

270 *When he got back to the Pentagon:* Some of this portrait of Gates comes from two articles I wrote about Gates at the time: Fred Kaplan, "The Professional," *New York Times Magazine,* February 10, 2008; and Fred Kaplan, "The Transformer," *Foreign Policy,* September–October 2010; the rest comes from interviews conducted since.

271 *The first glaring sign:* The article was Dana Priest and Anne Hull, "Soldiers Face Neglect, Frustration at Army's Top Medical Facility," *Washington Post,* February 18, 2007.

275 *By promoting Schwartz:* I wrote about the cultural change in the Air Force in Fred Kaplan, "Attack of the Drones," *Newsweek,* September 8, 2009; much else in this section comes from subsequent interviews.

276 *He also read an article:* The article was Paul Burka, "Agent of Change," *Texas Monthly,* November 2006.

277 *"continuing to strengthen":* Robert M. Gates, confirmation hearings, Senate Armed Services Committee, December 5, 2006.

277 *"In the years following the Vietnam":* Robert Gates, speech before the Association of the United States Army, October 10, 2007. I wrote about the significance of the speech at the time, in Fred Kaplan, "Secretary Gates Declares War on the Army Brass," *Slate,* October 12, 2007. The backstory on Scott and how the speech came to be written comes from interviews since.

278 *Scott got the idea:* Yingling gained notoriety for writing an article called "A Failure in Generalship" (*Armed Forces Journal,* May 2007), accusing the Army's general officer corps of lacking "professional character," "creative intelligence," and "moral courage," specifically for remaining silent while Bush and Rumsfeld sent "a nation to war with insufficient means," adding, "As matters stand now, a private who loses a rifle suffers far greater consequences than a general who loses a war." The article was widely circulated and reinforced the sense, shared by many junior officers, that their commanders were out of touch.

279 *"the surest means the Army":* Lieutenant Colonel John A. Nagl and Lieutenant Colonel Paul L. Yingling, "New Rules for New Enemies," *Armed Forces Journal,* October 2006.

281 *Geren had read:* I reported some of this bitterness on the part of junior officers in Fred Kaplan, "Challenging the Generals," *New York Times Magazine,* August 26, 2007. Geren read that article and heard similar reports elsewhere. (All of the material about Geren and the promotion board comes from interviews.)

282 *Among the forty colonels:* I covered the unique promotion board at the time in Fred Kaplan, "Promoting Innovation," *Slate,* November 21, 2007; Fred Kaplan, "Annual General Meeting," *Slate,* August 4, 2008, although I didn't have the full story until researching this book.

Chapter 19: "It Is Folly"

284 *"indirect colonial rule":* Roberto J. Gonzalez, "Toward Mercenary Anthropology?" *Anthropology Today,* June 2007.

285 *"a brutal war of occupation":* https://sites.google.com/site/concernedanthropologists.

285 *"an unacceptable application":* www.aaanet.org/pdf/EB_Resolution_110807.pdf.

285 *McFate rattled off several:* Montgomery McFate, "Building Bridges or Burning Heretics?" *Anthropology Today,* June 2007. See also McFate and Steve Fondacaro, "Reflections on the Human Terrain System During the First 4 Years," *Prism,* vol. 2, no. 4; Richard Shweder, "A True Culture War," *New York Times,* October 27, 2007.

285 *Kilcullen went further:* David Kilcullen, "Ethics, Politics, and Non-State Warfare," *Anthropology Today,* June 2007. In this reply to Gonzalez's article, Kilcullen, besides defending the humanitarian aspects of his work in Iraq, countered that

anthropologists held no unique wisdom for judging whether a particular war was itself legitimate. "Since support for government, in democracies, is expressed through the ballot box," he wrote, "the proper course of citizens who disagree with the war (including anthropologists) is to say so, and to vote for anti-war candidates at election . . . Once war is declared, the job of officials is to execute it effectively and humanely in line with the policy of the government of the day or, if they cannot support that policy, to resign." It is this view that Kilcullen would soon repudiate.

285 *"measurable data":* Email, Kilcullen to Houtman and Gusterson, July 29, 2007 (provided to author); and interviews.

286 *"I am very impressed":* Email, Houtman to Kilcullen, April 30, 2007 (provided to author). The sequence of Kilcullen's evolution comes from interviews.

288 *the "formulation of policy": US Government Counterinsurgency Guide,* January 2009, 36; and interviews. The backstory on the conference and the guide comes entirely from interviews.

289 *"should not be taken lightly":* Ibid., 3.

289 *"However great its know-how":* Ibid., 2.

290 *"will almost always need to co-opt":* Ibid., 29.

290 *It is folly:* Ibid., 37. A condensed version of this thought (including the word "folly") is also on pp. 3–4.

291 *"Unfortunately, there will inevitably": US Government Counterinsurgency Guide,* 40. The original draft, which did not contain this passage, was provided to author.

291 *"to bring about regime change":* Ibid., 43.

292 *"The biggest fucking stupid idea":* Quoted in Spencer Ackerman, "A Counterinsurgency Guide for Politicos," *Washington Independent,* July 28, 2008; background for the story comes from interviews.

292 The Huffington Post . . . *picked up:* "Rice Adviser: Iraq Invasion Was 'F*cking Stupid,'" *Huffington Post,* July 28, 2008.

292 *"did not seek to clear":* Dave Kilcullen, "My Views on Iraq," *Small Wars Journal,* July 29, 2008.

293 *Rice finally signed the guide:* The signatures and date are in *US Government Counterinsurgency Guide,* opening page.

Chapter 20: COIN Versus CT

294 *"I don't oppose all wars":* He made the speech at an antiwar rally in Chicago on October 2, 2002, action.barackobama.com/page/share/2002iraqfull.

295 *Soon after he won the November 2008 election:* Woodward, *Obama's Wars,* 33. The material on Riedel comes from interviews.

297 *On March 12:* The date comes from Woodward, ibid., 112; the account of the meeting comes from interviews.

298 *"The circumstances under which":* I was the journalist, reporting for the *New York Times Magazine.* Much of the material in this section about Gates comes from that profile ("The Professional," op. cit.) and another one I wrote, later, for *Foreign Policy* ("The Transformer," op. cit.). Much also comes from subsequent interviews.

298 *"covert action":* I was the journalist here, too, interviewing him for *Foreign Policy.* Kaplan, "The Transformer," op. cit.

299 *"deeply skeptical":* Testimony, Robert M. Gates, Senate Armed Services Committee, January 27, 2009; see also Fred Kaplan, "What Are We Doing in Afghanistan?" *Slate,* February 5, 2009.

300 *You could pay twenty Afghan:* When Obama learned a few months later that the Taliban were luring Afghan soldiers by paying them more, he doubled the latter's pay (the United States was financing the Afghan army's payroll). Even then, the cost-ratio between an American and Afghan soldier would be an enormous 10:1.

301 *"will take the fight":* Press conference, President Barack Obama, March 27, 2009.

303 *"fresh thinking":* Press conference, Robert M. Gates, May 11, 2009.

303 *In September 2003, Donald Rumsfeld signed:* Dana Priest and William M. Arkin, *Top Secret America: The Rise of the New American Security State* (New York: Little, Brown & Co., 2011), 236.

304 *By fusing all this intelligence:* Ibid., esp. ch. 11; Spencer Ackerman, "How Special Ops Copied al-Qaida to Kill It," *Wired* (*Danger Room* blog), September 9, 2011; Sean Naylor, "3-Star to Lead JSOC: Report Suggests Renewed Focus on Spec Ops," *Army Times,* February 27, 2006.

304 *A top-secret detention center:* Eric Schmitt and Carolyn Marshall, "Task Force 6-26: In Secret Unit's 'Black Room,' a Grim Portrait of US Abuse," *New York Times,* March 19, 2006.

304 *"This is how we lose":* Ackerman, op. cit.

304 *"No Blood, No Foul":* Schmitt and Marshall, op. cit.

305 *The questions he asked the "assessment team":* The questions are recited on the opening pages of the report. Headquarters, International Security Assistance Force, "COMISAF Commander's Initial Assessment," August 30, 2009, i. A leaked copy was reprinted in full in the *Washington Post*'s online edition, September 21, 2009, media.washingtonpost.com/wp-srv/politics/documents/Assessment_Redacted_092109.pdf.

305 *Among them were Fred Kagan:* The full list is in Laura Rozen, "Winning Hearts and Minds: All of McChrystal's Advisors," *Foreign Policy* (*The Cable* blog), July 31, 2009. The near-appointment of Nagl and the substance of the deliberations come from interviews.

306 *"The overall situation is deteriorating":* "COMISAF Commander's Initial Assessment," op. cit., 1-1.

307 *"shape / clear / hold":* Ibid., A-2.

307 *"better understanding":* Ibid., 1-2.

307 *"a condition where the insurgency":* Ibid., 2-2.

307 *"Progress is hindered":* Ibid., 1-2.

307 *"the weakness of state":* Ibid., 2-4.

307 *"have given Afghans little reason":* Ibid., 2-2.

307 *"must protect the people":* Ibid., 1-2.

307 *"by, with, and through":* Ibid., 2-4.

308 *"conventional force . . . poorly":* Ibid., 1-2; cf. also 2-11.

308 *"under-resourced":* Ibid., 1-3, 2-20.

308 *One in particular caught his attention:* Gates told me of Kagan's influence; see

Kaplan, "The Transformer," op. cit. The article in question was Frederick W. Kagan, "We're Not the Soviets in Afghanistan: And 2009 Isn't 1979," *Weekly Standard (The Blog),* August 21, 2009.

310 *He'd honed this craft during his time as deputy:* Scowcroft told me this, and Gates confirmed it, in my interviews for the *New York Times Magazine* profile. Kaplan, "The Professional," op. cit.

310 *That summer, he'd invited:* Kenneth T. Walsh, "Obama's Secret Dinner with Presidential Historians," *U.S. News & World Report,* July 15, 2009; Peter Baker, "Could Afghanistan Become Obama's Vietnam?" *New York Times* (Week in Review), August 22, 2009.

310 *The specter of Vietnam haunted:* Peter Spiegel and Jonathan Weisman, "Behind Afghan War Debate, a Battle of Two Books," *Wall Street Journal,* October 7, 2009; George Packer, "What Obama and the Generals Are Reading," *New Yorker* ("Interesting Times" blog), October 8, 2009. Soon after these articles appeared, the two authors wrote dueling op-ed pieces in the *New York Times:* Lewis Sorley, "The Vietnam War We Ignore," and Gordon M. Goldstein, "From Defeat, Lessons in Victory," both in the October 17, 2009, edition. The Vietnam parallels were further pursued in a piece that Goldstein cowrote with Bob Woodward, "The Anguish of Decision," *Washington Post,* October 18, 2009.

311 *McChrystal had listed a range of options:* Woodward, *Obama's Wars,* 192; Jonathan Alter, *The Promise: President Obama, Year One* (New York: Simon & Schuster, 2010), esp. ch. 21; and interviews.

312 *The vice chairman of the JCS:* Woodward, ibid., 235–36; Peter Bergen, *Manhunt: The Ten-Year Search for Bin Laden from 9/11 to Abbottabad* (New York: Crown, 2012), 173; and interviews.

313 *"President Karzai . . . is not an adequate":* Cable, Ambassador Karl W. Eikenberry to Secretary Hillary Clinton, US Department of State, "COIN Strategy: Civilian Concerns," November 9, 2009. There were two cables, sent on the same date; the second was much shorter and consisted of a few recommendations. Stories about the cables appeared in several papers within a few days. The full documents were reprinted in the *New York Times*'s online edition of January 25, 2010, to accompany an article by Eric Schmitt, "US Envoy's Cables Show Worries on Afghan Plans." See http://documents.nytimes.com/eikenberry-s-memos-on-the-strategy-in-afghanistan#p=1.

314 *Petraeus and Mullen had testified:* Admiral Mike Mullen, hearings, Senate Armed Services Committee, September 15, 2009.

315 *Western inspectors calculated:* Jon Boone and Ed Pilkington, "Fired UN Envoy Claims Third of Hamid Karzai Votes Fraudulent," *Guardian,* October 4, 2009; Peter Galbraith, "How the Afghan Election Was Rigged," *Time,* October 19, 2009 (Galbraith was another one of the monitors); "Focus on Karzai Following Afghan Election Fraud Report," *Voice of America,* October 20, 2009; Fred Kaplan, "Karzai Salesman," *Slate,* October 21, 2009. The "300 cups of tea" line is quoted in Fred Kaplan, "McChrystal: Gone and Soon Forgotten," *Slate,* June 23, 2010.

316 "not *fully resourced counterinsurgency":* Obama's order on Afghanistan-Pakistan

strategy, dated November 29, 2009, is reprinted in full in Woodward, *Obama's Wars,* 385–90; that it corresponded with what Obama told the advisers, and other details of the meeting, come from interviews.

317 *So he asked them, one at a time:* Alter, op. cit., 390; and interviews.

318 *Petraeus was asked afterward:* Woodward, op. cit., 338; and interviews.

Chapter 21: "Storm Clouds"

319 *It was headed up by a three-star:* The sections about Barno's command in Afghanistan and about Eikenberry's follow-up tour come mainly from interviews, but also from Christopher Koontz, ed., *Enduring Voices: Oral Histories of the US Army Experience in Afghanistan, 2003–2005* (Washington, DC: US Army Center of Military History, 2008), especially chs. 1–3.

321 *Led by Louis Hughes:* Ibid.; Beth Cole DeGrasse and Christina Parajon, "The Afghanistan Reconstruction Group: An Experiment with Future Potential," USIPeace Brief, September 2006, www.usip.org/publications/afghanistan-reconstruction-group-experiment-future-potential; and interviews.

323 *All in all, the NATO allies issued eighty-three:* Colonel Douglas V. Mastriano, *Faust and the Padshah Sphinx: Reshaping the NATO Alliance to Win in Afghanistan* (Carlisle, PA: Army War College, 2010); Center for the Study of the Presidency and Congress, *Mobilizing NATO for Afghanistan and Pakistan: An Assessment of Alliance Capabilities,* Washington, DC, 2010; " 'Caveats' Neuter NATO Allies," *Washington Times,* July 15, 2006; and interviews.

324 *"An operation that kills five":* US Army, *FM 3-24: Counterinsurgency,* 1-25.

325 *"for the support and will":* HQ, International Security Assistance Force, Kabul, Afghanistan, "Tactical Directive." The classified document was issued on July 1, 2009; unclassified excerpts were released July 6. www.nato.int/isaf/docu/official_texts/Tactical_Directive_090706.pdf.

326 "Protecting the people is the mission": HQ, ISAF, Kabul, "ISAF Commander's Counterinsurgency Guidance." www.nato.int/isaf/docu/official_texts/counterinsurgency_guidance.pdf. The document is undated; a historian at US Central Command told me it was issued on August 26, 2009.

328 *Sewall began work in November:* The section on Sarah Sewall's CIVCAS study comes entirely from interviews. As far as I know, the only published mention of it is Colonel Tim Ryan, "Chairman's Joint Lessons Learned Program," *JCAO Forum* (vol. 1, no. 2, Winter 2012), a publication of the Joint and Coalition Operation Analysis, a division of the Joint Staff J7 deputy directorate for joint and coalition warfighting; but it's wrong on most of the details.

330 *"We've got a government in a box":* Dexter Filkins, "Afghan Offensive Is New War Model," *New York Times,* February 12, 2010.

331 *forty-eight "focus districts" . . . eighty "key terrain districts":* These figures are cited in US Department of Defense, *Report on Progress Toward Security and Stability in Afghanistan,* April 2010; the rest of this section comes from interviews.

331 *Two days before the offensive began:* Dexter Filkins, "Afghans Try to Reassure Tribal Elders on Offensive," *New York Times,* February 11, 2010.

331 *McChrystal's staff figured that Marja:* Dianna Cahn, "Months After Marjah Offensive, Success Still Elusive," *Stars and Stripes,* July 10, 2010; Rajiv Chan-

drasekaran, " 'Still a Long Way to Go' for US Operation in Marja, Afghanistan," *Washington Post,* June 10, 2010; Carlotta Gall, "US Gains Evaporate, Taliban Go on Offensive," *New York Times,* May 17, 2010. There's also a very good, grim HBO documentary, *The Battle for Marjah,* directed by Ben Anderson.

332 *They brought together 160:* This section relies mainly on interviews, but also on Colonel Randy George and Dante Paradiso, "The Case for a Wartime Chief Executive Officer: Fixing the Interagency Quagmire in Afghanistan," *Foreign Affairs,* June 21, 2011, and on a longer, unpublished version of the article, "The Interagency Scrum in Afghanistan: Time for Unity of Command," provided by the authors.

334 *from "attacking the enemy in remote areas":* CJTF-82, 4 IBCT, 4th Infantry Division, "Towards the Tipping Point: The Separate, Connect, Transform (SCT) Strategy in N2KL," July 22, 2009 (provided to author); and interviews.

334 *One week after the signing:* The story was Dexter Filkins, "Afghan Tribe, Vowing to Fight Taliban, to Get US Aid in Return," *New York Times,* January 27, 2010.

335 *"This is classic counterinsurgency":* CNN, interview with Hillary Clinton, January 28, 2010.

335 *"we must focus on":* Quoted in Woodward, *Obama's Wars,* 386.

336 *"really stirred things up":* Joshua Partlow and Greg Jaffe, "US's Good Intentions Go Awry in Afghan Tribal Area," *Washington Post,* May 15, 2010.

337 *A few days later, McChrystal and his staff:* The article was Michael Hastings, "The Runaway General," *Rolling Stone,* July 8–22, 2010. It was posted on the magazine's website June 22 (the White House obtained an advance copy), and it appeared on newsstands June 25.

337 *President Obama obtained:* Mark Landler, "Short, Tense Deliberation, Then a General Is Gone," *New York Times,* June 23, 2010.

340 *Two years earlier, Biddle had written:* The article was Stephen Biddle, "The New US Army/Marine Corps Counterinsurgency Field Manual as Political Science and Political Praxis," *Perspectives on Politics,* June 2008.

341 *Through a mix of cajoling:* Spencer Ackerman, "Petraeus' First Big Afghanistan Gamble: Militias Local Cops," *Wired* (*Danger Room* blog), July 14, 2010; and interviews.

342 *"the ideal situation":* Galula, op. cit., 25. Galula even drew a sketch of what an ideal country for insurgents would look like; it's almost exactly the shape of Afghanistan.

343 *"secure and serve the population":* Unclassified portions of Petraeus's "Tactical Directive" were quoted in HQ, ISAF, press release, "General Petraeus Issues Updated Tactical Directive; Emphasizes 'Disciplined Use of Force,'" August 4, 2010, www.isaf.nato.int/article/isaf-releases/general-petraeus-issues-updated-tactical-directive-emphasizes-disciplined-use-of-force.html. The full "COIN Guidance" was issued as HQ, ISAF, Kabul, Afghanistan, "COMISAF's Counterinsurgency Guidance," August 1, 2010.

344 *In his first three months:* US Air Forces Central Combined Air and Space Operations Center, "Combined Forces Air Component Commander, 2007–2010 Air Power Statistics" (as of September 30, 2010), www.wired.com/images_blogs/dangerroom/2010/10/30-September-2010-Airpower-Stats.pdf.

344 *killing or capturing three hundred midlevel Taliban leaders:* Fred Kaplan, "A New Plan for Afghanistan: Less Counterinsurgency, More Killing and Capturing," *Slate,* October 13, 2010; I got these numbers from an ISAF official at the time.

344 *in late 2002, Rothstein had written:* Seymour M. Hersh, "The Other War: Why Bush's Afghanistan Problem Won't Go Away," *New Yorker,* April 12, 2004; the rest of the section on Rothstein comes from my interviews.

346 *"I have three main enemies":* Rajiv Chandrasekaran, "As US Assesses Afghan War, Karzai a Question Mark," *Washington Post,* December 13, 2010.

346 *But a few weeks later:* Joshua Partlow, "Karzai Wants US to Reduce Military Operations in Afghanistan," *Washington Post,* November 14, 2010.

346 *"Your president has put me in an* untenable *position":* Part of this quote and story comes from Joshua Partlow and Karen DeYoung, "Petraeus Warns Afghans About Karzai's Criticism of US War Strategy," *Washington Post,* November 15, 2010; part comes from my interviews.

347 *At Petraeus's urging, and with President Obama's:* In his first three years as president, Barack Obama launched nearly six times as many drone strikes on Pakistan as George W. Bush did in the previous five years (241 from 2009–11 compared to 42 from 2004–08). Casualties are harder to determine, but the most authoritative unclassified estimate puts the number at between 2,400 and 3,000, of whom 80 percent were militants. New America Foundation, Counterterrorism Strategy Initiative, *The Year of the Drone: An Analysis of US Drone Strikes in Pakistan, 2004–2012,* http://counterterrorism.newamerica.net/drones.

347 *But despite an impressive hit rate:* As late as January 2012, Ryan Crocker, US ambassador to Afghanistan, sent a top secret cable to the CIA, concluding that the persistence of enemy havens in Pakistan was jeopardizing the US war strategy. (Greg Jaffe and Greg Miller, "Secret U.S. Cable Warned About Pakistani Havens," *Washington Post,* February 24, 2012.)

The tale of Pakistan's role in the American adventure in Afghanistan is worthy of its own book. Pakistan's leaders have, at best, an ambivalent view of the Islamist militants in their midst. On the one hand, they regard al Qaeda insurgents as a threat to their own rule; on the other hand, many officers in the military's intelligence service have alliances with some militant groups, a relationship that was forged at Pakistan's very birth as a nation in 1947. See Husain Haqqani, *Pakistan: Between Mosque and Military* (Washington, DC: Carnegie Endowment for International Peace, 2005).

As for the Taliban on the Afghan border, Pakistan's military has fought some groups but protected others. Pakistan's officials uniformly see the bigger threat as India and are thus reluctant to place too many troops on the western border with Afghanistan, lest they leave themselves too exposed to India to the east. For the same reason, the Pakistanis have an interest in establishing a presence in Afghanistan—to secure a "defense in depth" against a possible invasion from India and, more immediately, to counter the economic foothold that India has established in Afghanistan in recent years—and they do this through not-so-covert sponsorship of the Haqqani network, one of the more militant of the insurgencies. To the extent the Pakistanis desire peace in Afghanistan, they want it only on their terms through their agents. In early 2010, the Pakistani government boasted of capturing two dozen Taliban leaders; but a few months later, US intelligence discovered that those specific leaders had been trying to set up peace talks—their sin being that they hadn't done so through Pakistan. On this, see Dexter Filkins, "Pakistanis Tell of Motive in Taliban Leader's Arrest," *New York Times,* August 22, 2010.

From the outset of his presidency, Obama was well aware of the conflict's regional dimension and appointed veteran diplomat Richard Holbrooke as his AfPak envoy. The two men were temperamentally very different—Obama cool, Holbrooke melodramatic—but this was one of the few personnel bones that the president threw to Hillary Clinton, who'd been a friend of Holbrooke's for years. (Had she won the 2008 presidential election, he almost certainly would have been her secretary of state.) At his first meeting with Karzai, Holbrooke launched into a screaming tirade, which may have worked with the likes of Slobodan Milosevic (in Bill Clinton's administration, Holbrooke had negotiated the Dayton Accords, which removed the Serbian dictator from power), but not with Karzai. The Afghan president refused to meet with him again. Holbrooke focused more on rallying the US civilian bureaucracy to the cause of Afghanistan, with uneven results. He died on December 13, 2010, and was replaced with Marc Grossman, a veteran diplomat of a lower key. Still, little progress was made. One limitation from the outset was that India's leaders refused to negotiate in any forum that regarded their country as one of three points in a triangle.

348 *McMaster linked up with the intelligence:* US Army, Center for Army Lessons Learned, Fort Leavenworth, interview with H. R. McMaster, Commander, CJIATF-Shafafkyat, HQ ISAF, Kabul, January 27, 2012; and interviews.

348 *His efforts resulted:* Matthew Rosenberg and Graham Bowley, "Intractable Graft Hampering US Strategy," *New York Times,* March 7, 2012; Dexter Filkins, "The Afghan Bank Heist," *New Yorker,* February 14, 2011; and interviews.

348 *A few nights before his farewell ceremony:* The guests were John M. Barry, *Newsweek*'s military correspondent, who was writing a profile of Petraeus, and Paula Broadwell, a former West Point cadet who was writing a hagiographical book about the general. The description comes from John Barry, "Petraeus' Next Battle," *Newsweek,* July 17, 2011, and from additional details provided to me by Barry.

Chapter 22: "A New American Way of War"

349 *He'd learned back in December 2010:* The date comes from Paula Broadwell, *All In: The Education of David Petraeus* (New York: Penguin Press, 2011), although the author doesn't report, or even speculate, why Petraeus didn't get the chairmanship.

356 *The eight-page document:* US Defense Department, "Sustaining US Global Leadership: Priorities for 21st Century Defense," January 2012, www.defense.gov/news/Defense_Strategic_Guidance.pdf.

357 *"As we look beyond the wars":* President Obama, press conference, January 5, 2012.

357 "conduct large-scale": See ch. 6.

360 *They include nine lieutenants:* The numbers are from Rick Hampson, "At West Point, a Quiet Place to Honor Warriors," *USA Today,* January 4, 2012; all other material in this section comes from interviews.

364 *The most often-cited models:* Examples of successful noncolonial counterinsurgency campaigns launched by outside powers, especially in the post-WWII era, are rare. See Erin Marie Simpson, *The Perils of Third-Party Counterinsurgency Campaigns,* PhD dissertation, Harvard University, June 2010.

364 *The successful COIN campaigns:* On Malaya, see Nagl, *Learning to Eat Soup with a Knife,* 75; on the Philippines, see Max Boot, *Savage Wars of Peace: Small Wars and the Rise of American Power* (New York: Basic Books, 2002), 125.

364 *"Vietnam was an extremely painful":* David Howell Petraeus, *The American Military and the Lessons of Vietnam,* PhD dissertation, Princeton, October 1987. He excerpted this section of the thesis in an article, "Lessons of History and Lessons of Vietnam," in the Autumn 1986 issue of *Parameters.*

Interviews

Names followed by asterisks were interviewed only by telephone and email. All others were interviewed in person, in some cases many times, and almost always followed up with several phone calls and emails. Military ranks are indicated only for active-duty officers, except for four-star generals, who are cited as "General," whether or not they're retired.

General John Abizaid
Clinton Ancker
Gary Anderson
Major General Joseph Anderson
Joel Armstrong*
Andrew Bacevich
David Barno
Stephen Biddle
Antony Blinken
Colonel Nichoel Brooks
David Buckley*
Lieutenant General John Campbell
General George Casey Jr.
General Peter Chiarelli
Alexander Cochran
Eliot A. Cohen
Conrad Crane
Terence Daly
William Darley
Janine Davidson
Lieutenant Colonel Ketti Davison
General Martin Dempsey
James Dobbins*
Daniel Dwyer*
Eric Edelman
Karl Eikenberry*
Andrew Exum
Michèle Flournoy
Colonel Charles Flynn
General John Galvin*
Robert M. Gates
Colonel Gian Gentile
Colonel Randy George
Pete Geren*
Celeste (Ward) Gventer*
Thomas X. Hammes
Derek Harvey*
Lieutenant General Frank Helmick*
James Hickey
Kathleen Hicks
John Hillen
Margaret Hivnor*
Major General William Hix*
Bruce Hoffman
Colonel Francis Hoffman
Donna Hopkins*
Jan Horvath
Frederick Kagan
Daniel Kaufman*
General Jack Keane
David Kilcullen
Andrew Krepinevich Jr.
Colonel Richard Lacquement Jr.*
David Lamm
Douglas Lute
Major General Sean MacFarland
Peter Mansoor*
Max Manwaring

Thomas Marks
Daniel Marston
General Stanley McChrystal
Gordon McCormick
Montgomery McFate
Brett McGurk
Major General H. R. McMaster
Colonel Michael Meese
Stephen Metz
Heidi Meyer*
Geoff Morrell
Admiral Mike Mullen
Major General John Michael Murray*
Jeffrey "Jeb" Nadaner
John Nagl
Lieutenant Colonel Suzanne Nielsen
Philip A. Odeen*
General Raymond Odierno
Douglas Ollivant
Meghan O'Sullivan
Jeremiah Pam*
Dante Paradiso
Jay Parker
William Perry
Ralph Peters*
Heather (Panitz) Peterson*
General David H. Petraeus
Joel Rayburn
Bruce Riedel
Hy Rothstein
Lieutenant General Robert Schmidle
General Peter Schoomaker
Benjamin Schwartz
Thayer Scott
Kalev Sepp
Sarah Sewall
Matthew Sherman
Erin Simpson
Emma Sky
Dale Steinhauser
Kyle Teamey*
James Thomas
Colonel John C. Thomson
John Waghelstein*
General William Scott Wallace
Huba Wass de Czege
Francis "Bing" West
Colonel Isaiah Wilson III
Edwin P. Woods*
Donald Wright*
Philip Zelikow

Acknowledgments

This book owes its existence to Alice Mayhew, the legendary editor at Simon & Schuster, who called me for lunch one day in 2010. I had no ideas for another book, but jotted down a few so she wouldn't feel that she'd wasted her time. Among them was this one, and I was stunned that I hadn't thought of it already. Thirty years ago, I'd written a book for Alice called *The Wizards of Armageddon,* about the small group of intellectuals, most of them strategists at the RAND Corporation, who invented the theory of nuclear deterrence. *The Insurgents* turns out to be a sequel of sorts, about the small group of intellectuals, most of them Army officers from West Point's Social Science Department, who revived the theory of counterinsurgency warfare. The new book's themes and structure are remarkably similar to the old one's, and I can't imagine anyone overseeing the project more astutely or supportively than Alice, who made just the right suggestions, and asked the probing questions I'd been evading, at crucial turns in its development.

I thank the entire team at S&S who helped make this happen: Jonathan Karp, Jonathan Cox, Karyn Marcus, Jonathan Evans, Larry Pekarek, Irene Kheradi, Renata DiBiase, Maureen Cole, Julia Prosser, Rachelle Andujar, Elisa Rivlin, as well as Phil Bashe and Tom McKeveny. I also thank Boris Fishman for his fastidious fact-checking (though any remaining errors are my own).

Additional support came from the New America Foundation, which awarded me a two-year Schwartz fellowship that covered the project's span. I thank in particular Steve Coll, Andrés Martinez, Rachel White, Faith Smith, and Caroline Esser. A weeklong media fellowship at Stanford University's Hoover Institution, for which I thank Mandy MacCalla, also proved highly useful.

I first delved into this book's topic, and cultivated many of its sources, while writing my War Stories columns for *Slate,* which has provided my main outlet this past decade. I thank all my editors and colleagues there, especially Jacob Weisberg, David Plotz, Julia Turner, Will Dobson, and June Thomas.

The book, of course, would be nothing without the people—more than one hundred of the story's characters—who agreed to talk with me, often at length, many of them repeatedly, face-to-face, on the phone, and in countless email exchanges. They include the subtitle's namesake, General David Petraeus, who, though he knew that I was not in the business of hagiography, gave very generously of his time under strenuous circumstances. (A complete list of those I interviewed can be found after the Notes.)

I thank the many public-affairs personnel who helped unearth materials and arrange interviews with senior officers and officials, especially Geoff Morrell, Jennifer

Harrington, Kathleen Jabs, Colonel David Lapan, Colonel Erik Gunhus, Lieutenant Colonel Lisa Garcia, and Major Toni Sabo.

I also thank Susan Lintelmann and Suzanne Christoff at the US Military Academy's special collections and archives for guiding me through the papers of Colonel "Abe" Lincoln and the West Point Social Science Department.

This is the third time in five years, and the fourth in thirty, that I've worked with Rafe Sagalyn, my literary agent, who has stood by throughout as taskmaster, counselor, and friend. I am grateful as well to his patient and able assistants, Lauren Clark and Shannon O'Neill.

I thank all my friends, especially fellow scribes with whom I've discussed issues of war and peace for years, in some cases decades: Deb Amos, Bill Arkin, John Barry, Ethan Bronner, Phil Carter, Andrew and Leslie Cockburn, R. C. Davis, Dan Ellsberg, H. D. S. Greenway, George Packer, John Pike, Peter Pringle, Gideon Rose, and Dan Sneider.

Finally, I thank, more than I can say, Brooke Gladstone, my best friend, my conscience, my life's love, my wife—and our children, Maxine and Sophie, still sources of astonishing joy.

Index

About the Author

Fred Kaplan is the "War Stories" columnist for *Slate* and the author of *1959: The Year Everything Changed, Daydream Believers: How a Few Grand Ideas Wrecked American Power,* and *The Wizards of Armageddon.* A former military reporter and Moscow bureau chief for the *Boston Globe,* where he was a lead member of the team that won a Pulitzer Prize for a series on the nuclear arms race, Kaplan has also written for the *New York Times,* the *Washington Post, The Atlantic, Foreign Policy, New York Magazine,* and others. He graduated from Oberlin College and has a PhD from MIT. He lives in Brooklyn with his wife, Brooke Gladstone.